D1500261

Wounds That Will Not Heal

WOUNDS THAT WILL NOT HEAL

Affirmative Action and Our Continuing Racial Divide

RUSSELL K. NIELI

ENCOUNTER BOOKS 𝑒 NEW YORK • LONDON

First American edition published in 2012 by Encounter Books,
an activity of Encounter for Culture and Education, Inc.,
a nonprofit, tax exempt corporation.
Encounter Books website address: www.encounterbooks.com

Manufactured in the United States and printed on
acid-free paper. The paper used in this publication meets
the minimum requirements of ANSI/NISO Z39.48 1992
(R 1997) (*Permanence of Paper*).

FIRST AMERICAN EDITION

LIBRARY OF CONGRESS CATALOGING-IN-PUBLICATION DATA
Nieli, Russell, 1948–
Wounds that will not heal: affirmative action and our continuing racial divide/
by Russell K. Nieli.
p. cm.
Includes bibliographical references and index.
ISBN-13: 978-1-59403-582-1 (hardcover: alk. paper)
ISBN-10: 1-59403-582-2 (hardcover: alk. paper) 1. Affirmative action programs—
United States. 2. Affirmative action programs in education--
United States. 3. Discrimination in employment—United States.
4. Racism—United States. I. Title.
HF5549.5.A34N54 2012
331.13'30973—dc23
2011025538

To the memory of Mohandas K. Gandhi and
Martin Luther King, Jr., who spoke to
our common humanity and taught us
the dignity and worth of all
God's children regardless
of race or class.

CONTENTS

INTRODUCTION 9

I

A NATION OF INDIVIDUAL CITIZENS OR A
CONFEDERATION OF CONTENDING TRIBES? 31

II

ARE RACIAL PREFERENCES AN ANTIDOTE TO RACISM? 97

III

THE CHANGING SHAPE OF THE RIVER: AFFIRMATIVE
ACTION AND SOME RECENT SOCIAL SCIENCE
RESEARCH 133

IV

DIVERSITY AND ITS DISCONTENTS: THE CONTACT
HYPOTHESIS UNDER FIRE 241

V

SELLING MERIT DOWN THE RIVER 275

VI

STILL AMERICA'S CONTINUING DILEMMA 383

INDEX 481

*Not only has the politics of rights spread to increasing num-
bers of groups in American society since the 1960s, it has also
expanded its goal. The relatively narrow goal of equalizing
opportunity by eliminating discriminatory barriers developed
toward the far broader goal of affirmative action—government policies or programs that seek to address past injustices against specified groups by making special efforts to
provide members of these groups with access to educational
and employment opportunities. An affirmative action policy
tends to involve two novel approaches: (1) positive or benign
discrimination in which race or some other status is actually
taken into account as a positive rather than negative factor;
and (2) compensatory action to favor members of the disadvantaged groups who themselves may never have been the victims of discrimination.*

—BENJAMIN GINSBERG ET AL., *WE THE PEOPLE:
AN INTRODUCTION TO AMERICAN POLITICS,*
SEVENTH ESSENTIALS EDITION (NEW YORK:
W. W. NORTON & COMPANY, 2009), PP. 128–30.

INTRODUCTION

R acial preferences in the U.S. first arose in response to the widespread rioting in the urban black ghettos of America during the late 1960s. As a result of these urban upheavals, concerned elites in the federal bureaucracy and federal courts, as well as in the top universities and law schools, concluded that much more had to be done to deal with the pressing problem of black poverty and alienation in America than could be achieved through the prevailing ideal of color-blind justice, which had done so much to inspire the 1950s and 1960s era civil rights movement.[1]

---

1. On racial preference policy as a response to urban rioting, see John David Skrentny, *The Ironies of Affirmative Action* (Chicago: University of Chicago Press, 1996); and Hugh Davis Graham, *The Civil Rights Era: The Origins and Development of National Policy, 1960–1972* (New York: Oxford University Press, 1990). Many would trace the transition from the color-blind civil rights ideal to color-conscious preferences to an address by President Johnson at Howard University in June 1965: "You do not take a man who, for years, has been hobbled by chains, liberate him, bring him to the starting line of a race saying, 'You are free to compete with all the others,' and still believe you have been fair. This is the next and more profound state of the battle for civil rights. We seek not just freedom of opportunity, not just legal equity, but human ability; not just equality as a right and theory, but equality as a right and result." Although Johnson himself at this time was probably thinking of a huge expansion of Great Society training and other programs rather than racial preferences—two years after this speech he issued Executive Order 11375 reaffirming in unmistakably clear and forceful terms the requirement for color-blind, nondiscriminatory, merit-focused hiring for all federal contractors—the speech was interpreted by many supporters of racial preferences and racial quotas as an endorsement of their ideas.

From the very beginning, however, racial preference policy was anathema to large segments of the American public, including many of those who had fought the good fight to end segregation and racial oppression in the Jim Crow South. For them, racial preferences were a shameful betrayal of the highest ideals of the civil rights movement, and of Justice Harlan's magisterial pronouncement in the *Plessy* case that "our Constitution is color-blind and neither knows nor tolerates classes among citizens." And today, more than four decades after their introduction, preferentialist policies continue to be a source of loathing and offense to their many critics, despite the notable shift in their supporters' preferred justifications from "compensatory justice" and "pressing social needs" to the sweeter sounding note of "diversity."

In *Wounds That Will Not Heal*, I address the continuing controversy over racial preference policies in America, particularly those in university admissions and in employment. Reworking a series of essays compiled over a period of more than three decades, I offer a no-holds-barred critique of race-based employment and university admissions policies, whose consequences for the social harmony and well-being of America, I believe, are almost wholly negative. Until they are removed, racial preferences, I contend, will continue to gnaw at the inter-ethnic norm of reciprocity and fairness, which is the very linchpin holding together racially and ethnicly diverse societies like the United States.

The fact that their supporters must continue to refer to racial preferences through an elaborate double-speak of euphemisms and code words—"affirmative action," "diversity," "goals and timetables," "race-sensitive admissions"—should tell us something. The need to speak in such euphemisms and code words indirectly acknowledges the fact that preferences based on race run counter to deeply ingrained ideals of justice and fair play in

America and require verbal dodges and prettifying obfuscations to be defended before the general public.

In his insightful study, *The Ironies of Affirmative Action*, political scientist John David Skrentny makes the telling point that toward the end of both world wars bills were introduced in Congress granting preferences in government employment to those who had recently served in the military. Without euphemisms or verbal dodges they were simply called "veterans preference bills." And they passed overwhelmingly.

Although one can dispute the wisdom of granting job preferences to veterans, even to those who have taken time out of their personal careers to serve their country in time of war (wise voices argue compellingly that there are more appropriate ways to reward veterans than through means compromising the worthy principle of merit-based selection),[2] it is clear that for many Americans granting job preferences *for the right reasons* breaches no generalized principle of justice. This is why job preferences for veterans can be called by their proper name—"preferences." But simply being a member of an "underrepresented" racial or ethnic minority group is not seen by most people in America as one of these "right reasons"—hence the need for deceit and deception by their defenders when racial preferences are publicly discussed. Does anyone have the slightest doubt about the legislative fate or the level of public support for an honestly labeled "Underrepresented Minorities Preference Bill"? For a "Racial Quota Employment Bill"? A "Minorities First Act"?

But advocates for racial preferences have other reasons for employing deceit and deception in the packaging of their wares than the perceived unfairness of such preferences and their lack of public support. Social philosopher Michael Walzer explained this all very well long ago in his book *Spheres of*

---

2. See Michael Walzer, *Spheres of Justice* (New York: Basic Books, 1983), p. 154 n.

Justice. "In our culture," Walzer wrote, "careers are supposed to be open to talents; and people chosen for an office will want to be assured that they were chosen because they really do possess, to a greater degree than other candidates, the talents that the search committee thinks necessary to the office. The other candidates will want to be assured that their talents were seriously considered. And all the rest of us will want to know that both assurances are true. That's why reserved offices [i.e., racial preferences and racial quotas in jobs and university admissions] in the United States today have been the subject not only of controversy but also of deception. Self-esteem and self-respect, mutual confidence and trust, are at stake as well as social and economic status."[3]

Does anyone really want to be told, "Congratulations, Ms. Jones, you're our newest affirmative action hire!"? Or presented with an equivalent announcement of acceptance to a prestigious college? The answer, of course, is no, and because no one wants to be told such things, no one is. And so a hiatus develops between what is actually going on—which must be hidden, suppressed, distorted, or denied—and open public discussion. Self-esteem and self-respect are on the line, as Walzer says, as well as the overall group image of those targeted for the preferences both in their own minds and in the minds of those in the nonbeneficiary categories. Despite the elaborate concealment and deception, however, most people come to understand pretty well exactly what is going on with all the harmful consequences that follow. One could hardly create a more devilish system than our current policies of racial preferences for reinforcing in the minds of all parties concerned the belief that blacks and other beneficiaries of affirmative action are intellectually inferior to whites and Asians.

---

3.   Ibid., pp. 152–3.

Economist and social critic Thomas Sowell, a long-time preference opponent, explains the matter this way in his book *Black Education: Myths and Tragedies*:

> The actual harm done by quotas is far greater than having a few incompetent people here and there—and the harm that will actually be done will be harm primarily to the black population. What all the arguments and campaigns for quotas are really saying, loud and clear, is that *black people just don't have it*, and that they will have to be *given* something in order to have something. The devastating impact of this message on black people—particularly black young people—will outweigh any few extra jobs that may result from this strategy. Those black people who are already competent, and who could be instrumental in producing more competence among this rising generation, will be completely undermined as black becomes synonymous—in the minds of black and white alike—with incompetence, and black achievement becomes synonymous with charity and payoffs.[4]

Having debated the issue of racial preferences in many forums, I can attest from personal experience that preference proponents have no answer to the charge that preference policies reinforce negative stigmas and negative stereotypes about the competence of their intended beneficiaries. Proponents will sometimes point out in this context that preference policies did not create the negative stigmas and negative stereotypes about the abilities of blacks and other oppressed minorities. Such debilitating stigmas and stereotypes, they will say, existed long before compensatory preferences came around and have deep

4.   Thomas Sowell, *Black Education: Myths and Tragedies* (New York: David McKay, 1972), p. 292 (emphasis in original).

roots in our racist culture. So don't blame racial preference policies for American racism, they say.

Much of what is claimed in this context is true, of course, since negative stigmas and negative stereotypes existed long before the late 1960s and early 1970s, when racial preference policies first came on the scene. But while racial preferences usually do not *create* negative stigmas and negative stereotypes (although they can), they most certainly *reinforce* and *perpetuate* existing stigmas and stereotypes about the abilities of blacks and other denigrated minorities, and they do so in a powerful way. And this surely must be considered an overwhelming strike against them. Preference proponents, I have found, typically sink into silence in the face of such unanswerable criticisms.

Some will feel that in the following material I have been much too harsh on preference policies and their supporters, that I look only at the downside of the policies, and that I ignore all the good that they have done. In response to such criticisms, I will just say that on balance not only have 40+ years of racial preference policies had overwhelmingly negative consequences, but that if one looks closely enough at the various "goods" they are supposed to have achieved, these "goods" almost always turn out to be so intimately tied to countervailing "bads" that their supposedly positive value cannot be unambiguously placed in any plus column.

It is said, for instance, that preference policies create greater diversity and an enriched cultural environment on competitive college campuses. But whatever truth such claims may contain, the cold fact is that one school's diversity gain is always purchased at the expense of another's diversity loss. Stanford siphons off black and Latino students who otherwise would have enrolled at UCLA or UC Riverside, thus depriving such schools of the diversity-enhancement value of these students.

And by upwardly ratcheting visible minorities into institutions one, two, or three degrees of selectivity above the level in which they would have enrolled in the absence of racial preferences, a stigma- and stereotype-reinforcement factor enters the equation that means good diversity is always being replaced by bad. The healthy kind of equal-status mixing is replaced by a very unhealthy mixing of people of very divergent talents and accomplishments. And these divergent talents and accomplishments differ by the readily visible factor of race. Negative stigmas and negative stereotypes are inevitably confirmed.

The same picture emerges from the employment arena. Preference policies, their supporters say, have been the major factor in creating a large and stable black middle class and a large number of successful black professionals who can serve as role models for black youth. The greatest growth in the black middle class, however, occurred in the 1940s and 1950s—long before the institution of racial preferences—as a result of the greater returns to formal education and the move of upwardly mobile Southern blacks into the more industrialized and less prejudiced regions of the North and Midwest. The best research by labor economists shows that very little of the growth in the black middle class since the 1940s can be attributed to racial preferences.[5] And while racial preferences in more recent years have no doubt made it easier for many blacks to become doctors, lawyers, MBAs, and other high-status professionals, they have done so by dramatically lowering the standards and expectations for black

---

5.   On the issue of black economic progress since the 1940s, see Finnis Welch and James P. Smith, *Closing the Gap: Forty Years of Economic Progress for Blacks* (Santa Monica, CA: Rand Corporation, 1986; and Ronald Ferguson, "Shifting Challenges: Fifty Years of Economic Change Toward Black-White Earnings Equality," *Daedalus* 124 (1995): 37–76.

entrants into medical schools, law schools, business schools, and other professional schools in America.[6]

The message sent out is that those in the beneficiary categories don't need to achieve at the same level required of their white and Asian classmates to gain entry to the prestige professions, and as a result they have less need to compete with such students and less incentive to do their best. They know that their race will count as a huge "plus factor" in applying to graduate and professional schools and corporate-sector jobs. Not surprisingly, black undergraduates achieve much lower grades and rank-in-class standings when matched with white and Asian classmates who have the same entering SAT scores and high school grade-point averages (GPAs). This "underperformance problem" has been well documented since the very beginning of racial preference policies in the 1970s, yet preference supporters claim to be baffled by it. "We don't know why black college students underperform their SAT scores and high school grades," they say, unwilling to acknowledge the obvious. To lay the blame for black underperformance on the disincentive effects of policies they have long championed would require a level of honesty and integrity that few possess.

This same disincentive dynamic is at work, studies suggest, among college-bound, black high school students, even those attending the highest-quality public schools in communities like Shaker Heights, Ohio, and Chapel Hill, North Carolina. These

---

6. This statement must be qualified in the case of lawyers. While racial preference policies have made it much easier for blacks to get into American law schools, UCLA law professor Richard Sander has made a powerful statistical case for his claim that the upward ratcheting of black students into competitive law schools that proceed at a pace too advanced for their individual needs leads to high drop-out rates, less law learned, and high rates of failure on state bar exams. Many more black lawyers would be produced, his statistical models indicate, if there were no racial preferences in law school admissions and blacks attended law schools where the white and Asian students had academic qualifications more similar to their own. Pedagogically it is a very unwise strategy, Sander believes, to place a student in a law school environment where the vast majority of the other students are better prepared or more academically talented. See the treatment of Sander's research in Chapter III.

students and their parents both know, as essayist Shelby Steele once put it, that mediocre performance can win for them what only excellent performance wins for their white and Asian classmates. And in virtually any mixed-race public school system in the country, when black students from middle- and upper-middle-class backgrounds are matched with whites from similar backgrounds, the black students do substantially worse on average in their grades and rank in class. It is difficult to avoid the conclusion that racial preference policies have lulled substantial segments of the black middle class into complacency and half-hearted performance in our increasingly education-focused world.

If I had to suggest an historical parallel to what I describe here as the overall disaster of post-60s racial preference policies it would be the high-rise public housing craze of the 1940s and 1950s. Like racial preference supporters in the late 1960s, the urban planners who sought to improve the lot of the inner-city poor by creating high-rise housing projects were not motivated by evil or depraved designs. On the contrary, they wanted to help the urban poor and believed that creating structurally sound, fire-safe modern high-rises was the way to do this. And no doubt the high-rises had some important advantages over the dwellings they replaced, which were often poorly ventilated, unsound firetraps, frequently lacking in the amenities of modern plumbing and modern heating. But "the projects," as they came to be called, often turned into urban nightmares, as high concentrations of delinquent youth, in combination with vast expanses of difficult-to-patrol vertical space, often turned the high-rises into scenes of deadly shoot-outs, gang wars, vandalism, and an all-pervasive climate of violence and fear. The final acknowledgment of their failure came when officials in cities like St. Louis and Chicago moved people out of some of the worst crime-infested projects to lower-density housing and had the high-rise buildings themselves demolished. Like prohibition, the high-rise craze was a noble experiment that failed—and at considerable cost in human suffering. Racial preferences, I contend, constitute a similar policy failure.

The material presented in this book draws on extensive social science research, including in some cases research going back to the 1930s. But the work as a whole is intended more as an exercise in social policy criticism than a new addition to social research more narrowly conceived. In this sense it stands in a venerable tradition of public policy critique that includes such spirited classics as Friedrich Hayek's *The Road to Serfdom*, Jane Jacobs's *The Death and Life of Great American Cities*, Edward Banfield's *The Unheavenly City*, Nathan Glazer's *Affirmative Discrimination*, and Arthur Schlesinger, Jr.'s *The Disuniting of America*. To all those of goodwill who sincerely believe that America's embrace of racial preferences over the past four decades has been a wholesome and healthy national project, I ask only that they confront the arguments and ideas presented in these pages with an open mind.

I ask them, too, to consider the material in the final chapter, which is the only one that does not deal directly with racial preference policy, but with the origin and development in the decades following the Second World War of a large black underclass in America's major cities. Part of the purpose of this chapter is to show the continuing relevance of the older theories of E. Franklin Frazier and Daniel Patrick Moynihan, which stressed the enormous difficulties of adjusting to a bewildering urban environment by involuntarily dispossessed rural peasants who lacked strong traditions of education, entrepreneurship, and self-improvement. Another purpose of this chapter is to draw attention to the extreme oppression and depravity of the Jim Crow system and to suggest that this might have something to do with why its victims were so ill-equipped to meet the task of preparing their offspring for the challenges of urban life.

The last chapter is in many ways the most important in the book, because it draws attention to the continuing dilemma of the very people—those "hobbled by chains," as Lyndon Johnson called them in his famous Howard University address—whose suffering and disadvantage provided much of the initial impetus in the late 1960s for white liberals and others to abandon Justice Harlan's commanding call for a color-blind justice and replace it with the racial quota and racial preference regime that has become so familiar to us today. The sympathy, pity, and guilt that privileged whites felt over the plight of the black urban poor were effectively hijacked by elements of the black middle class—and subsequently the Latino middle class as well—to serve their own middle-class ends, while the more pressing concerns of "the truly disadvantaged" were ignored.[7] For the latter, the worst consequence of this development was a general "civil rights fatigue," and a "we gave at the office" mentality. "We've given the blacks their quotas and preferences as compensation for their past mistreatment," the common thinking goes, and so our nation's debt to them is done.

It is hoped that the final chapter will explain better than most other accounts how past oppression, negative conditioning, and the involuntary nature of the black sharecropper exodus out of the rural South combined to produce in the second half of the twentieth century the explosive growth in America's cities of a downwardly mobile and painfully disoriented black underclass. And it is hoped that this will create some renewed sympathy toward, and better understanding for, today's Southern-origin

---

7.   The claim that racial preference policies have largely served to enhance the position of the black middle class, while having little or no effect upon the "truly disadvantaged" black poor, is made by William Julius Wilson in his influential—and now classic—study, *The Truly Disadvantaged: The Inner-City, the Underclass, and Public Policy* (Chicago: University of Chicago Press, 1987). Wilson writes from a social democratic perspective, although much of what he says on this matter is strongly endorsed by libertarian and conservative critics of current racial preference policies.

black poor—for those to whom history, fate, and human malice have dealt such a terrible hand.

The black underclass today continues to be, despite intense initial engagement by public and private agencies—and subsequent "benign neglect"—a second wound that will not heal, with all the attendant pain and suffering for those directly involved. As we direct our sympathy toward real sufferers and the truly lost, it is hoped that readers will come to reject even more forcefully the 40-year-old bait-and-switch game of racial preferences for the black and Latino middle class, which has done so little to help the truly disadvantaged while exacting such tremendous costs in terms of public generosity and racial goodwill. We need to do with our middle-class preferences what St. Louis and Chicago did to their crime infested high-rises—get rid of them and acknowledge that something better must be done.

The book seeks to achieve three main goals. First, it seeks to explain the continuing sense of outrage and betrayal that is felt by so many Americans—especially Asians, poor whites, and those "white ethnics" whose forbears often immigrated to the U.S. from many of the poorest regions of Southern and Eastern Europe—over policies of ethno-racial preferences from which their own kind have been systematically excluded. And not only excluded, but implicitly treated as if they were members of a historically privileged, discriminating, and oppressing class. This is the subject of the first chapter, which is a reworking of my first reflections on racial preference policies formulated not long after the policies were first introduced in the early 1970s. I know from extensive exposure of readers to an earlier version of the material presented in this chapter that it strikes a deep chord in many, with some standing and cheering—while others want to throw bricks and missiles at its author. The brick- and missile-throwers, I believe, are usually angered about the no-punches-pulled approach to revealing the corruption and hypocrisy of those wealthy whites who are eager to give away other people's education and job opportunities while retaining their own wealthy-white economic and social privileges.

The second major goal of the book is to direct attention to some of the most revealing social science research over the past 15 years that critically evaluates the claims of racial preference supporters. Much of this research is addressed to refuting the contentions of the three pro-affirmative action River Books sponsored by the Andrew W. Mellon Foundation. Additional weight is added to these critical studies by the fact that some of the most important of them were sponsored by the Mellon Foundation itself and written by people otherwise predisposed to favor racial preferences.

The book's most original input into this controversy, I believe, is the use of contemporary evolutionary biology and evolutionary psychology to explain why policies of racial preferences have so often reduced social harmony, intensified ethno-racial tensions, and ended in violence and murderous rage in the many countries where they have been introduced. The key to understanding these tendencies, I try to show, involves the sense among aggrieved parties that when ethno-racial preferences are introduced, a basic principle of inter-ethnic reciprocity and fairness is breached, with dire consequences for the public peace. This reciprocity and fairness principle, as I have said above, is the very linchpin holding together fragile, multiracial, multiethnic societies like our own.

We humans are by nature tribal in the sense that we have a powerful natural inclination toward ethnocentrism, xenophobia, and the favoring of those whom we consider "our own kind." The anthropologist Pierre van den Berghe, who first popularized the term "ethnic nepotism" in his study *The Ethnic Phenomenon*, states the matter in its simplest terms: "all social organisms are biologically programmed to be nepotistic, i.e. to behave favourably (or 'altruistically') to others in proportion to their real or perceived degree of common ancestry."[8] Along the same lines, the sociologist Stephen Sanderson writes: "Just as people behave more altruistically towards kin than non-kin, they behave more altruistically towards the members of their own tribe, nation, or ethnic group. People favour their own ethnic group and tend to look with disdain on the members of other groups. . . . Ethnic attachments seem to be universal, primordial human sentiments. Ethnocentrism—the view that one's own group is superior to all others and the focal point from which other groups should be judged—seems to have been implanted in the human biogram [genome] long ago, and may even have been inherited, to some extent, from our primate ancestors."[9]

I argue in this book that it is just because of this ingrained human tendency toward ethnic nepotism and xenophobia that the interethnic reciprocity and fairness norm of which I speak, which demands within the civic realm the abandonment of ethno-racial favoritism and partiality toward one's own group, is so crucial for expanding the circle of empathy and identity beyond one's parochial attachments. To achieve cooperative goals within the civic sphere we must each agree to give up the natural partiality we feel toward our own kin and clan and expand the "we-group" to which we identify to encompass all the participants in a larger, cooperative, reciprocity- and fairness-honoring civic community.

Human beings, I believe, are genetically predisposed to respond to the perceived mistreatment or derogation of their own ethno-racial group by outsider groups with a kin-and-clan

8.   Pierre van den Berghe, "Does Race Matter?" *Nations and Nationalism*, 1 (1995): 360.
9.   Stephen Sanderson, "Ethnic Heterogeneity and Public Spending," in Frank Kemp Salter, *Welfare, Ethnicity, and Altruism: New Findings and Evolutionary Theory* (London: Frank Cass, 2004), p. 74.

sensitivity and protectiveness that history shows often escalates into violence, ethnic riot, and outright civil war. Such violent and protective genetic predispositions would have had considerable survival value over the millennia of human evolutionary history when there were no organized governments or independent courts to protect against unfair treatment or to settle contentious disputes. Each tribe or ethnic group was on its own and had to fend for itself against the mistreatment by others. In-group loyalty and cooperativeness, combined with a willingness to fight against out-group aggressors and defectors from reciprocal agreements, would have had great survival value in the past for the tribe and its members.

Harmful breaches in reciprocity by an out-group would be deterred if they were automatically met by the murderous rage of the in-group. . For individuals and groups a capacity for ethnic rage and retaliation in the face of reciprocity defaults and assaults by rival tribes would have aided the group members in the Darwinian struggle for survival and enhanced the possibility that their genes passed into future generations. More pacifistic or indulgent tribes would have been endlessly exploited by their rivals and as a result would not have been reproductively successful enough to be the ancestors of those humans living today.

In the intergenerational struggle for survival, the dupes and saps would not even have had the consolation of finishing last. They wouldn't have finished the race at all as their genes would have come to a biological dead end. We today are the descendants of those who carried the genes for ethnic rage and moral opprobrium in the face of ethnic slights, not those who met the breaches of fairness and reciprocity directed against their tribe with moral indifference or apathy.

The violence and anger that racial preference programs have evoked around the world among those in the nonpreferred groups (and particularly their less-privileged members) are well known to us through the work of scholars such as Myron

Weiner, Thomas Sowell, and Donald Horowitz. Evolutionary psychology, I believe, helps us to understand at least some of the ethnic rage that these writers have so extensively documented, and why ethnic preferences tend to generate so much more heat and hostility than, say, college preferences for athletes or the children of wealthy donors (which, of course, also provoke controversy). This newer brand of psychology has certainly helped me personally, as a third generation Italian-American from the ranks of what Marxists used to call the "petty bourgeoisie" (shopkeeper class), with Sicilian grandparents who spent their earliest years in America as factory hands and garment workers, to understand better my own ethnic rage at affirmative action and that of so many other "white ethnics" whom I have known from similar backgrounds (including many Irish Catholics, Jews, Poles, and Germans).

The third purpose of the book is to draw attention to what I have called above the "second wound that will not heal"— the problem of the inner-city black underclass. The last chapter in the book stresses the brutality and inhumanity of the Southern segregation system—which I try to show was nothing short of a protracted white terror regime—and suggests that this fact, in combination with the rapid, push-driven, rural-to-urban migration out of the agricultural South in the 1950s and early 1960s, is largely responsible for the inability of so many Southern-origin rural blacks to adapt to the challenges of an achievement-oriented urban environment. The view presented here draws mostly from earlier, now "classic writers," whose works, I believe, still illuminate best this long-term problem. The insights of Daniel Patrick Moynihan, John Dollard, E. Franklin Frazier, William Julius Wilson, Charles Murray, and Christopher Jencks are drawn upon heavily. This last chapter seeks to gain sympathy for the plight of the black underclass with the same compelling logic and emotional force with which the first chapter tries to evoke loathing and contempt for the hypocrisy and corruption of white elites, who long ago lost interest in the black underclass but continue to support racial preferences in education and employment that mainly benefit—if they benefit at all—the black and Latino middle class.

This final chapter strives to combine appropriate moral feelings with clarity of understanding and vision, while bringing these together under the umbrella of an overarching theocentric humanism and dedication to the kinds of liberal principles that undermined slavery and Jim Crow. I do not offer in the book— and do not consider it appropriate to offer—a sanitized, value-neutral account of the topics under discussion. No punches are pulled in identifying those I see as the heroes and villains in the story. There are situations where moral anger and outrage are the proper responses to bad public policies and the evils and corruptions that sustain them. And I believe that the continuing support for racial preferences by so many wealthy white liberals and prominent black leaders, combined with their continued neglect of the situation of the underclass in our inner cities, are prime examples of two of them. The reader must decide the legitimacy and fairness of the many controversial claims I make in the book.

I have deliberately refrained from offering policy prescriptions for addressing the black underclass problem, knowing full well the fierce criticism made for such an absence when Daniel Moynihan submitted his famous report, *The Negro Family: The Case for National Action*. To suggest that Southern-origin blacks had been given a bad deal in America, that a significant portion of their contemporary problems stemmed from that bad deal, and that expanded public and private initiatives were needed to alleviate their current distress was not enough to prevent charges against the Moynihan Report that it failed to offer practical solutions, or even, more perversely, that it "blamed the victim"—a thoroughly ludicrous charge that ran against the entire thrust of the report. But I hesitate to offer policy prescriptions, believing, among other reasons, that they would inevitably be controversial and that I have already engaged in enough controversy for one book.

Which doesn't mean that I don't have my own ideas on the subject. I would like to see, for instance, a massive federal program to create a Civilian Infrastructure Corps on the lines of the New Deal-era Civilian Conservation Corps, by all accounts among the most successful of Franklin Roosevelt's New Deal initiatives. Such a new CCC-type organization would enroll hundreds of thousands of young men and women (over a million passed through the old CCC camps), teach them the importance of self-discipline, regularized work, and the manner of following the direction of supervisors, and like its New Deal counterpart, would undertake an urgent and important national task. That task, however, would not be conservation of natural resources, but the rebuilding of our collapsing bridges and decaying infrastructures. I would also like to see school vouchers universally available to the poor, and the black church become the builders of a nationwide Christian school system that would have a cultural impact among poor black youth at least as great as that engendered by the school system established by the Roman Catholic Church to deal with the children of Catholic immigrants in the period from the 1850s through the 1950s. The Rev. Eugene Rivers, Boston's dynamic black preacher and a paragon of down-to-earth common sense, perhaps summed up the situation best to me in a private dinner conversation. For many young black men and women in our Boston neighborhoods, Rivers explained, the choice is simple: "Crack or Church?"

But elaborating and defending such policy initiatives would require another book. Since this one has reached the limit in size that I think seemly for a policy critique, I resist the temptation to add further material on the crucial topic of "what is to be done?" And I reject most vehemently the view that "you can't criticize affirmative action unless you have something concrete with which to replace it!" Affirmative action has been a disaster on multiple levels. Like the excising of a deadly tumor, one need not "replace it" by anything to do a world of good. Much more may be necessary to achieve the ends we desire, but getting rid of racial preference policy and its poisonous effects on social harmony is a *sine qua non* for restoring the American body politic to sound health. The need to eliminate one debilitating wound that has not healed must not be confused with, or linked to, the need to address other festering sores. They are independent social evils that should be dealt with on their own terms.

As a final note, I should say something about the legitimacy of racial, ethnic, and sectarian-religious identities in our national life. America, as foreign observers often note, has been much more successful than many of the countries of Eastern Europe and Africa in integrating people of diverse identity-group backgrounds into a reasonably decent and humane society. This, in my view, is due in part to the widespread acceptance of the biblical view that "we are all children of God," and of the Jeffersonian ideal that, regardless of race or class, "all men are created equal" and endowed by their Creator with inalienable human rights. In addition to this ideological support, integration has been furthered by the fact that America, unlike, say, France, has allowed its people within the private and social realms to have hybrid identities, such as Irish-American, Polish-American, Chinese-American and the like, without imputing to such people disloyalty or lack of proper patriotic feeling.[10] In our racial, ethnic, and sectarian-religious identities we form our private and social *plu-*

---

10. A more elaborate treatment of the question "what holds America's diverse peoples together?" can be found in the long introductory essay, "Forging a Common Identity," in the volume edited by Carol Swain and myself, *Contemporary Voices of White Nationalism in America* (New York: Cambridge University Press, 2003), pp. 3–83.

ribus, while in the civic realm we are all *unum*—participants in the one same body politic. Our identities are thus multiple, or as the lucid theorist of assimilation Milton Gordon used to say, "layered," with an "inner layer" of an ethno-racial or sectarian-religious identity in the private and social realms co-existing quite comfortably with an outer layer of civic identity, where we are all equally citizens of the same nation state.

We have gotten it right in the past, in my view—and continue to get it right in the present—when we refuse to classify our population in the civic realm according to sectarian religious affiliations or religious identities, or to distribute government burdens and benefits according to such classifications. Even if such a policy were constitutionally permissible, it would be an invitation to unending civil strife to adopt it.

But while we have gotten it right with regard to the separation of church and state, we have not done the same with regard to the separation of race and state. In this area we have gone down the dangerous path of officially recognizing people in the civic realm, not as equal citizens of the United States, but as members of often contending and contentious ethno-racial tribes. Quota thinking and affirmative-action preferences within the civic and government-mandated realms reinforce this tribal mind-set within arenas where it has no place. The U.S. is a citizen republic, not a confederation of tribes. If there is one overarching purpose to the work that follows, it is to warn of the harm that this disastrous rejection of the color-blind ideal of the civil rights movement continues to do to our civic unity and our overall national health—including our willingness as a civic community to help those members of formerly oppressed ethno-racial groups that are genuinely in distress.

With this in mind I'll let the eloquent words and trenchant warnings of three very different U.S. Supreme Court Justices, from three very different eras, end this introduction. The first comes from John Marshall Harlan's lonely dissent in the *Plessy* case protesting the segregation of blacks from whites in Louisiana's public transportation system. The second is from William O. Douglas's dissent in the *Defunis* case dealing with racial preferences at the law school of the University of Washington. The final comes from Antonin Scalia's concurring opinion in the *Adarand* case, which overturned a federal set-aside law that had granted preferential treatment in federal contracting based on the racial identity of the contractors.

> *Our Constitution is color-blind and neither knows nor tolerates classes among citizens. In respect of civil rights, all citizens are equal before the law. The humblest is the peer of the most powerful. The law regards man as man, and takes no account of his surroundings or of his color when his civil rights as guaranteed by the supreme law of the land are involved. . . . The destinies of the two races in this country are indissolubly linked together, and the interests of both require that the common government of all shall not permit the seeds of race hate to be planted under the sanction of law. . . . The sure guarantee of the peace and security of each race is the clear, distinct, unconditional recognition by our governments, National and State, of every right that inheres in civil freedom, and of the equality before the law of all citizens of the United States without regard to race.*
> —PLESSY V. FERGUSON, 1896, 163 U.S. 537, HARLAN IN DISSENT

> *The Equal Protection Clause commands the elimination of racial barriers, not their creation in order to satisfy our theory as to how society ought to be organized. The purpose of the University of Washington cannot be to produce black lawyers for blacks, Polish lawyers for Poles, Jewish lawyers for Jews, Irish lawyers for Irish. It should be to produce good lawyers for Americans and not to place First Amendment barriers against anyone. . . . A segregated admissions process creates*

suggestions of stigma and caste no less than a segregated class-room, and in the end it may produce that result despite its contrary intentions. . . . It may well be that racial strains, racial susceptibility to certain diseases, racial sensitiveness to environmental conditions that other races do not experience may in an extreme situation justify differences in racial treatment that no fair-minded person would call "invidious" discrimination. Mental ability is not in this category. All races can compete fairly at all professional levels. So far as race is concerned, any state-sponsored preference of one race over another in that competition is in my view "invidious" and violative of the Equal Protection Clause.

—DEFUNIS V. ODEGAARD, 1974, 416 U.S. 312,

DOUGLAS, DISSENTING THE DECISION TO MOOT

In my view, Government can never have a "compelling interest" in discriminating on the basis of race in order to "make up" for past racial discrimination in the opposite direction. Individuals who have been wronged by unlawful racial discrimination should be made whole; but under our Constitution there can be no such thing as either a creditor or a debtor race. That concept is alien to the Constitution's focus upon the individual, and its rejection of dispositions based on race or blood. To pursue the concept of racial entitlement—even for the most admirable and benign of purposes—is to enforce and preserve for future mischief the way of thinking that produced race slavery, race privilege, and race hatred. In the eyes of government, we are just one race here. It is American.

—ADARAND V. PENA, 1995, 515 U.S. 200, SCALIA CONCURRING

I

A NATION OF INDIVIDUAL CITIZENS OR A CONFEDERATION OF CONTENDING TRIBES?

This first chapter represents my earliest attempt to come to grips with the reality of racial preferences. It focuses on the dramatic shift that took place in the early 1970s away from the civil rights era vision of a color-blind society to color-conscious "quota" thinking and other group-based understandings of human rights and government entitlements. For me this momentous change, coinciding with the very beginning of my graduate student days in Princeton's Politics Department, came as a great shock and a great betrayal.

At first I simply could not believe that overtly race-based preferences would ever find expression in our official national policy. Our government would never consent to classifying the American public according to racial and ethnic categories and distributing burdens and benefits on the basis of such classifications. That would stand the whole civil rights movement on its head. Perhaps a few guilt-ridden limousine liberals in Manhattan might support such a policy, I thought, but the entire white working class and white poor would rise up against it. And the black clergy and black civil rights leaders would never stand for it. They are Christians—most of them—and their foundational belief is that we are all children of God. They believe that we are all created in the image of God and must be respected because of this. They hold that categories like Jew or Greek have no meaning in the mind of our Creator and should have no place in public policy. This biblical understanding of human nature is the reason they fought so nobly in the '50s and '60s against racism, discrimination, and all manner of inter-tribal enmities and hostilities. One simply cannot imagine the black civil rights leaders—and black Christians more generally—abandoning their high principles for a few extra points on a civil service exam.

Ah, the callowness of youth! When reality finally did sink in by the mid-1970s, like many descendants of what were once called the New Immigrants—those mainly of Catholic and Jewish backgrounds who came to the United States before the First World War from many of the poorest areas of Eastern and Southern Europe—my response was one of shock and rage. In time the shock would diminish, but not the rage. My anger had the special moral intensity to it that only betrayed innocence can understand. Troubling questions arose: Was the civil rights movement really intended all along just as a cynical bait-and-switch game—a confidence trick by wily schemers to prey on the goodwill of decent Americans and swindle the naïve (as its segregationist critics had always charged)? Were my Sicilian grandparents, who came from Italy's poorest class of landless farm workers, somehow responsible for Southern slavery and Jim Crow? Must they—and their descendants—atone for all those "white-skin privileges" they enjoyed as garment workers and factory hands in Brooklyn? Does my Italian-American tribe—or the tribes to which the Irish, Polish, Jewish, and dozens of other European immigrants and their descendants belong— owe some kind of collective tribal debt to African-Americans and Latinos? And if so, who should pay whom, how much, and in what form?

These were the kinds of questions—mostly personal and rhetorical—that I asked myself in the mid-1970s, a time for me of still unjaded youth, when I first began to think systematically about racial preference policies and the radical transformation that had taken place in elite thinking on these issues since the days of the civil rights movement. The following essay, only slightly modified from the original, was my first attempt at an answer.[11]

Deeply rooted in our religious heritage is the conviction that every man is an heir to a legacy of dignity and worth. Our Judeo-Christian tradition refers to this inherent dignity of man in the biblical term "the image of God." . . . Every human being has etched in his personality the indelible stamp of the Creator. Every man must be respected because God loves him. The worth of an individual does not lie in the measure of his intellect, his racial origin, or his social position. Human worth lies in relatedness to God. An individual has value because he has value to God. Whenever this is recognized, "whiteness" and "blackness" pass away as determinants in a relationship and "son" and "brother" are substituted.

—MARTIN LUTHER KING, JR. (1967)

You guys have been practicing discrimination for years. Now it is our turn.

—JUSTICE THURGOOD MARSHALL (1974),
DISCUSSING THE DEFUNIS CASE WITH WILLIAM O. DOUGLAS.

Civil rights laws were not passed to protect the rights of white men and do not apply to them.

—MARY FRANCES BERRY (1985)

---

11. This chapter represents my first attempt to come to terms with the reality of racial-preference policies, particularly those in the employment arena. Its core ideas were conceived in the mid- and late 1970s, although they were first published later and went through subsequent revisions. In its present form the chapter is a revised version of the fourth chapter in my anthology, *Racial Preference and Racial Justice—The New Affirmative Action Controversy* (Washington, D.C.: Ethics and Public Policy Center, 1991), which was titled "Ethnic Tribalism and Human Personhood."

During the lengthy debate over the 1964 Civil Rights Bill (HR 7192), a number of Southern opponents of the bill, in an attempt to raise public fears, claimed that the section of the bill outlawing discrimination in employment would lead to the imposition by federal enforcement agencies of racial "quota" hiring in order to achieve a desirable "racial balance." The term "discrimination," it was pointed out, was not specifically defined in the bill, and so, it was held, might be interpreted by federal authorities to mean the lack of proportional representation of the members of various racial and ethnic groups in a given employer's workforce. This contention of the Southern opponents was, of course, nothing more than a scare tactic, as the clear wording of the bill precluded any such interpretation and made hiring based on racial or ethnic criteria of any kind, quota or otherwise, clearly illegal. Relevant sections of what were to become Titles VI and VII of the Civil Rights Act of 1964 read as follows:

Section 601

No *person* in the United States shall, on the ground of race, color, or national origin, be excluded from participation in, be denied the benefits of, or be subjected to discrimination under any program or activity receiving Federal financial assistance.

Section 703

(a) It shall be an unlawful employment practice for an employer:

(1) to fail or refuse to hire or to discharge *any individual*, or otherwise to discriminate against *any individual* with respect to his compensation, terms, conditions, or privileges of employment, because of *such individual's* race, color, religion, sex, or national origin; or

(2) to limit, segregate, or classify his employees in any way which would deprive or tend to deprive *any*

individual of employment opportunities or otherwise adversely affect his status as an employee, because of *such individual's* race, color, religion, sex, or national origin.

(b) It shall be an unlawful employment practice for an employment agency to fail or refuse to refer for employment, or otherwise to discriminate against *any individual* because of his race, color, religion, sex, or national origin, or to classify or refer for employment *any individual* on the basis of his race, color, religion, sex, or national origin.

(c) It shall be an unlawful employment practice for a labor organization:

(1) to exclude or to expel from its membership, or otherwise to discriminate against *any individual* because of his race, color, religion, sex, or national origin;

(2) to limit, segregate, or classify its membership, or applicants for membership, or to classify or fail or refuse to refer for employment *any individual* in any way which would deprive or tend to deprive *any individual* of employment opportunities, or would limit such employment opportunities or otherwise adversely affect his status as an employee or as an applicant for employment, because of *such individual's* race, color, religion, sex, or national origin;

(d) It shall be an unlawful employment practice for any employer, labor organization, or joint labor-management committee . . . to discriminate against *any individual* because of his race, color, religion, sex, or national origin in admission to, or employment in, any program established to provide apprenticeship or other training. [all emphasis added]

The language of the bill was clearly the language of persons and of individuals, and guaranteed to each and every one of them the right to be considered for employment and promotion on a strictly race-, ethnicity-, gender-, and religion-neutral basis. Here, of course, the law was continuing in the tradition of the 14th Amendment to the federal Constitution, which had also spoken of persons ("No State shall . . . deprive any person of life, liberty or property, without due process of law; nor deny to any person within its jurisdiction the equal protection of the laws"), as well as of the many state fair employment practice laws (FEP) after which Title VII of the 1964 Civil Rights Act was patterned.

In order to counter the scare tactics of the Southern senators, the supporters of the bill, led by Majority Whip Hubert Humphrey, and the two floor captains of Title VII, Senators Joseph Clark and Clifford Case, went on record again and again to reassure their colleagues that Title VII's guarantees against hiring discrimination applied to all people equally and not just to blacks or members of any particular racial or ethnic group. They also went on to stress the fact that any attempt to maintain a racial balance would not only *not* be required by the bill, but would be clearly illegal according to its provisions. Senator Humphrey was particularly forceful in speaking out against what he called at one point the "uninterrupted flow of nightmarish propaganda" and "wholesale distortions" that were attempting to mislead the public concerning the nature of the proposed bill and were responsible, in Humphrey's view, for the strong showing Alabama segregationist George Wallace had recently made in the Wisconsin presidential primary. (110 *Cong. Rec.*, pp. 11846–7)

In order to counter these distortions, Humphrey had his staff draft a carefully worded interpretive statement dealing with all the major provisions of the bill, and had the statement read and approved by all of the bill's floor managers in both houses of Congress. On the question of Title VII, the statement addressed itself specifically to the Southern charge that the bill would require the preferential hiring of Negroes:

[Title VII] does not provide that any preferential treatment in employment shall be given to Negroes or to any other persons or groups. It does not provide that any quota system may be established to maintain racial balance in employment. In fact, the title would prohibit preferential treatment for any particular group, and *any person*, whether or not a member of any minority group, would be permitted to file a complaint of discriminatory employment practices. (110 *Cong. Rec.*, p. 11848, emphasis added)

Senators Clark and Case had stressed earlier that Title VII would prohibit any attempt to maintain a racial balance, since this would involve hiring on the basis of race and would thus discriminate against individuals:

There is no requirement in Title VII that an employer maintain a racial balance in his workforce. On the contrary, any deliberate attempt to maintain a racial balance, whatever such a balance may be, would involve a violation of Title VII because maintaining such a balance would require an employer to hire or to refuse to hire on the basis of race. It must be emphasized that discrimination is prohibited as to *any individual*. (110 *Cong. Rec.*, p. 7213, emphasis added)

Senator Clark also had the Justice Department draw up a statement specifically addressing itself to a number of charges that had been made against Titles VI and VII of the bill by Senator Lister Hill of Alabama. In regard to the charge that the proposed law would require employees to maintain a racial balance, the Justice Department's interpretive memorandum offered the following rebuttal:

Finally it has been asserted Title VII would impose a requirement for "racial balance." This is incorrect. . . . No employer is required to hire an individual because that individual is a Negro. No employer is required to maintain any ratio of Negroes to whites, Jews to Gentiles, Italians to English, or women to men. . . . On the contrary, any deliberate attempt to maintain a given balance would almost certainly run afoul of Title VII because it would involve a failure or refusal to hire *some individual* because of his race, color, religion, sex, or national origin. (110 *Cong. Rec.*, p. 7207, emphasis added)

Senator Clark also had read into the *Congressional Record* a letter rebutting Senator Hill's arguments by Walter Reuther, the president of the United Auto Workers Union, who was one of organized labor's most outspoken supporters of the Civil Rights Bill. "Under the pending law," Reuther explained, "every Negro worker will have a fair opportunity for a job if he is qualified, and every white worker will know that he cannot be laid off or refused employment for a racial reason because discrimination against a white worker is just as forbidden as discrimination against the Negro." (110 *Cong. Rec.*, p. 7206)

While the criticisms of the Southern senators lacked all substance, and were essentially a tactical maneuver designed to instill fear and doubt into the public mind, they nevertheless reflected a peculiarly Southern way of thinking—or at least a way of thinking that was much more deeply ingrained in the American South than elsewhere—which was both incompatible with, and hostile to, the mode of thinking that had come to dominate American society under the impact of the civil rights movement of the 1950s and 1960s. These two contrasting modes of thought might be characterized by the terms "tribalism" and "personalism."

Tribalism can be defined as that mode of human consciousness that tends to view human beings not as unique persons but as depersonalized representatives of larger racial or ethnic collectives, with the collectives themselves being seen as singular or homogeneous entities rather than plural or diverse ones. It is a group-representation and group-identity principle that in all intergroup relationships is characterized by a stereotyping and deindividuating cast of mind. Personalism, on the other hand, is a mode of consciousness that seeks to view human beings as distinct and unique individuals ("persons"), who are capable of relating to, and communing with, all others of their kind on the basis of a group-unmediated, soul-to-soul relationship of mutual equality and respect. The early-twentieth-century Jewish philosopher Martin Buber famously called these latter "I-Thou relationships." The personalistic consciousness can engage in such relationships, the tribalistic cannot.

The two modes of consciousness are existentially and conceptually incompatible, with the latter, personalistic mode representing a higher, more differentiated type of thinking than the former, insofar as its terms and conceptual structures can be used to understand and to criticize the tribalistic mode of thought but the reverse is not the case. The personalistic mentality can understand—and criticize—the tribalistic, but the tribalistic cannot understand the personalistic.

It is something like the relationship between John Stuart Mill's higher and lower pleasures: a Socrates can comprehend the pleasures of the pig and the fool, but the reverse is not so. For people who had grown up, as the Southern opponents of the Civil Rights Act had, in a legally segregated and highly race-conscious society, where across the color line people tended to be viewed less as individual persons than as representatives of racial or ethnic tribes, it was not easy to comprehend a law in which individual persons were each respected as such, and racial and ethnic tribal associations were given no recognition whatever. When one views what has transpired in America since the late 1960s and early 1970s, particularly with regard to the government policy known as "affirmative action," it must certainly be seen as one of the grim ironies of modern American history that the Southern tribalistic mode of consciousness would not only come to dominate much of the country but would do so under the leadership of a national elite that claimed to be furthering the cause of "civil rights."

PERSONALISM EXPLAINED

According to the personalistic philosophy human beings are each individually centers of Meaning and Mystery. They are not Hegelian moments in a collective group history, nor are they faceless, depersonalized abstractions upon which to project one's stereotyped image of a group, be this image positive, negative, or some nuanced combination of the two. In claiming that each human being is a center of Meaning, personalism contends that human societies are not to be viewed as single, unified, collective worlds but as pluralities of many separate personal worlds, each interacting with, and communing with, other separate personal worlds in an ongoing drama of human history. While one can speak meaningfully of many collective and communal activities that these personal worlds engage in, each world remains in and of itself a separate and distinct unit of meaning, each with its own unique experiences, its own unique struggles, and its own personal time-frame of reference. Human persons according to the personalistic philosophy have an indissolvable unity to their being, to their life and thoughts, their actions and feelings, which groups of human beings simply cannot have, not even the most intimate group of the family.[12]

---

12. The view of human personhood developed here, which closely parallels both the thinking of Martin Luther King, Jr., and the spiritual universalism of early Quakerism, is similar in its philosophical and social implications to that developed by the British political philosopher Ernest Barker: "Now we may admire the nation moving and heaving: we may admire the surge of its thought: we may admire the philosophy of super-personal Group-persons—the Folk; the Fellowship; the *Verband*, in all its forms. It is, indeed, a philosophy which can ennoble the individual, and lift him above self-

When personalism contends that human beings are centers of Mystery, what is meant is that every person has a dimension of Depth to his being, and a private relationship to this dimension of Depth, which has about it something that is sacred. It is this dimension of Depth in each person and the special relationship that each person has to this dimension that form the basis of our public claims to a respect for personal privacy, a respect for conscience, and a respect for personal religious beliefs. The Depth in each person enters into a region that is mysterious and unfathomable, which the public has no right to enter.

It is sometimes charged that the personalistic outlook is "atomistic" or "antisocial," but this criticism is based on a complete misunderstanding. Persons are centers of Meaning and Mystery, and they are also centers of creativity and energy. From their vital centers outward then, persons engage other persons in society on various levels of intimacy and concern. Such

---

centered concern in his own immediate life. But it may also be a philosophy which engulfs his life, and absorbs his individuality; and it may end, in practice, in little more than the brute and instinctive automatism of the hive. We have to admit, after all, the justice of [Ernst] Troeltsch's saying, that the end of the idealization of Groups may be 'to brutalize romance, and to romanticize cynicism.' We have to confess that the cult of super-personal Beings has had some tragic results. . . . While it has grandeur and flame, it has also a cloud of smoke. Individualism is often used as a word of reproach; but it is good to see simple shapes of 'men as trees, walking' and to think in simple terms of human persons. Persons—individual persons—have a finitude or limit which can satisfy our intelligence, and an infinity or extension which can satisfy our faith. They have finitude or limit in the sense that, in any and every scheme of social order, each of them occupies a definite position, with its definite sphere of rights and duties, under the system of law which necessarily regulates their external relations with one another. They have infinity or extension in the sense that, *sub specie aeternitatis*, each of them is a 'living soul' (as nothing but the individual person is or can be) with an inner spring of spiritual life which rises beyond our knowledge and ends beyond our ken. If we look at Groups from this angle, we shall not call them persons. We shall call them organizations of persons, or schemes of personal relations, in all their successive phases, from the village or club to the State or the League of Nations. And because they are organizations or schemes, made by the mind of man, we shall regard them as constructed by the thought of persons, consisting in the thought of persons, sustained by the thought of persons, and revised or even destroyed by the thought of persons— but never as persons themselves, in the sense in which individuals are persons." Ernest Barker, from his Introduction to Otto Gierke's *Natural Law and the Theory of Society* (Cambridge, UK: Cambridge University Press, 1934).

social engagements can range anywhere from mutually self-interested business relationships up to the most intimate relationships of interpersonal love. Various social virtues, including charity, civic-mindedness, brotherly love, and certain forms of patriotism, are in no way antithetical to the personalistic perspective. The personalistic perspective, however, is incompatible with any kind of group-think that attempts to wrench the center of Meaning and Mystery out of individual persons and transfer it to a nation, a tribe, a class, or any other collective entity conceived of as a mysterious Super-Person. Personalism holds that whenever Meaning and Mystery are wrenched out of the Depth of individual souls and transferred to a collective entity of any kind, an ultimate violation is committed, with absurdity and mystification being the inevitable result, as one can readily discern from all the claptrap that has been written about a *Volksgeist*, a Race-Soul, the General Will, the National Destiny, and the like. The personalistic philosophy is hostile to any type of collective self-worship, to any type of group-deification, and to any and all types of political and social movements that demand of their adherents that they rate their nationality, their ethnicity, or their class affiliations higher than their individual humanity.[13]

Personalism, at least of the type outlined here, is thus the very opposite of "atomistic individualism." Atomized individuals are not persons, they are not centers of Meaning and Mys-

---

13. The tendency for racial, ethnic, and nationalistic loyalties to override basic human decency was the major theme of Reinhold Niebuhr's classic *Moral Man and Immoral Society*, a book that influenced a whole generation of social reformers, including Martin Luther King, Jr. Here are King's views on the matter: "Man's sinfulness sinks to such devastating depths in his collective life that Reinhold Niebuhr could write a book titled *Moral Man and Immoral Society*. Man collectivized in the group, the tribe, the race, and the nation often sinks to levels of barbarity unthinkable even among lower animals. We see the tragic expression of Immoral Society in the doctrine of white supremacy that plunges millions of black men into the abyss of exploitation, and in the horrors of two world wars that have left battlefields drenched with blood, national debts higher than mountains of gold, men psychologically deranged and physically handicapped, and nations of widows and orphans." *From Strength to Love* (New York: Simon and Schuster 1964), p. 111.

tery; rather, they are people who for one reason or another have been cut off from the deepest sources of their own unique personhood and, as a result, lack all sense of individual wholeness and human worth. In fact, atomized individuals are the very sorts of people who tend to become ethnic tribalists. Lacking all sense of their own personal meaning and worth, cut off from the Depth of their own being, atomized individuals will often try to fill the existential vacuum that they experience in their lives through the desperate appropriation of a group identity. This group identity then comes to take the place of the missing Depth in themselves and is worshipped as if it were a divinity.[14]

AMERICAN PERSONALISM: LIBERAL AND CHRISTIAN ROOTS

The type of personalistic thinking embodied in the 1964 Civil Rights Act grew out of two complementary strains in American thought, the first being the Christian religious tradition (and the related offshoots of Unitarianism and New England transcendentalism), the second being the liberal Jeffersonian tradition, especially as this was embodied in the Declaration of Independence. From the Christian religious tradition, personalism took over the idea that each human being is loved by God and has a separate inner relationship to God irrespective of whatever

---

14. The process by which the spiritually empty and forlorn seek desperately to overcome their emptiness through fanatical identification with a larger social group and its interests is a process that has perhaps nowhere been more profoundly analyzed than in the great novel of the Austrian writer Robert Musil, *The Man Without Qualities*. For a valuable psychoanalytic treatment of the same phenomenon, with Italian and German fascism in the background, see the classic work of Erich Fromm, *Escape from Freedom* (New York: Avon Books, 1941). Fromm's own view is well captured in one of the opening epigraphs to his book, a quotation from a work on human dignity by the Christian neo-Platonist Pico della Mirandola: "Neither heavenly nor earthly, neither mortal nor immortal have we created thee, so that thou mightest be free according to thy own will and honor, to be thy own creator and builder. To thee alone we gave growth and development depending on thy own free will. Thou bearest in thee the germs of a universal life" (from Mirandola's *Oratio de Hominis Dignitate*).

social relationships such a person may have. God, according to the Christian tradition, judges all men on the basis of their individual moral excellences and personal qualities, and this is the way all human beings are to view one another. Personalism also took over from the Judeo-Christian religious tradition the idea that each human being is created in the "image of God" and thus manifests in some way a godlike nature that commands the respect of all people. A final idea taken over from the religious tradition was the metaphor that all human beings are children of God and members of a single human family.

From the Declaration of Independence and the liberal tradition, personalism took over the notion that all human beings have individual human rights conferred equally upon all and that it is the responsibility of government to protect these rights. The key passage in the Declaration, of course, comes after the words "we hold these truths" ("We hold these truths to be self-evident, that all men are created equal, that they are endowed by their Creator with certain unalienable rights . . . that to secure these rights governments are instituted among men . . . "). The liberal tradition also provided personalism with the important idea of the citizen and the equality of rights of all citizens regardless of their ethnic or religious background. As sociologist Nathan Glazer explains, the United States became "the first great nation that defines itself not in terms of ethnic origin but in terms of adherence to common rules of citizenship. . . . The American polity has . . . been defined by a steady expansion of the definition of those who may be included in it to the point where it now includes all humanity."[15]

The influence of both of these traditions, the Judeo-Christian and the liberal-Jeffersonian, on the personalistic outlook of many of the supporters of the Civil Rights Act can be well

---

15. Nathan Glazer, *Affirmative Discrimination* (Cambridge, MA: Harvard University Press, 1975), p. 7.

illustrated by remarks taken from three key figures in the struggle for the law's passage: President Lyndon Johnson, Senator Joseph Clark, and the Reverend Martin Luther King, Jr. Shortly before signing the Civil Rights Bill into law on July 2, 1964, President Johnson went on national television to explain to the American public the nature and purpose of the new law. His remarks began with an allusion to the Declaration of Independence: "One hundred and eighty-eight years ago this week [i.e., July 4, 1776]," he stated, "a small band of valiant men began a long struggle for freedom. They pledged their lives, their fortunes, and their sacred honor . . . not only for political independence but for personal liberty." A few paragraphs later, Johnson drew attention to the great discrepancy that existed between the principles of the American founding and the actual status of the dispossessed in America, particularly the American Negro:

> We believe that all men are created equal, yet many are denied equal treatment. We believe that all men have certain unalienable rights, yet many Americans do not enjoy these rights. We believe that all men are entitled to the blessings of liberty, yet millions are being deprived of those blessings, not because of their own failures but because of the color of their skin.

Further on in the speech, Johnson invoked important tenets of the common religious tradition, suggesting that those who are equal before God should also be equal before the law and have an equal access to public accommodations and jobs:

> The purpose of this law [the Civil Rights Act] is simple. . . . It does not give special treatment to any citizen. . . . It does say that those who are equal before God shall now also be equal in the polling booths, in the classrooms, in the factories, and in hotels and restaurants, and movie theatres, and other places that provide service to the public.

Finally, at the close of his address, Johnson again invoked the biblical religious tradition, offering as a counter to the racial hatred in the land the ideal that all human beings are children of God and members of the same human family:

> Let us close the springs of racial poison. . . . Let us hasten
> that day when our unmeasured strength and our unbounded
> spirit will be free to do the great works ordained to this
> nation by the just and wise God who is the Father of us all.

Senator Joseph Clark, like many other supporters of the Civil Rights Bill, saw the bill as involving one of the key moral issues of the day. He went on the floor of the Senate in early April 1964 to explain to his colleagues just how central the moral issue was to him personally, especially in regard to Title VII, the fair employment practices section of the bill:

> The primary reason why I support it [the Civil Rights Bill]
> and why a majority of the Senate, I am confident, supports
> it, is that it raises as clearly as any piece of legislation which
> has come before the Senate since I have joined it . . . the
> clear issue of right and wrong. This is particularly true with
> respect to Title VII. (110 *Cong. Rec.*, p. 7203)

To support his view concerning the preeminence of the moral issue, Clark went on to quote from a statement made on behalf of over 30 different church and synagogue groups concerning the immorality of racial segregation and discrimination. The statement he quoted drew heavily from the personalistic strains in the religious tradition:

> The religious conscience of America condemns racism as
> blasphemy against God. It recognizes that the racial segre-
> gation and discrimination that flow from it are a denial of
> the worth which God has given to all persons. We hold that

God is the father of all men. Consequently in every person there is an innate dignity which is the basis of human rights. These rights constitute a moral claim which must be honored both by all persons and by the state. Denial of such rights is immoral. (110 *Cong. Rec.*, p. 7203)

Clark also quoted in this context an additional statement by a rabbinic group that had testified previously before his committee:

The major points of our statement, Mr. Chairman, have to do with [our] concern for the immorality of discrimination in the area of employment. . . . We believe that this kind of discrimination is blasphemous; it is an affront to our religious commitment and to our religious convictions, believing as we do that man is created in the image of God. (110 *Cong. Rec.*, pp. 7203–4)

Immediately following the above quotation, Clark explained how his own support of the Civil Rights Bill was intimately linked to his commitment to the national ideals of liberty and justice for all (i.e., the liberal-Jeffersonian ideal), and to a nation of one people, under God:

I speak only for myself when I say that if I opposed this bill, I would find it very difficult indeed at the next public meeting I attended to pledge allegiance to the flag of the United States of America, and to the Republic for which it stands, one nation under God, indivisible, with liberty and justice for all. (110 *Cong. Rec.*, p. 7204)

"BY THE CONTENT OF THEIR CHARACTER"

In the case of Martin Luther King, Jr., we have someone who was not only the most important public figure in the 1950s and early 1960s civil rights movement, but also perhaps more self-consciously committed than any other leading figure in the movement to the basic tenets of the personalistic philosophy and the personalistic mode of thought. In his book on the Montgomery bus boycott, for instance, Dr. King explained how he had first come to adopt the personalistic philosophy while a student at Boston University's School of Theology. Speaking of the impact upon his thought of two of his teachers, Edgar S. Brightman and L. Harold DeWolf, he wrote:

> It was mainly under these teachers that I studied personalistic philosophy—the theory that the clue to the meaning of ultimate reality is found in personality. This personal idealism remains today my basic philosophical position. Personalism's insistence that only personality—finite and infinite—is ultimately real strengthened me in two convictions: it gave me metaphysical and philosophical grounding for the idea of a personal God, and it gave me a metaphysical basis for the dignity and worth of all human personality.[16]

Throughout his life King invoked the rhetoric of the Declaration of Independence to weaken the forces of all racial, religious, and national attachments, at least insofar as they impeded the recognition of our individual personhood and universal rights as human beings. For instance, in a commencement address at Lincoln University he said the following of the American Dream:

---

16. Martin Luther King, Jr., *Stride Toward Freedom* (New York: Harper and Row, 1963), p. 82. King explains shortly after this passage that he was also influenced by his reading of Hegel's works. Although there were serious shortcomings in the Hegelian dialectic, he says, it "helped me to see that growth comes through struggle." But, he adds, "there were points in Hegel's philosophy that I strongly disagreed with. For instance, his absolute idealism was rationally unsound to me because it tended to swallow up the many in the one." (p. 82) One could perhaps find no better phrase to describe the spiritual and existential violation of human personhood involved in racial quota thinking, and the stereotyping mentality endemic to racially divided societies, than this last locution—"to swallow up the many in the one."

[The American Dream] is a dream of a land where men of all races, of all nationalities, and of all creeds can live together as brothers. The substance of the dream is expressed in these sublime words, words lifted to cosmic proportions: We hold these truths to be self-evident—that all men are created equal; that they are endowed by their Creator with certain inalienable rights; that among these are life, liberty, and the pursuit of happiness.[17]

And with specific regard to race, the principles of the Declaration were invoked with equal force in his telling account of the Montgomery bus boycott, *Stride Toward Freedom*:

Ever since the signing of the Declaration of Independence, America has manifested a schizophrenic personality on the question of race. She has been torn between selves—a self in which she has proudly professed democracy and a self in which she has sadly practiced the antithesis of democracy. . . . Indeed, segregation and discrimination are strange paradoxes in a nation founded on the principle that all men are created equal.[18]

Although Dr. King drew extensively in his political thought from the Declaration and the liberal-Jeffersonian tradition, it is clear that the most powerful source of his personalistic philosophy was that provided by the universalistic and personalistic strains in the biblical religion. In *Where Do We Go from Here: Chaos or Community*, which was published just a year before his tragic death, the Jewish and Christian roots of his thought were made unmistakably clear:

---

17. Martin Luther King, Jr., quoted in Kenneth L. Smith and Ira G. Zepp, *Search for the Beloved Community* (Washington, D.C.: University Press of America, 1986), p. 127.
18. King, Jr., *Stride Toward Freedom*, pp. 190–1.

> Deeply rooted in our religious heritage is the conviction
> that every man is an heir to a legacy of dignity and worth.
> Our Judeo-Christian tradition refers to this inherent dig-
> nity of man in the biblical term "the image of God." The
> image of God is universally shared in equal portions by all
> men. . . . Every human being has etched in his personal-
> ity the indelible stamp of the Creator. Every man must be
> respected because God loves him. The worth of an individual
> does not lie in the measure of his intellect, his racial origin,
> or his social position. Human worth lies in relatedness to
> God. An individual has value because he has value to God.
> Whenever this is recognized, "whiteness" and "blackness"
> pass away as determinants in a relationship and "son" and
> "brother" are substituted.[19]

One could hardly find a more succinct statement of the religiously grounded personalistic outlook or one more out of tune
with the type of ethnic tribalism that sees the ethnic group itself
as God and one's relatedness to this God as the major source
of one's being and worth. The God of the biblical religion is
seen as a force destructive to all racial and ethnic tribalism, a
force that breaks down all racial and social barriers between
human beings, and unites all men in a universal brotherhood of
mankind in which each human being is respected as a person of
individual dignity and worth.

Dr. King went on to explain shortly after the quoted passage
the special obligation of the Christian churches to proclaim the
sinfulness and injustice of the system of race subordination and
segregation in the Jim Crow South—a system, he claimed, that
denied the possibility of a shared communion in God between
people of different races, and thus denied the possibility of estab-

---

19. Martin Luther King, Jr., *Where Do We Go from Here: Chaos or Community?*
(Boston: Beacon Press, 1967), p. 97.

lishing a true community of equals. "The church has an opportunity and a duty to lift up its voice like a trumpet and declare unto the people the immorality of segregation," he wrote. "It must affirm that every human life is a reflection of divinity, and that every act of injustice mars and defaces the image of God in man. . . . A religion true to its mission knows that segregation is morally wrong and sinful. . . . It is unbrotherly and impersonal. Two segregated souls never meet in God. Segregation denies the sacredness of human personality."[20]

While King believed strongly that human laws were needed prohibiting segregation and discrimination, at the same time he believed that a change of heart was necessary for any genuine racial reconciliation to take place and that legislation alone could not achieve this. Such a change of heart could only come about, he believed, through the voluntary adoption of a religion of love such as that proclaimed by Jesus in the Bible.[21] Such a religion of love, rooted in the idea that all human beings are created in the image of God and ought to be treated accordingly, was the foundational belief of his personalistic philosophy and the driving force behind his entire life's mission.

Biblical religious themes as the basis of Dr. King's personalistic philosophy can also be seen in the famous "I Have a Dream" speech of August 1963. The magnificent climax to that speech draws upon the Genesis creation story and its depiction of all human beings as ultimately children of the same universal God: "When we allow freedom to ring, when we let it ring from every village and every hamlet, from every state and every city, we will

---

20. Ibid., pp. 97, 99.
21. "The ultimate solution to the race problem lies in the willingness of men to obey the unenforceable. . . . A vigorous enforcement of civil rights will bring an end to segregated public facilities, but it cannot bring an end to fears, prejudice, pride and irrationality, which are the barriers to a truly integrated society. These dark and demonic responses will be removed only as men are possessed by the invisible inner law which etches on their hearts the conviction that all men are brothers and that love is mankind's most potent weapon for personal and social transformation." Martin Luther King, Jr., *Where Do We Go from Here: Chaos or Community?* (Boston: Beacon Press, 1967), pp. 100–1.

be able to speed up that day when all of God's children—black men and white men, Jews and Gentiles, Protestants and Catholics—will be able to join hands and sing in the words of the Old Negro spiritual, 'Free at last, free at last; thank God almighty, we are free at last.'"

The most often quoted lines from that speech also drew heavily upon the biblical theme of judgment: "I have a dream that my four little children will one day live in a nation where they will not be judged by the color of their skin, but by the content of their character." Human beings, it is wished here, will someday be able to view one another, not in terms of artificial differences such as skin color or race, but in terms of personal moral worth, the same criterion that God uses in his judgment of people.

King had many times before this historic speech invoked the same biblical themes in his church sermons. Here, for instance, is what he had to say about the lesson of the Good Samaritan story in a sermon titled "On Being a Good Neighbor":

> Too seldom do we see people in their true *humanness*. A
> spiritual myopia limits our vision to external accidents.
> We see men as Jews or Gentiles, Catholics or Protestants,
> Chinese or American, Negroes or whites. We fail to think
> of them as fellow human beings made from the same basic
> stuff as we, molded in the same divine image. The priest and
> the Levite saw only a bleeding body, not a human being like
> themselves. But the Good Samaritan will always remind us
> to remove the cataracts of provincialism from our spiritual
> eyes and see men as men. If the Samaritan had considered
> the wounded man as a Jew first, he would not have stopped,
> for the Jews and the Samaritans had no dealings. He saw
> him as a human being first, who was a Jew only by accident.
> The good neighbor looks beyond the external accidents and

discerns those inner qualities that make all men human, and
therefore, brothers.[22]

ABOLITIONIST PERSONALISM

The civil rights movement of the 1950s and early 1960s did not,
of course, invent the personalistic mode of thought, nor was it
original in applying biblical and liberal-Jeffersonian themes to
a struggle for personal rights. Both of these ideas and practices
had been taken over from the earlier antislavery movement, and
it is probably safe to say that nothing did more to weaken the
influence of ethnic and tribalistic modes of thought in America
than New England abolitionism and the Christian and transcen-
dentalist philosophy that often undergirded it.

Two antislavery writers can be taken to illustrate some of the
themes discussed so far. The first, Samuel Sewall, was a Puritan
merchant whose "The Selling of Joseph," first published in 1700,
was one of the first antislavery tracts to appear in America. The
biblical teaching that all human beings are of the same blood—
the doctrine derived from both the creation story in Genesis and
chapter seventeen of the Book of Acts—was seen by Sewall as
incompatible with the manner in which black Africans were
being treated in America. Although he apparently believed Africans to be physically quite ugly in appearance, and doubted that
they could be integrated into white New England society, Sewall
nevertheless held that they were children of God and should be
treated with a respect commensurate with their status as such:

It is most certain that all men, as they are the sons of Adam,
are co-heirs, and have equal right unto liberty, and all other

---

22. Martin Luther King, Jr., *Strength to Love* (New York: Simon and Schuster, 1964),
p. 23.

outward comforts of life. God "hath given the earth . . . unto
the sons of Adam" (Psalm 115). "And hath made of one
blood, all nations of men, for to dwell on all the face of the
earth . . . that they should seek the Lord. Forasmuch then as
we are offspring of God" (Acts 17: 26–7). These Ethiopians,
as black as they are, seeing they are the Sons and Daughters
of the First Adam, the Brethren and sisters of the Last Adam,
and the offspring of God. They ought to be treated with a
respect agreeable [i.e., a respect commensurate with their
divine dignity].[23]

The second example is that of William Lloyd Garrison, who
developed further the biblical and religious argument against
slavery, although he went much further than Sewall in carrying
out its implications. The fact that all men are of one blood (i.e.,
that they constitute a single human race), that they have all been
created by a loving God, and that what counts in the eyes of
this God is an individual's moral virtue rather than his wealth
or skin color—all these were seen by Garrison as facts incompatible not only with the institution of slavery,but also with the
many laws in free states prohibiting interracial marriage. The
standard of matrimony Garrison believed should be the degree
of moral worth and mutual affection of the people involved, not
their race or ancestry:

> If [the Creator] has made "of one blood all nations of men
> for to dwell on all the face of the earth," then they are one
> species, and stand on a perfect equality; their intermarriage
> is neither unnatural or repugnant to nature, but obviously
> proper and salutary, it being designed to unite people of dif-
> ferent tribes and nations. As civilization, and knowledge, and

---

23. Quoted in Louis Ruchames, ed., *Racial Thought in America*, vol. 1 (Amherst:
University of Massachusetts Press, 1969), pp. 47, 51.

republican feelings, and Christianity prevail in the world, the wider will matrimonial connections extend. . . . An unnatural alliance is not that which joins in wedlock an African descendant with an American, or an Indian with a European, who are equal in moral worth. . . . The standard or matrimony is erected by affection and purity, and does not depend upon the height, or bulk, or color, or wealth, or poverty, of individuals.[24]

Garrison also quotes from the famous passage in Saint Paul's Letter to the Galatians, the passage often quoted in recent times by feminist writers, where all human beings are said to be one in Christ:

I call upon the spirits of the just made perfect in heaven, upon all who have experienced the love of God in their souls here below, upon the Christian converts in India and the islands of the sea, to sustain me in the assertion that there *is* power in the religion of Jesus Christ to melt down the most stubborn prejudice, to overthrow the highest walls of partition, to break the strongest caste, to improve and elevate the most degraded, to unite in fellowship the most hostile. . . . "In Christ Jesus, all are one: there is neither Jew nor Greek, there is neither bond nor free, there is neither male nor female"(Galatians 3:28).[25]

Because of his great faith in the power of the Christian religion to transform people's attitudes and behavior, Garrison, unlike Sewall, believed that black Africans, once freed from slavery, could eventually be assimilated into American society.

---

24. Ibid., pp. 308–9.
25. Ibid., pp. 312–13.

The liberal-Jeffersonian tradition and the themes of the American Revolution are also prominent in Garrison's writings, and can be seen, for instance, in the very first issue of the *Liberator*, where the aims and purposes of the periodical were set forth to the public:

> I determined, at every hazard, to lift up the standard of emancipation in the eyes of the nation, within sight of Bunker Hill, and the birthplace of liberty. That standard is now unfurled. Assenting to the "self-evident truth" maintained in the American Declaration of Independence, "that all men are created equal, and endowed by their Creator with certain inalienable rights—among which are life, liberty, and the pursuit of happiness," I shall strenuously contend for the immediate enfranchisement of our slave population. . . . On this subject, I do not wish to think, or speak or write, with moderation. . . . I will not equivocate—I will not excuse—I will not retreat a single inch—AND I WILL BE HEARD.

The mixture of biblical religious themes with the spirit of '76 was, in Garrison's case, of course, a very volatile combination, and both traditions would eventually go on to inspire the Northern armies in the American Civil War. The civil rights movement of the 1950s and early 1960s absorbed much of the driving spirit of this earlier abolitionism, but it was to add to it the important additional element of Gandhi-inspired nonviolence. It was this third element, most prominently displayed in the figures of Martin Luther King, Jr., and the early members of the Student Nonviolent Coordinating Committee (SNCC) that lent to the civil rights movement of this period much of its high moral tone and ultimately elevated it to a moral level considerably above that of most of the earlier abolitionism.

It was this moral elevation, and the genuine Christian commitment of several of its leaders, that enabled the 1950s and

1960s era civil rights movement to draw into its fold people from many different racial, ethnic, religious, and ideological backgrounds. Indeed, the moral elevation of the movement sometimes rose to the level of the saintly and heroic. One can get a good sense of the high moral tone and basic Christian orientation of many in the movement from the following "Commitment Blank," which Martin Luther King, Jr., and his aides required all demonstrators to sign before participating in the marches in Birmingham, Alabama:

COMMANDMENTS FOR THE VOLUNTEERS

I hereby pledge myself—my person and body—to the nonviolent movement. Therefore I will keep the following ten commandments:

1) Meditate daily on the teachings and life of Jesus.

2) Remember always that the nonviolent movement in Birmingham seeks justice and reconciliation—not victory.

3) Walk and talk in the manner of love, for God is love.

4) Pray daily to be used by God in order that all men might be free.

5) Sacrifice personal wishes in order that all men might be free.

6) Observe with both friend and foe the ordinary rules of courtesy.

7) Seek to perform regular service for others and for the world.

8) Refrain from the violence of fist, tongue, or heart.

9) Strive to be in good spiritual and bodily health.

10) Follow the directions of the movement and of the captain on a demonstration.

I sign this pledge, having seriously considered what I do and with the determination and will to persevere.

It was the genius of Martin Luther King, Jr., that was able to bring together the noblest strains in the biblical and liberal traditions and inspire millions in their lofty promises through the power of his magnificent oratory. Subsequent revelations of great personal flaws in the man cannot detract from the courage he showed in the face of incessant threats of racist violence, nor from the truth and goodwill of the message he preached of racial reconciliation and universal Christian love.

DETRIBALIZATION AND THE IMMIGRANT EXPERIENCE

The American experience after the Civil War was marked by the influx of successive waves of immigrants from many diverse lands. The immigrants generally shared the hope of advancing economically and being accepted into the larger society on an equal footing with the descendants of the older immigrants of English, Scottish, Welsh, and German origin. The open-market economy and the corresponding opportunities it offered for personal advancement gave birth to a peculiarly American work and achievement ethic that shared with the earlier Christian and liberal traditions the idea that individuals should be judged by what they individually do in life, rather than by what their ancestors did or by what ethnic group they belonged to.

There were counterforces at work, of course, ranging from the mild genealogical snootiness of the Daughters of the American Revolution to the terrorist-prone WASP racism of the Ku Klux Klan. But the personalistic mode of thought had taken strong root in America, and as the children of the first-generation immigrants learned to speak the English language and to adopt the ways of the American culture, they came to be accepted more and more into the general society and to be judged individually, rather than as representatives of their respective ethnic groups. This process was never complete, of course, and ethnic-tribalistic modes of consciousness always retained a considerable hold, sometimes harmlessly and with genuine social benefits.[26] But the personalistic viewpoint—the view that human beings are to be judged by their own characteristics and their own achievements, and not by their ethnic-tribal affiliations—was a powerful ideal that generally had a least some effect in shaping people's attitudes and actions.

The personalistic mode of thought, as it relates to the work and achievement ethic, can be well illustrated by the comments of a prominent black journalist in the early 1940s. The writer in question, a feisty and gifted columnist for the *Pittsburgh Courier*, was objecting to the fact that while individuals in the press were generally respected as such and not seen as representatives of their respective racial, ethnic, or religious groups, in the case of the Negro this was not the case. Only in the case of Negro individuals, the writer protested, was it thought relevant or appropriate to identify a person according to race, ethnicity, or ancestry:

> This [sinister policy of identifying individual Negroes as such] is a subtle form of discrimination designed to segregate these individuals in the mind of the public and thus bolster the national policy of biracialism. Thus, Paul Robeson is not a great baritone, he is a great "Negro" baritone. Dr. Carver is not just a great scientist, he is a great "Negro" scientist. Anne Brown is not merely a great soprano, she is a great

---

26. Ethnic-tribal affiliations, when properly integrated into, and counterbalanced by, a more encompassing or more universal understanding of humanity, can promote many salutary benefits to both individuals and the larger social order. Chief among these is a sense of rootedness and belonging to a shared history and culture, which, like our membership in the "little platoons" of our family, can be instrumental in helping us expand the circle of our empathy and identity beyond the narrow confines of our individual interests and predatory selves. It is when ethnic-tribal affiliations lose their sensitivity for ever expanded circles of empathy and identity—and place the tribe itself in the position of Supreme Being and Ultimate Concern—that a devilish distortion in consciousness takes place that leads to the kind of murderous aggression and distorted patriotism that produced the devastation of the First World War and the instigation by fascist nationalists of the Second.

"Negro" soprano. Langston Hughes is not a poet merely, he is a "Negro" poet. Augusta Savage is a "Negro" sculptor, C.C. Spaulding is a "Negro" insurance executive, R.R. Wright, Sr., is a "Negro" banker, J.A. Rogers is a "Negro" historian, Willard Townsend is a "Negro" labor leader, etc., etc., *ad infinitum*. No other group in this country is so singled out for racial identification, and no one can tell me that there is not a very definite reason for it. No daily newspaper refers to Mr. Morgenthau as "Jewish" secretary of the treasury, or New York's Herbert H. Lehman as the "Jewish" governor, or Isador Lubin as a "Jewish" New Dealer. Mayor Rossi is never identified as the "Italian-American" executive of San Francisco, nor is the millionaire Giannini called an "Italian" banker. There would be considerable uproar if Senator Robert F. Wagner were termed "New York's able German-American solon," or Representative Tenerowicz dubbed "Detroit's prominent Pole." When has a Utah legislator in Washington been labeled "Mormon"?

One could go on and on, but the point is that "our" daily newspapers carefully avoid such designations except in the case of so-called Negroes. I cannot recall when I have seen a criminal referred to as a Jew, an Italian, a German or a Catholic, but it is commonplace for colored lawbreakers or suspects to be labeled "Negro."

Personally, I shall not be convinced of the sincerity of these white editors and columnists who shape America's thinking unless they begin treating the Negro in the news as they do other Americans. Those who continue this type of journalism are the worst sort of hypocrites when they write about democracy and national unity.[27]

---

27. George S. Schuyler, in *Pittsburgh Courier*, 13 June 1942, as cited in Gunnar Myrdal, *An American Dilemma* (New York: Harper and Row, 1944, 1962), p. 1184. Schuyler is a much underappreciated black writer who held what today might be called

The writer was expressing here, of course, the same aspiration that many Jews, Italians, Poles, and others had previously expressed of being accepted as equals into a multiracial, multiethnic, and multireligious culture that was respectful of individual differences and individual achievements. This seems to have been the dominant aspiration of the vast majority of black Americans, along with the vast majority of other Americans, at least up until the late 1960s, although a minority of black separatists and black nationalists, it is true, never accepted it.

A very similar point to that of the *Pittsburgh Courier* journalist was made a few years later by the distinguished historian Frank Tannenbaum. In his influential study of slavery in the Western hemisphere, *Slave and Citizen*, Tannenbaum wrote:

It is not enough to say, as we often do [in the U.S.], that there are so many Negro doctors, lawyers, politicians, businessmen, and scholars. It is requisite that there should not be Negro doctors, Negro lawyers, or Negro scholars. Their professional standing must overshadow their racial origin. It is only when we can say he is a great actor, a great scholar, a great lawyer, a great citizen, that the step has been taken which endows the Negro with the moral worth as a man which obliterates the invidious distinction and sweeps away the condescending fawning of the better-than-thou attitude. When the time does come that a Negro judge on the bench is a judge and not a Negro judge, when a Negro scholar is a scholar and not a Negro scholar . . . the gap between legal equality and moral acceptance will be obliterated.[28]

"socially conservative" views on a number of prominent social and political issues of his day.

28. Frank Tannenbaum, *Slave and Citizen* (New York: Alfred A. Knopf, 1947), pp. 113–14. We have clearly come to the point in the arena of professional sports where the hopes of Tannenbaum and the *Pittsburgh Courier* journalist have largely been met. Managers, players, and sports fans alike look today primarily to the merit and achievement of professional athletes and rarely place blacks, whites, Latinos, and

THE GREAT CONTRACTION

The early and mid-1960s marked a high point in post-Reconstruction American history in the public understanding of, and respect for, the dignity and worth of individual human persons. It is often hard for people today to remember just what this period was like, so far have we strayed from its motivating spirit. It was a period in which progress was being made on several fronts by many black Americans, and for the vast majority of people of all races and ethnicities this progress was cause for rejoicing. Black faces seen in banks and business enterprises where they had never been seen before gave to all people of goodwill, black and white alike, the feeling that they lived in a society that was at least a little more just and humane than the society that had existed before. A very similar feeling had been unleashed two decades previously by President Truman's order abolishing segregation in the military, and by Jackie Robinson's breaking of the color barrier in professional baseball. These were developments about which all fair-minded Americans could feel a genuine satisfaction and pride. The early and mid-1960s was also a period when questions regarding a person's race, ethnicity, and national origin were often deleted from government questionnaires, as such questions were generally viewed as irrelevant to any legitimate government purpose, and the mere solicitation of such information was frequently held to be an affront to the dignity of human persons and a threat to the principle of equality before the law.

---

members of other races and ethnicities in separate mental categories, at least not when their status as athletic professionals is at issue. Unfortunately, one cannot say the same for people in occupations where racial preferences have been in play. Regrettably, for many whites and Asians terms like "black doctor," "black lawyer," and "black accountant" do connote a better-than-thou attitude, one suggesting that the doctor in question may be a racial-preference recipient—"an affirmative-ation hire"—and perhaps not up to meeting the white and Asian standards. Worse still, there is rationality to this better-than-thou attitude perhaps most tellingly revealed in anecdotal reports of black patients in municipal hospitals requesting to be treated by white doctors.

All this, however, was to change in the late 1960s and early 1970s with the emergence of the policy known as "affirmative action." It was at this time that a radical change in consciousness was taking place, both inside and outside the government, which could be seen in the very terms and conceptual structures that were thought legitimate to interpret human reality. One might characterize this change as a shift from the personalistic language and personalistic mode of thought that had characterized the 1964 Civil Rights Act and the black protest movement that had preceded it to the depersonalizing logic of racial and ethnic tribalism. The death of Martin Luther King, Jr., who in many ways epitomized the personalistic ideal in its Christian form and who, at the time of his assassination in April 1968, was organizing a march on behalf of the poor of all races, might be taken as symbolic of the passing of this older ideal of a universal citizenship and universal personhood. By the late 1960s, a new militant spirit, one often combined with a strong anti-white animus, had taken hold of many black, Hispanic, and American Indian spokesmen, and it became clear to all by this time that the days when Italian housewives, Jewish college students, and Irish priests would walk arm in arm with Southern blacks in defense of universal principles of justice and individual rights were now a thing of the past.

In the 1950s and early 1960s the black protest movement was a genuine civil rights movement, and represented the convergence of an ethnic-parochial interest (i.e., the social and economic interest of black people), with a universal-human ideal (i.e., equal rights for all, regardless of race or ethnicity). A decade later this was no longer the case, as black groups, often joined in coalition with Hispanic groups and women's groups, sought favored treatment for the members of their own particular groups, regardless of what deleterious effect this might have on other people and regardless of how unjust or unfair these other people might perceive this favored treatment to be. The attitude of many of the black and Hispanic militants was essentially this: "Look, you white folks [or 'white Anglos'] have been screwing us for three hundred years now. It's about time we started screwing you for awhile." Militant feminists often took a similar attitude with regard to white males. The universal-human ideal, it seems, had lost most of its appeal and increasingly gave way to self-seeking power politics, ruthlessly pursued by well-organized racial, ethnic, and gender interest groups, which cared little for those they had to step on in the pursuit of their goals.

The period of the very late 1960s and early 1970s proved to be a period of unprecedented ethnicization and tribalization in the American public consciousness. It was a period when many Americans desperately sought their "roots," not in a common humanity or in a universal God, nor in a common national heritage (from which many had become estranged as a result of the unpopularity of the Vietnam War), but in their respective genealogies and ethnicities. This was true not only of Americans of African, Spanish, and Asian ancestry but also of many people of white European and Mideastern backgrounds as well.

With the liberal tradition in abeyance and the universalistic strains in the Judeo-Christian religion ceasing to have any significant influence over people's minds, the net effect of the increasing interest in genealogy and ethnicity was to erect new barriers between people where previously such barriers had been greatly weakened or in some cases had not existed at all. Ethnic-tribal modes of thought, unmodified by any wider identity or commitment, were to be given a new legitimacy and preeminence in America, and the practice of classifying the whole population according to racial and ethnic criteria, at one time viewed in most places outside the South with near universal horror, and identified in the minds of many with South Africa and Nazi Germany, was to become the order of the day.

There was, of course, a counterattack, led both by individuals and by the organizations of those ethnic groups who found themselves placed at a disadvantage vis-à-vis those groups that were officially favored. A new convergence of ethnic-parochial interest and universal-human ideal came to be represented by Polish-American organizations, Italian-American organizations, and Jewish-American organizations, plus a number of other groups, with the Jewish groups being the most active and influential, owing in part to bad historical memories of the effect of racial classifications and quota systems in both Europe and America. None of these groups, however, either individually or collectively, could stem the tide of racial and ethnic classification or the preferential treatment of persons based on such classifications.

The actual policy of affirmative action in employment, it should be understood, had nothing to do—at least in its inception—with any laws passed by Congress, and indeed was in clear violation of federal statues. What happened was that the federal bureaucracy, led by the Equal Employment Opportunity Commission (EEOC) and the Office of Federal Contract Compliance (OFCC), aided and abetted along the way by the federal courts, simply rewrote through "interpretation" Titles VI and VII of the 1964 Civil Rights Act, as well as President Johnson's antidiscrimination Executive Orders 11246 and 11375, substituting ethnic-tribal categories (e.g., "Hispanic," "Oriental," "black," etc.) for the personalistic language of the documents in questions. Terms such as "person," "individual," "*any* employee," "*all* qualified applicants," and the like, were cynically reinterpreted to mean in effect only those persons, individuals, or employees who were members of officially designated racial and ethnic "minority groups" as such groups were defined by the EEOC. It was only as members of certain racial and ethnic groups that individuals could claim the right of protection under legislation that was originally written to insure to all Americans that they would be treated in all employment situations, in the language of President Johnson's Executive Order 11246, "*without* regard to their race, creed, color, or national origin."[29]

The federal bureaucrats, using such euphemisms and code words as "underutilization," "goals," "timetables," and the like, began to pressure employers into giving special preference to people who fit into certain racial, ethnic, and gender categories, at the expense of people who did not and who were denied all manner of redress for such action. The approach of the federal courts was even more direct, insofar as a finding that an employer had discriminated in the past was seen as a justification, under a blatantly dishonest reading of Section 703(g) of the 1964 Civil Rights Act, for the hiring of new people on a racial or ethnic quota basis. One might have supposed that being guilty of discriminating against people in the past was even more reason not to discriminate against people in the future—that, for instance, discriminating against two people in the past because they were black and then discriminating against two people in the present because they were white would mean that a total of four people had been discriminated against. And this is exactly what critics of affirmative action, including such black critics as

---

29. The cynicism, dishonesty, and blatant disregard for public law that federal bureaucrats have displayed in their efforts to transform the meaning of the 1964 Civil Rights Act is well captured in the following remark by a staff member of the Equal Employment Opportunity Commission. Speaking in 1970 to representatives of the *Harvard Law Review*, the staffer boasted: "The anti-preferential hiring provisions [of the 1964 Civil Rights Act] are a big zero, a nothing, a nullity. They don't mean anything at all to us." Quoted in Elliot Abrams, "The Quota Commission," *Commentary*, Oct. 1972, p. 54. When one considers that the EEOC was explicitly set up by the Civil Rights Act to enforce the provisions of its hiring section, one gets a sense of the truly frightening lengths to which affirmative-action supporters have gone in the pursuit of their policies. For an excellent account of the radical transition from the color-blind understanding of antidiscrimination law to the highly color-conscious policies of racial preferences, see Nathan Glazer, *Affirmative Discrimination* (New York: Basic Books, 1975).

Bayard Rustin, have strenuously argued. But within the logic of affirmative action, two plus two equaled zero. It is the logic of tribal warfare.

Consider, for instance, the following, scenario:

> A small Southern town is polarized along racial lines. Early on a Friday evening, members of the local Ku Klux Klan go down to the local shopping mall, abduct the first black person they see, steal his wallet, and give all his money away to the first white person to come along. Upon hearing this, members of the local black community are incensed, and many among the more militant youth vow to get even. Consequently, on the following week members of the local Black Defense League go down to the same shopping mall, abduct the first white person they see, steal *his* wallet, and give all *his* money away to the first black person to walk by.

One has in the above account an *exact* parallel to the logic and underlying mentality of affirmative action. What most affirmative action programs in employment are really saying is this: Because of the discrimination in the past against person A, which worked to the unmerited benefit of person B, it is now necessary to give special preference to person C at the expense of person D. Person A and person C are not the same person, nor are they necessarily related to each other in any way at all except for the fact that they both have the same black, brown, or yellow skin color, or both have ancestors who were born in foreign countries where the official language spoken is Spanish. Similarly, person B and person D are not the same person, nor are they necessarily related to each other in any way at all except for the fact that they both have the same white skin color—and their ancestors were born in foreign countries where the official language spoken is *not* Spanish.

Put in such terms, the policy sounds clearly absurd,[30] and indeed it is absurd, although an impression to the contrary seems to have been created in the minds of the federal judges and federal bureaucrats who initially developed the policy by their tendency to view all black and Hispanic people as poor and underprivileged and all white people, by contrast, as rich and privileged. (On this latter point, it would seem the judges and bureaucrats generalized from their own circumstances and apparently assumed white people were all more or less like themselves and their friends). The tradition of giving a break to the underdog is in many contexts a praiseworthy one, and on grounds of justice, at least, many would not object to a hiring

---

30. Even this characterization does not capture fully the arbitrariness and absurdity of the policy. According to the guidelines of the Equal Employment Opportunity Commission—America's official race classification board—an Arab American with the complexion of, say, an Anwar Sadat, would be considered "white," as would the very darkest-skinned Turk, Sicilian, or Sephardic Jew. Steven Plaut, an economics professor at Oberlin, has well captured the arbitrariness and injustice of the current system when he writes:

> I have always been disturbed by the fact that many ethnic groups who have been the victims of discrimination in the past because they were minorities (e.g., Jews, Italians, etc.) are now the victims of discrimination because they have been designated by some bureaucrat as belonging to the "majority."

Plaut, however, has successfully outfoxed the affirmative-action bureaucrats, for although he himself is of Jewish origin, he has been able to turn their Nuremberg-like laws to his own advantage. As he explains:

> For years, I have been listing myself as an Asian American or Oriental American on "affirmative-action" questionnaires. I am a Jew, whose ancestors, culture, and "roots" originated in the Middle East, i.e., Asia. The fact that I and my immediate ancestors were not born in Asia should be irrelevant; the same holds true for many Japanese and Chinese Americans. And I defy anyone to prove that Asia ends at the Himalayas. Ethnic identity, as pointed out above, is subjective, and only the worst racist would deny me my self-definition because of the pigmentation of my skin (a rather pale, insipid shade). I urge all other potential Asian Americans to follow my example.
>
> If I should ever be pressed about this, I am prepared to alter my self-definition. It seems that my ancestors on my father's side (hence my surname) lived in Spain until they were forcibly expelled in the fifteenth century, migrating to central Europe. So, you see, I am also a "Spanish surnamed" American, an Ibero American, or—if you will—an Hispanic. Steven Plaut, article title in quotes with comma after *Midstream* Feb. 1980, p. 49.

policy that gave some degree of preference to poor and under-privileged people over rich and privileged ones (some call this "class-based affirmative action"). But the great socioeconomic diversity in America, of course, does not conform to any simple ethnic or racial stereotype. According to the Census Bureau, for instance, there are two and a half times as many white people in America below the poverty line as black people, and a full 25% of all black families have family incomes above the national average for whites.

One can say in their favor that some of the federal judges and bureaucrats who favored affirmative action harbored a genuine sympathy for the plight of the poor and disadvantaged, especially for those who had been victims of racial and ethnic discrimination. Where they went wrong was in abandoning the suffering person as the unit of concern and transferring their sympathy to a very heterogeneous group of people, whom they saw only in terms of a stereotyped image. Indeed, the rhetoric of affirmative action is one in which language has cut loose from flesh-and-blood reality and gone on to create its own fantasy world of images, symbols, and depersonalized mental abstractions. Terms such as the "black," the "white," the "Mexican American," the "Oriental," the "Puerto Rican," etc.—terms meaning everyone in the group and yet no one—were to become the basis for a general mystification that was to desensitize people to the personal-discrete nature of all human reality and all human suffering.

FEEBLE DEFENSES

Supporters of preferential hiring on the basis of race and ethnicity will sometimes pay lip service to the older, personalistic ideal of a color-blind society but will then try to defend race- and ethnic-conscious hiring policies as an interim or temporary measure that is supposedly necessary to bring about such a society. This idea, for instance, was expressed in a federal circuit court decision in 1973: "Our society cannot be completely color-blind in the short run if we are to have a color-blind society in the long run." It is never explained, however, just how race-conscious policies in the short run can bring about color blindness in the long run. Why, for instance, should people who have been encouraged—or, indeed, required by law—to see other people not as persons, but as group representatives, suddenly at some future date begin seeing them as individuals? The idea is absurd on its very face. Institutionalizing ethnic and color consciousness only habituates the practice, and ingrains it that much more deeply in the public mind. The idea that you can get human beings to think of other human beings as persons in the long run by having them think of them as group representatives in the short run is akin to the idea that you can get young males to view young females as persons, not as sex objects, by subjecting them in their formative years to heavy does of government-sponsored porn films. As Miro Todorovich, a leading critic of affirmative action in education, has remarked, it is a policy of prescribing whiskey to cure alcoholism.

The inevitable effect of race- and ethnic-conscious hiring policies is to legitimate ethnic and racial stereotyping both as a way of thinking and as a manner of human beings relating to one another. Such policies only serve to undermine that ongoing openness to new experience and new encounters, which alone is an antidote to a prejudicial frame of mind. In addition, such policies provoke deep resentment in those persons not of the favored race or ethnicity, and they will frequently take out their very legitimate anger, not on the federal judges and federal bureaucrats who instituted the policies, or on the various black, Hispanic, and feminist leaders who support them, but on the individual blacks, Hispanics, and women they encounter daily, many of whom, according to opinion polls, are opponents of affirmative action.[31]

Many people try to justify preferential hiring based on race and ethnicity as a mode of rectifying the "present effects of past discrimination." This, however, is a rather feeble defense, as preferential hiring programs are rarely, if ever, means-tested, and it is not quite clear just what "effects" are being rectified. Very often it is the best-off among the targeted racial and ethnic minority groups who take advantage of such programs. In some cases, the actual beneficiaries of preferential programs would seem to have been the victims of nothing more serious than affluence.[32] But even if preferential hiring *were*

---

31.   A June 1977 *Gallup Opinion Index* survey revealed that 64% of the "nonwhites" and 82% of the females questioned believed that "ability as determined by test scores" should be the main consideration in hiring and university admission decisions rather than preferential treatment based on ethnicity or gender.

32.   This is probably most common in the area of preferential admissions to prestige universities. Joseph Adelson, for instance, describes the following case of preferential treatment in graduate school admissions in his own department of psychology at the University of Michigan: "One afternoon several years ago, while serving on our admissions committee, I came across the applications of two young women. One was an ambassador's daughter who has been educated in private secondary schools, and was attending a most prestigious Ivy League university. The other might have stepped out of a Harriet Arnow novel. She had been born in Appalachia, the daughter of a poor farmer. The farm failed, the family moved north, her father died, the family survived on welfare and odd jobs, she married young, bore a child, was divorced, began attending a municipal university and ultimately was graduated with an excellent record. With respect to objective measurements—test scores and the like—these two young women were more or less evenly matched. It was the ambassador's daughter who, being black, was offered an invitation. . . . The welfare child, being white, was not admitted, did not come close."

Adelson goes on to describe what the admissions committee found when it began to take a closer look at the individual economic backgrounds of the so-called minority applicants: "This past year our admissions committee decided to give some attention to the socioeconomic status of all plausible candidates. What we found was startling: of the five minority finalists, three were attending elite private colleges, and two were at selective state universities. Only one had received scholarship help. Three of the five came from affluent—not merely comfortable—families, and one of these gave every evidence of being rich. The committee member who interviewed most of them reported back to our faculty, somewhat ruefully, that their average family income was considerably higher than that enjoyed by the faculty itself." (Joseph Adelson, *Commentary*, May 1978, p. 27)

means-tested and, say, the income and educational level of a job applicant's parents were taken into account in an attempt to favor the disadvantaged, it is not at all clear why such a program should be limited to those of only certain racial and ethnic backgrounds but not others. Does socioeconomic disadvantage that may arguably be attributed to racial and ethnic discrimination against one's ancestors have any greater claim to public concern than socioeconomic disadvantage that is not so attributable? Many would answer no, but even if this were not the case, it would seem that many poor Irish Americans, poor Polish Americans, poor Jewish Americans, poor Greek Americans, poor Italian Americans, poor Portuguese Americans, poor Slavic Americans, poor Hungarian Americans, poor Czech Americans, poor Ukrainian Americans, poor Arab Americans, poor Turkish Americans, poor Armenian Americans, poor Gypsy Americans, and indeed virtually every poor person in America who is of Southern European, Eastern European, North African, or Middle Eastern ethnic background would have a legitimate claim to preferential treatment, since their socioeconomic deprivation could arguably be attributed to past discrimination against their ancestors.

Perhaps the most common defense of preferential hiring in recent years is the so-called role-model argument. Women, Hispanics, and particularly black people, it is said, need same-race (or same-gender) role models in various occupations in order to be convinced that they can succeed in a competitive employment world where most important positions in the past have been held by white males. It is necessary, the argument goes, to weigh the injustice done to the better-qualified applicants who are not hired because of affirmative action programs against all the good that is done by the additional minority and women role models that are created.

Such an argument may enjoy a superficial appeal at first glance, but the appeal evaporates once one reflects that affirmative-action role models are not genuine and are soon recognized as such by all concerned. The role actually modeled by affirmative-action recipients is that of a patronized black, Hispanic, or female who is of inferior qualifications in comparison to the best qualified applicant for a job or promotion, and who would not have gotten to where he or she is except for the existence of an official policy of government favoritism. Affirmative-action role models, it would seem, serve only to perpetuate the prejudiced view that blacks, Hispanics, and women are grossly inferior to Caucasian males and incapable of competing with them on an equal plane. Affirmative-action role models also undermine all the positive influences of those genuine role models—i.e., those blacks, Hispanics, and women who really have competed successfully with white males—because of the inevitable tendency of observers to lump the two types of achievers together.

The situation, it would seem, is particularly damaging for many young blacks, who often lack self-confidence in unfamiliar arenas where they must compete with whites because of the long-time dominance of white-supremacy thinking. Supporters of affirmative action apparently believed that such negative effects of affirmative-action role models could be significantly offset by keeping preferential hiring policies secret. People, they believed, would be given preference on the basis of their race, ethnicity, or gender, but this would not be publicly admitted, and indeed, would be officially denied. Dissimulation and denial have, in fact, been a characteristic feature of most affirmative-action programs, but they do not seem to have had much of their intended effect. Most people, both those in the preferred groups and those in the non-preferred groups, have generally understood quite well exactly what is going on. What proponents of the role-model argument have failed to grasp is that, with regard to any positive inspirational value, quality counts much more than quantity. A large quantity of low-quality role models has distinctly negative value. Affirmative-action role models negatively affect public perceptions of the competence of their intended beneficiaries and reinforce stereotypes of black and Hispanic inferiority and incompetence. They also negatively affect incentives for those in the beneficiary categories to achieve at their maximum since they know that standards will be lowered for them.

MYTHOLOGIES AND PATHOLOGIES

Since affirmative action in employment is in blatant contradiction to the plain meaning of the 1964 Civil Rights Act and contrary to certain moral and ethical precepts that have deep roots in America's liberal and Christian past, it became necessary for supporters and defenders of the program to devise certain legitimizing social and legal mythologies, which seem to have had considerable success in confusing a good number of people. The legal myth holds that affirmative action, in the sense of preferential hiring based on racial, ethnic, and gender criteria, was mandated by President Johnson in 1965 in his Executive Order 11246 and is provided for in Title VII of the 1964 Civil Rights Act. This, of course, is the exact opposite of the truth. What is true in the myth is that President Johnson did indeed use the words "affirmative action"[33] in his executive order, but the term was used in a sense directly opposite the meaning the term would take on in the 1970s. By "affirmative action" Johnson meant that contractors doing business with the federal

---

33. The term "affirmative action" is also used in the 1964 Civil Rights Act in Section 706(g), where it refers to forms of redress for acts of discrimination against individuals—redress such as hiring or reinstatement, the granting of back pay, or similar acts of "affirmative action." The usage of the term here was apparently taken over from the 1935 National Labor Relations Act (Wagner Act), where employers could similarly be required to reinstate employees, grant back pay, and take other such "affirmative action" to compensate union members who had been fired or otherwise adversely treated because of union activities. Needless to say, the racial and ethnic quota hiring often mandated by courts under this section is inconsistent with the explicit letter, spirit, and legislative history of the Civil Rights Act.

government would make a special effort both to advertise their nondiscrimination policies more broadly and to ensure that all employees and applicants for employment were treated on a strictly race-, ethnicity-, and religion-neutral basis. "Affirmative action," in other words, meant affirmative nondiscrimination, i.e., scrupulous ethnic neutrality and color-blindness. The relevant section of the executive order reads:

> The contractor will not discriminate against *any* employee
> or applicant for employment because of race, creed, color or
> national origin. The contractor will take *affirmative action*
> to ensure that applicants are employed, and that employees
> are treated during employment, *without* regard to their race,
> creed, color, or national origin. (Section 201.1; emphasis
> added)

Executive Order 11246 did not include a ban on the use of gender in the making of employment decisions, so to rectify this oversight, Johnson two years later issued another executive order, No. 11375, which reaffirmed the merit-based imperative of both the 1964 Civil Rights Act and his earlier executive order, and extended the scope of his earlier order to include a ban on sex discrimination as well:

> It is the policy of the United States government to provide
> equal opportunity in federal employment and in employment
> by federal contractors *on the basis of merit* and *without* dis-
> crimination because of race, color, religion, sex or national
> origin.
>   The Congress, by enacting Title VII of the Civil Rights
> Act of 1964, enunciated a national policy of equal employ-
> ment opportunity in private employment, *without* dis-
> crimination because of race, color, religion, sex, or national
> origin.

Executive Order 11246 of September 24, 1965, carried forward a program of equal employment opportunity in government employment, employment by federal contractors and subcontractors, and employment under federally assisted construction contracts *regardless of* race, creed, color, or national origin.

It is desirable that the equal employment opportunity programs provided for in Executive Order 11246 expressly embrace discrimination on account of sex. (Executive Order No. 11375; emphasis added)

Supporters of preferential hiring in the federal bureaucracy realized, however, that few people ever read presidential executive orders, and they guessed—and guessed correctly—that if they simply set down their own laws mandating preferential or quota-like hiring, the federal courts would eventually back them up and would act as though a policy that was explicitly prohibited by the Civil Rights Act of 1964 was actually required by it.[34] They also suspected—again correctly—that neither Congress nor the president would do anything to interfere out of fear of being denounced in the media by the so-called "civil rights groups" either as racist bigots or, at the very least, as insensitive to the plight of "minorities." And so, in 1971, the policy of affirmative action in employment was given birth by bureaucratic

---

34. A number of federal court decisions effectively rewrote Title VII of the Civil Rights Act of 1964, the most important being *United Steelworkers of America v. Weber* (decided June 27, 1979). The majority opinion in this case, written by Justice William Brennan, must surely rank as one of the most blatantly dishonest judicial decisions ever handed down by an American court. It has been the subject of numerous commentaries and of at least three elaborate and devastating refutations, one by Justice Rehnquist in his impassioned 37-page dissent, another by Carl Cohen in *Commentary* ("Justice Debased: The *Weber* Decision," Sept. 1979, pp. 43–53), and a third by Bernard D. Meltzer in *The University of Chicago Law Review* ("The *Weber* Case: The Judicial Abrogation of the Antidiscrimination Standard in Employment," Spring 1980, pp. 423–66). These three critiques contain valuable information on the legislative history of the 1964 Civil Rights Act as well as on the personalistic mode of thought embodied in that act.

fiat, the key document in question being Revised Order No. 4 of the Labor Department's Office of Federal Contract Compliance. This was the document that spoke of "goals," "timetables," "deficiencies," "good-faith efforts," "underutilization," "result-oriented" policies, and the like, and helped set the style for the mystification and double talk that would become the stock-in-trade of most affirmative-action programs.[35]

The social mythology that affirmative-action supporters created has also been touched upon previously. It consists of at least four interrelated mythic elements, each of which is usually presented as the unspoken premise of various arguments and moral appeals rather than as explicitly stated facts. The first element might be described as the myth of the socioeconomically homogeneous white majority. If one is going to place a person at an employment disadvantage because of that person's race, then it is certainly easier on one's conscience if the person put at a disadvantage is from a rich and privileged background

---

35   Revised Order No. 4 was issued in December 1971. It summarized and clarified a policy that the OFCC had been gradually developing, though without clarification as to its true intentions, since May 1968. The ultimate intentions of the OFCC's affirmative-action policy first became clear in early 1970 with the issuance of its Order No. 4, which stated that federal contractors must devise affirmative-action plans that included:

> an analysis of areas within which the contractor is deficient in the utilization of minority groups and further, goals and timetables to which the contractor's good faith efforts must be directed to correct the deficiencies and thus to achieve prompt and full utilization of minorities at all levels and in all segments of his work force where deficiencies exist.

Regarding Order No. 4 (1970) and its 1971 elaboration and revision, Kenneth C. McGuiness and his colleagues write: "These revisions significantly altered both the direction and the purpose of the compliance program. What was at first an effort to provide equal employment opportunity for all groups had become a program to provide minorities and women with a share of the existing jobs, commensurate with their representation in the work force and/or the population. Success was to be measured in the number of jobs won for minorities and women, and not by the establishment of nondiscriminatory employment practices. . . . The purpose of the program had become, not equal employment opportunity, but simply equal employment. Equal opportunity was considered a distant, although worthy goal. For the present, the program had become the vehicle for establishing and monitoring preferential treatment." See Kenneth C. McGuiness, ed., *Preferential Treatment in Employment* (Washington, D.C.: Equal Employment Advisory Council, 1977), p. 21.

rather than from a poor and underprivileged one. Hence, to justify a policy of discriminating against white people, white people must be identified with wealth and privilege. The fact that there are 25 million white people in America who are below the official poverty level and many more in very humble, lower-middle-income circumstances, and the fact that many of these people must also apply for jobs in competitive job markets were facts that the myth propagators sought to eliminate from public awareness.

The second mythic element complements the first, and might be described as the myth of the socioeconomically homogeneous black and Hispanic minorities. To justify preferential treatment in favor of black people, Hispanic people, and certain other people officially designated as constituting a "minority group," the people in these groups naturally had to be conceived of as economically and culturally deprived. The fact that there is a sizable black and Hispanic middle and upper-middle class in America and the fact that the members of these groups are much more likely than their poorer brethren to be the ones applying for the most competitive and high-prestige jobs where the greatest degree of racial and ethnic preference is generally given, were once again facts that the myth propagators sought to shield from public awareness.

The third element in the mythology was what might be called the myth of the ethnicly homogeneous white majority. All white people, according to this myth, are ethnicly more or less the same and can be adequately viewed in terms of the White Anglo-Saxon Protestant model. Since WASPs were never discriminated against in America to any significant degree, and since WASPs in the past have enjoyed social and economic privileges that, in some cases at least, were purchased at the expense of racial and ethnic discrimination against others, the more white people could be viewed as WASPs, the easier it would be to justify the withdrawl of certain of their rights and privileges. The myth, of course, deliberately tried to obscure the fact that many present-day WASPs are quite poor, that in any event WASPs constitute a distinct minority among white people in America (less than a third according to some definitions and estimates), and that America is a nation whose "white" people come from literally dozens of different ethnic and national-origin backgrounds. The myth also, of course, tried to obscure the fact that, unlike most WASPs, most white immigrants to America from the various nations and regions of Eastern and Southern Europe, North Africa, and the Middle East, often experienced widespread ethnic discrimination in employment and other areas of life, discrimination that was widespread roughly up until the end of the Second World War.

The fourth element in the social mythology is what might be termed the myth of the ethnicly homogeneous Hispanic minority. In reality, of course, as Nathan Glazer and others have stressed, Spanish-speaking people and their descendants in America do not constitute a single ethnic group, but a whole host of ethnic groups, with widely varying group histories and group traditions. Historically speaking, the amount of ethnic discrimination that was typically experienced by the members of these different groups varied considerably from group to group, with the members of the better-off groups, such as the Spaniards, probably experiencing less discrimination on average than the members of many of the Eastern European, North African, and Middle Eastern ethnic groups. But since the public image of Hispanics in America, at least among many non-Hispanics, is largely conditioned by the history of Mexican Americans (who on average experienced perhaps the greatest degree of ethnic discrimination), as well as by the recent history of Puerto Ricans (who, in aggregate per capita terms, are among the poorer Hispanic groups in America), it apparently served the interest of the propagators of the myth to lump all Spanish-speaking people and their descendants under a single term.

Each element in the social mythology of affirmative action was consciously or unconsciously intended to desensitize the mind of the observer to the vast diversity of people in America and to the individual personal nature of every human being and every human life. The social mythology also sought to inject into public consciousness what is perhaps the most perverse idea of the many perverse ideas that the ethnic-tribal mind-set has bequeathed to mankind—the idea of collective and congenital blood guilt. Given the history of this idea, with its use, for instance, to justify black slavery as just punishment for the biblical sin of Ham and to persecute Jews throughout the centuries for their alleged collective and congenital responsibility in the murder of Christ, one might have thought such an idea would have had little appeal to those who had been victims of racial and ethnic prejudice. Its success within a modern American context is something truly alarming.

According to this way of thinking, all people who have white skin partake of a collective blood guilt for all the heinous crimes committed in the past by white people against blacks, Hispanics, and the members of various American Indian tribes. The guilt for such crimes, according to this view, is not only transmitted along genealogical lines but has a peculiar race-specific infectiousness about it that contaminates all people with white skin. Even descendants of white abolitionists, for instance, would be seen to share in this blood guilt, as would the descendants of the many millions of post-Civil War white immigrants, despite the fact that most of their ancestors had to cope with ethnic discrimination of their own, had little or nothing to do with Southern slavery, Jim Crow laws, or the persecution of Mexicans or Indians, and generally settled in the industrial areas of the country outside the South, where few Mexicans, Indians, or blacks resided. The collective and congenital guilt idea, like the various other elements in the affirmative-action social mythology, was rarely stated in explicit terms but assumed a prominent background existence, usually as an unarticulated premise or assumption of various proaffirmative-action arguments and appeals.

Some of the elements in the social mythology can be well illustrated by a few quotations from the famous Kerner Commission report on the causes of the urban rioting of the late 1960s. This report was written at the very beginning of the period when influential intellectuals and government bureaucrats were considering the desirability of abandoning the national policy of racial and ethnic neutrality in hiring, substituting instead one of racial and ethnic favoritism. The document is invaluable for understanding the psychology and motivation of the type of upper-middle-class, guilt-ridden, white "liberal"[36] of the late 1960s era, who helped to institute the policy of affirmative action, and it contains one of the earliest uses of the actual phrase "affirmative action" in a sense that seems to be at least approaching the meaning it would later acquire.[37]

36. The term "liberal" is set in quotation marks here and throughout this chapter to stress the fact that affirmative action is anything but a liberal policy and those who support it, regardless of how they classify themselves, have ceased to be liberals in any meaningful sense of the term. From the British Levellers of the seventeenth century to the American welfarists of the New Deal, Fair Deal, and Great Society, liberals have always endeavored to view human beings as individual persons with individual human rights and individual human needs, rather than as members of classes, castes, or ethnic groups whose rights and privileges are contingent upon their membership in such groups. One cannot be both a liberal in any of its many past meanings and a supporter of race-based classifications and the allocation of government benefits and burdens on the basis of those classifications (just as one cannot be a liberal and a supporter of a regime that classifies people as aristocrats, commoners, and clergy and allocates rights and obligations according to these class distinctions). Liberalism is incompatible with ethnic tribalism and tribal-based categorization schemes just as it is with class-based systems of hierarchy and hierarchical privilege.

37. *Report of the National Advisory Commission on Civil Disorders* (New York: New York Times Company/Bantam Books,1968). The phrase "affirmative action" appears in a subsection of chapter 17 titled "Opening the Existing Job Structure": "Federal, state and local efforts to ensure equal opportunity to employment should be strengthened by . . . linking enforcement efforts with training and other aids to employers and unions, so that affirmative action to hire and promote may be encouraged in connection with investigations of both individual complaints and charges of broad patterns of discrimination." (p. 419). It is not clear in this statement whether "affirmative action" means simple redress for people who have actually been the

The conclusion of the Kerner Commission was set forth in a famous sentence in the introduction to its report, in a line allegedly penned by commission vice-chairman John Lindsay, which stated:

> Our nation is moving toward two societies, one black, one white—separate and unequal.

Here, of course, one can see the tendency toward the racial stereotyping of the population that would become a characteristic feature of affirmative-action programs. One ethnicly and socioeconomically homogeneous white group, which is thought of as rich and privileged, is pictured as standing over an equally socioeconomically and ethnicly homogeneous black group, which is thought of as uniformly poor and underprivileged. Social status and economic well-being are seen to run along strict racial lines, with little consciousness of the vast diversity to be found among the enormous black and white populations actually found in America.

The commission also set forth its view regarding the collective guilt of "white society" for the deplorable conditions in the

---

victims of racial discrimination—where the redress takes the form of "make-whole" efforts on the part of the institutions that have victimized them through specific acts of employment discrimination (and where the discrimination itself is not simply alleged but substantiated in a formal fact-finding process) or whether "affirmative action" refers to special consideration in the awarding of jobs based on racial identity where the special consideration is not related to specific discriminatory acts by specific employers in relation to their individual past victims. The first meaning of "affirmation action" would parallel its use in the National Labor Relations Act (where employees fired for antiunion activities were entitled to being reinstated and their employers subject to other acts of "affirmative action" to bring about redress). The redress required is always victim- and violation-specific and does not permit racial proxies for actual victims. If this is the meaning, the Kerner Commission's recommendation would be consistent with the both the spirit and letter of the 1964 Civil Rights Act. But it is the second meaning that seems to be aimed at, where the special hiring and promoting under affirmative-action plans is not victim- or violation-specific and sweeps into its fold whoever meets certain racial criteria.

inner-city ghettos where many black Americans were forced to live:

> What white Americans have never fully understood—but what the Negro can never forget—is that white society is deeply implicated in the ghetto. White institutions created it, white institutions maintain it, and white society condones it.

Now if one asks in this context just *who* is white society, the answer, of course, is all white people. All white people are seen as collectively responsible for the degradation and despair in the black urban ghetto, and they are supposed to feel guilty for their past sins in having created it. The sin and guilt is not personal, but collective and congenital. It is a racial guilt. The commission fully realized, as indicated in the first line of the quotation, that many "white Americans" were rather far removed from the situation in the inner-city ghetto and had little understanding of its problems. But in the commission's view this fact served only to heighten their guilt, as it rendered them less concerned about the evil conditions that lurked there, for which all white people were seen as collectively responsible.

When we try to understand the motivations of the supporters of affirmative action, certainly the easiest motive to grasp is that of the leaders of various black, Hispanic, and women's groups. These groups, in their support for preferential hiring, were simply playing the typical American game of interest-group politics. They sought special favors for the members of their respective clienteles, with little regard for the rights of those who would have to be shoved aside, much as labor unions and business associations do when attempting to promote the self-interest of their respective members. Other ethnic groups in the past had acted in a similar manner (the Irish, for instance, in many northern cities during the age of machine politics), and however regrettable this may have been—however sickening the fact that these ethnic and gender interest groups often spoke in the exalted name of "civil rights"[38]—the motivation of their members was certainly transparent enough for all to see.

The situation is much more complicated, however, when we consider the motivation of the high-ranking federal bureaucrats and judges who instituted the affirmative action policy, as well as their supporters among the intellectual elite in the universities and the news media, the great majority of whom are white males. It is the psychology of the contemporary upper-middle-class white male "liberal" that is so complicated, yet an understanding of it is crucial in order to grasp how a policy such as affirmative action could have come into being.

The upper-middle-class white "liberal" who supported affirmative action seems to have been stirred initially by two very different passions. The first of these was a genuine sympathy and compassion for the plight of the black poor in America— for those who were at the very bottom of the socioeconomic ladder and who had often suffered in their own lifetimes from

---

38. The understanding of this term has been so corrupted by recent history that it's worthwhile to introduce here a simple dictionary definition. The term "civil" in "civil rights" comes from the Latin *civilis* and French *civil* and means "of or belonging to citizens," "of or pertaining to the whole body or community of citizens," "of or pertaining to the individual citizen," or "becoming or befitting a citizen" (*Oxford English Dictionary*). A civil right is a right that each citizen has solely by virtue of his citizenship, whether in a republic, commonwealth, or other political body. It is not a right conferred on the basis of ethnic, tribal, or genealogical relationships. The Fourteenth Amendment to the U.S. Constitution laid the foundation for the modern American understanding of civil rights by granting to "all persons born or naturalized in the United States" equal status as citizens and the full and equal political rights citizenship confers. Much confusion has been created by the common use of the term "civil rights group" to describe a number of groups that have little interest in promoting the rights of citizens. To speak of the NAACP or La Raza as a "civil rights group" is no more accurate than to confer such a label upon the Polish American Congress or the Sons of Italy. Calling such a group a "civil rights group" is akin to describing the Sheet Metal Workers Union or the National Association of Realtors as a "distributive justice group." The fact that such groups are still routinely called by such an honorific title is an indication of the deep moral and spiritual confusion that reigns within large segments of our population in the post-civil rights era.

the meanest of prejudices and the vilest of social practices. This sympathy and compassion was then extended by the white "liberal" to cover black people in general and subsequently the members of certain other ethnic groups as well, particularly Mexican Americans, Puerto Ricans, and American Indians.

The second force at work in the mind of the upper-middle-class white "liberal" was a deeply rooted sense of guilt. This sense of guilt in most cases had nothing to do with any awareness of any specific wrong that either the white "liberal" himself or any of his ancestors had actually committed against black people or the members of any other ethnic group. In many cases, of course, no such specific wrong existed. The source of the white "liberal's" sense of guilt, rather, was something much more immediate, having to do with the moral uneasiness he felt about his own privileged position in society. Growing up amid relative wealth and privilege and discovering so many in radically different circumstances, the upper-middle-class white "liberal," like many privileged people, felt a sense of guilt and uneasiness over his own personal circumstances and the realization of the fact that he may have been no more deserving of his relative wealth and privilege than the poor and degraded were deserving of their poverty and degradation. Even people from very modest circumstances will sometimes have similar feelings when confronting, for instance, a wretched beggar on a city street.

This combination of guilt about one's own privileged socioeconomic position and compassion for the plight of the poor and downtrodden can often lead to morally praiseworthy activities of great benefit to society. A person motivated by such feelings, for instance, might decide that it was his obligation to give away much of his wealth and earnings to those more in need of them than himself, or he might decide to dedicate his spare time and energy to any number of charitable activities. With regard to underprivileged blacks, for instance, he might choose to make large contributions to the United Negro College Fund or to other black charities; he might decide to adopt a black orphan, or at least spend time as a tutor or a Big Brother to a fatherless black child in need of personal attention; he might lend large sums of money to a promising black enterprise in need of start-up capital; or he might reach out in any number of ways to help individual black people in distress.

But the compassion and concern for the downtrodden of the typical affirmative-action-supporting white "liberal" was to stop at that very point where any significant degree of his own personal sacrifice was called for. It was at this point that he was seized by what can only be described as a kind of demonic self-righteousness and hypocrisy, which induced him to try to expiate his own sense of guilt, not by giving up any of his own wealth or privilege—not, for instance, by giving up his own job or promotion entitlement and recruiting a poor black or Hispanic person to take his place—but by using government power to force other people, usually people considerably less well off than himself, to sacrifice *their* jobs, *their* lives, and *their* promotion entitlements. And when these other people then complained about such treatment—when the Brian Webers, that is, the Stuart Marshes, the Wendy Wygants, the Memphis fire fighters, and the like, complained about the discrimination against them—they were denounced by the affirmative-action-supporting white "liberals" for their insensitivity to the plight of the poor and oppressed.

In the 53rd chapter of the Book of Isaiah, we read of a Suffering Servant who takes upon himself the burden of the entire world's sin and guilt in order that man might be restored to God through his great personal suffering and sacrifice. The affirmative-action-supporting white "liberal," one might say, took upon himself the sin and guilt, if not the "world," at least that of "white society," but when it came to the question of personal suffering and sacrifice, he delegated that task to others, whom he would then confront as his moral inferiors.[39]

In addition to the three forces of guilt, compassion, and self-righteous hypocrisy, two other forces come into play in the motivation of the upper-middle-class white "liberal," which might be designated as "romanticism" and "fear." Both forces are intimately related and proceed from the peculiar manner in which poor and oppressed people have frequently been viewed in Western society, particularly by those on the left side of the political spectrum. Poor and oppressed people are, of course, exactly that—they are poor and oppressed. They are not necessarily noble people, or virtuous people, or wise people. Indeed, they are sometimes the very opposite, as the effect of poverty and oppression is frequently to brutalize people, to keep them in ignorance, and to fill them with hatreds and animosities, which they not infrequently take out both on fellow sufferers and upon innocent third parties who did them no wrong.

But the upper-middle-class white "liberal" tends to romanticize the victims of poverty and oppression and to see them as possessing a certain inner moral purity that elevates them in his mind above the general lot of better-off people, almost endowing them with a kind of secular holiness. The culmination of this type of thinking is found in Marxism, where the masses of poor

---

39. Consider in this context the biting remark of Mike Fontham, the attorney for the plaintiff Brian Weber, the white factory worker passed over for a job promotion to a lower-seniority black because of a racial preference program at a Kaiser Aluminum plant in Gramercy, Louisiana: "Look what's happening. A bunch of bureaucrats in Washington and a bunch of high-level corporate executives all decided to achieve some social goal. But how many of them are saying, 'I'm giving up my job?' *That* would be affirmative action! But instead they're saying some schmoe in the plant has to give up *his* job." (Cited in Steven V. Roberts, "The Bakke Case Moves to the Factory," *New York Times Magazine*, 25 Feb. 1979, p. 101).

and oppressed factory workers are seen as nothing less than the saviors and redeemers of mankind. The idea that something said by such people could be mean-spirited, or misinformed, or simply nonsense is seen by the white "liberal," and even more so by his compatriots on the far left, as bordering on a profanation. What is said by the poor and oppressed—or more typically, by those not-so-poor-and-oppressed people who claim to be their spokesmen—is treated with a special deference and generally exempted from the moral and intellectual scrutiny that would be accorded to statements made by almost anyone else. Indeed, many a white "liberal" and his far left brethren are so lacking in any cultivation of their own inner faculties of moral and spiritual discernment that morality and justice will not infrequently come to be associated in their minds with whatever spokesmen for poor and oppressed people demand.

The upper-middle-class white "liberal," one might say, views the poor and oppressed much the way medieval Catholic peasants sometimes viewed the holy orders of priests and monks. In just thinking about them, he can experience a sense of his own unworthiness and guilt, and he fears nothing more than being outside their good graces. This fear is particularly strong when attention is turned to black people, whose disapproval the white "liberal" fears with an intensity bordering on horror. The thought of black people conjures up in his mind all the imagery and symbolism of the Civil War crusade against slavery and the subsequent struggles against the Ku Klux Klan and Jim Crow. Opposition to what black people or their spokesmen demand is thus closely associated in the white "liberal's" mind with evil and the forces of extreme depravity. The thought that black people or their spokesmen might disapprove of him, that they might think of him, for instance, as a racist or a bigot—or merely as lacking sufficient concern to extirpate racism and bigotry—is enough to shake the white "liberal" to his foundations and instill terror in his soul.[40] It

40. Consider in this context the following account of a gathering of left-liberal student leaders at Rutgers University in the winter of 1988. The class origin of the students isn't mentioned, but given the fact that they were able to fly around the country to attend a college conference and were politically on the left suggests that most came from middle- to upper-middle-class backgrounds.

Encouraged by the rebirth of campus activism, students from a score of institutions began in January, 1987, at Hampshire College, to lay the foundation for a national student organization designed to radically transform American society. Eventually the National Student Convention '88 (NSC) was planned and held at Rutgers University, Feb. 5–7, 1988.

The organizers had expected about 200 activists at Rutgers. . . . Contrary to these expectations, Rutgers was swamped by almost 700 registrants representing approximately 130 institutions. . . . Overall, the assembled multitude was over 95 per cent white, geographically diverse, a mixture of the modish and those expressing reverence for the sixties through dress and hairstyle. . . . In addition to students, a host of New Left elder statesmen attended.

On the convention's last day, when the campus delegates were supposed to debate and vote on a constitution and various workshop-generated proposals, a twenty-five member Students of Color Caucus declared that insufficient care and skill had been devoted to assuring the presence of greater numbers of nonwhite students. The caucus . . . demanded that the convention postpone any vote on a proposed constitution until new outreach efforts were undertaken. If this were not acceptable to the delegates, Students of Color would disassociate itself from the organization.

Pandemonium ensued. Privately, the conveners said their considerable outreach efforts had aroused little enthusiasm among black and Hispanic student groups about the prospect of joining a multiracial, multi-issue organization in which their interests might frequently be subordinated to other pressing concerns. Publicly, they remained mute on the issue. Some students spoke against the caucus's proposal. Nevertheless, with widespread white guilt clearly evident, a voice vote of those assembled . . . easily carried the day for the caucus's demands. Regional delegates were chosen to conduct the outreach. . . . But there was no adequate attempt to create a temporary national organizing committee to whom outreach efforts should be reported and which in turn would plan the demonstrations or the next convention. . . .

Finally, since the assembly just voted itself insufficiently representative of student radicalism, there was no logical rationale to vote on the myriad positions and proposed actions that had been discussed at workshops earlier. Students drifted aimlessly about the gym and eventually began to leave for home. (Milton Mankoff, "Rutgers, DSA, and the Revival of the New Left," *Tikkun*, May/June 1988, pp. 85–6)

"Pandemonium" is the correct term to describe the phenomenon under observation here. Pandemonium, a Miltonian coinage (literally: "place of all evil demons"), is the capital of hell in Milton's great epic literary myth, *Paradise Lost* (I, 756; X, 424), and it symbolizes the moral depravity and social chaos that result when mankind is cut off

is roughly equivalent to the medieval Christian's fear of being denounced by the clergy as a heretic, excommunicated from the church, and denied access to the holy sacraments. It was the successful exploitation of this fear, it would seem, that was at least partially responsible for the incredible success of black and Hispanic groups, both in muting opposition to affirmative action and in gaining such tremendous leverage over important segments of the federal bureaucracy and federal judiciary.

To the five forces of compassion, guilt, self-righteous hypocrisy, romanticism, and fear, a sixth would have to be added in the case of federal bureaucrats, which is simply a desire for power. A vast bureaucratic empire has been built up to enforce the policy of affirmative action, with the mandarins who rule over this empire wielding a degree of power and influence that would be the envy of many a petty prince. Almost every major corporation and university in the country has been brought under the control of this empire, which successfully intimidates employers into maintaining in their workforces whatever racial, ethnic, or gender balance the government bureaucrats deem appropriate. When the human will-to-power, the *libido dominandi*, combines with the other five forces mentioned, the result can be a potent mixture indeed.[41]

---

from the redeeming power of God's grace. For Marxists, leftists, and left-liberals of various persuasions, the poor and oppressed of society—the wretched of the earth—are seen as the carriers of a moral purity and a secular power of redemption closely paralleling the redemptive power that traditional Christians derive from the death and resurrection of Jesus and the sacraments of the Christian church. To be estranged from these is to fall into sin, and when this ensues on a mass scale, all manner of guilt, confusion, and chaos break out.

41. It would take a writer of genius with the consummate skill and psychological acumen of a Tolstoy, a Dostoyevsky, or a Shakespeare—or possibly a northern version of William Faulkner—to adequately plumb the depths of the soul of the contemporary, guilt-ridden, white "liberal" in its confrontation with issues of race in America. I have offered here only the crudest outline of some of its more salient and more easily recognizable tendencies in their most blatant waywardness, hypocrisies, and distortions.

PERSONALISM AND PUBLIC POLICY

When discussing the issue of preferential hiring, both supporters and opponents of affirmative action almost invariably wind up in a position of appearing to give at least tacit approval to the materialist-careerist ethic that exerts so powerful a force in modern American life. One might characterize this ethic as one in which higher- and better-paying jobs are sought, not merely for the increases they provide in the ease and conveniences of life, or for the more challenging and fulfilling nature of the tasks they offer, but as ends in themselves and for the status and social prestige that go along with them. In premodern times in the West, materialist and careerist attitudes were at least partially kept in check by the counter-pressures of the dominant Christian religious ethic, which always condemned the pursuit of wealth as an end in itself and viewed status-seeking as a form of vanity that constituted both a moral and social evil. Part of the reason the affirmative-action debate over jobs has generated so much heat in American society is precisely because these older religio-ethical restraints have largely been abandoned in modern times, allowing questions of material and career advancement to assume a hypertrophic significance in many people's lives totally out of proportion to the actual importance of such questions in the overall scheme of things.

There are, to be sure, numerous criticisms that can and should be made of modern Western careerism and materialism, particularly in their tendency to equate the value and worth of human beings with their degree of economic and careerist "success." But having made such criticisms, it is still necessary to have guidelines for a fair employment policy once one accepts the basic proposition that there is something radically wrong with any policy, such as the current policy of affirmative action, that encourages hiring on the basis of race and ethnicity. I would like to suggest three fundamental principles, each closely related, that can serve as a guide to evaluating any future government policy in the area of employment, or indeed, in any number of other areas as well. All three principles are closely in tune with the basic thrust of the 1950s and early 1960s civil rights movement and are based on the key idea of the human person as the inviolable unit of public policy concern. The three principles might be designated: 1) the Self-Representation Only Principle; 2) the Underdog Equality Principle; and 3) the Ethnicity Indifference Principle.

The Self-Representation Only principle holds that in the eyes of government each person is to be seen as representing only himself and his own personal history rather than anyone else or anyone else's history—or any group of people or any group's history. What this means apropos any government ameliorative or compensatory program is that no one who is himself privileged is to be considered underprivileged merely because many *other* people of the same race or ethnicity are underprivileged; nor is any person who is genuinely underprivileged to be considered privileged merely because many other people of the same race or ethnicity are privileged. The Self-Representation Only Principle holds that the only human deprivation that public policy has any business concerning itself with is that deprivation, in terms of economic, educational, or cultural disadvantage, which is actually borne by actually deprived human beings. (The Self-Representation Only Principle could also be called the No Proxy Principle)

The second principle, the Underdog Equality Principle, holds that all involuntarily disadvantaged people, commensurate with their degree of disadvantage, have an equal claim to government compassion and concern, and an equal right to the benefits of any government program designed either to improve their life opportunities or alleviate their individual distress. The Underdog Equality Principle also holds that the historical reason or reasons for a person's involuntary deprivation—whether, for instance, it can arguably be attributed to racial or ethnic discrimination rather than class discrimination, regional poverty, abusive family situations, bad luck, or some other cause or causes—is not a relevant consideration. The Underdog Equality Principle explicitly rejects racial and ethnic criteria as a basis for determining underdog status, on the grounds that all such criteria are both overinclusive and underinclusive, allowing many top dogs to claim status as underdogs, while denying to many genuine underdogs the right to claim title as such.

The third principle, the Ethnicity Indifference Principle, holds that racial and ethnic identities, in the same manner as religious identities, are strictly private affairs, to be accorded no official status in American public law. The principle holds that all persons born or naturalized in the United States are to be viewed by the government equally as citizens thereof, and are to enjoy all rights and benefits under public law *without* regard to race or ethnicity. Racial and ethnic affiliations—like religious affiliations—may be very important in peoples' personal lives and conducive to their general welfare, but they are to be given no official recognition by the state.

All of the three enumerated principles, as applied to a preferential government hiring program, can be seen at work in the various programs that have existed in the past on state and local levels to encourage the hiring of the physically handicapped. Such programs might be taken as models for any government policy designed to improve the life situation of the economically and culturally deprived. One obviously has no claim to special consideration because one's grandfather was physically handicapped, or because one belongs to the same ethnic group as someone else who is physically handicapped, or because the ethnic group to which one belongs has a substantially higher proportion of physically handicapped persons than the public at large. And so it might be with a government policy to encourage employers to give special breaks to economic and cultural underdogs. While competency and ability should certainly be the main consideration for most job hiring, it would not be inconsistent with our sense of justice or with the demands of economic efficiency for government policy to encourage, on a voluntary basis, small deviations from the meritocratic principle in order to give a slight preference to those most in need of a job, or to those for whom a given employment position would represent the greatest step up the economic ladder. Such preference, however, would have to be given strictly on the basis of deprivation, not on the basis of race.

CONCLUSION

It is important to keep in mind in discussing the affirmative-action debate that the issues go much deeper than the simple question of employment policy, touching the very roots of the American political order. And that political order, like all political orders, is inherently precarious. The poison of ethnic tribalism brought chaos to the Balkans and to other areas of Eastern Europe in the early decades of the twentieth century; it has led to bloodbaths in Armenia, India, Nigeria, Burundi, Uganda, Lebanon, Sri Lanka, and many other nations of Asia and Africa; it has periodically convulsed such otherwise stable nations as Belgium and Canada; and in the form of German National Socialism it was to lead to one of the most brutal and genocidal regimes the world has ever known. America must not think that it is automatically immune to the fate of these other lands. One simple fact can be extracted from all these tragic histories, and that simple fact is this: the principle of ethnic tribalism, if not counter-balanced by, and integrated into, a more encompassing human vision—such as that all men are created equal, that we are all part of the same *human* race, that in the eyes of God there is no Jew or Greek—is a principle of social chaos[42] and, ultimately, a formula for civil war.[43]

42. Consider in this context a remark by the ever-wise Thomas Sowell:

> A multi-ethnic society like the United States can ill-afford continually to build up stores of inter-group resentments about such powerful concerns as one's livelihood and one's children [i.e., employment quotas and busing]. . . . We must never think that the disintegration and disaster that has hit other multi-ethnic societies 'can't happen here.' The mass internment of Japanese Americans just a generation ago is a sobering reminder of the tragic idiocy that stress can bring on. We are not made of different clay from the Germans, who were historically more enlightened and humane toward Jews than many other Europeans—until the generation of Hitler and the Holocaust. The situation in America today is, of course, not like that of the Weimar Republic. History does not literally repeat, but it can warn us of what people are capable of, when the stage has been set for tragedy. We certainly do not need to let emotionally combustible materials accumulate from ill-conceived social experiments. (Thomas Sowell, *Commentary*, June 1978, p. 43)

43. As explained in the chapter introduction, the ideas presented here, although they did not appear in a published form until much later, were first developed in the early and mid-1970s during my graduate student days at Princeton. They were greatly influenced by the theocentric humanism and spiritual universalism of thinkers such as William James, Henri Bergson, Martin Buber, Rudolf Otto, Reinhold Niebuhr, Paul Tillich, Jacques Maritain, Karl Jaspers, Eric Voegelin, Ram Dass, Simone Weil, Mohandas Gandhi, and Martin Luther King, Jr. Looking back, from the vantage point of four decades of elapsed time, there is little here that I would wish to change, though my arguments for and against racial preferences would be much more detailed and analytically sophisticated were I writing on this topic today. I am also less convinced than I once was that class-based affirmative action in employment is a good idea or that it could be administered with any degree of honesty or integrity. The most valuable and enduring feature of this essay, in my view, is its analysis of the corruption of soul in those privileged whites who continue to support racial preferences—the guilt-ridden, "limousine liberals" as they are derisively called by critics—a topic I take up again in Chapters II and III of this book, where the focus shifts to assessing racial-preference policies at elite educational institutions rather than in the employment arena.

II

ARE RACIAL PREFERENCES AN ANTIDOTE TO RACISM?

Andrew Koppelman is a distinguished legal scholar and professor of law who currently teaches at Northwest Law, the law school of Northwestern University. His area of specialty is anti-discrimination law, particularly as it applies to issues of race, gender, and sexual orientation. I got to know Andy during the early 1990s, when he taught in Princeton's Politics Department. Though holding widely divergent views on the issue of racial preferences, we came to respect each other's intellect and depth of conviction, and if not coming to agreement on the issues dividing us, we at least came to understand better why each side thinks as it does.

While at Princeton, Professor Koppelman circulated a chapter-length manuscript for comments among colleagues and friends titled "What Anti-Discrimination Law is Against." Much of the substance of this manuscript was later incorporated into his book *Antidiscrimination Law and Social Equality*, which was published by Yale University Press. I was one of those honored to offer reader comments. The letter I present below contains my extended remarks.

The main issue I address in the letter is the claim that racial preference policies serve to combat the racist understanding that certain types of jobs are mainly for whites and not suitable for black capacities or interests. This was one of the major claims in Koppelman's circulated manuscript. Affirmative action preferences, and the more aggressive recruitment and favoring of blacks for occupations from which they have previously been excluded, are seen according to this view as striking a blow against racism and the exclusive association in the public mind of high-status and high-paying positions with whites. In addition to serving as a form of compensation for past acts of racial exclusion, preferences are said to help undermine the view that blacks should occupy a subordinate "place" in the American income and occupational hierarchy.

Offering two definitions of the highly charged word "racism," I try to show in my reply to Koppelman that racial-preference policies serve to heighten rather than reduce racist ideas and racist understandings. Insofar as affirmative-action policies bring into the workplace blacks who have been hired under lower standards than those applied to others, or encourage the admission to competitive colleges of black candidates who are less qualified or less academically accomplished than competing white or Asian candidates, such policies almost certainly strengthen racism. This is the case, at least, if we define racism either as a) the negative stereotyping of the members of any racial or ethnic group, or b) the harboring of intense hatred or hostility that is directed toward any such group.

Besides the racism issue, I also contest the claim, implicit in many of Koppelman's arguments, that racial-preference policies have had a great impact in reducing black/white income disparities. Most labor economists, I point out, believe the effects of preference policies have been very modest in terms of expanding the growth of the black middle class and in reducing black/white income differences. Blacks began to catch up with whites in terms of income and job status long before such policies came on the scene, in part because of features inherent in a competitive market economy. Statistical models show no jump in overcoming the black/white wage gap that can be attributed to policies in the post-1960s preference era.

I conclude with the wise counsel of social philosopher Michael Walzer, who stresses the importance in addressing past racial exclusion of building upon, rather than challenging, the understandings of social justice that are widely shared by members of all races in America.

A REPLY TO PROFESSOR ANDREW KOPPELMAN

Dear Andy,

I have now had time to look over again the manuscript you were kind enough to share with me, "What Antidiscrimination Law is Against," and offer the following comments, for whatever they may be worth (probably not much). I will naturally be critical of what you say, but as you know pretty well my general views on these issues, I'm sure this will not come as any great surprise.

RACIAL PREFERENCES AS WEAPONS AGAINST RACISM: THE NEED FOR CLEAR DEFINITIONS

The weakest part of your presentation, it seems to me, is your failure to specify adequately the meaning of the term "racism." The term as you use it combines such a high level of moral affect with such a low level of intellectual or definitional precision that the net effect is to diminish both your own and the reader's capacity for rational and humane reflection on the critical issues which are involved here. I am, of course, not a value-neutralist, and by itself have no objection to the use of morally charged language (as you know, I use it myself, though perhaps not always with the greatest wisdom). Indeed, I would say that people who do not have a well-developed moral, aesthetic, and spiritual sense, which is only cultivated by our use of evaluative terminology, are in some sense less that fully human. However, as the term "racism" is used in this manuscript I think the effect is to create considerably more heat than light (or perhaps a better metaphor is a nuclear explosion—the blast is so intense that it temporally blinds all who look at it too directly and prevents people from seeing what is going on). Some clear definitions are called for here, particularly when you make the claim, which I find highly dubious, that race-conscious policies will somehow help to overcome racism.

If I might supply a definition that I think captures at least one meaning of the term as it is used in your manuscript, I would say that racism is a type of thinking that imputes to many or all of the members of a diverse racial, ethnic, kinship, clan, or tribal group certain very negative characteristics—characteristics which are most often attributed to innate, biogenetically determined factors rather than to environmentally supplied ones—which in point of fact are only possessed by a much smaller subset of that group's population. The essence of racism in this sense is what we might call "negative stereotyping," "negative imaging," or "negative associating." So understood racism is at once a moral failing (because it does not distinguish human beings on the basis of individual merit or culpability, but in a truly tyrannical fashion, lumps the good with the bad, the innocent with the guilty); an intellectual failing (because it overgeneralizes and fails to make relevant and important distinctions); and a formula for social disharmony and political disaster (because it undermines the sense of open-minded fairness, and mutual respect across ethnic divides that is needed to maintain the peace in any multi-racial, multi-ethnic society).

Now if this is your prime meaning of racism—and I think it is—then it seems to me that you have failed to make the case that racial preferentialism can reduce racism, and you offer only the flimsiest of rebuttals to the standard stigma-reinforcement argument on this issue such as that which [Supreme Court Justice William O.] Douglas presents in *DeFunis* and Antonin Scalia in his article on "The Disease as Cure." Since stigma-reinforcement arguments against preferentialism are also made by virtually every black critic of affirmative action (e.g., Stephen Carter, Thomas Sowell, Shelby Steele, Carol Swain, Alan Keys, Glenn Loury, Walter Williams, etc.), I think this is a topic that calls for a great deal of reflection. Yet insofar as I can extract any kind of reasoning on this matter from your manuscript, you seem to be saying that black people are already negatively stigmatized by racist whites in America (and most white Americans appear in your account to be racists—i.e., they are strongly predisposed to stereotype blacks negatively), so that given this state of affairs, preferentialist policies cannot be blamed for an evil which would surely exist with or without them. "If blacks," you write, "will be stigmatized whether or not they are the beneficiaries of preferential treatment, either for being in those positions or for not being in them, then the stigma factor may be a wash rather than an argument against preferential treatment." ms. 45

I may well have misunderstood or misstated your argument here as it appears to me so obviously fallacious. It assumes that social stigma is an all-or-nothing affair when in fact the degree of social stigma in any given society (i.e., the pervasiveness and intensity of the negative images and negative stereotypes of any particular group) can display virtually any level of development from the most mild to the most extreme depending upon such factors as the percentage of the population that harbors negative views of a given ethnic group; how negative these negative views are; and how deeply ingrained the negative views are in each person. The claim made by opponents of preferentialist policies is that regardless of their supposedly benign intentions, within the context of contemporary American society such policies inevitably strengthen the belief in black inferiority in the minds of those who already assume or suspect that blacks are inferior, and just as inevitably create doubts and suspicions regarding black inferiority in the minds of those who are predisposed to think otherwise. I don't believe you have really addressed this kind of stigma argument at all.

In saying that preferentialist policies encourage and reinforce negative assessments of black ability (i.e., that they encourage racism), one is not, of course, saying that such policies are the only factor influencing such assessments. But that they are *a* factor—and a very important one—seems to me almost self-evidently true. Consider, for instance, what [Yale Law professor] Stephen Carter—certainly a very moderate and thoughtful observer—has to say about existing policies of preferentialist admissions to colleges and professional schools and the effects such policies have on the public images of college athletes and blacks:

> When a person admitted because of membership in a special category does not succeed, that lack of success is often attributed to others in the same category. The stereotype of the dumb jock exists because of the widespread perception (a correct one) that athletes are frequently admitted on paper records for which other students would be rejected. When people of color are admitted in the same fashion, the damage is worse, because the double standard reinforces an already existing stereotype, and because the stereotype, like the program, sorts explicitly according to race. Consequently, if our success rate at elite colleges turns out to be lower than that of white students (as, thus far, it is) we can scarcely avoid having the fact noticed and, in our racially conscious society, remembered as well. *This risk is a predictable consequence of double standards and cannot be avoided.* Stephen Carter, *Reflections of an Affirmative Action Baby* (New York: Basic Books, 1991), p. 86, emphasis added.

Carter himself goes on to defend a very modified and highly restricted form of preferences, though he acknowledges that even in the restricted form he recommends there will be some unavoidable stigmatization created by such policies. His reasoning in this matter as far as I can see is unassailable. William O. Douglas makes a similar point about preferential admissions to law schools:

> A segregated admissions process creates suggestions of stigma and caste no less than a segregated classroom and in the end it may produce that result despite its contrary intentions. One other assumption must be clearly disapproved, that blacks or browns cannot make it on their individual merit. That is a stamp of inferiority that a state is not permitted to place on any lawyer. . . . So far as race is concerned, any state-sponsored preference of one race over another in that competition is in my view "invidious" and violative of the Equal Protection Clause.
> —*Defunis v. Odegaard*, 416 U.S. 312, 1974.

The only way I can imagine getting around the stigma problem is if preferences were restricted exclusively to toss-up situations where two or more applicants are equally qualified, none being noticeably better than the other. We know, however, that this is not how affirmative action works in the real world, nor is it ever likely to work in this way (and if it could be made to work in this way, preferentialist policies would have only marginal social effects, certainly not the socially transformative ones you wish for them).

That current preferentialist policies in hiring, promotions and other employment settings, as well as in college, university, and professional school admissions, increase racism (in the sense of negative stereotyping) rather than simply leaving the amount of existing racism unaffected seems to many of us a fact so obvious and elementary that what is really needed is an explanation of how anyone could fail to grasp it. If I may venture a speculation here, I would say that those who fail to comprehend this elementary fact do so because they have transformed in their own minds the empirical question of whether or not blacks are cognitively and intellectually inferior to whites—a question that can obviously only be determined by facts and evidence—into a question that is somehow determinable on *a priori* moral and philosophical grounds. As such people are not open to the possibility that the inferiority doctrine may be true, they cannot appreciate how much personal experience plays with others in determining their attitudes towards black competence and black intellectual ability. They cannot see that for many people the existence on the job or in school of blacks who are on average significantly less qualified than the whites or Asians they meet will start them thinking that the inferiority doctrine may well be correct, while exposure to blacks on the job or in school who are as competent as the whites or Asians they come in contact with will have the opposite effect (i.e., it will help to disconfirm and discredit such beliefs).

Stephen Carter makes a similar point (he quotes a black friend to the effect that blacks on the job who are as good or better than their white colleagues have a powerful disconfirming effect on negative images of blacks, while those who are less qualified have a powerful effect in reinforcing and sustaining such images). In this context, the greatest harm of current preferentialist policies, as Charles Murray puts it, is "[that they segment the] whites and blacks who come in contact with each other so as to maximize the likelihood that whites have the advantage in experience and ability."

Glenn Loury makes a related point about the "rationality" of discrimination in employment situations where dual standards of selection have been applied. "If, in an employment situation," Loury writes, "it is known that differential selection criteria are used for different races, and if it is further known that the quality of performance on the job depends on how one did on the criteria of selection, then in the absence of other information it is a rational statistical inference to impute a lower perceived quality of performance to persons of the race that was preferentially favored in selection. Using race as a criterion of selection in employment, in other words, creates objective incentives for customers, co-workers, etc., to take race into account after the employment decision has been made" ("Beyond Civil Rights," *The New Republic*, October 7, 1985). I think there is very considerable anecdotal evidence that the process Loury describes here is actually taking place, and that in many situations in the business and professional worlds not only whites and Asians, but blacks as well avoid dealing with black people whose competence has not yet been established. My mother's stories [which I related to you earlier] about how many of the black patients in the Florida hospital in which she worked would actively request to be treated by white doctors is only one manifestation of this perverse-but-rational logic at work.

Perhaps the best way to illustrate the points that the critics of preferentialism are making here is with a few simple statistics. The table below gives the mean SAT test scores for incoming freshmen at Berkeley over the eleven year period 1978–1988 subdivided into racial and ethnic categories. The scores represent the means on a 1600 point scale adding the math and verbal scores together. For present purposes I limit the discussion only to the preferential admissions of blacks setting aside the equally important issue of Hispanic preferences. I don't know how typical Berkeley's policies of preferential admissions are, though I suspect they are not dramatically different from those one would find at comparable schools like Rice, Duke, Brown, Tufts, etc.—i.e., schools that are just one small step below the most competitive elite institutions (Harvard, Princeton, Yale,

Stanford). The very top quality black students, who are in *very* short supply, are inevitably siphoned off by the upper elite institutions leaving very few such students available for the next tier of schools to recruit.

You will notice that from 1978 to 1983, the average Asian and the average white scores on the SAT were separated by a modest gap of between 54 and 91 points (the white scores always being higher), but that a rapid convergence began in 1984 such that by 1986 the Asian average was actually slightly higher than the white average, and this pattern continued in the two following years. At the beginning of this 11 year period, both white and Asian students who attended Berkeley would probably have noticed that the white students on average were better prepared academically than the Asians, though the difference was quite small (indeed all of the measured test score difference was probably the result of the lower English verbal skills

SAT Scores for Berkeley Entering Freshmen by Race/Ethnicity, 1978–1988			
Year	Blacks	Asians	Whites
1978	878	1080	1155
1979	898	1087	1162
1980	879	1125	1179
1981	902	1098	1189
1982	910	1122	1180
1983	933	1119	1183
1984	923	1189	1204
1985	936	1204	1227
1986	952	1254	1232
1987	938	1281	1261
1988	979	1269	1267
(Source: Office of Student Research, University of California)			

of the Asians resulting from the disproportionate percentage of Asians reared in families where English was not spoken in the home), and although we cannot conclude definitively from the data given, a reasonable hypothesis as to the distribution of test scores would suggest that both Asians and whites who attended Berkeley during this period would have come in contact with many Asian students who were at least as good if not better academically than was the average white student at Berkeley. In the last few years that are represented in the table, both Asians and whites who attended Berkeley would very likely notice that neither group was statistically superior or statistically inferior to the other (again we are making a reasonable assumption about distributions based on the simple averages given in the table), and the possession of Asian or Caucasian racial features would thus come to be seen as of little predictive value in determining who were the weaker and who the stronger Berkeley students. Any negative images about Asian intellectual competence that a white student might have brought to Berkeley would quickly be dispelled.

When we look at the data regarding black/white differences, however, the situation is radically different. Over the entire 11 year period represented in the table the entering black freshmen at Berkeley have had SAT scores that on average ranged from 250 to 323 points below the average score for entering white freshmen. The situation has changed little from 1978, the first year represented in the table, when the black/white gap in SAT averages was 277 points. Now as you know a 250 to 300 point gap in the math-plus-verbal SAT score represents a huge difference in terms of intellectual preparation and intellectual development. Put in terms of high school performance, a typical student scoring a 1250 on the SAT (roughly the average score for an Asian or white entering Berkeley in the late 1980s) would be the kind of student who during his high school career took almost all honors-level courses, received mainly A-level grades in those courses, and graduated in the top 5% of his high school graduating class.[44] A typical student scoring 950 on the SAT, on the other hand (roughly the average score for a black freshman entering Berkeley in the late 1980s) would be the kind of student who took many middle-track rather than honors-track or Advanced Placement courses in high school, probably received as many B-level grades as A-level grades, and wound up in the middle-to-upper-middle level of his high school graduating class (but not the top level). I am envisioning here a large, mixed-race, predominantly middle-class public high school, which is the sort of institution from which universities like Berkeley typically recruit their students whether white, black, Asian, or Hispanic (contrary to a widely shared belief, few black high school graduates who have gone to inner-city ghetto schools can meet even the drastically lowered standards of admissions that are applied to blacks at the more competitive colleges, and insofar as they go on to college, even the better among such students usually wind up going either to community colleges or to the less competitive four year schools).

Now what do you think is going to be the effect of a situation such as that at Berkeley on a) the image of blacks in the minds of the white and Asian students; and b) the self-image of the black students in their own minds? The answer is obvious: the white and Asian students cannot help but notice that while there are some good black students at Berkeley, the bulk of the blacks who attend Berkeley are grossly inferior academically to the average Asian or white. The possession of black racial features under such circumstances becomes a highly significant

---

44. Note: In 1995 the College Board recentered SAT scores, raising the mean of each test to 500 from the much lower mean that had prevailed in years immediately previous to 1995. Converting pre-1995 scores to the higher scores after the 1995 recentering requires the use of the College Board conversion tables, but a rough rule of thumb is to add 70–100 points to the older math-plus-verbal score to get its newer equivalent (e.g., a 1220 on the older SAT might be equivalent to about a 1300 on the newer scoring system).

marker insofar as it says that the bearer of such features has gotten into Berkeley under a much lower standard of admission than is applied to whites and Asians, and that there is a good chance such a person will wind up near the bottom of the class. (Studies show that SAT scores actually *overpredict* somewhat black performance in colleges, no doubt due in part to the fact that so many blacks are in institutions where the bulk of whites and Asians are better prepared than they are, and under such circumstances, there is little incentive to working very hard in order to graduate, let us say, in the bottom 30% of the class, when you can do a minimal amount of work in most colleges nowadays and still manage to graduate, say, in the bottom 10%. Under such circumstances subcultures of lower-achieving blacks might well be expected to develop on campus that place lesser value on academic excellence—just as such subcultures develop among the recruited athletes.)

The stories one reads about white students at competitive colleges passing over black students when they seek lab partners or when they seek help on homework assignments are fully comprehensible once one understands this perverse-but-rational logic that preferentialist policies must inevitably create. Just as athletes will be associated with intellectual inferiority and stupidity at institutions where they are admitted under significantly lowered academic standards than those applied to non-athletes, so blacks or any other ethnic group so favored will be associated with like deficiencies. There is no getting around this. It is an iron law of dual standards.

As far as the black self-image is concerned, I simply cannot imagine how the experience of being at an institution where 80% of the white and Asian students do better than the average black can have an impact other than a negative one. Black people themselves often internalize the image of intellectual inferiority projected by the larger society (cf. the Howard and Hammond article in my anthology), and spending four years in various classroom situations where most of the smart kids are either white or Asian, and most of the really dumb kids black, can hardly contribute to the creation of a positive attitude toward black intellectual abilities. On the contrary, it may lead many black students to thinking, perhaps subconsciously, that there may be something to the claims that blacks are much less intelligent than whites.

In his article in *The New Republic* on "Affirmative Racism," Charles Murray has described a similarly perverse process going on among his affirmative action supporting white liberal friends, who he calls (without rancor) "the new racists." Such people have an impeccable record on civil rights, Murray assures us, and they genuinely want to see blacks integrated into the mainstream of American life. Nevertheless, these "new racists," he explains, display a critical feature of the old racism: they *think* about blacks very differently than they do whites. He writes:

> Among the new racists, lawyers have gotten used to the idea that the brief a black colleague turns in will be a little less well rehearsed and argued than the one they would have done. Businessmen expect that a black colleague will not read a balance sheet as subtly as they do. Teachers expect black students to wind up toward the bottom of the class.

Murray then goes on to explain the inevitable results that preferentialist policies will produce in time even among many of the liberals who support such policies given the fact that most people eventually come to develop an image of a group that depends upon the members of that group whom they actually know and with whom they have come into contact.

> In years past virtually every ethnic group in America has at one time or another lagged behind as a population, and has

eventually caught up. In the process, the ones who breached the barriers were evidence of the success of that group. Now blacks who breach the barriers tend to be seen as evidence of the inferiority of that group. And that is the evil of preferential treatment. It perpetuates an impression of inferiority. . . . [And] it is here that the new racism links up with the old. The old racism has always openly held that blacks are permanently less competent than whites. The new racism tacitly accepts that, in the course of overcoming the legacy of the old racism, blacks are temporarily less competent than whites. It is an extremely fine distinction. As time goes on, fine distinctions tend to be lost.

I think what Murray says here is already happening, and that those with the sociological and historical knowledge, the patience, and the high level of motivation needed to make the "fine distinctions" he talks about in this area are a rapidly diminishing breed.[45]

----

45. Note: After extensive discussions with Harvard psychologist Richard Herrnstein, Murray in the early 1990s came to modify the culture-and-history interpretation of black intellectual deficiencies that he had adopted when he wrote these words in 1984. He came to believe that along with such environmental factors as past racism, genes probably play some kind of role in explaining poor black academic performance, though he was noncommittal and uncertain as to the relative weights of genetic and nongenetic factors: "It seems highly likely to us," he and Herrnstein wrote in their book *The Bell Curve*, "that both genes and the environment have something to do with racial differences [in IQ scores]. What might the mix be? We are resolutely agnostic on that issue; as far as we can determine, the evidence does not yet justify an estimate." *The Bell Curve* (New York: The Free Press, 1994), p. 311. It is important to get the exact wording here because, contrary to a widespread understanding, nowhere in Murray and Herrnstein's controversial book is it suggested that the environmental factors are unimportant in explaining black/white IQ differences or that they are any less important than genetic factors (although it is stated that many specific environmental factors that are thought to be important are not really as important as generally believed). Regardless of his changing view on the genes vs. environment controversy, Murray never seems to have altered his conviction that racial-preference policy has had—and continues to have—a harmful effect on interracial relations and that it encourages the belief among all parties concerned that blacks are less capable than whites.

BREACHING THE RECIPROCITY AND FAIRNESS NORM

Defining "racism" in terms of negative imaging, negative associating, and negative stereotyping, etc., is certainly useful for
many purposes, but I think that in trying to understand certain
types of racial and ethnic clashes in the United States and elsewhere such a definition is perhaps too narrow (because "too
intellectual, or "too cognitive"). When the European settlers in
the West in the nineteenth century claimed that the only good
Indian was a dead one—and the Indians reciprocated by expressing similar feelings toward white Europeans—or when we survey all the inter-ethnic violence and mayhem around the world
in this century we soon see that the racism-as-overgeneralization
model doesn't really get to the historical and emotional core of
many racial and ethnic conflicts. For instance, if we look at the
relationships that exist (either currently or in the recent past)
between the Ibos and the Hausas in Nigeria, between the Serbs
and the Croats in the former Yugoslavia, between the Kurds
and the Arabs in Iraq, between the Greeks and the Turks in
Cyprus, between the Armenians and the Azerbaijanis in Western
Asia, between the Tamils and the Sinhalese in Sri Lanka, in each
of these cases (and the list, unfortunately, could be expanded
manyfold) we see that the members of different ethnic or tribal
groups are fully capable of hating the members of rival groups,
often with a murderous or genocidal passion, even though they
probably have developed no elaborate inferiority doctrine and
are probably well aware of the fact that all sorts of personal
differences exist among the members of their ethnic enemies.
For certain purposes, therefore, I would propose a second definition of racism: racism, I would say, refers to any of a variety
of enmities, hostilities, or hatreds of people of a different race,
ethnicity, or tribe, regardless of the extent to which such enmities, hostilities, or hatreds are related to any ideology of inferiority or any cognitively deficient process of overgeneralization
or stereotyping.

The reason I propose this second definition of racism is because of my strong belief that in trying to formulate public policies that will lessen that bad thing which we call racism, and in trying to articulate principles and ideas that can further the common good, we want to make absolutely certain that the policies we formulate will not only not increase racism in the sense of increasing negative stereotyping and negative imaging, but that they will also not increase racism in the sense of increasing inter-ethnic or inter-racial tension, hostility, or bitterness. Put in more positive terms, I would say that it is imperative that we seek policies that will help to promote cooperation, understanding, and friendship among people of all the diverse racial, ethnic, and religious groups that are to be found in America. And preferentialist policies, I contend, must, by their very nature, undermine efforts to further such cooperation, understanding and mutual friendship because they breach a widely shared inter-ethnic, inter-racial, and inter-religious norm of reciprocity and fairness that has evolved over time in America, and because the breach of this norm inevitably produces a deeply felt hostility and sense of grievance and wrong on the part of many of the people in the non-preferred groups (particularly the poorer and less fortunate members of these non-preferred groups) that can only serve to poison race relations and to sap the moral and spiritual vitality of any people so racially, ethnicly, and religiously diverse as our own.

While the fairness and reciprocity norm of which I speak is widely understood and has become very deeply ingrained in America, it seems clear to me that you yourself do not understand it—or more precisely stated, do not understand the motivation and thought processes behind it—and as a result of this lack of understanding, you tend to attribute to base and sinister motives in others their opposition to the various preferentialist schemes which you support. (If I may speculate here once again, I would suggest that your lack of understanding of this commonly accepted norm is intimately tied to your relatively privileged socio-economic position in life as a member of the more comfortable and secure segment of the middle class, as well as to your diminished level of ethnic consciousness and ethnic loyalty. Poor and lower-middle-class whites, as well as whites of whatever socio-economic class who display high levels of ethnic identity and ethnic loyalty, almost without exception understand this norm very well.) Let me take a little time, therefore, to explain how this norm works in America, and why a breach of it is so bitterly resented even by people who harbor no special animus or ill-will toward the members of those groups on behalf of whom a breach of the norm is demanded.

The reciprocity and fairness norm I am talking about has evolved over time in America as a highly functional and creative response to a simple fact of human nature, namely, the fact that we all tend to show a natural human partiality toward those whom we regard as our "own kind"—i.e., toward our own family, our own close relatives, our own friends, our own extended kinship group, our own ethnic group, our own race, etc. This natural partiality, to be sure, has some beneficial aspects to it (as you correctly remark at one point in your manuscript in your discussion of partiality toward the members of one's family), but it just as certainly harbors the potential for great danger when systems of cooperation must be worked out within the polity that will lead to harmonious relationships between people who belong to many different (and potentially rivalrous) kinship groups, friendship groups, tribal groups, racial groups, and religions.

Most people are naturally inclined to show partiality or preference to those with whom they identify closely and whom they see as members of their own kind rather than members of any outsider group. In employment situations, for instance, the practice of showing special consideration toward one's relatives, one's close friends, one's co-religionists, or the members of one's tribal or ethnic group is probably universal, and can certainly be seen today in America, either where fair employment practice laws are successfully evaded or where such laws, as in the case of very small businesses, do not apply. To give just one example (which I may or may not have related to you in conversation), a friend of mine who worked for many years in the sales division of a large Fortune 500 company explained to me the hiring situation that existed in the various sales offices in the New York City area with which he was familiar. In the district offices where the district manager was Irish, he explained, a majority of the people hired were Irish; in district offices where the district manager was a Jew, the majority of people hired were Jews; in the district offices where the district manager was Italian, a majority of the people hired were Italian. My friend explained this situation as a simple case of preferentialist hiring (it was not simply due to word-of-mouth transmissions of job openings): the district managers simply gave preference to members of their own ethnic group even though better qualified members of out-groups had sought employment.

Now, as I say, most people, given the chance, would hire in this kind of preferentialist manner, just as most nation-states, given the opportunity, tend to favor the products of their own manufacturers (i.e., through subsidies and tariff protections) over goods produced by foreign peoples. Government employment in this regard is no different from private-sector employment: whenever it was legal to do so (and even in many cases where it was not), those in control of government in America, whether at a local, state, or national level, have generally sought to give special preference to their "own kind," whether family, friends, co-religionists, members of the same ethnic group, people from the same geographic region, or members of the same political party.

This special preference may or may not have been accompanied by high levels of animosity toward the members of various nonpreferred groups (just as the in-group preferences nation-states display toward the people in their own manufacturing industries may or may not be accompanied by high levels of out-group animosity toward the people of various rival nations). Such a practice, however, obviously has many disadvantages both in terms of economic and administrative efficiency, as well as (and this may be more important), in terms of creating that sense of common purpose and common humanity among diverse peoples that is so necessary for social harmony in any nation as demographically diverse as America. It was, I think, to combat these disadvantages of preferentialism that the fairness and reciprocity norm to which I have referred developed among reformers and others in the latter part of the nineteenth century, and as far as government employment was concerned, became institutionalized, first in federal, state, and local civil service laws, and then, beginning in the late 1940s, in the passage of many state and local "fair employment practice laws," which covered both government and private sector employment. (I think the term "fair employment practice law" captures a major objective of anti-discrimination legislation which your own analysis tends to neglect—i.e., that the laws not only intend to discourage employment practices considered by most people to be in some sense unfair or bad, but to encourage those considered by most people to be positively fair or good. This dual purpose is well reflected in the opening sentence of Lyndon Johnson's Executive Order 11375: "It is the policy of the United States Government to provide equal employment opportunity in federal employment and in employment by federal contractors on the basis of merit and without discrimination because of race, color, religion, sex, or national origin.")

As I say, both the civil service laws dating back to the nineteenth century, and the FEP laws which came into vogue in many states beginning in the late 1940s (Title VII of the 1964 Civil Rights Act being a late instance of an FEP law), reflect this norm of reciprocity and fairness. This norm has the form of a social contract and if put into words might be stated something like the following:

> In order to achieve a more perfect harmony and union among our diverse peoples and achieve certain long-run economic benefits that will be of advantage to all, within certain clearly specified contexts I will give up acting upon the natural partiality which I feel towards *my* own kind, if—but only if—you and others give up acting upon the partiality which you feel toward *your* own kind. Employment in government and large-scale corporations is one of these specified contexts. Here the reciprocity principle demands that we renounce nepotism, amicism, ethnic preferences, racial preferences, religious preferences, cronyism, and the like in order that we may further employment practices which we can all accept as reasonably fair and just, and which we can all relate to in a positive manner.
>
> Such fair and just employment practices will usually be based upon merit or seniority, but we may also want to give special consideration to those among our diverse people who may be physically handicapped, or who may have taken time out from their careers to protect us all through active duty in the military. In promising to give up acting upon our natural partiality in these clearly specified contexts, it is to be understood that there will remain many private areas of our lives where we retain the right to act upon our natural partiality without hindrance from government or other rule-enforcing agents. It is also to be understood that if others do not live up to their part of the reciprocity agreement in those contexts where we have agreed that the reciprocity principle is to apply, and seek instead one or another form of preferential treatment for members of their own group, then I will no longer feel bound by the nonpreferentialist principle. Under

such circumstances I will consider those who have fraudulently used this principle to further their own selfish ends to be unscrupulous deceivers whom I will henceforth consider my hostile rivals if not my outright enemies.

Such, I believe, is the reciprocity principle underlying the thinking of most Americans with regard to ethnicity-, race-, and religion-based public benefits, at least most Americans who occupy the lower, working, or not-so-comfortable section of the middle class, and who belong to one of the various European-origin ethnic groups. Many Asians, many Hispanics, and a not-insignificant number of blacks also feel a kinship with this norm. (The reciprocity principle, of course, does not accurately reflect the complex thought processes of the politically influential, white "limousine liberals," whose tangled complex of compassion, guilt, self-righteous hypocrisy, romanticism, and fear I have tried to analyze in the article appearing in my affirmative-action anthology.) The reciprocity principle involved here, you will note, is structurally very similar to the principle that lies behind most international trade agreements. It says in effect that all parties to the agreement will give up whatever in-group partiality and out-group hostility they may have maintained in the past in order to join in a process of mutual accommodation and mutual benefit that will both further good will among the parties and produce certain important long-term economic benefits that improve the living standards of most of the people involved.

To illustrate the fairness and reciprocity principle as it actually influences people's thinking, I offer below a few illustrations drawn from Jonathan Rieder's important ethnographic study of the lower-middle class Jews, Italians, and blacks living in the Canarsie section of Brooklyn (*Canarsie: The Jews and Italians of Brooklyn against Liberalism*, Cambridge, MA: Harvard

University Press, 1985). The first comes from a Jewish school teacher who explained to Rieder the sense of betrayal he felt when national policy in the area of ethnic and racial relations turned away from strict neutrality to a regime of compensatory preferences. "Black demands for equality of results rather than of opportunity began to alienate even fervent supporters of the black struggle for justice," Rieder explains. He then goes on to describe the reaction to this development of many of the lower-middle-class Jews of Brooklyn (many of whom in the past had been politically far to the left, having enthusiastically embraced New Deal welfarism in the 1930s and Debsian-style socialism in the 1920s):

> Their new status as opponents of civil rights measures pained countless progressive Jews, who felt torn not simply between cupidity and ethics but between commitment to justice for blacks and disapproval of specific means of redress. One Jewish educator specified the visceral universalism that he felt should guide the good society: "As a Jew, I believed anything that helped someone getting the short end of the stick would help the Jews. I couldn't go to medical school because of the quotas. . . . I was pro-civil rights. I supported the Selma march, and the civil rights movement in its early phase. But, when someone tries to take something from me to benefit others, I'll fight it. . . . I changed with the notion of not offering equal rights and opportunities but compensation. That's reverse discrimination. It's a gut reaction with me." (pp. 111–12)

While the above statement of the Jewish educator may be lacking in precision and articulateness, Rieder's concept of "visceral universalism," I think, well captures the man's feelings. The man clearly believes that in America people are entitled to whatever job or whatever place in a professional school they can attain on the basis of religion-, ethnicity-, and race-neutral criteria of selection, and that such neutral principles are the way people of diverse religions, ethnicities, and races can get along best in America. The man does not want to keep black people or Hispanic people in any assigned "place," and indeed, one could hardly imagine him objecting, let us say, to the great success Asian Americans have shown in getting into elite universities and professional schools through their superior academic performance even though such success has been gained at the expense of many aspiring Jews. The man, no doubt, feels strong loyalty toward his own people, but he is willing to forgo acting upon this loyalty in the arena of public policy in return for the application of a neutral principle upon which both Jews and non-Jews can agree.

Another aspect of this "visceral universalism" (which only a warped ideologue would confuse with racism) is represented in Rieder's book by the comments of an Italian housewife. The woman in this case is objecting to the fact that while efforts were being made to set aside a special day in the Canarsie school system to celebrate Black Solidarity, Italians and Jews, who constituted a majority of the local population, were denied similar opportunity to set aside their own day for cultural celebration. Rieder writes on this:

> The residents of Canarsie viewed themselves not as abstract whites but as members of specific ethnic groups. As a result, they felt blacks were demanding unfair helpings of cultural dignity. A housewife sketched an elemental ideal of justice. "If you close schools on Martin Luther King Day, or Black Solidarity Day, then you must close the schools for Jewish Solidarity Day and Italian Solidarity Day. It's all a matter of fairness. I believe in black pride, but don't step on my white Italian pride."

This woman clearly believes that in the public arena no single ethnic, racial, or religious group is to be favored over any other, and that if official public celebration or recognition is established for any one group it must be established as well for all other groups that seek such treatment. Here we have a somewhat different type of reciprocity principle than that operating in the areas of employment or professional school admissions, but it draws upon many of the same thought processes and moral intuitions that are operative in the latter areas.

Rieder explains very well in his book the fundamental clash that took place in Canarsie over the decade of the 1970s between the neutralist principles that most Canarsie residents adhered to with regard to the place of race and ethnicity in the public arena and the alien preferentialist principles supported by New York's white, upper- middle-class liberal elite. "A consensus prevailed in Canarsie," Rieder writes, "on the rightful place of ethnicity in a democratic society." He goes on:

> The local theory of pluralism forbade the dominance of a single group in public life, defined the individual as the proper unit in affairs of state, and reserved a space in private life for regional culture, ethnocentric prejudice, and communal lifestyle. But as they nervously watched the twists and turns of the civil rights movement, Canarsians became persuaded that a different, and quite dangerous, notion of race had triumphed in public discourse. The use of explicit terms of race to allocate goods, assign blame, and apportion respect threatened to rend the fabric of society with communal passion. Concepts like compensation and restitution imposed more than financial burdens. By implying that all whites shared equal liability for past wrongs, racial remedies bestowed judgments of guilt and innocence, shame and virtue. Canarsians were too close to their own humble origins to think of themselves as exploiters. (pp. 121–2)

I think Rieder's remarks here explain very well why there is a class bias on the preference issue among people who are in the nonbeneficiary categories. Supporters of preferences, as I have tried to emphasize in my anthology article, are almost always drawn from the relatively privileged segments of the white ethnic groups—most often they are people who feel somewhat ambivalent or guilty about their class privileges and try to expiate their guilt through their support for help-the-black-underdog public policies whose costs and burdens are almost always disproportionately borne by poor and lower-middle-class whites. When these poor and lower-middle-class whites then complain, as they inevitably do, the privileged white liberals (i.e., the Tom Wickers, the John Lindsays, the William Hudnuts, the Howard Glicksteins, etc.) denounce them in the most uncharitable of terms for their lack of compassion and their Neanderthal-like bigotry.

In recent years I have come to believe—reluctantly to be sure, as I don't like to accuse people of wrongdoings they have not committed—that a substantial portion of the privileged white liberals who support preferentialist policies actually feel good about the situation that is created when such policies help to provoke ugly public displays of hostility toward blacks on the part of poor and lower-middle-class whites (cf. the Boston busing episode). Just as many among the lower segment of Southern white society always felt good about public displays of irresponsibility and immorality on the part of the lowest class of Southern blacks because such displays helped to reinforce and confirm their own sense of moral and social superiority over the group immediately beneath them on the social ladder, so in like manner many of the more economically privileged and secure among the white middle-class liberals actually feel good about the ugly displays of mean-spiritedness and bigotry on the part of the white ethnic lower-middle class ("the Archie Bunkers") because such displays help to reinforce and confirm the sense of moral and social superiority that they want to feel over the group immediately beneath them on the social ladder. I know this is a very harsh judgement, and it certainly doesn't apply to all the privileged white liberals who support preferences, but is seems to me to apply to a very substantial portion of them. (Indeed, I would suspect very possibly a majority. It is the way, I think, that most upper-middle-class, liberal Manhattan WASPS, and most upper-middle-class, liberal Long Island Jews whom I have known feel toward the lower-middle-class Jews and Italians of Brooklyn that Rieder describes).

While I am on the issue of "visceral universalism," I should say something about the response to preferentialism on the part of the one white person I have known in my life who displayed the least bigotry or antipathy toward black people. I am referring here to my late mother, who was not only committed in principle to a policy of nondiscrimination regarding black people but who had a genuine and heart-felt affection for black people that was surely unusual for a white person. This unusual affection, I learned later in life, was the product of two formative experiences she had in her childhood and adolescence. (In both instances black people actively befriended her and treated her with great kindness, once when she was a little girl growing up on her grandmother's farm, the other time when she was a teenager attending a new high school on Long Island, where she was snubbed by most of the other whites in the school.) I suppose the supreme test of her nonbigoted affection for black people came some years back when my sister—her only daughter—was engaged to marry a young black man (a very dark-skinned black man). I don't think ninety-nine out of a hundred white mothers in a similar position would have accepted this situation with the equanimity and support that my mother did (this was at a time when black-white marriages were much less common than they have become over the past several years). My mother reached out to my sister's boyfriend and his mother, made all the preliminary plans for the wedding, and was very much looking forward to her mulatto grandchildren. (As it turned out, the wedding and engagement were eventually called off, and my mother died two years ago never having experienced the joy of grandchildren).

Regarding the issue of preferences in employment and professional schools, my mother had the exact same gut-universalist reaction as the Canarsie teacher that Rieder quotes. "It's just not fair" was how she responded to such policies, and I am sure she would have had the same response regardless of the races, ethnicities, or religions that were singled out for special treatment. (Like many other white Americans, however, my mother was a strong supporter of such programs as Head Start even though she was well aware of the fact that in many areas the vast majority of the beneficiaries of such programs were blacks and Hispanics. The difference here, of course, is that programs like Head Start are applied to the poor of all races, ethnicities, and religions, and thus respect the norm of inter-racial, interethnic, and inter-religious reciprocity and fairness.)

At one point in your discussion you seem to me to be so eager to convict antipreferentialist whites of racism that you accept not merely an unlikely but a thoroughly impossible interpretation of why many whites can support certain types of deviations from meritocracy but not others. Responding to Michael Walzer's observation that "the policy of veteran's preferences in civil service employment seems to have been widely accepted," you pose the ominous question, "What does it reveal when a departure from meritocracy stirs outrage and indignation only when blacks benefit from it?" Two pages later you give us the answer to your question in the form of a quotation from Derrick Bell's *Race, Racism and American Law*:

> If one recognizes that racism is part of the shared structure
> of meaning in the U.S., this anomaly becomes more under-

standable. The singling out of affirmative action among all the deviations from meritocracy that are institutionalized in the United States for special opprobrium is best understood as one manifestation of "the unstated understanding by the mass of whites that they will accept large disparities in economic opportunity to other whites as long as they have a priority over blacks and other people of color for access to those opportunities." In short, the norms that racial preference violates are, to a certain and perhaps decisive extent, racist ones.

This is, if I may be pardoned here for my own lack of charity, a completely ludicrous, thoroughly off-the-wall interpretation of the current racial situation in America. About the best that can be said for it is that it may accurately reflect the situation that existed in the Deep South around the turn of the century when the white alliance between lower-class populists and middle-class conservatives institutionalized the Jim Crow system. (cf. C. Vann Woodward's *The Strange Career of Jim Crow*). But where, I am inclined to ask, have you and Bell been for the last 30 years? I have had a fair amount of experience with lower-class white people in recent times, from the most overtly bigoted to those with racial views similar to those of my mother. This was the result of the fact that for many years I was out of academics and worked in a number of factories as a night watchman and security guard, during which time I got to meet and discuss with them their views on race and related matters of numerous truck drivers, fork lift operators, janitors, security guards, boiler operators, electricians, secretaries, manual laborers, hair dressers, packers, waitresses, etc.

In my several years of working as a security guard in a number of different factories and offices, I never met a single white person whom I felt needed the assurance that he would be promoted ahead of blacks before he would be willing "[to] accept large disparities in economic opportunity." As a number of important studies of public attitudes have shown (see especially Jennifer Hochschild's *What's Fair?*, and a number of articles by Robert Lane), white Americans in recent years, including most poor and lower-middle-class white Americans, simply do not question the desirability of a competitive capitalist economic system and the highly variable status order and opportunity structure that such a system inevitably produces, and this, I think, you will find to be the case in states and cities that are essentially all white as it is for regions that have more substantial black populations.

I never met a white person, no matter how overtly hostile to black people, who thought it was unfair that black people should have done so well in areas such as football, basketball, boxing, music, entertainment, or any of the other areas of American life where black people have been very successful through their competitive efforts. This is a quite remarkable fact, considering that many working-class people relate much more readily to sports or entertainment figures than they do, say, to corporate lawyers, college presidents, CEOs, and the like, and I certainly have met many working-class people who regret—but who do not think it unfair—that blacks practically monopolize such sports as boxing and basketball. As far as "other people of color" are concerned, I have never met a white person—again no matter how overtly bigoted—who thought it unfair that Japanese, Chinese, or Asian Indians have done so phenomenally well in various scholastic pursuits in America, or that Koreans and members of other Asian groups have come to dominate the small-business field in a number of large cities.

What this tells me is that white people, even very bigoted ones, can accept the advancement of blacks or any other racial, ethnic, or religious group in America, within virtually any area of endeavor, so long as that advancement takes place within the accepted rules of the game—that is, the advancement of the members of the group respects the conditions set up by the widely shared norm of racial, ethnic, and religious reciprocity and fairness.

Your interpretation of the veterans' exception to the meritocracy principle seems to me to be wrong on its very face. The U.S. military is one of the most racially, ethnicly, and religiously integrated institutions in American society, and blacks have been joining the military in droves since the time of the First World War. In recent decades blacks have been overrepresented in the military ranks, and no doubt among the veteran population as well. Whatever else one may attribute a white person's support of veterans' benefits to, one can hardly explain it as a result of a pro-white bias, or an anti-black prejudice, for the simple reason that any employment policy that gave special advantages to veterans would almost certainly have the effect of disproportionately benefiting blacks. A preference for veterans, however, does not breach the racial reciprocity norm, which is why, no doubt, whites can support it in large numbers. (I agree with Walzer, however, that there are better—and certainly fairer—ways to show appreciation for veterans than job preferences, but I would feel this way even if we were a country like Japan, where almost everyone identifies themselves as belonging to the same ethnic group). One can make a similar remark with regard to special preferences for college athletes. Whatever reasons may be involved, at many institutions white acceptance of such preferences can hardly be the result of racial bias for the simple reason that particularly in the more popular college sports like football and basketball a vastly disproportionate percentage of the recipients of such preferences are blacks.

THE LIMITS OF THE PREFERENTIALIST PROJECT

I would like to make one final point about the scope and limits of the "anti-discrimination project" that you envision. You already know my views about the harmful social and psychological effects that preferentialist policies have both on beneficiaries and on nonbeneficiaries. But I would also like to say something about the very limited economic effect that such policies are likely to have based on the experience of such policies in the past. Although their capacity to do extensive social and psychological harm is very great, in the economic realm preferentialist policies have done little more in the 20 years they have been with us than help a relatively small percentage of mainly better-off blacks to rise up in the world at a somewhat faster pace than they would have done in the absence of such policies. As you yourself acknowledge at one point, they have had very little effect in helping the black underclass ("the truly disadvantaged") in the name of whom such policies are often defended. But such policies have also had very little effect in furthering the growth of the black middle class, which has indeed grown by leaps and bounds since the 1940s, but owing to forces generally unrelated to preferences.

It is well known among labor economists that the great growth of the black middle class, and the increasing convergence of black incomes and white incomes, occurred in the three decades *before* preferentialist policies were instituted in the early 1970s. Since 1970, blacks have made, in aggregate economic terms, comparatively modest progress vis-à-vis whites, and even those labor economists (such as Jonathan Leonard) who have taken the most optimistic view of the positive effects of preferentialist policies on black incomes would concede that those effects are relatively small compared to other factors. No labor economist knowledgeable about the relevant research in this area would endorse the view that preferentialist policies have either had in the past or are likely to have in the future a *major* transformative effect (as opposed to a rather modest one) on the distribution of jobs and income among the different racial and ethnic groups in America.

One of the best treatments of this issue is that of economists Finis Welch and James P. Smith in their Rand Corporation study *Forty Years of Economic Progress for Blacks.* Welch and Smith show in their study tremendous economic progress for blacks in terms of catching up to white norms over the period 1940–1980 with the bulk of the progress occurring during the decades of the 1940s and 1950s. These were, of course, pre-affirmative action decades, yet the pace of catch-up Welch and Smith show was much faster then than in the 1960s and 1970s, when civil rights policies and then preferences were instituted. Economists like Welch and Smith who look at the great black economic progress in the pre-quota era between 1940 and 1970 attribute this progress to the large movement of blacks out of the low-paying regions of the agricultural South into the better-paying urban-industrial regions of the country and to the significant improvement in the black returns on education, which were apparently due to more meritocratic employment practices. Credit for some of the convergence of the black/white income distributions over the 1940–1970 period can probably be attributed to state and local FEP laws as well as to FEP requirements placed upon federal contractors by the federal executive (beginning with FDR), but most of the black improvement probably had little to do with explicit government policies. State FEP laws were often more symbolic than rigorously enforced, and in the decade of the 1940s, when the greatest black progress occurred, few states had such laws.

Most of the economic progress of blacks from the 1940s onward, economists like Welsh and Smith argue, came from improved education for blacks throughout the nation and the decision of individual blacks to leave the cotton- and tobacco-growing regions of the South and the low-paying occupations of maids and janitors in order to take the higher-paying jobs that offered themselves in the burgeoning Northern, Midwestern, and Western industrial regions. Welch and Smith show how little convergence of white and black incomes there really was between 1970 and 1980, when preferentialist policies became widespread. "Affirmative action," Welsh and Smith write, "apparently had no significant long-run impact, whether positive or negative, on the male racial wage gap. The general pattern is that the narrowing of the racial wage gap was as rapid in the 20 years prior to 1960 (and before affirmative action) as during the 20 years afterward. This suggests that the slowly evolving historical forces we have emphasized in this report that enhance the labor-market skills of blacks—education and migration—were the primary determinants of long-term black economic improvement. At best, affirmative action has marginally altered black wage gains about this long-term trend." James P. Smith and Finis Welch, *Closing the Gap: Forty Years of Economic Progress for Blacks* (Santa Monica, CA: Rand Corporation, 1986).

Free-market economists have long told us how market forces tend to dissolve prejudices insofar as prejudiced employers in any competitive industry will be at a competitive disadvantage if they arbitrarily refuse to hire the best available workers because of racial, ethnic, or other criteria unrelated to productivity and merit. Unprejudiced employers reap benefits by hiring on purely economic and efficiency grounds. There are complications to this rosy picture to be sure, especially if an employer operates in a climate like the Jim Crow South, where fellow workers or customers may be prejudiced against persons of certain races or ethnicities. But there is a good deal of truth in the rosy picture, especially as it played out in the more competitive and more industrial regions outside the segregated South.

It seems clear that preferentialist policies, contrary to the impression many of their supporters have of them, are responsible for very little of the great economic progress blacks have made over the past 50 years, and what progress can be attributed to them has been attained at a heavy cost in terms of harmonious race relations and public goodwill. Even if I were not against such policies on moral grounds (i.e., because they breach a widely shared norm of reciprocity and fairness that I believe is reasonably just and worthy of retaining), I would have to admit that from a simple cost/benefit perspective such policies have been a very bad deal. Relatively meager economic benefits have been achieved at huge costs—moral, psychological, and political. The cause of racism, I believe—in both senses that I have defined the term here—has certainly been furthered by such policies, and there is really very little to show for them.

CONCLUDING REMARKS

Well, this communication has gone on too long. Let me conclude with a statement from Michael Walzer. "In general," Walzer says at the end of his discussion of preferences in *Spheres of Justice*, "the struggle against a racist past is more likely to be won if it is fought in ways that build on, rather than challenge, understandings of the social world shared by the great majority of Americans, black and white alike."

Walzer is a very wise and thoughtful man—he's my favorite intellectual on the left—and I can only say to his remarks here, Amen! As a final word I would add the equally wise injunction of Hippocrates: "Above all, do no harm!"

PS: Good luck to you, Andy, on your book!

III

THE CHANGING SHAPE OF THE RIVER: AFFIRMATIVE ACTION AND SOME RECENT SOCIAL SCIENCE RESEARCH

Racial preferences in college admissions have been at least as contentious as those in the employment field. William Bowen and Derek Bok, former presidents of Princeton and Harvard, have been the figures most influential over the past two decades in defending admissions preferences at America's elite institutions of higher learning. In their enormously influential 1998 study, *The Shape of the River,* they tried to convince an often skeptical public that racial preferences at America's leading colleges and universities have few of the drawbacks critics usually attribute to them and have produced great benefits not only for the students receiving the preferences but also for their classmates and American society more generally.

In the years since the publication of *The Shape of the River* a good deal of research has been done relating to affirmative-action policies at competitive colleges and other institutions of higher learning, much of it suggesting that Bowen and Bok's original conclusions were much too sanguine. At least three subsequent studies sponsored by the Andrew W. Mellon foundation—the same group that sponsored *The Shape of the River* and which until 2009 William Bowen headed—have found evidence regarding academic performance and student attitudes on college campuses that confirm many of the claims preference critics have long been making.

In this chapter I summarize some of the research since the publication of *The Shape of the River* that indicates a huge downside to preference policies both at the undergraduate and professional-school levels. This research suggests that a) white and Asian students deeply resent racial preference policies and hold those who benefit from them at a considerable "social distance"; b) support for racial preferences among the black and Hispanic public is much less than generally thought; c) the upward ratcheting of black students into more competitive undergraduate institutions lowers their grade-point average and discourages many from pursuing careers in the natural sciences and in college teaching; d) the independent "school effect" of attending a more prestigious college in terms of future earnings may be small or nonexistent once one takes into account the motivation and multiple background factors of the students who attend them; e) racial-preference policies cause whites to look down upon blacks as their intellectual inferiors and help promote racial self-segregation on college campuses; f) whites and Asians who have attended colleges with substantial percentages of blacks and Hispanics experience no net benefit in terms of later job market outcomes compared with whites and Asians who have attended less ethnically diverse colleges; and g) the upward-ratcheting system in law school admissions often results in black students attending institutions too competitive for their individual needs, leading to high drop-out rates and high rates of failure on state bar exams.

If racial-preference policies have such harmful consequences, why do they continue to be supported by people like William Bowen and Derek Bok? To answer this question I draw heavily on the brilliant analysis of white narcissism and white guilt by the essayist Shelby Steele, who claims that many privileged whites who support policies ostensibly intended to help blacks are less concerned with whether those policies actually achieve their goals than with whether they make their supporters feel good about themselves and morally cleansed and uplifted in supporting them. They are above all concerned with protecting themselves against charges of racial insensitivity and racism. Given the enormous power of this dynamic, meaningful change in college preference policies, I conclude, is not likely to come about any time soon regardless of the verdict of social science research.[46]

Social science research has not always been kind to supporters of affirmative action. Though little known outside a narrow circle of specialists, over the past several years a growing body of research by sociologists, economists, and political scientists has been accumulating that seriously calls into question many of the most cherished assumptions of affirmative-action supporters regarding the effects of race-based preferences in university admissions. The great irony in the matter is that some of the research that has proved most damaging to the case for racial preferences in higher education has come from studies sponsored by some of the very same organizations that have been the most active in the past in their support of the affirmative-action initiatives at our nation's leading universities and colleges.

Organizations such as the Andrew W. Mellon Foundation, which funded William Bowen and Derek Bok's *The Shape of the River*[47] (the academic establishment's unofficial defense of affirmative action), the liberal Ford Foundation, the Russell Sage Foundation, and the Princeton-based Council of Ivy Group Presidents have been uniformly supportive of affirmative action in higher education and have often been in the forefront of efforts to convince a generally skeptical public of the great

46. This chapter is based on an updated and substantially expanded version of an article bearing the same title that appeared in the journal *Academic Questions* in the fall of 2004 (17:4, pp. 7–59).
47. *The Shape of the River* (Princeton: Princeton University Press, 1998).

social and economic benefits of greater "diversity" in university admissions. That some of the most important research these organizations have funded in recent years would turn out to refute several of the key arguments in favor of the policies they have long cherished was no doubt something the organizations themselves never bargained for. And at least in the case of the deep-pocketed Mellon Foundation, they don't seem to have accepted what their own researchers have discovered with any degree of grace or candor.

To get a sense of the irony of the matter, imagine a situation in which the Cato Institute, the Heritage Foundation, the Independent Institute, and the American Enterprise Institute all shelled out big chunks of money to sponsor a number of research projects on the relationship between tax policy and economic growth, only to have their researchers discover that countries with very high marginal tax rates and large public sectors had much higher growth rates and more lavish living standards than countries following a low-tax, small-government model. One would perhaps not be too surprised if they reacted in the same way that Mellon and the rest have done: keep quiet about the matter, do little to publicize their researchers' findings, and hope that nobody outside a circle of reliable ideological soulmates ever reads their researchers' reports.

ATTENDING AN ELITE UNIVERSITY: NO SPECIAL TICKET TO RIDE

One of the more damaging pieces of research to the case for affirmative action made in *The Shape of the River* comes from a study by economists Stacy Berg Dale and Alan Krueger. The study, which was funded by the Mellon Foundation, bears the prosaic and disarmingly unsensational title "Estimating the Payoff to Attending a More Selective College: An Application of Selection on Observables and Unobservables." It was first published as a Working Paper of the prestigious National Bureau of Economic Research and later, in slightly modified form, as an article in the *Quarterly Journal of Economics*, a peer-reviewed economics journal jointly published by MIT and Harvard.[48] The "insider" nature of those writing the article is well reflected in the fact that Dale was employed at the time as a full-time Mellon Foundation research associate working out of the organization's Princeton office, and by the fact that the College and Beyond survey used by Dale and Krueger was a "restricted access database" compiled by the Mellon Foundation itself.[49] Indeed, the C&B database formed the basis for most of the analysis in *The Shape of the River*. Its prosaic title notwithstanding, the Dale/ Krueger study is a real blockbuster in terms of its authors' iconoclastic conclusions and the sobering implications of these conclusions for our understanding of elite universities and their role as supposedly unique vehicles of upward mobility in America.

What Dale and Krueger set out to determine was the effect on a student's post-graduation income that can be attributed to the level of selectivity of the particular college or university that a student attends. In terms of future earnings, what difference does it make, the authors ask, if one attends a first-tier institution like Yale, Princeton, Duke, or Swarthmore, where the average SAT scores are the highest, rather than a second-tier school like Vanderbilt, Northwestern, Kenyon, or Emory, where the

---

48. NBER Working Paper # 7322 (Cambridge, MA: National Bureau of Economic Research, Cambridge, Aug. 1999; "Estimating the Payoff to Attending a More Selective College: An Application of Selection on Observables and Unobservables," *The Quarterly Journal of Economics,* Nov. 2002, pp. 1491–527. The page numbers in the text refer to this latter journal article unless otherwise indicated.

49. In a highly unusual move, the Mellon Foundation designated the results of its College and Beyond survey as a "restricted access database," and it has been reluctant to make the data available for reanalysis by scholars known to hold views critical of affirmative action in higher education. Robert Lerner, a distinguished sociologist who has written one of the most intelligent scholarly criticisms of *The Shape of the River*, was specifically turned down in his request for access to the Mellon database. See Lerner's article "The Empire Strikes Back," available online at www.ceousa.org/bok.html.

degree of selectivity is considerably less? Are there advantages to attending these second-tier schools rather than the third-tier and fourth-tier schools immediately beneath them on the selectivity scale? It is well known—and well-established in the economics literature—that attending a more selective college is positively correlated with at least a moderately greater lifetime earnings potential, but much of this difference can be easily attributed to the fact that smarter people with higher grades and higher standardized test scores—and often with wealthier and better-connected parents—are the people who attend these schools. People who already have the highest earning potential often attend the most selective colleges, and much of their post-college success can be attributed to the superior talents and special personal factors that they bring with them to college rather than to the superior schooling or superior contacts that they make while in school. Assuming one attends some four-year college or other, after controlling for initial input factors, how much of a difference does it really make whether one attends a school that warrants a Most Competitive, a Highly Competitive, a Very Competitive, a Competitive, or a Less Competitive rating in the Barron's *Profiles to American Colleges*? These are the kinds of questions that Dale and Krueger set out to answer, and their answers clearly undermine the notion that elite universities provide some sort of unique pathway to wealth, power, and occupational prestige in America.

A major aim of the analysis presented in *The Shape of the River* was to show that for both whites and blacks—but particularly for blacks—the "school effect" of attending an elite college was very substantial, even after controlling for SAT scores and other obviously important input factors like a student's high school grades, race, gender, family socioeconomic status, and the like. At any given SAT level, the Bowen and Bok data showed, both blacks and whites who attended a more selective institution incurred a substantial earnings advantage later in life. "Black students admitted to the most selective of the [28] C&B schools,"[50] Bowen and Bok wrote, "did not pay a penalty in life after college for having attended such competitive institutions. On the contrary, the black (and white) matriculants with academic credentials that were modest by the standards of these schools appear to have been well advised to go to the most selective schools to which they were admitted. . . . After holding SATs constant, black students who attended the more selective schools gained an earnings advantage." (p. 144)

In addition to this earnings advantage, black students who attended the more selective colleges among the 28 C&B schools were also shown in the Bowen and Bok study to incur many other advantages (after controlling for initial input factors), including increased graduation rates, increased participation in certain civic and community affairs, and increased student satisfaction with their college experience. It was these advantages that were at the heart of the Bowen and Bok defense of racial preference policies at elite universities, and without these policies, it was suggested, the black community would have been deprived of a large segment of its leadership, business, and professional class. The message of *The Shape of the River* was as stark as it was clear: eliminating affirmative action at elite universities would decimate the black middle class.

Long before the Dale/Krueger research, critics of the Bowen and Bok study were quick to point out that only a small segment of the black middle class and of black political and business leaders are the products of Ivy League colleges or other first-tier universities in America. Many more black congressmen,

---

50. The C&B database contains information on students entering the following schools as freshmen in 1976 and 1989. Liberal Arts Colleges: Barnard, Bryn Mawr, Denison, Hamilton, Kenyon, Oberlin, Smith, Swarthmore, Wellesley, Wesleyan, Williams. Research Universities: Columbia, Duke, Emory, Miami, Northwestern, Pennsylvania State, Princeton, Rice, Stanford, Tufts, Tulane, University of Michigan (Ann Arbor), University of North Carolina (Chapel Hill), University of Pennsylvania, Vanderbilt, Washington University, Yale.

black business leaders, black professionals, black mayors, and the like are the product of state universities and comparable private institutions than the kinds of elite universities with which William Bowen, former Princeton president, and Derek Bok, former Harvard president, are most intimately acquainted. It has been estimated, for instance, that the 100 most selective colleges and universities in America turn out only about 4 percent of the approximately 100,000 black B.A.s produced in the United States annually, the remaining 2,500+ four-year colleges turning out the other 96 percent.[51] The vast majority of black college students attend institutions where racial preferences are either very small or don't exist at all.[52] Bowen and Bok, critics charged, were employing a British "Oxbridge" model to understand upward socioeconomic mobility in the United States, although the model is invalid because of the many diverse avenues to wealth, power, education, and occupational prestige in America.[53]

Whatever truth may have remained in the Bowen and Bok claims after such criticisms (which were never really answered by the authors of *The Shape of the River*) has been called into question by Dale and Krueger's subsequent inquiry. Dale and Krueger proposed a simple hypothesis: since admissions committees seek to admit to their institutions not only students with the highest grades, highest standardized test scores, and other easily measurable academic indicators but also those who most excel in such not-so-easily-measurable personal qualities as maturity, motivation, self-discipline, and the like, could it be

---

51. Stephen Cole and Elinor Barber, *Increasing Faculty Diversity: The Occupational Choices of High Achieving Minority Students* (Cambridge, MA: Harvard University Press, 2003), p. 206.
52. See the important article by Thomas J Kane, "Racial and Ethnic Preference in College Admissions," in Christopher Jencks and Meredith Phillips, eds., *The Black/White Test Score Gap* (Washington, D.C.: Brookings Institution Press, 1998), chap. 12.
53. This is one of the many criticisms of the Bowen and Bok book made by Stephen and Abigail Thernstrom in "Reflections on the Shape of the River," *U.C.L.A. Law Review*, 46:5, June 1999, pp. 1583–1631. This article presents a wealth of empirical material critical of the Bowen and Bok position on racial preferences.

that these latter qualities are at least partially responsible for the positive school effect on future earnings of attending elite universities that past researchers have found? Common knowledge and common experience show that these personal qualities play a major role in terms of achieving one's occupational goals, and it just might be the case, Dale and Krueger surmised, that part of the advantage of attending an elite institution was simply a reflection of the fact that the most selective colleges and universities, given the huge number of applicants they receive, were able to choose students with the highest levels of these difficult-to-measure attributes. Admissions officers have before them, Dale and Krueger point out, an array of documents, including essays by applicants, recommendation letters from teachers and guidance counselors, personal interview material, etc., by which they try to ascertain these important personal qualities, but none of this information figures in the regression models economists and sociologists usually construct to figure out an independent school effect of attending a more competitive institution. Such analyses may thus seriously overstate the elite-college advantage. What may appear to be an independent school effect may really be a simple reflection of the fact that people who attend the most selective colleges often have qualities that would make them more likely to succeed financially and occupationally regardless of the institutions they attend.

The Dale/Krueger theory sounds plausible enough, but how is it to be tested? Here is where Dale and Krueger got creative. Using two different types of econometric models, they tried to incorporate as well as possible proxy measures for these important personal motivational factors, usually not observable by the social scientists looking at a typical database (hence the designation "unobservables") but possibly vaguely known and partially ascertainable by both admissions officers and the applicants themselves. In what they call the Matched Applicant Model (which they present in three variants), Dale and Krueger take advantage of the fact that many students do not attend the most selective colleges they were admitted to but, for a variety of reasons, often choose to attend an institution lower on the selectivity list. Whether for financial reasons ("they gave me more money"), geographic reasons ("it's much closer to home"), or a host of personal reasons ("my father went there," "my two best friends are going"), some people who are deemed worthy by admissions officers of attending a first-tier college wind up at a second- or third-tier institution, just as many deemed worthy by admissions officers of attending a second- or third-tier institution often wind up at colleges less selective than these. Why not, Dale and Krueger ask, match students who were admitted to, and rejected by, an array of schools of comparable selectivity but who wound up attending differently ranked schools? Look at just these matched students, consider all the other factors that influence future earnings contained in the C&B database, and see if the positive school effect on future earnings of attending a more selective institution still holds. Are students who could have attended a more selective institution but chose not to at a future-earnings disadvantage over similar students facing similar choices who went to the most selective school to which they were accepted?

These are the questions Dale and Krueger address in their Matched Applicant Model, and their results were startling, probably to themselves and most certainly to the Mellon Foundation, which funded their work. Although they use three separate measures for matching school selectivity (SAT-score intervals, Barron's rankings, an exact-match model), in none of the three matched applicant models they developed could they discover *any* independent, positive effect on future earnings associated with attending a more selective school. In fact, the one model they did construct that showed a statistically significant selectivity effect—the Exact-Match Model—showed a *negative* effect on future earnings of school selectivity. Other things equal, attending a more selective college was associated with a 10.6 % *lower* future income! Dale and Krueger sum up their findings in the following words:

> A major concern with past estimates of the payoff to attending an elite college is that more selective schools tend to accept students [who already come] with higher earnings capacity. This paper adjusts for selection on the part of schools by comparing earnings and other outcomes among students who applied to, and were accepted and rejected by, a comparable set of institutions. . . . Since college admissions decisions are made by professional administrators who have much more information at their disposal than researchers who later analyze student outcomes, we suspect that our selection correction addresses a major cause of bias in past wage equations. After we adjust for students' unobserved characteristics, our findings lead us to question the view that school selectivity . . . is an important determinant of students' subsequent incomes. . . . The effect of school-SAT score was not significantly greater than zero in any version of the matched-applicant model that we estimated. . . . Students who attend more selective colleges do not earn more than other students who were accepted and rejected by comparable schools but attended less selective colleges. (*Quarterly Journal of Economics*, Nov. 2002, pp. 1523, 1509).

To many these results seem counterintuitive. Others things being equal, it seems as if attending a more elite institution should count for something. One would assume that the higher prestige of a more selective school and the more intense academic atmosphere provided by such an institution would impact positively on future earnings, at least to some degree. Dale and Krueger, however, offer powerful rejoinders to such conjectures. First of all, they say, most schools have a large array of student peer groups, ranging from those primarily focused on studying hard, getting good grades, and advancing student career potential to those minimally focused on these things. At whatever institution they attend, students will be able to seek out their own kind and spend their time encouraging one another to do what they are most inclined to do, be it working hard or partying. Thus the overall atmosphere of the school probably doesn't matter much, Dale and Krueger conclude. "An able student who attends a lower tier school can find able students to study with, and, alas, a weak student who attends an elite school can find other weak students to *not study* with." (p. 1520)

That a degree from a more selective college has more prestige than one from a less selective college is something Dale and Krueger hardly doubt, nor do they deny that employers often look at a college's level of selectivity when making initial employment decisions. But Dale and Krueger find that students who attend a more selective college incur a considerable disadvantage in terms of their relative grades and final class ranking because of the increased academic competition in such schools. In all three of their Matched Applicant Models they found that students who attended a college whose average SAT score (on a 1600 point scale) was just 100 points higher than those of student matches incurred a rank-in-class penalty of between 5 and 8 percentile intervals. And they show clearly that students who graduate with a higher rank in class earn more money than those with a lower ranking. Thus students who attend a less prestigious institution may offset any earnings disadvantage that derives from this fact by the premium that accrues to the higher rank in class they are likely to attain in such an institution. "The improvement in class rank among students who choose to attend a less selective college," Dale and Krueger write, "may partly explain why these students do not incur lower earnings. Employers and graduate schools may value their higher class rank by enough to offset any other effect of attending a less selective college on earnings." (p. 1512)

As an alternative means of accounting for motivational factors, Dale and Krueger employ what they call the Self-Revelation Model. This model assumes that students who are more aggressive in the application process in terms of applying to schools that are more difficult to gain admission to are more likely to rate high on any scale of motivation and ambition even if they don't get accepted to the most selective schools to which they apply. The example they give is Steven Spielberg, who attended the California State Long Beach film school though only after trying unsuccessfully to gain entry to the more prestigious UCLA and USC film schools. From an early age Spielberg had ambition, drive, and a high opinion of his career potential, and this was clearly reflected in the stretch of his application net. Whereas the Matched Applicant Model assumes that college admissions officers may know more than econometricians about a student's motivation, ambition, and future potential, the Self-Revelation Model assumes that the applicants themselves may reveal important information about these qualities through the very pattern of their applications. The model takes into account both the number of applications submitted (assuming the more applications, the more persistence and drive the student has), and the average selectivity of the schools applied to.

When the number and selectivity of the schools applied to are entered into the regression equation as rough proxies for unmeasured personal qualities, and these are then added to the other student inputs known to affect future income, Dale and Krueger find that the advantage of attending a more elite university shrinks almost to zero. In terms of future earnings the more highly motivated and ambitious are no less successful for having attended a non-elite institution than an elite one. The result of the Self-Revelation Model thus reinforces the conclusions drawn from the three Matched Applicant Models.

Because of the relatively small numbers of blacks attending the institutions surveyed, Dale and Krueger were not able to construct a separate Matched Applicant Model that was limited to blacks. They were, however, able to construct a separate Self-Revelation Model for black students. The results of this model were similar to those for white applicants: the positive school effect on future income drops precipitously when a proxy measure for motivational "unobservables" in the form of student application behavior is added to the statistical model. And since admissions officers at selective institutions look for the same motivational factors in black and Hispanic applicants as in whites and Asians, there is every reason to believe that the results of the three Matched Applicant Models would apply to all races. "There is no evidence," Dale and Krueger conclude, "that the relationship between school selectivity and subsequent earnings is different for black students." (NBER Working Paper, p. 28)

The Dale and Krueger study is in one sense very narrow in scope. It looks almost exclusively at future income as the object to be explained, and it is not concerned with most of the other benefits that supporters of affirmative action attribute to racial preferences in higher education. Nevertheless, their conclusions cast doubt on one of the most important benefits that affirmative action policy is said to confer. Their bottom line is that almost all of the differences apropos future income of attending a more selective college or university are attributable to the initial differences that entering students bring with them—including both the easily quantifiable factors like academic skills, aptitude test scores, and parental income, as well as the not-so-easily quantifiable factors like motivation, maturity, ambition, and self-discipline.

The implication of their findings for affirmative action policy is clear: if the black and Hispanic students who now get preferentially admitted to places like Columbia, Princeton, and

Yale wound up instead under a color-blind admissions policy at schools like Tufts, Vanderbilt, and Tulane, they wouldn't do much worse in terms of future earnings than they would at the top-rated schools. They might even do a little better. And at the lower-tiered schools most would wind up with substantially higher grades and class ranks than at the more prestigious institutions. Although Dale and Krueger do not speculate beyond earnings outcomes, there is reason to believe that at least some of the other benefits of attending a more selective university claimed in the Bowen and Bok study, including certain leadership advantages and increased graduation rates, may also be at least partially the result of the "unobservables" that entering students bring with them rather than the independent school effect of attendance at an elite institution. Although former presidents of Harvard and Princeton may be loath to admit it, elite universities offer no special ticket to wealth, power, and influence in America, although they are, of course, a source of great social prestige for those attending them.

Dale and Krueger do acknowledge one very important exception. Students coming from low-income families—defined as those in the bottom quarter of the national income distribution—do benefit in terms of future earnings from attending a highly selective college compared to a less selective one. On this basis Krueger, in a follow-up article in *The New York Times*, suggested that high-end colleges should practice something like class-based affirmative action and make special efforts to recruit students based on their socioeconomic disadvantage. "My advice to elite colleges," he wrote, is this: "Recognize that the most disadvantaged students benefit most from your instruction. Set financial aid and admission policies accordingly."[54]

---

54. Alan B. Krueger, "Students Smart Enough to Get into Elite Schools May Not Need to Bother," *New York Times*, 27 Apr. 2000.

In the same *Times* article Krueger offered advice to all college applicants that can be described as nothing less than sage wisdom: "Don't believe that the only school worth attending is one that would not admit you. That you go to college is more important than where you go. Find a school whose academic strengths match your interests and which devotes resources to instruction in those fields. Recognize that your own motivation, ambition and talents will determine your success more than the college name on your diploma."[55]

WHY DO SO FEW BLACKS BECOME COLLEGE PROFESSORS?

The Dale and Krueger study touched only briefly on the fact that students entering elite universities with lower-than-average high school grades and SAT scores generally wind up with lower-than-average college grades and class ranks. This issue would attain greater prominence in another study sponsored by the Mellon Foundation titled *Increasing Faculty Diversity: The Occupational Choices of High-Achieving Minority Students*, which was published in 2003 by Harvard University Press. Conducted by sociologists Stephen Cole and Elinor Barber, the study represented a serious blow to defenders of affirmative action at elite colleges and universities and immediately touched off efforts by Mellon and other sponsoring organizations to distance themselves from some of its analyses and central conclusions.

The Cole/Barber study owed its inception to conversations in the early 1990s between Elinor Barber, a research associate in Columbia University's Provost Office, and Neil Rudenstine, then the president of Harvard. Like many academic adminis-

---

55. Ibid.

trators, Rudenstine and Barber were concerned about the very small number of blacks in university teaching—at the Ivy League institutions blacks typically make up only 2 to 3 percent of the faculty. They agreed that a thorough study of the problem was in order, and an initial grant of $80,000 was obtained from the Council of Ivy Group Presidents to review existing literature on the problem and prepare a formal proposal for a larger study. Stephen Cole, a seasoned sociologist on the faculty of SUNY-Stony Brook, who had worked previously in the area of the sociology of education, was recruited to work with Barber on the project. The bulk of the funding for the study was provided by a $400,000 grant from the Mellon Foundation, and a subsequent grant of $75,000 was obtained from the Ford Foundation. The Russell Sage Foundation in New York City also kicked in by providing Cole with a Visiting Scholar appointment that allowed him to complete the data analysis and write up the final report. Barber died unexpectedly in 1999 just as the final research results were being completed and written up, leaving Cole to fend for himself in the face of the heated controversy that the study touched off among affirmative action-supporting administrators and foundation heads.

A major conclusion of the study—i.e., that affirmative action policy was contributing to the lower grades received by black and Hispanic students, which in turn discouraged many from pursuing careers in academia—was so distasteful to those who had funded the project that some tried to discredit its authors and findings. The executive director of the Council of Ivy Group Presidents, for instance, obliquely suggested to a reporter for the *The Chronicle of Higher Education* that Cole and Barber—both liberal academics—might have some kind of biased "ideological position" that explains their final antiaffirmative-action conclusions. "There are a whole lot of data in here," he told the *Chronicle*'s reporter, "and if one started out with an ideological position—whatever it was—you could find a whole lot to support that."[56] Similarly, the vice-president of the Mellon Foundation warned readers of the report to be "cautious about putting much weight on certain findings." None of the four Ivy League presidents that the *Chronicle*'s reporter contacted were willing to comment on the study.

Cole himself told the *Chronicle* reporter that there was "no chance" he would ever receive Mellon Foundation funding again, "and I don't care." Despite his attempt to put up a strong front, however, Cole seems to have been deeply hurt by the criticism of his work from the funding organizations and has come to see *their* stance, not that of himself and Barber, as politically and ideologically driven. "I was trained at a time before social science became so politicized," he told the *Chronicle*, referring back to his graduate student days in the early 1960s when he was a student of Robert K. Merton and Paul Lazarsfeld at Columbia University. "I believe that social science should be objective and value-free, and you should design a study to answer a question and whatever the answer is, that's what it is."

The Cole/Barber study was based on the results of an extensive questionnaire ultimately filled out by 7,612 graduating seniors at 34 colleges and universities, most of which were considerably above the national norm in selectivity. The study focused on the average-to-above-average students at these institutions since it was known from past research that lower-achieving students rarely seek careers in university teaching or research. Four types of institutions were included in the study: all eight Ivy League institutions; 13 of the most selective liberal arts colleges (e.g., Amherst, Williams, Swarthmore, Bowden); nine large state universities (e.g., Rutgers, Stony Brook, Chapel

---

56. Robin Wilson, "The Unintended Consequences of Affirmative Action," *The Chronicle of Higher Education*, Jan. 31, 2003; available online at http://chronicle.com.

Hill, University of Virginia); and four historically black institutions (Xavier, Howard, Florida A&M, North Carolina A&T). The questionnaires were given only to arts and science majors since the purpose of the study was to determine how to increase faculty diversity in these areas, and in the case of the state universities and historically black institutions, only those students with a 2.8 average or higher were included. This latter restriction was intended to conserve scarce project resources and was based on the sensible assumption that students with grades lower than this would almost certainly not choose a career in academics. The response rate—and hence the reliability of the survey—was high, with seven out of ten students contacted responding to the questionnaire.

Many of the results and conclusions of the Cole/Barber study are noncontroversial and involve well-known facts. For instance, the small number of blacks and Hispanics in academics is seen primarily as a "pipeline problem" resulting from the much lower levels of academic performance of black and Hispanic students at every level of the American educational system, from elementary school through graduate school. Unless this situation changes, the authors suggest, we will never see the black and Hispanic presence in the better colleges approaching the levels that liberal administrators would like. The pipeline problem, however, is not one that universities can do much to fix, at least not in the short run, so Cole and Barber focus much of their attention on those aspects of current academic practice that can affect the number of black and Hispanic students choosing academia as a career. Affirmative-action policy comes under scrutiny in this context because their research shows that it makes an inevitably bad situation (given the pipeline problem) significantly worse.

The Cole/Barber reasoning goes something like this: People who seek to become college professors are overwhelmingly recruited from those who were excellent students in their undergraduate institutions in terms of their *relative* grades. Whereas students who get mainly Bs and Cs are likely to choose careers in business or in teaching at the primary or secondary school level, those who choose careers in academia—like those who choose careers in medicine—are usually drawn from students who get mostly As and A-s and outshine in their academic performance a large portion of their peers. The critical factor, Cole and Barber believe, is the relative standing students have among their immediate classmates. Among those black and Hispanic students who expressed an initial freshman-year interest in becoming a college professor, Cole and Barber found that there is a much greater persistence with this intention at the somewhat less selective schools in their study than at the Ivy League institutions and the most highly selective private colleges. The lower relative grades received by the black and Hispanic students at these latter institutions, Cole and Barber contend, convinced many that they were not smart enough for a career in academics and that they had best choose a less intellectually demanding occupation. Had these same students—many with SAT scores in the 90th percentile or higher in terms of national norms—attended institutions that were somewhat less selective than the top-rated schools that they actually did attend, they would have gained more academic self-confidence and would have been more likely to persist in their desire to become a college professor. A student with, say, a 1350 SAT score who had a freshman-year intention to become a college professor is much more likely to follow through with this intention, Cole and Barber found, if that student attended an upper-middle-level school like Rutgers or Stony Brook than a top-ranked school like Columbia or Yale, where they are more likely to have received a lower class ranking.

To illustrate with a few numbers: Of black students receiving 1300 or higher on the SAT, Cole and Barber found that only 28 percent received grade-point averages of A or A- at the Ivy

League universities, and an even lower number—12 percent—received such averages at the elite liberal arts colleges in their study. Among this same group of high-SAT blacks, however, fully 44 percent of those attending the state universities in their study and 55 percent of those attending the historically black colleges and universities (HBCUs) attained A and A- level grade-point-averages. The *relative* grade problem is even greater than that suggested by these figures since grade inflation has been a stronger trend at the elite colleges and universities than at less selective institutions. Blacks with 1300+ SAT scores are thus getting fewer grades of A or A- at the very institutions where A and A- grades are most prevalent. Cole and Barber show that blacks with high SAT scores were likely to attain substantially higher grades and a much higher rank-in-class rating if they attended a university with students more similar to themselves in terms of past academic performance than one where most students exceeded them in this department. For this reason, Cole and Barber found that of those black students who indicated having a freshman-year interest in pursuing an academic career more than 30 percent of those attending the less selective institutions in their study persisted with this interest through senior year, while the comparable figure for those expressing the same freshman-year interest who attended the Ivy League universities and elite private colleges was only half this. The fall-off in interest, in other words, was much greater for those attending the most elite colleges and universities than for those attending less selective institutions.

Cole and Barber summarize their findings in the following words:

> The best-prepared African Americans . . . are most likely to attend elite schools, especially the Ivy League. Because of affirmative action, these African Americans (those with the highest scores on the SAT) are admitted to schools where, on average, white students' scores are substantially higher,

exceeding those of African Americans by about 200 points or more. Not surprisingly, in this kind of competitive situation, African Americans get relatively low grades. It is a fact that in virtually all selective schools where racial preferences in admission is practiced, the majority of African American students end up in the lower quarter of the class. . . . African American students at the elite schools—the liberal arts colleges and the Ivy League—get lower grades than [comparable] African American students at the non-elite schools (state universities and HBCUs). Lower grades lead to lower levels of academic self-confidence, which in turn influence the extent to which African American students will persist with a freshman interest in academia as a career. African American students at elite schools are significantly less likely to persist with an interest in academia than are their counterparts at the non-elite schools. (pp. 124, 212)

Cole and Barber thus found considerable evidence in support of those who have claimed that affirmative action "mismatches" black students in terms of institutions and SAT scores and that this has a harmful effect on the ability of those students who expressed a desire to become college professors to persist with their initial intentions. This was a far different message from that of *The Shape of the River*, which had pooh-poohed the "mismatch" theory and claimed that the effects of placing black students in institutions where most of the white and Asian students were academically better prepared was almost wholly salutary for the black students.

STEREOTYPE VULNERABILITY AND THE BLACK UNDERPERFORMANCE PROBLEM

The "pipeline problem" that Cole and Barber devote many pages to explaining is generally well known, at least in barest outline. In terms of scholastic performance, black and Hispanic students at every level of the educational system do much worse on average than their white and Asian counterparts, with the blacks usually doing worse than the Hispanics. The discrepancy begins even in preschool, where black three- and four-year-olds score a full standard deviation behind whites on simple word-recognition tests like the Peabody Picture Vocabulary Test. The average black child enters elementary school with significantly weaker counting, vocabulary, and reading skills than the average white child. The gap widens throughout the K-12 years, such that by the age of 17 the average black high school student achieves scores in math, science, and English on the comprehensive National Assessment of Educational Progress test that are roughly comparable to those of the average white and Asian 13-year-old. The black/white and black/Asian gap on the SAT is equally stark, with blacks trailing whites and Asians on each of the sections of the test by approximately 100 points (1 SD).

Because of these persistent discrepancies between the test scores of blacks and whites—and more recently blacks and Asians—many critics of standardized testing have said that such tests do not measure the true ability of members of the lower-scoring minority groups. The SATs and other standardized tests, it is frequently charged, are culturally biased and do not reflect the true potential of those who have not grown up in a white, middle-class household. The implication of much of this criticism is that blacks, on average—and probably Hispanics as well—will do better in terms of their college performance than their lower test scores would indicate.

This question was comprehensively addressed many years ago by economist Robert Klitgaard in an outstanding study of affirmative-action policy at elite universities that was published in 1985.[57] Klitgaard surveyed all the available research

---

57. Robert Klitgaard, *Choosing Elites* (New York: Basic Books, 1985).

on the relationship between scores on SAT tests and student performance in terms of college grades, and he found—what all subsequent research has confirmed—that the SAT is not predictively biased against blacks. Blacks do not do any better in college in terms of their grades and class ranks than whites with the same SAT scores. On the contrary, Klitgaard found that when blacks and whites are matched for SAT scores, the blacks in college actually do significantly *worse* than whites in terms of their college grades. The SATs, in other words, *overpredict* black performance in college, and in this sense are biased in favor of blacks, not against them. Put another way, blacks do not seem to do as well in college as one might expect given their measured scholastic ability as determined by the SAT. Whites and Asians substantially outperform blacks with the same SAT score. "If a black and a white have the same test scores and prior grades," Klitgaard found, "the black will on average do about a third to two thirds of a standard deviation worse in later academic performance than the white" at the most competitive academic institutions. (p. 161)

Since Klitgaard's seminal work, which focused primarily on the most selective of America's universities and colleges, two problems have come into focus regarding black college students; they have come to be designated the "underpreparation problem" (i.e., before entering college blacks and Hispanics do not learn as much in high school or score as high on standardized tests as whites and Asians), and the "underperformance problem" (i.e., blacks, and to a lesser extent Hispanics, do not do as well in college as whites and Asians with the same SAT scores and high school grades). Although many college administrators are reluctant to admit it, both common sense and recent research suggest that affirmative-action policy is deeply implicated as a contributing source to both of these problems, particularly as they affect the higher-scoring blacks who enter our more competitive universities and colleges.

The underperformance problem was a major concern of Bowen and Bok in *The Shape of the River*, and considerable attention was devoted to it. "At almost every college in our sample," Bowen and Bok write, "black students are not only performing less well academically than whites but also performing below the levels predicted by their SAT scores. In fact, this underperformance turns out to be even more important than lower [entering SAT] scores in explaining the gap in class rank between blacks and whites." (p. 88) Bowen and Bok found that in terms of his/her final grade-point average the average black student in the 28 selective colleges in their survey graduated at only the 23rd percentile, while the average Hispanic graduated at the 36th percentile (the average white graduated at the 52nd percentile). Only about half of this rank-in-class gap they found could be attributed to the lower SAT scores and lower high school grades that entering black and Hispanic freshmen brought with them to college. The rest was the result of "underperformance." If blacks and Hispanics had performed equally well in college with whites of the same SAT scores, the average black graduate, their statistical model predicted, would have wound up at the 38th percentile instead of the 23rd—a very large difference—while the Hispanic students would have raised their average percentile ranking from 36th to 44th. For some reason many of the black and Hispanic students at the highly selective colleges studied in the C&B survey seemed not to be living up to their demonstrated potential, and for the black students especially, the degree of underperformance was huge.

Just why this underperformance should exist has been the source of much speculation, though one theory that has gained wide acceptance in recent years is that propounded by Stanford psychologist Claude Steele. In a series of articles based on experiments carried out at Stanford and other universities, Steele and his colleagues have focused on what they call "stereotype vulnerability" to explain why blacks often do worse in college courses than their SAT scores would indicate. Steele has shown that higher-achieving black students at competitive universities like Stanford are often sensitive to the fact that white students and faculty sometimes hold negative stereotypes about their academic competence. This problem, says Steele, is most acute among those black students who have most closely identified with the domain of academics—rather than, say, the domain of sports or social life—and it is for this reason, he says, that stereotype threat and the resulting underperformance it produces are most acute among the higher-achieving members of the black cohort at elite universities.

Stereotype vulnerability can negatively impact black students, according to Steele, either by causing them to "disidentify" with the domain of academics—that is, to invest less psychologically in learning and getting good grades and more in nonacademic activities—or it can lead to heightened anxiety and psychological stress, which have a demonstrated harmful impact on a student's test performance. Through a series of ingenious experiments Steele and his colleagues have shown that when black students at Stanford are given a difficult verbal test and told that it is designed to measure "your verbal abilities and limitations," they do substantially worse than their white classmates who have similar SAT scores. When the same test is given to Stanford blacks and told by the experimenter that the test is specifically *not* designed "to evaluate your ability" but merely to help understand better "the psychological factors involved in solving verbal problems," the black students do just as well as comparable white students. Test anxiety caused by fears of being negatively stereotyped by whites, Steele concludes, causes many blacks to "choke" on important exams, and this he believes, is a major cause of much of the black underperformance seen at elite institutions of higher learning.[58]

Steele is reluctant to speculate on whether affirmative-action policies at competitive institutions exacerbate the "stereotype threat" problem, although the answer would seem self-evident.[59] It is hard to see how lowering the standards of admission to highly competitive colleges and universities for a people long thought of as intellectually inferior can fail to have the effect of reinforcing negative stigmas and negative stereotypes regarding the intellectual competence of those people. And by its very logic the current system of racial preferences

---

58. Claude M. Steele and Joshua Aronson, "Stereotype Threat and the Test Performance of Academically Successful African Americans," in Jencks and Phillips, eds., *Black-White Test Score Gap*, pp. 401–30.

59. Claude Steele is reluctant to acknowledge the obvious antiaffirmative-action implications of his own research—one suspects out of a desire to maintain good relations with his affirmative-action-supporting friends and colleagues. In the spring of 2001, Steele gave a public lecture on the Princeton University campus in which he discussed his research on stereotype vulnerability. In the question-and-answer period after the lecture I specifically asked Steele if it was not likely that the negative stigmas and negative stereotypes that black students must labor under would be "reinforced, strengthened, and perpetuated" at the elite colleges and universities by the affirmative-action policies at these institutions. At first Steele tried to evade the question by answering a related but different question—i.e., whether affirmative-action policies have *created* the negative stigmas and stereotypes that exist about blacks in America (answer: they don't, the stigmas and stereotypes existed long before affirmative action). I immediately saw where he was going with his response and quickly interrupted, "Wait a minute! I'm not asking whether affirmative action *creates* negative stigmas and stereotypes but whether it *reinforces* and *perpetuates* those which already exist in the culture. Isn't it likely that affirmative action policies will have this effect?" Recognizing that he had to give a direct answer to an obviously disturbing question, he conceded that "some" affirmative-action policies probably have this harmful effect, although he made no effort to distinguish which ones would and which ones would not fall into the stereotype-reinforcing category. On this issue, isn't it reasonable to speculate that the lower the level of racial preference at an institution, and the closer that entering black and Hispanic students are to their white and Asian classmates in terms of test scores and high school grades, the less stereotype vulnerability the black and Hispanic students will face? The mismatch hypothesis seems commonsensical here. For those who doubt this, ask yourself this question: Would a black student with, say, a 1200 SAT score and a 3.5 GPA face the same level of stereotype vulnerability at a school like Rutgers, where students typically have SAT scores in the 1100s and GPAs around 3.4, as at Princeton or Yale, where SAT scores average around 1450 and most students have GPAs of 3.8 or higher?

guarantees that the typical black and Hispanic student on elite college campuses really will be intellectually inferior to his typical white and Asian classmates, at least in terms of past academic performance as measured by factors such as SAT scores and high school grades. This can hardly be a confidence-builder for the black and Hispanic students.

Shelby Steele—Claude Steele's brother and a long-time critic of affirmative action policy—has no trouble seeing the obvious here. "The accusation that black Americans have always lived with," Shelby Steele writes, "is that they are inferior . . . and this accusation has been too uniform, too ingrained in cultural imagery, too enforced by law, custom, and every form of power not to have left a mark." He continues:

> So when today's young black students find themselves on white campuses, surrounded by those who historically have claimed superiority, they are also surrounded by the myth of their inferiority. . . . And today this myth is sadly reinforced for many black students by affirmative action programs, under which blacks may often enter college with lower test scores and high-school grade-point- averages than whites. "They see me as an affirmative action case," one black student told me at UCLA. . . . A black student at Berkeley told me that he felt defensive every time he walked into a class and saw mostly white faces. When I asked why, he said, "Because I know they're all racists. They think blacks are stupid."[60]

---

60. Shelby Steele, *Second Thoughts about Race in America* (New York: Madison Books, 1991), pp. 87, 89.

Many years before Steele's remarks, Thomas Sowell had similar comments on the psychological harm that racial-preference policies would have on their intended beneficiaries. In his book *Black Education: Myths and Tragedies*, Sowell gives eloquent voice to the devastating effect that affirmative-action policies would likely have both on black self-confidence and on the image of blacks in the minds of whites:

> The actual harm done by quotas is far greater than having a few incompetent people here and there—and the harm that will actually be done will be harm primarily to the black population. What all the arguments and

Bowen and Bok saw clear evidence of stereotype vulnerability at work in their study of blacks at the C&B colleges. The black/white rank-in-class gap followed the pattern suggested by Claude Steele whereby those black students with the highest SAT scores—and thus presumably most committed to the domain of academics—showed the poorest performance when matched with whites of similar SAT scores. A subsequent study by the Mellon Foundation of 11 of the most selective colleges and universities in their database, which Bowen co-authored with researcher Fredrick Vars, showed a similar pattern: as one moved up the SAT scale black underperformance increased.[61] In both *The Shape of the River* and the Bowen and Vars study it is suggested that stereotype vulnerability has something to do with this pattern, but none of the authors of these studies were willing to acknowledge the obvious—i.e., that across-the-board racial preferences at America's most select universities almost certainly exacerbates this psychological problem and the harmful academic effects that flow from it.

In *The Shape of the River*, however, Bowen and Bok do acknowledge that "the academic performance of a number of black students [in the C&B schools] seemed clearly affected by difficulties in adjusting to new environments." They then quote a statement by a black student in one of these schools—a statement

campaigns for quotas are really saying, loud and clear, is that black people just don't have it, and that they will have to be given something in order to have something. The devastating impact of this message on black people—particularly black young people—will outweigh any few extra jobs that may result from this strategy. Those black people who are already competent, and who could be instrumental in producing more competence among this rising generation, will be completely undermined as black becomes synonymous—in the minds of black and white alike—with incompetence, and black achievement becomes synonymous with charity and payoffs. Thomas Sowell, *Black Education: Myths and Tragedies* (New York: David McKay, 1972), p. 242.

61. Frederick E. Vars and William G. Bowen, "Scholastic Aptitude Test Scores, Race, and Academic Performance in Selective Colleges and Universities," in Jencks and Phillips, *The Black/White Test Score Gap*, pp. 457–89.

they say is "similar to many others." "When I arrived at campus for the first time," the student explains, "I was a little bit intimidated. I said, 'Wow, I wonder if they made a mistake accepting me; am I going to fit in?' [I had] those kinds of feelings. And will I be the dumbest person here?" (pp. 82–3) Bowen and Bok spend a good deal of effort in their book trying to refute Thomas Sowell's "fit" hypothesis, but it seems difficult to deny when reading such statements that affirmative-action policy places many black students in competitive academic environments where they have doubts about "fitting in" because of the superior academic credentials of their white and Asian classmates. In Sowell's terminology, they are severely "mismatched" for the institutions they attend. If this doesn't contribute to heightened stereotype vulnerability it is difficult to imagine what would.

Many years ago, the dean of Harvard College, John B. Fox, Jr., noted that black students who enrolled in Harvard in the 1970s—the first full decade of affirmative-action preferences— seemed to suffer much more from self-doubt about their academic competence than other Harvard students. "In the 1970s," he explained,

> when [Harvard] College first found itself with a significant
> number of minority students, it began to seem that certain
> problems of self-confidence—shared to some degree by most
> students—afflicted minority students disproportionately.
> Minority students reported experiencing even more academic
> stress than their non-minority counterparts. . . . Dr. Jeffrey
> Howard has described it as "in the first year . . . a rapid and
> unchecked erosion of their confidence in their capacity to
> compete."[62]

---

62. Cited in Klitgaard, *Choosing Elites*, p. 188.

Things haven't changed much since the 1970s, but it is at least clear now through Claude Steele's work that "a rapid and unchecked erosion" in minority students' "confidence in their capacity to compete" can have severe consequences in terms of their ability to learn. "Underperformance" is—at least in part—a direct consequence of institutional mismatch, just as Thomas Sowell told us it would be more than thirty years ago. The villain here is clearly affirmative action, however reluctant certain educators may be to acknowledge this fact.

RECENT RESEARCH ON STEREOTYPE VULNERABILITY

At least two major studies in recent years—both funded by the Mellon Foundation—have taken up the issue of stereotype vulnerability, and both have concluded that a) at least for a certain portion of black college students stereotype vulnerability is a major reason for their relatively poor academic performance in college compared with similarly qualified whites and Asians; and that b) affirmative-action policy plays an important role in intensifying the stereotype vulnerability to which these students are subjected. The first results come from the Cole/Barber study already mentioned. Like all other researchers who have looked into the problem, Cole and Barber found that when black students are matched with white students for SAT scores, the black students wind up with substantially lower grades in most of the colleges they surveyed. This performance gap persisted pretty much intact even after controlling statistically for all sorts of additional background variables such as family socioeconomic status, field of major, gender, type of high school attended, and the like. They also found—again consistent with other researchers—that the performance gap was greatest for blacks with the highest SAT scores. As SAT scores rise, so does the black/white performance gap.

The most interesting finding of the Cole/Barber study, however, was the huge difference between institutions in terms of the degree of black underperformance. The underperformance problem, they found, was most acute at the most elite colleges and universities in their study, while it was much less severe at the less selective state universities, and didn't exist at all at the historically black colleges and universities.[63] For instance, among white students who had SAT scores in the 1200–1299 range, 33 percent earned grade-point-averages of A or A- at the predominantly white institutions in their study. Among blacks with comparable SATs, however, only 14 percent of those attending the elite institutions earned A or A- level GPAs, while 23 percent of those at the state universities earned grades in this range. At the HBCUs more than a third—38 percent—of blacks in the 1200–1299 SAT range achieved A or A- level GPAs (i.e., 5 percentage points *higher* than comparable whites at the predominantly white colleges and universities).

Cole and Barber conclude that something at the predominantly white institutions was retarding black performance, and it seemed to be greatest at the most selective schools. After surveying a variety of possible explanations, they come to the conclusion that Claude Steele's stereotype vulnerability dynamic seemed to be at work, and that the degree of harm done by

63. Since there are not enough white students at the HBCUs with which to compare black performance, the HBCU "underperformance" figure given by Cole and Barber is determined by comparing HBCU blacks of a given SAT interval with similar whites at the predominantly white institutions. That the greater success of high-SAT blacks in getting A and A- grades at the HBCUs is not an artifact of differing grading policies is shown by Cole and Barber by the fact that the grades at the HBCUs are much lower than that at the more grade-inflated state universities and elite institutions. A black student with a 1200–1299 SAT is more likely to get an A or A- GPA at an HBCU than will a comparable white at one of the predominantly white institutions in the Cole/Barber study despite the fact that proportionally there are many more A and A- range grades given out at the predominantly white institutions. Nevertheless, since the black/white performance comparisons are not at the same schools, what Cole and Barber say about the lack of black underperformance at the HBCUs must be viewed with some caution.

stereotype threat was directly related to a school's level of selectivity and the corresponding degree of affirmative-action preferences it accorded to minority students. They write on this:

> Just as Claude Steele argues that an unintended consequence
> of remedial programs is to trigger a fear of stereotyping,
> we believe that an unintended consequence or side effect of
> affirmative action programs is also likely to do so. . . . One
> condition that can contribute to the fear of activation of this
> negative stereotype [about the intellectual ability of African
> Americans] is the possible belief on the part of minority students that they were admitted to a selective school because
> of affirmative action programs and that they "don't really
> belong" in these schools. (pp. 209, 249)

Cole and Barber offer a number of possible ways to reduce the stereotype threat and underperformance problem, including better mentoring and advising, closer supervision of student progress, more pep talks, additional tutoring, etc. But they also suggest that high school guidance counselors should direct black students, like all students, to those institutions where they are likely to shine academically. "Instead of recommending that minority students go to the most prestigious school they can get into," they write, "high school guidance counselors . . . should try to reduce some of the lack of fit between the level of academic preparation of minority students and the schools where they enroll." (p. 249) At least in terms of the underperformance problem and depressed black grades, they find much to support Thomas Sowell's mismatch theory and propose better matching of students and institutions as a simple remedy to the problem.[64]

---

64. A number of studies (including that of Cole and Barber) indicate that blacks do better both academically and socially at the historically black colleges and universities than do comparable blacks at predominantly white institutions.

While Cole and Barber do not recommend scrapping affirmative-action programs wholesale, they do recommend that, if they are retained, more successful efforts must be made at concealment and deceptive labeling lest knowledge of the very existence of such programs lead to the activation of negative stigmas and stereotypes about the academic competence of the intended beneficiaries. "If colleges and universities continue to practice race-sensitive admissions," they advise, "they should try to reduce to a minimum any negative psychological effects

---

Summarizing the results of many studies of student life at black colleges, educational researcher Jacqueline Fleming writes: "Previous research makes it clear that Black students adjust better to Black colleges than to predominantly White colleges. Black students who attend predominantly Black schools tend to have higher average grades, a richer learning environment, better relationships with faculty members, exhibit better cognitive development and display greater effort and engage in more academic activities than Black students who attend White schools. In Black schools, Black students show better social adjustment, have more extensive social support networks, show greater social involvement, and engage in more organizational activities." Jacqueline Fleming, "SATs and Black Students," *Review of Higher Education*, 25 (2002): 281–96, 287.

UCLA sociologist Walter W. Allen finds similar advantages of the black colleges in his literature survey: "The salutary effect of Black students attending a historically Black university speaks volumes about the importance of the social-psychological context for student outcomes. In this respect, previous research demonstrates unequivocally the profound difference that historically Black and predominantly White campuses represent for African-American students. On predominantly White campuses, Black students emphasize feelings of alienation, sensed hostility, racial discrimination, and lack of integration. On historically Black campuses, Black students emphasize feelings of engagement, connection, acceptance, and extensive support and encouragement. Consistent with accumulated evidence on human development, these students, like most human beings, develop best in environments where they feel valued, protected, accepted, and socially connected. The supportive environments of historically Black colleges communicate to Black students that it is safe to take the risks associated with intellectual growth and development. Such environments also have more people who provide Black students with positive feedback, support, and understanding, and who communicate that they care about students' welfare." Walter W. Allen, "The Color of Success: African-American College Student Outcomes at Predominantly White and Historically Black Public Colleges and Universities," *Harvard Educational Review*, 62 (1992): 26–44, 39–40. Neither Allen nor Fleming say much about the effects of racial-preference policies on predominantly white campuses, but it is hard to believe that they contribute to blacks feeling more "valued, protected, accepted, and socially connected." Adjusting to a white-majority campus, difficult under any circumstances, is almost surely a more daunting task when the white and Asian students look down on the members of your race for needing affirmative-action preferences to compete with other groups.

that affirmative action programs may have. We suggest that scholarships that are earmarked for minorities not be labeled as such, but rather awarded in the same way as non-affirmative action scholarships are awarded. The idea is to increase the minority students' belief that they have been admitted to the college because of their high academic qualifications and ability, rather than because of the need of the college to maintain ethnic diversity among the student body." (p. 250)

Hearing such recommendations, some may conclude that Cole and Barber are immoral Machiavellians with little concern for academic integrity or truth. With regard to affirmative action they seem to be recommending the academic equivalent of a false advertising swindle or accounting fraud. It can be argued, however, that they are merely proposing that elite colleges and universities carry out more successfully the policies of concealment and obfuscation apropos racial preferences that almost all of them have been practicing from the very beginning of their introduction of affirmative-action programs. Bowen and Bok, for instance, openly acknowledge that most elite institutions employing racial preferences have been reluctant to admit what they are doing out of a concern to avoid controversy and to prevent stigmatizing the intended beneficiaries of their programs.

"The very existence of a process that gives explicit consideration to race," Bowen and Bok write, "can raise questions about the true abilities of even the most talented minority students ('stigmatize' them, some would say). The possibility of such costs is one reason why selective institutions have been reluctant to talk about the degree of preference given black students. . . . Some of these institutions may . . . be concerned that the standing of black students in the eyes of white classmates would be lowered if differences in test scores and high school grades were publicized."(pp. 264–5) Bowen and Bok, however, do not say whether they approve of this reluctance on the part of academic institutions to talk honestly and openly about their affirmative action policies, but from the general tone of their comments it would seem that they acquiesce in the practice. Cole and Barber seem to do likewise, though apparently with many more misgivings than *The Shape of the River* authors.

Evidence confirming stereotype vulnerability theory also comes from an extensive study carried out by sociologist Douglas Massey and his colleagues. The study sets out to solve "the puzzle of minority underachievement" through a longitudinal survey of 3,924 students who first began their college careers in the fall of 1999 as freshmen in one of 28 selective colleges and universities. Each student was initially interviewed in a face-to-face format and asked to respond to more than 150 separate interviewer questions. Topics included the students' neighborhood background, high school experiences, attitudes toward people of different races and ethnicities, self-esteem—to name just a few. A roughly equal number of blacks, Hispanics, whites, and Asians were included in the survey. The preliminary results, which extend to the completion of the students' first semester of their freshman year, were published in 2003 in a volume by Princeton University Press titled *The Source of the River*, the title reflecting the fact that most of the colleges chosen in the survey were the same as those included in the Bowen and Bok study.

Most of the students in the Massey study did reasonably well during their first semester, with 97 percent passing all their courses and less than a third having to drop a course. Nevertheless, there were substantial differences in ethnic group performance, with the results repeating a familiar pattern: whites and Asians did the best, Latinos did significantly worse, and blacks wound up at the bottom. "During the very first semester of college," Massey and his colleagues write, "there are clear and significant differences in academic performance that emerge between groups. Whether measured in terms of grade point average, courses dropped, or courses failed, whites and Asians perform significantly better than Latinos and blacks. In general, the grades earned by Latinos in their first college courses averaged about a quarter of a grade point lower than those of whites, whereas the grades earned by black students were more than a third of a point lower. Likewise about a quarter of all Latinos and a third of all blacks ended up dropping a fall-term class, compared with only a fifth of white and Asian students." (pp. 193–4) Overall, the average white and Asian student achieved a B average (roughly 3.3 on a 4.0 scale), the average Latino a B- (3.05), and the average black a C+ (2.95).

Much of the difference in the grades of the four ethnic groups, Massey and his colleagues found, could be attributed to differing levels of entering preparation as measured by such things as high school GPA, the number of AP courses taken, and the students' self-estimate of their academic preparation. The white and Asian students admitted to the 28 colleges they surveyed were on average more intellectually advanced and simply better prepared for academic work than the blacks and Latinos. But these differences in initial preparedness explained only part of the first-semester grade gap that the Massey team found. Few of the other factors that they included in their statistical model to explain the gap seemed to make a big difference, but there was one exception—a positive score on one of their two indices of "stereotype threat" showed a substantial and statistically significant effect in depressing black and Latino grades. Those students who expressed both a lack of self-assurance regarding their ability as students as well as a high level of concern about what their teachers thought of them were found to be most at risk for the grade-depressing effects of stereotype threat. While the number of students who fell into this category was small (only around 9 percent for blacks and an even lower percentage for Latinos), the effects of stereotype threat for these students could be severe. The Massey team writes:

> We found clear and consistent statistical evidence that stereotype vulnerability worked to undermine the academic performance of black and Latino students above and beyond whatever deficits they experienced with respect to academic, financial, social, or psychological preparation for college. . . . For those students possessing the relevant psychological dispositions . . . the effects on performance can be profound. . . . Our analysis suggests that stereotype vulnerability has a pronounced influence on the risk of course failure. . . . In their first term of college work, those who [were most predisposed to stereotype vulnerability] earned significantly lower grades and failed courses at much higher rates than other minority students. (p. 195)

Although they never criticize affirmative action policy directly—in the introductory chapter of their study they characterize it as "the great social experiment of affirmative action"—the Massey team found clear evidence that racial-preference policies, and the considerable resentment they provoke among whites and Asians, is a major contributor to the saliency of stereotype threat on campus. Stereotype threat, they say, "may be particularly salient in selective colleges and universities, where minority students are widely perceived by white faculty and students to have benefited from a 'bending' of academic standards because of affirmative action." The psychological harm to black students, they believe, may be particularly strong because of the negative stereotype of black intellectual ability that is so deeply ingrained in American culture and history. African Americans, they explain, "are stereotyped as being intellectually inferior in U.S. society . . . [and] every time black students are called upon to perform academically in the college setting, they are at risk of confirming this negative valuation, both to themselves and to others." (pp. 10–11)

The bottom line for Massey and his colleagues is that the "puzzlement of minority underachievement" is best explained by two overarching factors: "To a great extent," they write, "early differences in grades earned is explained by different susceptibilities to stereotype threat and by the different levels of preparation for college that students in different [racial and ethnic] groups bring with them when they arrive on campus." (p. 191) Blacks and Hispanics lag behind whites and Asians in their freshman college grades, Massey and his colleagues contend, primarily because they enter college with lower high school grades and SAT scores, and because they have debilitating doubts about their academic competence.

One could, of course, with equal truth say that to a great extent the freshman year differences in grades earned at selective colleges by members of different racial and ethnic groups is a direct result of affirmative-action policy. Abandon affirmative action and everything would change. Replace the racial-preference regime with a more meritocratic system based on past academic performance and in one fell swoop the initial-preparation problem (blacks and Hispanics enter selective colleges with much lower grades and test scores than whites and Asians); the stereotype threat problem (blacks and Hispanics fear being thought inferior by higher-scoring white and Asian classmates and by college instructors); the underperformance problem (blacks and Hispanics choke on exams and don't put their all into academic work as a result of their fear of failure and fear of being negatively stereotyped); and the white and Asian resentment problem (whites and Asians don't like affirmative action and act condescending toward, if not contemptuous of, its black and Hispanic beneficiaries); all these problems would disappear in an instant, or at least be greatly mitigated, if affirmative action policy were abandoned.

And as we shall see, the additional problem of "perverse incentives" (blacks and Hispanics know they don't have to achieve at the same level as whites and Asians to get into good colleges and professional schools) would disappear as well. There's a bonus here, too: abandon affirmative action and college administrators would no longer feel compelled to tell lies about what they are doing. With affirmative action ended, the "pipeline problem" could then come into view as the real 800-pound gorilla in this show and the problem most worthy of focusing public attention upon.

DIVERSITY, YES; RACIAL PREFERENCES, NO! RACIAL ATTITUDES ON CAMPUS

One of the most unexpected findings of the study by Massey and his colleagues was the considerable degree of resentment that white and Asian students often harbor toward black and Hispanic beneficiaries of racial preferences. Student respondents were presented with a "social distance" scale. They were asked to rate how close they felt toward whites, blacks, Latinos, and Asians "in terms of your ideas and feelings about things." Besides giving their closeness ratings to members of "the group in general," eight other subcategories for each ethno-racial group were given, including "the middle class," "the rich," "the poor," "professionals," "business owners," "young women," "young men," and "affirmative-action beneficiaries." Most students, regardless of their own racial or ethnic background, gave relatively high closeness ratings to the middle class and professional members of all of the four ethno-racial groupings, and there was no indication of any "extreme out-group distance" felt by one ethno-racial group for another when the target being assessed was "the group in general."

There was, however, a considerable amount of social distance expressed by many white and Asian students both to the black and Latino poor and to blacks and Latinos who had benefited from affirmative action. "Whites and Asians," Massey and his colleagues report, "tended to perceive a great deal of [social] distance between themselves and blacks who benefited from affirmative action." (p. 143) They also tended to rank each group in terms of their academic promise "with Asians on top, followed by whites, Latinos, and blacks." (p. 152) Blacks and Latinos tended to be seen as "academically underqualified," while Asians were seen as overqualified.

Massey and his colleagues found these responses deeply troubling for two reasons. First, they believe that if whites and Asians think of blacks and Latinos as intellectually inferior to themselves, the demon of stereotype threat will be fed and nurtured in a powerful way. In such an environment, blacks and Latinos will develop defenses and anxieties that are sure to have a harmful effect on their academic performance. But beyond this, the quality of race relations as a whole, Massey and his colleagues argue, will surely be impacted negatively if such perceptions are widespread. If whites and Asians look upon black and Latino students on campus as their intellectual inferiors, and assume an attitude of condescension or resentment, racial tensions on campus will surely increase. "Such perceptions of distance from 'affirmative-action beneficiaries,'" Massey and his colleagues write, "carry important implications for the general tone of race relations on campus because one stereotype that emerges . . . is that without affirmative action most black and Latino students would not be admitted. To the extent that such beliefs are widespread among white students at elite institutions, they will not only increase tensions between whites and minorities on campus; they will also increase the risk of stereotype threat by raising anxiety among minority students about confirming these negative suspicions." (pp. 143, 145)

The problem Massey and his colleagues draw attention to here may be much more serious than they think. This is because the question asked on their social distance survey was specifically worded in terms of "affirmative action" rather than "racial preferences," "racial quotas," or other terms more clearly associated with special consideration or special privileges based on race. We know from many years of polling that the phrase "affirmative action" means different things to different people, and for some people, at least, it is not associated with any kind of controversial policy or with a policy that any reasonable person would oppose. It is a nice-sounding phrase that is sometimes responded to positively even by people who indicate strong opposition to any kind of racial preferences, even the most modest in scope. For many, "affirmative action" seems to mean nothing more than outreach or welcoming policies, or such policies combined with rigorous enforcement of nondiscrimination norms. A 1996 Roper poll, for instance, asked a random sample of 1001 University of California faculty members the following question:

> The term "affirmative action" has different meanings to different people. I'm going to read two definitions of the term "affirmative action." Please tell me which one best describes what you mean by the term. First, affirmative action means granting preferences to women and certain racial and ethnic groups. Second, affirmative action means promoting equal opportunities for all individuals without regard to their race, sex, or ethnicity.

In the Roper survey, 37 percent of respondents chose the first statement (the preferentialist understanding) as best describing what "affirmative action" means to them, while a larger percentage—43 percent—said the second statement (the color-blind and gender-blind meaning) was closer to what they understand by the term (14 percent said neither statement captured what they mean by "affirmative action"). For many of the respondents "affirmative action" thus meant nothing more controversial than a systematic policy of nondiscrimination, which was the original meaning of the phrase in the famous executive order issued by Lyndon Johnson in 1965.[65]

A June, 2003 Gallup poll captures the dilemma even more forcefully. Respondents in a representative national sampling of 1,385 adults were asked the following question: "Do you generally favor or oppose affirmative action programs for racial minorities?" Almost half of all whites who had an opinion on the matter expressed support for "affirmative action programs for minorities"—47 percent favoring, 53 percent opposing—while a clear majority of all the respondents (whites plus non-whites) expressed such support.

In the same survey, however, Gallup asked the following question about race-based admissions to colleges and universities:

Which comes closer to your view about evaluating students for admission into a college or university?

a) An applicant's racial and ethnic background should be considered to help promote diversity on college campuses, even if that means admitting some minority students who otherwise would not be admitted?

---

65. Executive Order No. 11246, issued by President Johnson on September 24, 1965, required all federal contractors to follow a policy of strict nondiscrimination in all areas of employment. The "affirmative action" section of the executive order reads as follows: "The contractor will not discriminate against any employee or applicant for employment because of race, creed, color, or national origin. The contractor will take *affirmative action* to ensure that applicants are employed, and that employees are treated during employment, without regard to their race, creed, color, or national origin. Such action shall include, but not be limited to the following: employment, upgrading, demotion, or transfer; recruitment or recruitment advertising, layoff or termination, rates of pay or other forms of compensation, and selection for training, including apprenticeship. The contractor agrees to post in conspicuous places, available to employees and applicants for employment, notices to be provided by the contracting officer setting forth the provisions of this nondiscrimination clause" (emphasis added).

 b) Applicants should be admitted solely on the basis
of merit, even if that results in few minority students being
admitted.

To this question only 23 percent of whites among those expressing an opinion chose alternative "a" (i.e., that racial and ethnic background should be given special consideration in college
admissions to help promote diversity), while the remaining 77
percent—a substantial majority—opposed this idea. Although
47 percent of whites with an opinion had said they supported
"affirmative action programs for minorities," only half this
amount—23 percent—said they favored special consideration
of race to enhance diversity on college campuses. Among Hispanics who had an opinion only 38 percent supported alternative "a", although 77 percent had said they favored "affirmative
action programs for minorities." Here too, among those with
an opinion there were twice as many supporters of "affirmative-
action programs" as those saying they favored special consideration for race in admissions to college. (Only blacks showed
majority support for race-based college admissions, though just
barely, with only 53 percent of those who had an opinion supporting alternative "a").

 What it all adds up to is this: Questions that ask about
"affirmative action" do not capture the full level of public
opposition to racial preferences, whether in college admissions
or elsewhere. Many people who will respond favorably to an
"affirmative-action" question ("Sure, I support it") are apparently thinking of issues like outreach and aggressive nondiscrimination—if the phrase conjures up anything at all in their
minds—and do not support even the mildest forms of race-based
preferences. If Massey and his colleagues had asked their student
respondents to express their level of closeness to "beneficiaries
of racial preferences in college admissions" it is almost certain
that they would have gotten responses expressing much greater

social distance than even the very substantial level of such distance their question did evoke. Indeed, student responses would probably have indicated a greater level of social distance toward "racial preference beneficiaries" than that found in any of the 140 response categories listed in Massey's tables (the current leader on the social distance scale is that expressed by blacks toward "rich whites" and "rich Asians," who are apparently seen as objects of disdain).

The level of student disapproval of race-based preferences may be gauged by the results of a survey conducted in 1999 by the research firm Angus Reid.[66] In telephone interviews with a representative sample of 1,643 students in 140 different American colleges, the study found overwhelming opposition within this group to racial preferences in employment and college admissions. To the statement, "No one should be given special preferences in jobs or college admissions on the basis of their gender or race," almost one in five student respondents said they "moderately agreed" with the statement (18.7 percent), while fully two out of every three (66.7 percent) said they "strongly agreed" with the statement. Less than 15 percent said they disagreed with the statement, with more than two out of three of these saying they disagreed only moderately, not strongly (a mere 4.6 percent said they "disagreed strongly"). In all, 85 percent of the students in the survey disagreed with granting racial and gender preferences in employment and college admissions, with most saying they disagreed strongly.

The high level of student opposition to both racial and gender preferences is no doubt a reflection of the triumph of the meritocratic ideal in America. It gains a special poignancy among students in the most selective colleges and universities since most have gained admissions only after an arduous four-year trial-by-

---

66. Cited in Stanley Rothman, Seymour Martin Lipset, and Neil Nevitte, "Racial Diversity Reconsidered," *The Public Interest*, spring 2003, online at www.thepublicinterest.com, p. 4.

ordeal in which they have had to struggle through demanding high school honors and Advanced Placement courses, countless hours of study, harrowing exams and standardized tests, and a senior year of applications and personal essays, to be followed by months of anxious waiting. The universal expectation is that if you have academic talent, work hard, and focus your energies on your school work, you will be appropriately rewarded, and your reward will be commensurate with your academic performance. That's the basic trust, and many students view it as the fundamental social contract under which they live.

For many high-achieving students affirmative action in college admissions dashes this trust, and nowhere does this become more evident than in the early spring of senior year when high school students receive final word on whether or not they have been admitted to the colleges of their choice. It is at this time that many students first learn of the enormous degree of racial preference that elite universities often accord to black and Hispanic students. They watch with bewilderment and dismay as some of their much better qualified white and Asian classmates get the thin letters of rejection from some of the very same elite institutions that have sent out the fat letters of acceptance to some of their much less qualified black and Hispanic peers. "It's not fair," they say, and their resentment can oscillate in its focus between the individual students who benefit from racial preferences and the institutional policies that support them.

The great social distance regarding "affirmative-action beneficiaries" that Massey and his colleagues found among the entering white and Asian freshmen is no doubt explained by many individual high school experiences of this kind. The resentment and perception of unfairness that such experiences can evoke are well captured in a poignant description by a Princeton undergraduate of his own experiences in the college admissions process. The account is taken from the concluding paragraph of a term paper the student wrote, which was highly critical of affirmative-action policy in America:

> I'll close with a personal anecdote. In my high school
> graduating class, five were admitted into the class of 2005
> at Princeton. Of those, one was of a minority. While I was
> lucky enough to be one of those five, many others in my
> high school with much higher grades and SAT scores than
> the admitted minority were passed over. In many ways, the
> situation disgusted me. I knew that countless students had
> worked much harder than the minority student, but they had
> not been admitted *only because* they were not black. While I
> had never fostered any ill will towards that student, I found
> that I resented the fact that she could matriculate because
> she was black; really, though, my anger could only be
> directed at the cause of the problem—race-preference—and
> not the minority student. We seek a society where race does
> not matter, but affirmative action, as my high school experi-
> ence testifies, only intensifies the importance of race. I look
> forward to the day when affirmative action ends and race
> truly *does not matter*. In the meantime, society seems vigor-
> ously keen on becoming *more* race-conscious in a misguided
> attempt to become *less* race-conscious.

The conclusion of Massey and his colleagues that white and Asian students have negative attitudes toward affirmative-action beneficiaries and that this stance will have negative consequences for the academic performance of the stereotype-vulnerable students and for the quality of race relations on campus has obvious implications for the affirmative-action debate. One of the major arguments of those who support "race-sensitive admissions" is that such policies produce an enriching racial diversity on campus that contributes to the overall educational experience of students of all races and ethnic backgrounds. A more racially representative student body, it is maintained, helps to further tolerance and racial understanding, facilitates interracial friendships, and improves the overall educational environment of all students on campus, not just the minority students. Students, it is said, learn from one another, and by working and studying together students of different races and ethnicities learn important lessons that they will carry with them throughout life. If the findings of Massey and his colleagues are correct, however, this "diversity" rationale for race-based admissions policies would be seriously undermined. There are good diversities and bad diversities, and diversities created artificially through racial preferences—ones that increase "social distance" and reinforce negative stereotypes—are obviously in the "bad" category.

One of the early attempts to test the "diversity rationale" for affirmative-action policies was made by social scientists Stanley Rothman, Seymour Martin Lipset, and Neil Nevitte. Using the Angus Reid telephone survey previously referred to, the Rothman group explored the relationship between the degree of enrollment diversity on college campuses (as measured by the percentage of black students) and several important outcome variables, including student satisfaction with their university experience, the overall quality of education, the strength of the work ethic on campus, and the proportion of students complaining of having personally experienced discrimination. The survey utilized the random sample of students, faculty, and administrators at the 140 colleges and universities polled by the Angus Reid group.

What Rothman and his colleagues found would be deeply disturbing to affirmative-action supporters. Virtually none of the promised benefits of larger black enrollments was supported by their study's findings. Not only did increased black enrollment not have the intended beneficial outcomes, but it seemed on balance to have clearly harmful effects:

When student evaluations of the educational and racial
atmosphere were correlated with the percentage of black
students enrolled at a college or university, the predicted
positive associations with educational benefits and interracial
understanding failed to appear. The statistically significant
associations that did appear were the opposite of those predicted. . . . As the proportion of black students rose, student
satisfaction with their university experience dropped, as did
their assessments of the quality of their education and the
work ethic of their peers. In addition, the higher the enrollment diversity, the more likely students were to say that they
personally experienced discrimination. The same pattern
of negative correlations between educational benefits and
increased black enrollment appeared in the responses of faculty and administrators. Both groups perceived decreases in
educational quality and academic preparation as the number
of black students increased. Faculty members also rated students as less hard-working as diversity increased.[67]

Rothman and his colleagues found more mixed results in
regard to discrimination and minority relations than in regard
to some of the other items surveyed. "Among faculty and
administrators," they write, "higher minority enrollment was
significantly associated with perceptions of less campus discrimination and among administrators, more positive treatment of
minority students." These findings, however, were offset, they
say, "by the absence of similar results among students, who
reported more personal victimization as diversity increased."
Students, Rothman and his colleagues found, were generally

67. Stanley Rothman, Seymour Martin Lipset, and Neil Nevitte, "Does Enrollment
Diversity Improve University Education," *International Journal of Public Opinion
Research*, 15: 1, 2003, pp. 8–26. A less technical version of this paper appears as
"Racial Diversity Reconsidered," in *The Public Interest*, spring 2003 (available online
at www.thepublicinterest.com). The quotations in the text are taken from the online
version of *The Public Interest* article.

much less enamored of greater "diversity" on college campuses (i.e., a higher percentage of black students) than college administrators, with faculty assessments somewhere between these.

Those in the Rothman group believe that affirmative-action policy is involved in these negative views of black enrollment diversity, and they offer as evidence the fact that a very different assessment is given of the value of larger Asian enrollments. Unlike a larger black and Hispanic presence on campus, a larger Asian presence, they found, was sometimes viewed in a positive light by college students and others. In terms of the outcome variables explored in the study, "the increased presence of Asian Americans seems to have at least some positive impact," Rothman and his colleagues report. They speculate that the difference lies in the absence of racial preference given to the entering Asian students. "Since higher percentages of black and Hispanic students," they write, "are produced in part by affirmative action, while the same is not true for Asian-American students, it may be that affirmative action places students in academic environments for which they are unsuited, leading to tension and dissatisfaction all around." Once again, we see evidence confirming Sowell's "mismatch" hypothesis.

Rothman and his colleagues see their study as providing strong evidence against what they call the "diversity model" of campus relations put forth by Bowen and Bok and other defenders of current affirmative-action policy in higher education. They criticize much of the previous research in this area for asking questions that are often too vague to interpret meaningfully (example from a study directed by Harvard researcher Gary Orfield: "Do you feel that diversity enhances or detracts from how you and others think about problems and solutions in classes?"), and for failure to appreciate the effect of political correctness and socially expected response patterns on the level of candor with which respondents will answer questions pertaining to race. They believe their own study overcomes these problems.

Perhaps the worst shortcoming of the Bowen and Bok study is its tendency to equate a generalized support for the value of demographic diversity on college campuses with support for all elements in that diversity and for all policies intended to achieve that diversity. "The vast majority [of the respondents in our study]," Bowen and Bok write, "believe that going to college with a diverse body of fellow students made a valuable contribution to their education and personal development." (p. 280) It is well and good to know all this, of course, but a vague genuflection before the value of "diversity" really tells us very little about what students actually think about the more important and controversial issues dealing with race and college life.

It is clear from the work of the Massey and Rothman groups that white students view the presence of Asian students on campus very differently from the way they view the presence of black students, and that the difference is almost certainly connected with the lower academic qualifications of many of the black students and the sense that many blacks have benefited unfairly from affirmative-action programs. Incredibly, Bowen and Bok never thought to place on their lengthy questionnaire any kind of question soliciting the views of their respondents to affirmative-action policy and its beneficiaries. Their respondents were never even asked the crucial question of whether or not they favored "race-sensitive admissions" as a way of increasing racial diversity on campus. They were never asked how distant or close they felt to "beneficiaries of racial preferences in college admissions." They were never asked whether they believed that the average black or Hispanic student they met in college was equally qualified academically with the average white or Asian student, and if not, whether they thought this situation had any effect on the quality of race relations on campus. One suspects that the reason for the omission of such crucially important questions from Bowen and Bok's survey was simply a fear of the answers.

Bowen and Bok, along with most other defenders of the diversity rationale, proceeded as if no difference existed in public perceptions between the kind of diversity that a merit system might produce and the contrived, artificial, end result-focused diversity that comes about through a process of conscious racial engineering, racial preferencing, and racial-quota thinking. An analogy with professional sports might be helpful. Most sports fans appreciate the ethnic diversity existing nowadays on professional baseball teams, where more Hispanic and Asian players have added to a racial makeup at one time dominated exclusively by whites, and subsequently by a mixture of blacks and whites. Many sports fans would no doubt be pleased if basketball (a black-dominated sport), ice hockey (a white-dominated sport), and horse-racing (an Hispanic-dominated sport) became more baseball-like in this regard. Sports fans seem to appreciate the fact that blacks like Tiger Woods and the two Williams sisters gained prominence in such traditionally all-white country club sports as golf and tennis. Many golf fans also seem to like the fact that more Europeans, South Americans, and Asians are now seen on the American golf tour.

But how many sports fans would thrill to the prospect of greater diversity in any of these sports if it meant lowering entrance standards for the members of underrepresented racial and ethnic groups or otherwise departing from meritocratic standards? What would professional athletes themselves think of such an arrangement? Would they revel in the greater "diversity" of their sport? How would white hockey players, for instance, respond to an affirmative-action program in which being black or Asian was considered a huge "plus-factor" in determining who makes the hockey team? Would the situation be any different if diversity on a college or high school sports team was at issue rather than diversity in professional sports? How, for example, would high school athletes react to an aggressive affirmative-action program that sought to enhance racial diversity on their high school sports teams? How would their classmates and parents react? Would it make any difference whether the target of the affirmative action program was a varsity or a junior varsity team? Would it make any difference if the target were an intramural team?

It doesn't require any special genius to figure out the answers to any of these questions. In all cases a policy of race-based preferences would have a disastrous effect on the morale of the teams involved; those selected under the higher standards would look down on those who made the team by way of racial preferences; the beneficiaries of the racial preferences would acquire an inferiority complex and become vulnerable to "stereotype threat"; and everywhere disappointed aspirants from the "over-represented" groups would decry the system as "unfair." And for all these reasons those implementing the preference system would have a powerful incentive to speak in euphemisms and prettifying obfuscations and lie about what they are actually doing.

Many years ago political philosopher Allan Bloom gave an acute description of the pattern of black/white relations on elite college campuses that he had observed during his many years of teaching under the affirmative-action plans at Cornell and the University of Chicago.[68] Bloom saw clearly from the very beginning of America's embrace of racial preferences that the phenomenon that would later be called "stereotype vulnerability"

---

68. Allan Bloom, *The Closing of the American Mind* (New York: Simon and Schuster, 1987).

or "stereotype threat" unleashed a powerful dynamic on college campuses that not only had a negative effect on the learning environment, but also had a chilling effect on the quality
of social relationships between the lower-achieving blacks who
were preferentially admitted to elite colleges and the higher-
achieving whites and Asians.

At the nation's premier universities, Bloom observed, "white
and black students do not in general become real friends with
one another." This is a terribly disappointing development, he
says, especially when one considers the great success universities
have had since the Second World War in integrating members of
formerly excluded groups, including the Irish, Jews, Catholics,
Asians, and women. The black/white divide, he says, is "the
one eccentric element in this portrait, the one failure." (p. 91)
The better universities, he explains, are formally integrated, and
blacks and whites are used to seeing one another on campus and
act politely in each other's company. "But the substantial contact, indifference to race, soul to soul, that prevails in all other
aspects of student life simply does not usually exist between the
two races." (pp. 92–3)

Bloom blames the situation on affirmative action. "Affirmative action," he says, "now institutionalizes the worst aspects
of [racial] separatism." (p. 96) In the better universities, Bloom
explains, "the fact is that the average black student's achievements do not equal those of the average white student . . . and
everybody knows it." Those who know it best are the black
students themselves, who react to the situation with defensiveness and self-segregation on campus. The black students know
"that everyone doubts their merit, their capacity for equal
achievement," and, as a result, they "avoid close associations
with whites, who might be better qualified than they are and
who might be looking down on them." They adopt a simple
defensive strategy: "Better to stick together, so these subtle but
painful difficulties will not arise." (p. 96) Segregated cafeterias

and eating clubs are but one manifestation of this phenomenon. Whites too, says Bloom, react to the situation with their own form of self-segregation and try to avoid intimate black/white contacts and discussion topics that will be fraught with tension and uneasiness. The result, he says, is a bad situation all around. The intimate interracial friendships and better understanding between the races, which affirmative action is supposed to produce, do not come about.

Anyone with intimate knowledge of the racial scene at elite colleges and universities in recent years will detect a powerful ring of truth in what Bloom says. For example, John McWhorter, who for many years was a professor of linguistics at Berkeley, has described black/white relations on the Berkeley campus in the late-1990s in terms almost identical to those of Bloom, although McWhorter, who is black, writes with an even greater sense of sadness and disappointment than does Bloom. "At Berkeley," McWhorter explains, "I have had occasion to teach large numbers of both black and other students. I spent a long time resisting acknowledging something that ultimately became too consistent and obvious to ignore, which was that black undergraduates at Berkeley tended to be among the worst students on campus, by any estimation." This, he says, has had horrible consequences for the quality of black/white and black/Asian relations on campus. He explains further:

> With it widely known among a student body that most minority students were admitted with test scores and GPAs which would have barred white and Asian applicants from consideration, it is difficult for many white students to avoid beginning to question the basic mental competence of black people as a race. This is especially true when most black students are obviously of middle-class background . . . A white person need not be a racist to start wondering why

black students need affirmative action even when growing up
no poorer than they did. . . . This can only leave many young
whites with a private suspicion that blacks simply aren't as
swift, which will in turn encourage suspicion in black students, and thus perpetuate interracial alienation on campus
and undermine the mutual respect that successful integration requires. . . . [Alienating racial encounters] like these
subvert the goal of peaceful integration, and importantly,
unexpressed renditions of these encounters lurk underneath
interracial contacts campus-wide all year long.[69]

There is one arena, however, where the kind of critique
offered by Bloom and McWhorter clearly does not apply and
where true black/white friendships really do flourish on elite
college campuses. These are among the recruited college athletes on the varsity sports teams. In this arena, however, such
contacts flourish precisely because the participants can escape
the harm done by race-based affirmative action programs and
devote much of their energies to activities where strict meritocratic principles reign supreme. However negatively one may
view contemporary policies of athletic recruitment on college
campuses, they clearly do produce the rare oases of integration
amid the desert of self-segregated student social groups.
Recruited athletes on college campuses are generally certain of
two things. First, they know a) that they have been recruited to
play a college sport under the same highly relaxed set of academic standards that applies to all athletic recruits, regardless
of their race or ethnicity (i.e., admissions officers at selective
institutions will reach down just as far academically for a top-

69. John McWhorter, *Losing the Race: Self-Sabotage in Black America* (New York:
The Free Press, 2000,) pp. 89, 229–30. McWhorter's solution to the problem is the same
as Bloom's: "Black students often come to a selective campus wary that white students
suspect them of being affirmative-action admits and thus not equally qualified. A simple
solution would be to eliminate the policy that makes the white students' suspicion—let's
face it—usually correct." (p. 236)

quality white or Asian athlete as for a comparable black or Hispanic athlete); and they know b) that both their recruitment to the team and their subsequent play will be based purely on performance, not on their capacity to contribute to a team's "diversity." On the sports teams black and Hispanic athletes work together with white and Asian athletes in a common project under a set of standards that all can consider fair. No one has any reason to look down on the members of any racial or ethnic group as athletically inferior because all have been judged by a common set of standards. No one has any reason to experience "stereotype threat."

It is perhaps no accident that two of the most prominent white politicians in the post-civil rights era known to have the greatest rapport with black people—i.e., Bill Bradley and the late Jack Kemp—were both products of the college and professional sports world. In an earlier generation the intimate contact between blacks and whites that so many yearn to see on college campuses and elsewhere was most prominently displayed in another arena of strict meritocracy—the world of jazz musicians (it is partially for this reason that the saxophone-playing Bill Clinton seems to have such natural rapport with so many black people). The conclusion seems inescapable here, and recent social science has confirmed it more and more: if true friendships—"indifference to race, soul to soul"—are to flourish between blacks and whites on college campuses, they must be based on mutual respect and a system of race-blind selection that focuses on genuine talent and performance, not on race.

WHY DO SO FEW BLACKS BECOME SCIENTISTS AND ENGINEERS?

Long before the Cole and Barber study looked into the question of why so few blacks become college professors, several researchers had taken up the even more pressing question of why so few blacks become scientists and engineers. In the past these professions have often been popular with members of previously disadvantaged minority groups because of their great social prestige and financial rewards, plus the greater fairness that reigns within them in determining objective merit. The small number of non-Asian minorities in most of these fields has been an ongoing concern for many college administrators. Although Asian freshmen are the most likely to say they want to major in a science or engineering field, numerous studies have shown that college-bound blacks and Hispanics express an interest in these fields in at least the same proportion as whites—in some surveys they show an even greater interest. Yet of the black and Hispanic freshmen who express an initial interest in majoring in engineering or a science, an extremely high proportion of them change their minds after a year or two of study and switch into a nonscience major.

Many students of all races, of course, fail to carry through with their freshman-year intention to major in engineering or a laboratory science once they realize how demanding the course work in these disciplines usually is and how much easier it is to get a degree in a nonscience field like business or the humanities. But the hard-science falloff or "nonpersistence rate" among blacks and Hispanics is considerably higher than that for whites or Asians, and college administrators have wanted to know why.

One of the most important studies looking into this problem was conducted by a group of researchers led by Dartmouth psychology professor Rogers Elliott.[70] Elliott and his colleagues surveyed the progression of students from the class of 1992 who entered as freshmen four Ivy League colleges (Dartmouth, Cornell, Yale, and Brown), and they looked at a host of background

---

70. Rogers Elliott, A. Christopher Strenta, Russell Adair, Michael Matier, and Jannah Scott, "The Role of Ethnicity in Choosing and Leaving Science in Highly Selective Institutions," *Research in Higher Education*, 37 (1996): 681–709.

factors that might predict both the students' intention to pursue a natural science major and their propensity to stick with that intention through graduation. Like other researchers, the Elliott group found black and Hispanic freshmen having as high an initial interest in majoring in a natural science as whites, but the proportion following through with their intention and going on to get a degree in one of these fields differed greatly among the various ethno-racial groups. While approximately 70 percent of Asians and 61 percent of whites initially expressing an intention to major in a natural science persisted with their intention through graduation, only 55 percent of Hispanics did and only 34 percent of blacks. The "nonpersistence rate" for blacks (66 percent) was 1.7 times that for whites (39 percent), and more than twice that for Asians (30 percent). The Elliott group also found that while relatively few students who initially failed to express a science-major intention changed their minds later in their college careers and switched into a science, among those who did switch and wound up with a hard science degree at the end of college the usual ethnic pattern was observed: 14.9 percent of Asians not initially intending to be science majors switched into a science, 8.6 percent of whites, 5.8 percent of Hispanics, and only 2.5 percent of blacks.

While the Elliott group's study suggests that there may be ethnic or cultural factors involved in explaining the differing falloff rates, the most important factor, their regression equations showed, is simply the differing levels of preparation and achievement in math- and science-related fields that students brought with them from high school. The SAT math score—one of the best predictors of freshman-year grades in the hard sciences—differed substantially by ethnic group among those initially expressing a desire to major in a natural science. Among freshman-year science aspirants the Asians had the highest average SAT math score (721), followed closely by the whites (714), while Hispanics (653) and blacks (607) lagged far behind. These numbers, of course, reflect the huge affirmative-action boosts in admission given to blacks over whites and Asians and the somewhat lesser boosts given to Hispanics. But regardless of their race, students with high math SAT scores and other indications of past math/science achievement in high school (like grades in high school science courses) were found to be much more likely to persist in their initial desire to major in a hard science than those with lower scores. Black and Hispanic falloff rates were much higher than those for whites and Asians mainly because of their "entering credentials" deficit—the white and Asian students were simply better prepared.

The Elliott group, however, didn't end its inquiry with this simple insight. They knew from other studies that at many colleges less competitive than the four Ivy League institutions they surveyed blacks seemed to have an easier time sticking to a major in a laboratory or hard science, and many of the graduates of these less prestigious institutions often went on to successful careers in science, engineering, and medicine. Some even went on to get Ph.D.s in their field from very respectable universities. The historically black colleges and universities (HBCUs)—schools like Morehouse, Fisk, Spellman, and Howard—were known to turn out as many as 40 percent of all blacks with science and engineering degrees in the U.S. despite enrolling only about half that proportion of the country's black undergraduates. Elliott and his colleagues suspected that there was a "mismatch factor" involved in explaining the high black falloff rate at the Ivy institutions they surveyed, since they knew that blacks who successfully completed science and engineering programs at the HBCUs and other colleges less selective than the Ivies were often no better prepared in terms of their science and mathematics background than those Ivy-attending blacks in their study who dropped out of science.

"We think it certain that more of the black students in our sample," they wrote, "would have persisted in science had they been, say, at Howard" and "more of them would also have per-sisted at any of several majority white institutions." (pp. 700–1). They came to this conclusion after looking at a different data set that examined the relative math SAT scores of the students who successfully completed a degree in the natural sciences at 11 col-leges of differing overall selectivity. The pattern they found at each of the 11 colleges was almost always the same: A majority of natural science majors were drawn from the students whose math SAT scores were among those in the top third of their institution, while very few such majors came from students in the bottom third of the SAT math range.

However, the SAT math scores of the black students in the four Ivy League schools, including those of many who either dropped out of natural science or never intended to major in it to begin with, were often higher than those earning science and engineering degrees at other schools. The Elliott group con-cluded that a student intending to major in a natural science is more likely to persevere in that intention if the student matricu-lates at an institution where the student's entering credentials (math SAT score, high school grades, etc.) are closer to the middle or top third of student ranges in the school they attend rather than at the bottom. A student whose academic creden-tials place him in the upper part of his college freshman class is more likely to persist with an intention to major in a hard science than a student with equal credentials who enrolls in a more competitive institution where most of the other students are academically better qualified.

The reason for this mismatch effect, Elliott and his col-leagues believe, is because natural-science instruction is hierar-chical, always building on what had to be learned—and learned well—before. Enrolling in a highly competitive college where most of the other science students are better prepared and pro-ceeding at a rapid rate in the acquisition of new knowledge is not a formula for success for those starting out behind. The science programs at Ivy League schools are no place to play catch-up. However, those with a real desire to become scientists and engineers who may not have reached the top of the charts by the end of their high school days still have a good chance of succeeding in their career goals, the Elliott researchers believe, if they choose a college where the other students are more similar to themselves academically. The mode of teaching at less selective colleges will presumably be more geared to students at their level, and they will not be intimidated by a pace of instruction that threatens to overwhelm them.

Within this context the Elliott group asked serious questions about the wisdom of current affirmative-action programs at America's most competitive colleges and universities—at least insofar as they impact black and Hispanic students who intend to major in the natural sciences and engineering. To the question "Why do so few blacks pursue careers in science and engineering?" the Elliott group gave an answer virtually identical to the answer Cole and Barber would give to the question of why blacks seldom pursue careers in academia: There is a "pipeline" and "entering credentials" problem that is made much worse by the current American system of racial preferences and the skills-mismatching it creates. As Elliott said in his testimony before the U.S. Civil Rights Commission (September 2008), where he explained the results of his team's research: "Race preferences in admissions in the service of Affirmative Action are harming the aspirations particularly of blacks seeking to be scientists by creating this huge mismatch . . . The differences are largest at the most elite universities because they have very high . . . admissions standards, levels which minorities, especially blacks, don't come close to meeting."[71]

71. U.S Commission on Civil Rights, "Encouraging Minority Students to Pursue Careers in Science, Technology, Engineering and Math," Sept. 12, 2008, p. 35, www.nealgross.com.

The mismatch problem as a contributor to the high "non-persistence" rate of blacks and Hispanics intending to major in hard sciences has been explored in a number of other studies, including one that made use of the same College and Beyond database used by Bowen and Bok in *The Shape of the River.* University of Virginia psychologists Frederick Smyth and John McArdle looked at data from 23 of the competitive colleges and universities in the College and Beyond survey and combined the C&B data with additional information about the students at these 23 institutions compiled by UCLA's Higher Education Research Institute in its ongoing Cooperative Institutional Research Program survey.[72]

Smyth and McArdle focused their attention on the 5,047 entering freshmen at these 23 C&B institutions who initially expressed an interest in majoring in either science, math, or engineering (SME). Not surprisingly, they found important differences in the average SAT math scores of the SME intenders that reflected familiar patterns. The Asians who intended to major in the SME subjects had substantially higher SAT math scores than the whites, the whites substantially higher than the Hispanics, and the Hispanics higher than the blacks. Men, too, on average, had higher scores on their math SATs than women. This fact alone, combined with parallel differences in high school grades, accounted for much of the observed differences in the proportion of the SME intenders within each group who persisted in an SME major until graduation. The combined black and Hispanic persistence-until-graduation rate (38 percent)[73] was much lower than the white (55 percent), and lower still than the Asian (63 percent).

---

72. Frederick Smyth and John McArdle, "Ethnic and Gender Differences in Science Graduation at Selective Colleges with Implications for Admission Policy and College Choice," *Research in Higher Education*, 45 (2004):353–81.
73. This is a combined figure for blacks and Hispanics (plus the very tiny number of Native Americans in the C&B database).

Like the earlier Elliott study, Smyth and McArdle found evidence of an "institutional mismatch" effect as well as an "entering credentials" effect. Those with SAT math scores substantially below average for the SME intenders at the institutions where they were enrolled were at a heightened risk of not carrying through with their initial intention to major in a science, math, or engineering field. This mismatch factor was shown to affect disproportionately the blacks, Hispanics, and American Indians in their study. Linking their own results to the earlier study of the Elliott group, they write: "Elliott and his colleagues concluded that race-sensitive admission, while increasing access to elite colleges, was inadvertently causing disproportionate loss of talented underrepresented minority students from science majors. Our findings for the College and Beyond students are consistent with this inference." (p. 373)

Smyth and McArdle estimated that if all of the black and Hispanic students in their survey who expressed a freshman-year intention to major in an SME subject had attended one of the 23 schools where their math test scores and high school grades equaled the average among the students at that school with similar SME intentions, there would have been a substantial increase in the number of blacks and Hispanics sticking with SME subjects until graduation. Their mathematical model predicted that eliminating the harmful mismatch effect would have produced 45 percent more black and Hispanic females with science, math, or engineering degrees and 35 percent more males. (p. 373)

Results similar to those of the Smyth/McArdle study and the Elliott group study were reached by UCLA education professor Mitchell Chang and his colleagues in their study of students who intended to major in four biomedical-related fields—biology, health sciences, psychology, and chemistry.[74] The Chang team

---

74. Mitchell J. Chang, Oscar Cerna, June Han, and Victor Sáenz, "The Contradictory Roles of Institutional Status in Retaining Underrepresented Minorities in Biomedical and Behavioral Science Majors," *The Review of Higher Education*, 33 (2008):433–64.

looked at data collected in 2004 and 2005 by UCLA's Higher Education Research Institute as part of two ongoing longitudinal projects funded by the National Institute of Health. In all, 2,964 students were surveyed from 159 different institutions, with the institutions spread out among those with a predominantly white and Asian clientele, those serving mostly Hispanics, and the historically black colleges and universities. Their main interest was discovering what factors led students with an initial interest in majoring in a biomedical-related science to stick with that intention at least until completion of their first year of college.

Like all other researchers, they found that past preparation and achievement—as measured by such factors as the number of math and science courses taken in high school, high school grade-point average, and SAT scores—played a major role in a student's decision to persist with an initial intention to major in one of the four science fields examined. Other factors that played a positive role in science-major retention included membership in a campus preprofessional organization and a stated desire to find cures for diseases. However, the Chang group also found a substantial mismatch penalty involved when students attended more selective institutions. Students of all ethnic groups, including whites and Asians, were more likely to abandon their initial intention to major in science if they attended a highly competitive college or university. The falloff was greatest, however, for blacks, Hispanics, and American Indians (the "underrepresented minorities" in their study), whose chances of sticking with their freshman-year intention fell very sharply the more competitive the institution they attended.

For every 10-point increase in the average SAT score of the entering freshmen in the institutions surveyed (adding the math and verbal scores together), the chances of a student from an underrepresented minority sticking with a projected science major was reduced by 3 percent. "All things being equal," they write, "a URM [underrepresented minority] student has a 30% higher chance of departing from a biomedical or behavioral science major if he or she attends an institution where the average undergraduate combined SAT score is 1100 versus one with an average of 1000." (p. 449)

Chang and his associates, however, found one important exception to this rule. At the historically black colleges and universities, the higher the standards of the institution, the greater the science-retention rate. "Rather than increasing the risk of departure in the biomedical and behavioral sciences, attending an HBCU where students have higher average test scores may improve URM students' chances of persisting in those majors." (p. 449) They do not explain just why this is so, although part of the reason would seem to be that the HBCUs have developed over the years a special expertise in educating black students with spotty high school records and are more focused on effectiveness in undergraduate instruction than preeminence in research. (In this sense they would act like the Catholic schools in the inner city). Probably there also exists what statisticians call a "restriction of range" factor, since even the most selective HBCU institutions have students with typical SAT scores only modest by national standards (math-plus-verbal SAT scores at schools like Spellman and Morehouse typically average around 1000). The difference in past achievement and SAT scores between the better and less prepared students across the various HBCUs is thus probably much less than that across the more academically diverse institutions with white or white-plus-Asian majorities.

The Chang team sums up the most important finding of its research in the following words:

There does seem to be a mismatch occurring in science education at the college level. The problem, however, is

> not only an issue of poorly prepared URM students failing
> among high achievers . . . The problem is that all students,
> irrespective of their race, academic preparation, or motiva-
> tion, are at greater risk of failing among high achievers at
> highly selective institutions where the undergraduate student
> body is mostly White and Asian. In other words, even highly
> capable and talented White and Asian students—who would
> otherwise continue in a biomedical or behavioral science
> major at less selective institutions—are leaving the sciences
> at higher rates at more selective institutions. (p. 454)

The conclusion of the Chang team thus parallels that of Elliott
and his associates: A student who wishes to succeed as a biomedical science major is advised to choose a college or university where the student's entering academic credentials are not
too far below those of the typical science major at the institution chosen. The lowering of standards for black and Hispanic
students at our more competitive colleges and universities and
the resulting credentials mismatch that ensues almost certainly
reduces the number of these "underrepresented minority" students who go on to complete a program in the biomedical and
laboratory science fields.

PERVERSE INCENTIVES: REWARDING UNDERACHIEVEMENT

As previously noted, each year black students typically score
about 100 points lower than whites and Asians on each of
the sections of the SAT exam (a 200-point gap on the math-
plus-verbal score and a 300-point gap when the newer writing test scores are added). This gap was even greater in the
mid-1970s when data on the matter first became available (the
gap then on the math-plus-verbal score was almost 250 SAT

points), but it began to close after this time until the late 1980s, when progress in this direction stopped. Hispanics, too, score substantially lower on the SATs than whites and Asians, with average Hispanic scores much closer to the black mean than to that of the whites and Asians. These SAT-gap figures actually understate the real distance between the achievement levels of the four ethno-racial groups, since smaller proportions of the lower-scoring groups actually take the SAT. Compared with whites and Asians, a larger portion of black and Hispanic students either drop out of high school before the period in which the SAT is normally taken or do not take the SAT because they do not intend to go to college (or intend to go to a noncompetitive institution that does not require the SAT). Students in these latter categories, of course, would be among the lowest achievers. If the same proportion of 17-year-old black and Hispanic students took the SAT as whites and Asians the existing gap would be larger.

The racial gap at the highest SAT levels, where the "right-tail" colleges and universities recruit most of their entering classes, is even more extreme. In 2006, for instance, while constituting 10.3 percent of all SAT test takers, blacks comprised only 1.6 percent of those who scored 700 or above on the verbal part of the SAT and only 1.0 percent of those scoring 700 or above on the math. Thirty-nine times as many whites as blacks scored 700 or above on the verbal SAT and 53 times as many on the math SAT.[75] The racial gap among those scoring 750 or above—where schools like Princeton, MIT, and Yale recruit many of their students—was even more skewed. Since the nation's most selective colleges and universities choose most

---

75. "A Large Black-White Scoring Gap Persists on the SAT College Admission," *Journal of Blacks in Higher Education*, 2006, www.jbhe.com/53_SAT.

of their incoming student body from those who have scored at these very high levels, college administrators are faced with the choice of either forming an entering class that is well below the 5–7 percent black representation range they desire, or lowering their standards substantially for black entrants. Virtually all elite institutions choose the latter option (Caltech may be the one exception).[76]

If elite colleges enroll only the most academically talented and accomplished students, they will be drawing from a pool that is overwhelmingly white and Asian—and among the whites disproportionately Jewish.[77] If they are unwilling to have an

---

76. On Caltech as a partial outlier, see Stephan and Abigail Thernstrom, *America in Black and White* (New York: Simon and Schuster, 1997), p. 400; and Russell Nieli, "Why Caltech Is in a Class by Itself," Minding-the-Campus website, Dec. 9, 2010, www.mindingthecampus.com.

77. The Asian advance on the SATs since the 1970s has been nothing short of spectacular, with the Asian/white gap at the high end substantial and the Asian/black gap enormous. In 1995, for instance, for every thousand Asians taking the SAT, 18 scored 700 or above on the verbal test, as did 13 out of every thousand whites. The comparable figure for blacks was less than 2 per thousand. The results on the math portion of the SAT were even more ethnicly skewed. More than 140 out of every thousand Asian test-takers scored above 700 on the math test, as did 58 out of every thousand whites, while only 6 out of every thousand black test-takers scored this high. Although the total number of blacks taking the SAT in 1995 was considerably greater than the total number of Asians taking the test, among those scoring 700 or above Asians exceed the number of blacks by a factor of 8 to 1 on the verbal portion (1,476 vs. 184), and on the math by a factor of more than 18 to 1 (11,585 vs. 616). (These figures are taken from the College Entrance Examination Board, *1995 National Ethnic/ Sex Data*, as tabulated in Thernstrom and Thernstrom, *America in Black and White*, p. 399, Table 4.). Asians since this time have continued with their steady advance, producing an ever-widening ethnic gap especially on the math SAT. Among SAT test-takers in 2010, approximately 23 percent of Asians scored 700 or above on the math SAT, compared with only 6 percent of whites and 1 percent of blacks (inferred from the table "SAT Percentile Ranks, 2010 College-Bound Seniors, College Board, http://professionals.collegeboard.com).

On Jews: Although the College Board doesn't routinely publish figures on religious or ethno-religious demographics, it did publish such figures in one year (2002), indicating that on average Jews had a combined math-plus-verbal SAT score of 1161, 100 points higher than that of the average white test-taker. This is a very substantial difference and suggests a huge difference far out on the right tail of scores of the overall test-taking population, where Jewish overrepresentation is enormous. This largely

entering class that is only 1–3 percent black, they will have to resort to huge racial preferences, even if they must conceal this fact from a skeptical public—or lie about it, as they typically do.[78]

Tempting as it may be for some to think so, these huge racial gaps cannot be explained simply by differing levels of family income or family education. Even after taking all such factors into consideration, huge gaps remain. For instance, in a study by the College Board of 1995 test takers, white students whose parents never went beyond high school outperformed in their SAT scores black students from families in which at least one parent had a graduate degree (873 vs. 844). A similar situation obtained between Asians and blacks with these same family characteristics, where the gap was even greater (890 vs. 844). Blacks from relatively affluent families earning more than $70,000 per year scored 849 on the SAT, while whites from very poor families earning less than $10,000 per year scored twenty points *higher* (869). Not surprisingly, poor Asians, many of whose parents were immigrants and who often lived in households where no English was spoken, performed much more poorly than the affluent blacks on the SAT verbal (343 vs. 407), but they significantly outscored them on the math portion of the test (482 vs. 442).[79] These are old figures, and the College Board has not published more recent data cross-tabulating SAT

---

explains why Jews, comprising only 2 percent of the American student-age population, often comprise as much as 20 percent of the student body at several Ivy League schools and other elite undergraduate institutions.

78. "A leading educator once remarked to me that there were two issues about which many university presidents deluded themselves or lied: preferential admissions for athletes and affirmative action." Robert Klitgaard, *Choosing Elites* (New York: Basic Books, 1985), p. 187.

79. The figures are taken from the College Entrance Examination Board, *1995 National Ethnic/ Sex Data*, as tabulated in Stephan and Abigail Thernstrom, *America in Black and White*, Simon and Schuster, N.Y., 1997, p. 407, Table 7.

scores by household income and race. But this older pattern almost certainly persists today as black SAT scores continue to stagnate while high-scoring Asians increase their distance from both blacks and whites.

It is because of these huge racial gaps, coupled with the near-universal belief among administrators at elite colleges and universities that their institutions must have a "decent" representation of black and Hispanic students, that the degree of racial preferences given to members of these groups is so large. By checking off the box that says "black" on their college applications, high school students in effect are accorded a "plus factor" boost equivalent to roughly 100 points on each of the sections of the SAT, and perhaps half a grade letter on their high school GPA. Absent affirmative action, the proportion of blacks at the most elite universities would probably plummet—at least in the short run—from the current 5–10 percent range to the 1–3 percent range. Hispanic declines would be somewhat less, though still very steep.[80]

The reason for these huge differences in group performance are multiple and controversial, and the theories that are out there to explain them include in their focus everything from culture, to genes, to family structure, to group psychology, to child-rearing practices.[81] Differences in nutrition, neo-natal care, public health, the neighborhood crime situation, and the ambient levels of lead and other toxic environmental pollutants have also been

---

80. For projections on the effect of doing away with race-based preferences on the racial composition of highly competitive colleges and universities, see William Bowen and Derek Bok, *The Shape of the River* (Princeton: Princeton University Press, 1998), pp. 15–52; and Thomas Espenshade and Alexandria Walton Radford, *No Longer Separate, Not Yet Equal—Race and Class in Elite College Admission and Campus Life* (Princeton: Princeton University Press, 2009), pp.12–13, 339–78.

81. Discussion and evaluation of some of these theories are presented in Christopher Jencks and Meredith Phillips, eds., *The Black/White Test Score Gap* (Washington, D.C.: Brookings Institution Press, 1998).

suggested by reputable researchers as contributing to these pronounced racial differences in academic performance. Whatever
constellation of factors may be involved, however, it is becoming increasingly clear that the racial preference regime that has
been in place now for over 40 years is not only a result of these
persistent racial gaps but also a major contributor to their per-
petuation and seeming intractability. Mention has already been
made of the tendency of racial preferences to reinforce negative stigmas and stereotypes about the academic competence of
their intended beneficiaries, and about the harm this can have
in terms of heightened "stereotype threat" and similar vulner-
abilities. The harm done by preferences, however, may be much
greater in terms of their tendency to distort the incentive structure under which black and Hispanic students work for admission to the more prestigious colleges and graduate schools.

Considering the central importance that incentive structures
have in the analyses of economists and other social scientists, it
is remarkable that so little has been done in this area to illuminate the effects of across-the-board racial "plus-factoring" on
student motivation and work ethic. Bowen and Bok hardly take
up this issue at all—they mention in a single page of their 400-
page book the possibility that "the willingness of leading graduate and professional schools to admit black candidates who
did not rank at the very top of their classes" may reduce the
incentive for black students at the better colleges to strive for
top ranking. But they quickly drop the issue, saying that they
"know of no way to test this hypothesis." (p. 85) One suspects
that here, too, a fear of the answer drives the reticence of Bowen
and Bok (and others) to face this issue squarely.

It is difficult to see how an across-the-board system of racial
preferences would *not* have a harmful effect in terms of student motivation and work ethic. Affirmative-action supporters
sometimes claim that even with racial preferences in place at
all major universities, colleges, and graduate programs, there is

still a marginal payoff to getting higher grades for the minority students who receive the racial preferences.[82] Whether in high school or college, black and Hispanic students, it is argued, will always find that their higher grades are rewarded by acceptance to more highly rated colleges and graduate/professional schools, even if they are automatically given a substantial boost in the admissions process. They will thus have every incentive to strive to do their best, it is claimed, and thus there is no "perverse incentives" problem with current affirmative-action practices.

Such arguments would make sense if most high school and college students were singularly focused on putting all their efforts and energies into attending the most prestigious colleges and graduate programs to which they could gain admission, with no consideration for alternate uses of their time and effort. But this is not how most adolescents and young adults, including many of the most academically gifted, typically conduct their lives. For even the most highly motivated of students, school work is often dull and demanding, and less appealing certainly, than alternative ways to spend one's time such as

---

82 See the Bowen and Vars article, "Scholastic Aptitude Test Scores, Race, and Academic Performance in Selective Colleges and Universities," p. 475n (footnote #27). Against those who see racial-preference policy as creating disincentives to work hard for those in the beneficiary categories, Bowen and Vars respond: "Even if affirmative action were to shift upward career prospects for black graduates, the *marginal* payoffs to academic achievement should remain constant." This is true, of course, and if typical black students acted like profit-maximizing business firms in a competitive market—or like Weber's inner-worldly Puritan ascetics—one would expect no fall-off in their efforts to strive relentlessly to gain admission to the most prestigious graduate and professional schools possible, even ones well out of reach for their equally smart or smarter Asian and white classmates. However, if the ultimate goals that black students set for themselves in terms of graduate and professional schools are heavily influenced by the goals and aspirations of their white and Asian classmates, and if they can attain these goals with less study and more leisure time than these classmates and peers, then one would expect a considerable fall-off in black effort in response to the racial preferences they receive. I'll let the reader judge whether the typical American teenager and young twenty-something he/she knows who has academic talent conforms more to the profit-maximizing-firm model presupposed in the Bowen/Vars response or to the account of John McWhorter in the text describing his own education. In deciding this issue, it should be kept in mind that blacks on average receive much less pressure from home to get top grades than do whites and Asians.

sports activities, socializing with friends, partying, pursuing a hobby, or watching television or movie videos. If a talented black or Hispanic student knows that he need not work as hard or perform as well in the classroom as an equally talented—or more talented—white or Asian student to get into the same college or graduate school, the black and Hispanic student will have every reason to work less and devote more time to fun-producing activities.

The logic here is simple and commonsensical and is well laid out by John McWhorter in his reminiscence about his own days as a student in a Philadelphia private school. "I can attest," McWhorter writes,

> that in secondary school I quite deliberately refrained from working to my highest potential because I knew that I would be accepted to even top universities without doing so. Almost any black child knows from an early age that there is something called affirmative action which means that black students are admitted to schools under lower standards than white; I was aware of this from at least the age of ten. And so I was quite satisfied to make B+'s and A-'s rather than the A's and A+'s I could have made with a little extra time and effort. Granted, having the knack for school that I did I was lucky that my less-than-optimum efforts still put me within reach of fine schools. However, there is no reason that the same sentiment would not operate even in black students who happen to be less nerdy than I was . . . If every black student in the country knows that not even the most selective schools in the country require the very top grades or test scores of black students, that fine universities just below this level will readily admit them with even a B+/B dossier by virtue of their "leadership qualities" or "spark," and that even just a better-than-decent application file will grant them admission to solid second-tier selective schools, then what incentive is there

for any but the occasional highly driven student to devote his most deeply committed effort to school?[83]

McWhorter's final verdict on affirmative action is devastating: "In general," he says, "one could think of few better ways to depress a race's propensity for pushing itself to do its best in school than a policy ensuring that less-than-best efforts will have a disproportionately high yield." (p. 233) McWhorter does not believe that affirmative action is the cause of all the problems that blacks have with academic achievement. At the heart of these problems, he believes, is what he describes as a "cult of anti-intellectualism" and a preoccupation with victimhood in the black community that severely undermines the strivings of black students to perform to their maximum in the intellectual arena. He also agrees with Claude Steele's theory of "stereotype vulnerability," but believes it has been greatly exaggerated as a factor in explaining the poor academic performance of blacks. Cultural factors are more important, McWhorter contends, than the psychological factors that Steele stresses.

While affirmative action may not be the underlying cause of all the difficulties blacks face in the intellectual arena, it nevertheless greatly exacerbates these difficulties, McWhorter believes, by skewing the incentive structure black students face, especially the more talented black students who aim to go to the more prestigious colleges and professional schools. Since the degree of racial preferences given in colleges, universities, and graduate/ professional programs is known to vary directly with the ranking of the institution (i.e., the more prestigious the institution, the greater the degree of "plus-factoring" preferences), McWhorter's theory here would offer a further explanation (along with "stereotype threat") for why the degree of "underperformance"

---

83. John McWhorter, *Losing the Race—Self-Sabotage in Black America* (New York: The Free Press, 2000), p. 233.

among black college students increases as black SAT scores rise. The better a black student is in relation to his black classmates the greater the degree of "plus-factoring" bonus he can count on receiving in relation to his white and Asian classmates, and the less need he thus has to match those nonpreferentially treated classmates in terms their academic performance. Since black students respond to the incentive structures in which they have been placed, the performance gap between blacks and the nonpreferentially treated whites and Asians—i.e., the degree of "underperformance"—will increase the higher a black student stands academically among his black peers.

Outside the affirmative-action context, few have any difficulty understanding the compelling logic of what McWhorter has to say here. To give a salient example: Nancy Weiss Malkiel, a leading academic dean at Princeton University, has led a protracted and in many ways courageous effort over many years to put an end to the continuing grade inflation that has plagued Princeton, like most other elite universities, since the early 1970s. Her efforts culminated in late April 2004 when the faculty senate passed a resolution recommending a limit on A+, A, and A- grades to 35% of all grades. In a *New York Times* interview published shortly after the faculty vote, Dean Malkiel, who hopes that Princeton will set an example in the national effort to combat grade inflation, explained the logic behind her anti-grade inflation stance. Grade inflation and grade compaction, she told the *Times*, must be seen as "part of inflationary patterns of evaluation in the larger culture. . . . When students get the same grade for outstanding work that they get for good work, they are not motivated to do their best." (*New York Times*, 5 June 2004, B-2)

Malkiel explained further to the *Times* interviewer how her early experiences as an undergraduate at Smith College at a time before grade inflation—when As and A-s were very few and Cs very common—had taught her the value of an honest grading system in motivating students "to do their best." The ironic fact here is that Malkiel has been a leading defender of Princeton's affirmative action policy over the years, though one suspects more out of bureaucratic necessity than passionate conviction. In any case, the logic of her anti-grade inflation position bears a close resemblance to the logic of McWhorter and other opponents of affirmative action. The McWhorter position could be rephrased as follows: If, because of affirmative action, good work by black and Hispanic students receives the same level of reward from undergraduate and graduate school admissions committees as outstanding work by their white and Asian classmates, the black and Hispanic students will not be motivated to do their best.

Essayist Shelby Steele has made a similar point. "The top quartile of black American students," Steele writes, who often come "from two-parent families with six-figure incomes and private school educations, is frequently not competitive with whites and Asians even from lower quartiles. But it is precisely this top quartile of black students that has been most aggressively pursued for the last thirty years with affirmative-action preferences. Infusing the atmosphere of their education from early childhood is not the idea that they will have to steel themselves to face stiff competition but that they will receive a racial preference, that mediocrity will win for them what only excellence wins for others. Out of deference, elite universities have offered the license *not* to compete to the most privileged segment of black youth . . . And because blacks are given spaces they have not won by competition, whites and especially Asians have had to compete all the harder for their spots. So we end up with the effect we always get with deferential reforms: an incentive for black weakness relative to others."[84]

---

84. Shelby Steele, *A Dream Deferred* (New York: Harper Collins Publishers, 1998), pp. 126–7.

Another way to think about the problem is this: Imagine that admissions committees throughout the United States at both the undergraduate and graduate/professional school level adopted the strictest of race-blind admissions policies and did not even know the race or ethnicity of their applicants. Applicants were always judged on the basis of their scores on standardized tests and their grades in high school or college. Assume that these policies were generally well-known and understood by all. But imagine too, that it became the general practice in all mixed-race secondary schools and colleges for classroom teachers to automatically raise by a substantial degree the grades of black and Hispanic students on all tests, term papers, and classroom work. A paper or test that was of a quality that would earn a B if handed in by a white or Asian student would automatically be given an A- if handed in by a black or Hispanic student. Similarly, the standard of quality that would garner a B+ for a white or Asian student would garner a straight A for a student who was black or Hispanic. Assume that the Educational Testing Service followed a similar policy. Although ETS never revealed to colleges and graduate schools the race of their test takers (and institutions of higher learning were prohibited from inquiring about the race of their applicants), ETS automatically added to the scores of black and Hispanic test-takers a 100-point bonus on each of the sections of the SAT and a comparable boost (about 1 SD) on the other standardized tests ETS administers (GRE, LSAT, etc.). As in the case of the color-blind admissions committees, imagine that students everywhere understood how this "plus-factoring" system worked in both the classroom and at ETS.

The incentive structure faced by black and Hispanic students under this imagined system would be identical to that of our current affirmative-action regime. At least for those who are focused on going to a good college or graduate school, it makes little difference whether the automatic boost one gets for being black or Hispanic takes place at the classroom level and on the ETS scoring system or in the admissions offices of the nation's undergraduate colleges, graduate schools, and professional schools. The perversity of the system in terms of undermining the incentives for blacks and Hispanics "to do their best" would be the same in both cases. Under both systems all but the most highly self-motivated black and Hispanic students—or those receiving the greatest degree of grade pressure from home—would have good reason to cut themselves a good deal of slack and leisure time in their academic pursuits and let the whites and Asians toil away to get their good grades. Under both systems, a talented black or Hispanic student need not work as hard or perform as well as a comparably talented white or Asian student to get into a good college or graduate school. Under both systems one would expect a substantial black and Hispanic "performance gap" to develop even if there were no harmful cultural or psychological factors at work to make matters worse. And under both systems one would expect the black-white and black-Asian difference in learning and performance to increase as one ascended the scale of black talent.

When the perverse incentives of the affirmative-action system are added to the "cultural disconnect" that McWhorter and others have drawn attention to and when to these two factors are added the "stereotype threat" dynamic that Claude Steele has explored, the result can be the extreme gaps in learning that we see among so many black students, even those from economically and educationally privileged backgrounds. Berkeley anthropologist John Ogbu was asked a few years before his untimely death in 2003 to go to Shaker Heights, an affluent mixed-race community in suburban Cleveland, to find out why black students in the Shaker Heights public school system did so poorly compared with their white counterparts. Ogbu holds a "cultural impediments" view of black underachievement similar to that of McWhorter; he is the researcher who first brought attention to the fact that for many black youngsters in the inner-city ghetto working hard in school was shunned not only as nerdy and "uncool" but also as "acting white." And he saw much of his cultural impediments theory confirmed even among the middle-class black students in Shaker Heights whose parents were well-educated and economically quite comfortable.

The title of Ogbu's study of the situation, *Black American Students in an Affluent Suburb—A Study of Academic Disengagement*, well summarizes his findings.[85] By all accounts, including those of several black teachers, black administrators, and the black students themselves, black students in Shaker Heights, Ogbu found, take their academic work much less seriously on average than do the whites; they are less focused on their studies; and they display what Ogbu calls a "low effort syndrome" or working just hard enough to get by. Ogbu does not speculate on the effect that the affirmative-action policies at America's better colleges may have on these tendencies, but it is hard to imagine that such policies do not negatively impact the work ethic of the more academically talented black students in communities like Shaker Heights and other integrated suburbs.

Ogbu's findings are also consistent with those of a much larger research project carried out by developmental psychologist Laurence Steinberg and his colleagues. The Steinberg team, which consisted of psychologists, sociologists, psychiatrists, and educational researchers from Stanford, Temple, and the University of Wisconsin, surveyed more than 20,000 students and their families in nine largely middle-class high schools in Wisconsin and Northern California.[86] One finding of the Steinberg team,

---

85. John U. Ogbu, *Black American Students in an Affluent Suburb: A Study of Academic Disengagement* (Mayway, NJ: Lawrence Erlbaum Associates, 2003). Ogbu's seminal article on the "acting white" phenomenon, co-authored with Signithia Fordham, is titled "Black Students' School Success: Coping with the Burden of Acting White," *The Urban Review*, 18:3 (1986), pp. 1–31.
86. Laurence Steinberg, *Beyond the Classroom* (New York: Simon and Schuster, 1996.)

consistent with much other research, is that the typical American high school student doesn't work very hard and is only moderately interested in doing well in school. What Ogbu calls "low-effort syndrome" and "academic disengagement" were found to be common in the typical American high school, and this was true for whites as well as blacks. The typical American high school student works as hard as need be to avoid academic trouble, while only a minority strive for academic excellence or are focused on getting into a highly competitive college.

Of the minority who are academically focused, however, Steinberg and his colleagues found—much to their surprise— huge ethnic differences. "Of all the demographic factors we studied in relation to school performance, ethnicity is the most important," they write, with Asian students clearly outshining all other groups in terms of the amount of time they spend on homework, how attentive they are in class, how strongly they value academic success, and how likely they are to have academically-oriented peers. (pp. 86 ff.) White students stood considerably behind the Asians on these measures, and the Hispanics and blacks considerably behind the whites.

Paralleling these trends, the Steinberg team found clear differences in the level of the demands that parents placed on their children in terms of acceptable school performance. Asked what would be the lowest grade they could come home with without their parents getting angry, the typical Asian said A-, the typical white somewhere between B and C, and the typical black or Hispanic C-. (p. 161) Steinberg also found a yawning gap between the Asian students, on the one hand, and the black and Hispanic students on the other, in terms of their belief in how harmful not doing well in school would have on their future. While members of all groups expressed belief in the value of a good education, "many Black and Latino students don't really believe that doing poorly in school will hurt their chances for future success." (p. 91)

Other researchers, including Abigail and Stephen Thernstrom,[87] have found similar patterns distinguishing the four ethno-racial groups studied by the Steinberg team. Asians seem to work the hardest in high school and to be the least focused on social life, partying, sports, and other kinds of diversion that compete with school work, while Hispanics and blacks display the opposite pattern (whites usually come out in the middle). Blacks seem to be particularly enamored of television watching and spend twice as many hours before the TV screen as whites. While it is beyond question that there are important cultural, psychological, and historical factors at work that account for much of these differences, it is difficult to avoid the conclusion that the disincentives of the affirmative-action system also come into play. Asians work harder, in part, because they and their parents know that to get into a good college they have to work harder than an equally talented black or Hispanic student. But like John McWhorter, the more academically talented black and Hispanic students, along with most of their middle-class parents, know that there is this thing called "affirmative action" that allows blacks and Hispanics to attend highly rated colleges and universities with much lower grades and test scores than those of their white and Asian peers. To repeat McWhorter's indictment, "one could think of few better ways to depress a race's propensity for pushing itself to do its best in school than a policy ensuring that less-than-best efforts will have a disproportionately high yield." Perhaps, too, it is no accident that the black respondents in the Bowen and Bok study, looking back many years later on their days as undergraduate students, were much more likely than their white counterparts to say that they

---

87. Stephen and Abigail Thernstrom, *No Excuses* (New York: Simon and Schuster, 2003).

wish they had studied more in college.[88] The affirmative action regime clearly seems to be part of the problem here.

DO UNDERGRADUATE AFFIRMATIVE-ACTION PROGRAMS BENEFIT WHITES AND ASIANS IN THE POST-COLLEGE EMPLOYMENT ARENA?

Defenders of racial-preference policies in college admissions often claim not only that such policies help white and Asian students gain a better understanding of blacks, Latinos, and members of other ethno-racial minorities but also that this enhanced cultural knowledge is a great economic asset in a globalized economy. Affirmative-action policies, it is said, by furthering cultural knowledge, have a positive effect on the post-college job performance of all parties involved, including whites and Asians, and help to make American businesses more competitive in the global marketplace. Originally employed in a quite different form within the medical school context by Justice Lewis Powell in his *Bakke* decision, this line of reasoning proved persuasive

---

88. Bowen and Bok write: "More than half (57 percent) of all black graduates in the '76 cohort felt that they didn't study enough while in college; 40 percent of their white classmates expressed the same regret." "The members of the '89 cohort expressed essentially the same set of views; an even higher fraction of black graduates wished that they had studied more [65 percent vs. 41 percent for whites]." "These retrospective expressions of regret by African American respondents need to be thought about in the context of the debate over factors affecting their academic performance . . . especially the suggestion that peer group pressures discourage studying." (Bowen and Bok, *The Shape of the River*, p. 208). Even more than the issue of peer group pressures, we need to think about this underperformance within the context of an all-pervasive U.S. preference regime that makes it much easier for black college graduates to get accepted to graduate schools, professional schools, and jobs in the corporate and government sectors than their white and Asian classmates. Blacks in college know that they don't have to do as well academically as their white and Asian peers to get accepted to the same post-graduate programs and same jobs after college. It's hard to imagine that this isn't a factor in the decision some blacks make about how hard they will work in college.

to Justice Sandra Day O'Connor in her majority ruling in the *Grutter* case (2003), where she claimed that ethno-racial diversity in higher education was a truly "compelling" state interest that could override the constitution's otherwise central demand for a color-blind system of university and professional school admissions in all state-sponsored institutions.

Summarizing and endorsing the arguments of several of the amicus briefs that had been submitted to the court, O'Connor wrote: "Numerous studies show that student body diversity promotes learning outcomes and 'better prepares students for an increasingly diverse workforce and society' . . . These benefits are not theoretical but real, as major American businesses have made clear that the skills needed in today's increasingly global marketplace can only be developed through exposure to widely diverse people, cultures, ideas, and viewpoints." (*Grutter v. Bollinger*, 539 U.S. 306)

To critics, some of the claims implied in O'Connor's decision seemed wrong on their very face since many of the countries that have been most successful in the globalized economy in recent years—including Norway, Taiwan, Japan, and South Korea—are countries with unusually homogeneous workforces in terms of race, ethnicity, religion, and language, and outside their companies' global marketing departments, their workforces and corporate management generally consist of people who have attended schools with others very much like themselves. There is an extensive management literature on this topic, which suggests that racially and ethnicly diverse workforces, while they may sometimes produce beneficial cross-fertilization of ideas, often encounter severe problems with communication, group cohesiveness, lack of common purpose and common goals, diminished trust, and general difficulties in staff members getting along. These latter disadvantages often outweigh any potentially positive effects of diversity.[89]

Some of the most successful international companies have been those run by members of a single, homogeneous ethnic group that can easily avoid such problems—often very cohesive groups like the Hong Kong Chinese, Ashkenazic and Sephardic Jews, Lebanese Christians, and Indian Gujaratis that combine ethnic homogeneity with extensive past experience as middlemen traders, money lenders, or entrepreneurs. Ethnic homogeneity in such groups leads to greater trust, understanding, and ease of communication, all of which contribute to lower transaction costs in conducting business. Racial, ethnic, regional, linguistic, and religious diversity within a workforce is more often than not seen by those who run large companies as a challenge to be managed rather than a source of organizational strength. The diversity-improves-international- competitiveness claim is thus highly dubious—the preponderance of evidence around the world suggests that ethno-racial homogeneity, not heterogeneity, is more likely to improve local and international competitiveness.[90]

89. For a good summary of the extensive management literature see Francis Miliken and Luis Martins, "Searching for Common Threads: Understanding the Multiple Effects of Diversity in Organizational Groups," *Academy of Management Review*, 21(1996):402–33.
90. See, for instance, Joel Kotkin, *Tribes: How Race, Religion, and Identity Determine Success in the New Global Economy* (New York: Random House, 1993); Francis Fukuyama, *Trust: The Social Virtues and the Creation of Prosperity* (New York: The Free Press, 1995); Janet Landa, "A Theory of the Ethnically Homogeneous Middleman Group: An Institutional Alternative to Contract Law," *The Journal of Legal Studies*, 10 (1981):349–62; Amy Chua, *World on Fire* (New York: Doubleday, 2003); Ivan Light, *Ethnic Enterprise in America* (Berkeley: University of California Press, 1972); Thomas Sowell, *Race and Culture: A World View* (New York: Basic Books, 1994); Edna Bonacich, "A Theory of Middlemen Minorities," *American Sociological Review* 38 (1972): 583–94; Robert Silin, *Leadership and Values: The Organization of Large Scale Taiwanese Enterprises* (Cambridge, MA: Harvard University Press, 1976); Alice

On the more specific issue of whether in America today whites and Asians benefit in the contemporary labor market from the greater exposure to blacks and Latinos facilitated through their college's affirmative-action programs, there is at least one important study on this question, and its conclusions are hardly consistent with the claims made by affirmative-action supporters. The study, by Duke University economists Peter Arcidiacono and Jacob Vigdor, carries particular weight since it is based on an analysis of 30 selective colleges and universities taken from the same database used by Bowen and Bok to draw their pro-affirmative-action conclusions in *The Shape of the River*—the Andrew W. Mellon Foundation's College and Beyond survey.[91]

Arcidiacono and Vigdor looked at what they call the "little-tested hypothesis that increasing minority representation in elite colleges generates tangible benefits for majority-race students"—where "majority-race students" is interpreted to mean Asians as well as whites and "minority representation" refers to the proportion of blacks and Hispanics in an undergraduate college's student body (Native Americans were also included in the minority category, but they are almost everywhere an insignificant part of the composite statistic). The "tangible benefits" Arcidiacono and Vigdor looked at involve four outcome variables from the College and Beyond dataset: (1) the likelihood

Amsden, *Asia's Next Giant: South Korea and Late Industrialization* (New York: Oxford University Press, 1989); and Werner Sombart's classic, *The Jews and Modern Capitalism* (New York: E.P. Dutton, 1913).

91. The institutions surveyed were the following: Barnard, Bryn Mawr, Columbia, Denison, Duke, Emory, Georgetown, Hamilton, Kenyon, Miami University (Ohio); Northwestern, Oberlin, Penn State, Princeton, Rice, Smith, Stanford, Swarthmore, Tufts, Tulane, University of Michigan (Ann Arbor), University of North Carolina (Chapel Hill), University of Notre Dame, University of Pennsylvania, Vanderbilt, Washington University (Saint Louis), Wellesley, Wesleyan University, Williams, and Yale. Peter Arcidiacono and Jacob Vigdor, "Does the River Spill Over? Estimating the Economic Returns to Attending a Racially Diverse College," Dec. 23, 2008, pp. 1–23, at http://econ.edu/~psarcidi.

of completing college; (2) the level of income in the post-college years; (3) satisfaction with one's job; and (4) the level of general satisfaction with one's life after college. Based on the rhetoric one hears among affirmative-action supporters—including Justices Powell and O'Connor—one would expect at least some evidence of a positive effect on one or more of these outcome variables as colleges enroll greater proportions of minority students.

But Arcidiacono and Vigdor found almost nothing to confirm the optimistic claims that white and Asian students benefit from having attended colleges with higher percentages of blacks and Hispanics. "Our empirical results cover a broad range of outcomes, including earnings, educational attainment, and satisfaction with both one's life and one's job," they write. "Across these varying specifications, we fail to find any significant evidence that white or Asian students who attend more diverse colleges do better later in life." "In general, we find that the type of diversity increase brought about by affirmative action policies—which brings lower-scoring minority students into potential contact with higher-scoring majority-race students—is if anything detrimental to majority-race students." While black and Hispanic students may derive some benefit from racial-preference policies, "the majority-race students do not benefit and may in fact endure a cost." (pp. 17–19) Whites and Asians do not earn more, do not learn more, and show no indication of having been more satisfied with their life, their college experience, or their job for having attended a college with a higher percentage of blacks and Hispanics. Looking across the 30 C&B institutions, they find that higher minority enrollment often leads to lower scores by whites and Asians on these desirable outcomes.

The result of their analysis, Arcidiacono and Vigdor say, "strongly suggests that the predominant policy tool designed to increase the representation of minority groups, affirmative action, has a negative net impact on students not directly targeted by the program." If this is the case, they conclude, preferential admissions for certain groups "should be understood for what they are: redistributive mechanisms that create benefits for the targeted racial groups but costs for others." (pp. 19–20)

Arcidiacono and Vigdor do not believe that it is simply the higher percentage of black and Hispanic students on a college campus that has negative effects for whites and Asians. Rather, it is the fact that at so many of the nation's most competitive colleges the actual black and Hispanic students on campus are much less academically qualified than other students, and this fact seems to be decisive in reducing the achievement level—in college and beyond—for their white and Asian peers. It is the high numbers of black and Hispanic students in combination with their lower achievement levels that has the harmful effect. The lower-scoring blacks and Hispanics, when present in sufficient numbers, seem to have a deleterious spill-over effect on their higher-scoring white and Asian peers. Although Arcidiacono and Vigdor do not speculate on the causal mechanisms involved, it may be that the lower-scoring minority students have an adverse effect on the overall intellectual atmosphere and work ethic on campus that affects a much wider circle of students. If this is so, the effect would be similar to what many claim results from large numbers of academically deficient athletes on college campuses. Large numbers of "dumb jocks" affect the overall campus intellectual environment and negatively impact the campus work ethic. This, in turn, would affect future job prospects and other developments that affect later life satisfaction.

Arcidicono and Vigdor show that the negative outcomes for whites and Asians of having more blacks and Hispanics on a college campus disappear when the focus is on whites and Asians attending colleges with weak or non-existent affirmative action programs—a situation often found in those institutions below the highest levels of competitiveness and prestige.[92] The researchers conclude that if one of the goals of integration within the American college and university system is to benefit majority-race students in tangible ways, it is not being furthered by a policy of placing black and Hispanic students in institutions where their academic credentials are inferior to those of their white and Asian peers. "Policies that introduce disparities between the academic backgrounds of minority and non-minority students," they write, "are unlikely to generate benefits for non-minorities, and may in fact be costly in the aggregate." (p. 17)

"A policy of maximizing the benefits of diversity accruing to majority-race students," Arcidiacono and Vigdor conclude, "would involve reducing or eliminating cross-race differences in admission standards"—that is, it would dispense with racial-preference programs and institute a uniform standard of college admissions, placing black and Hispanic students in institutions where they are academically competitive with others. When "minority students are transferred from campuses where their academic background is comparable to their peers of other races

---

92. It is easy to forget in the controversy over affirmative action that the vast majority of four-year colleges and all community colleges have high rates of acceptance and do not practice racial preferencing. In a widely cited study, Harvard economist Thomas Kane found that "the use of race in college admissions appears to be limited to the most selective 20 percent of four-year institutions." At these institutions, however, race was seen to weigh heavily in admissions decisions: "being black or Hispanic has approximately the same effect on one's chances of admission as two-thirds of a grade point performance in high school [e.g., an "A-" vs. a "B" in a student's grade-point average] or roughly 400 points [out of 1600] on the SAT test." Arcidiacono and Vigdor draw upon the Kane study in formulating their own conclusions. (Thomas Kane, "Racial and Ethnic Preferences in College Admissions," in Jencks and Phillips, eds., *The Black-White Test Score Gap*, pp. 431–56, 451–2.) Similarly, large admissions boosts at the more highly competitive colleges were found in a more recent study by Thomas Espenshade and Alexandria Walton Radford, *No Longer Separate, Not Yet Equal—Race and Class in Elite College Admission and Campus Life* (Princeton: Princeton University Press, 2009). On an all-other-things-equal basis, Espenshade and Radford found that at the eight highly selective colleges they studied, on a 1600-point scale being black over being white confers a 310 SAT point admissions advantage; the black-over-Asian advantage was 450 points.

to campuses where their credentials are on average significantly worse than those of their peers," Arcidiacono and Vigdor write, the effect is generally "detrimental to majority-race students." While the authors do not believe that this kind of "mismatching" necessarily hurts black and Hispanic students in terms of the four outcome variables they explore, they clearly believe that it harms their white and Asian peers. Justices Powell and O'Connor are clearly wrong, they believe, to suggest otherwise. (pp. 17–20)

MISMATCHING STUDENTS IN LAW SCHOOL

The affirmative action preference regime doesn't end, of course, at the level of the undergraduate college. Law schools, medical schools, business schools, and many graduate programs in the arts and sciences pursue goals of racial and ethnic "diversity" with equal or greater zeal than those championed at the elite undergraduate institutions. And as at the undergraduate institutions, "diversity" and "affirmative action" at the graduate and professional school level come to be defined primarily in terms of blacks and Hispanics. A "diverse" student body according to an unwritten rule of thumb is one in which black and Hispanic students each comprise at a minimum 5–7 percent of a school's overall enrollment (roughly half, that is, of each group's share in the general American population). A school with a substantially smaller proportion of these two targeted minorities would not be considered "diverse" by academic administrators, and a decrement involving blacks and Hispanics cannot be made up by increased enrollment of other underrepresented groups.

Members of many other demographic groups may be grossly underrepresented at elite graduate and professional schools— e.g., poor whites from Appalachia, born-again Christians from the Bible Belt, military veterans, people who have grown up on farms or ranches, working-class "white ethnics," non-Hispanic urban Catholics, Mormons, Muslims, people from small towns, married students with children, etc.—but they count for little or nothing in the way most academic administrators set their "diversity" goals. An increased number of the members of these other groups will not be seen as offsetting a low black or Hispanic enrollment.

Affirmative-action programs at graduate and professional schools are like their counterparts at undergraduate institutions in yet another way—such programs have been shrouded in secrecy and are routinely misrepresented to the general public by academic administrators. As in the case of undergraduate programs, supporters of affirmative-action policies at graduate and professional schools have generally shown little interest in a fair evaluation of the costs and benefits of the policies, and little in the way of high-quality research has been done on the effect they have on those they are intended to help. An exception is the continuing research of Richard H. Sander.

Sander, an economist and professor of law at UCLA Law School, published a path-breaking study in the November 2004 issue of the *Stanford Law Review* on the effect of affirmative-action policies on blacks seeking to enter the legal profession. A lifelong Democrat who has been active in the enforcement of antidiscrimination housing law—and who is also the concerned parent of an mixed-race black/white child—Sander was troubled by the unwillingness of most law school administrators to discuss openly the nature of their affirmative-action programs or to submit them to honest evaluation by competent researchers. Sander's own view on affirmative action is pragmatic, in the sense that he believes racial-preference policies at law schools would be fully justified if they can be shown to work in the way their defenders claim they do and if they actually produce more and better minority attorneys. He has no objection to racial preferences on moral, legal, or constitutional grounds. His research, however, has led him to conclude that the conventional wisdom propounded by affirmative-action supporters is totally mistaken, and that at least in the case of blacks in law schools, current affirmative-action policies do great harm to the career prospects of many of those they are supposed to benefit.

Sander's research is based on analysis of several large databases, including the huge Bar Passage Study (BPS) compiled in the period from 1991 to 1997 by the Law School Admission Council. This study contains extensive information on over 27,000 students who first entered law school in 1991. Almost 95 percent of the nation's accredited law schools participated in the study, which tracked the progress of the 1991 cohort of law students over a six-year period—enough time for most to graduate, take the bar exam (in some cases multiple times), and land their first job. Included in the BPS database is information on the entering students' race, undergraduate grade-point average, score on the Law School Admissions Test (LSAT), grades and class rank obtained in law school, and performance on state bar exams. What Sander found in his analysis of the BPS data is riveting.

For instance, at all but the few historically black law schools, from the most elite national institutions down to the lowest state schools, the black/white gap in the academic credentials of entering students is enormous. Using a 1000-point scale that gives 400 points for a perfect undergraduate grade-point average (4.0 x 100) and 600 points for a perfect LSAT score—a formula Sander says is similar to that used by many law schools in assessing applicants for admission—Sander shows that entering black law students are typically two full standard deviations behind their white counterparts in their level of academic accomplishment. This is an enormous difference, which guarantees that there will be almost no overlap between black and white students—the higher achieving blacks will barely equal the lowest achieving whites.

This huge "credentials gap," Sander shows, exists at all levels of the law school hierarchy.[93] The most elite law schools, he says, believe they must all have a certain healthy percentage of black students—in practice, 6–8 percent—and given the fact that there are relatively few blacks who score at the same level as the highest-scoring whites and Asians, to meet their goals they are willing to accept black students with test scores and grades that would not meet their normal admissions threshold. At the 14 most elite schools in his study, whites had a median academic index of 875 (equivalent to an undergraduate GPA of 3.75 and an LSAT score of 170), while the black median was only 705 (equivalent to an undergraduate GPA of 3.05 and an LSAT score of 160). The median black score was 2.3 standard deviations below the median score achieved by whites.

The preference regime, however, does not stop at the first-tier institutions, because the law schools below them on the selectivity scale, Sander says, also want 6–8 percent blacks in their entering classes and fear they will be called racists if they have substantially fewer blacks. They thus face a dilemma caused by the fact that almost all of the black students who could have met their admissions standards without preferences have been admitted to—and usually wind up enrolling in—the more elite institutions that lie above them. The first-tier law schools thus siphon off black students who, in the absence of racial preferences, would be attending second- and third-tier institutions, causing a shortage of qualified blacks at these places. The second- and third-tier institutions then, likewise fearful of being called racist, respond to this situation by granting huge racial preferences of their own, and in the process deprive the fourth-

93. His conclusions on this score are thus different from the studies of affirmative-action policies at undergraduate institutions where preference polices seem to be important primarily at the more competitive schools (and unimportant or nonexistent at the vast majority of schools).

and fifth-tier law schools of students who could meet their own admissions criteria. This preference-granting process proceeds to the very bottom of the law school pecking order, where the lowest-ranked schools feel compelled to admit a significant number of blacks who have such poor academic qualifications that were they white or Asian, they would not be admitted to any of America's 182 accredited law schools.

There is thus a "cascading effect" at work in which black applicants are shuffled into law schools that are usually one or two levels of selectivity above the ones they would have gained entry into if all law schools had observed race-blind admissions policies. Sander describes this cascading process in the following words:

> Affirmative action . . . has a cascading effect through American legal education. The use of large boosts for black applicants at the top law schools means that the highest-scoring blacks are almost entirely absorbed by the highest tier. Schools in the next tier have no choice but to either enroll very few blacks or use racial boosts or segregated admissions tracks to the same degree as the top-tier schools. The same pattern continues all the way down the hierarchy. . . . At the bulk of law schools, the very large preferences granted to blacks only exist in order to offset the effects of preferences used by higher-ranked schools. . . . The use of these preferences by elite schools give nearly all other law schools little choice but to follow suit. [The result is that] blacks are consistently bumped up several seats in the law school hierarchy, producing a large black-white gap at nearly all law schools in the academic credentials of students. (pp. 149–51)

This upward ratcheting seems unjust to most critics of affirmative action, but Sander, who avoids normative controversies in his study, focuses on what he sees as the great practical harm that a system-wide policy of racial preferences will have on black students both in law school and on the state bar exams. Upward ratcheting results, he says, in a serious mismatch of blacks with the law schools they attend, such that many find themselves in academic environments that are too competitive for their individual abilities and needs. The result, he says, is that they are frequently overwhelmed by the law school material, get very poor grades, wind up graduating at the very bottom of their law school classes (if they don't drop out or flunk out before graduation), learn much less law in law school, and have much greater difficulty passing the state bar exams.

The statistics Sander compiles are stunning: At the most elite law schools in the BPS database, 52 percent of blacks—more than half—had first-year grades that placed them in the bottom 10 percent of the grade distribution, while only 8 percent of blacks did well enough to place in the top half. The median black student at these elite schools had first-year grades equivalent to those of whites at only the 5–6th percentile of the white distribution. The situation was much the same throughout the entire law school system. At the 163 law schools surveyed in the BPS database the median black grade-point average at the end of the first year was equivalent to those of whites at the 7–8th percentile. In terms of grades, the typical black in other words did more poorly in his first year at most American law schools than all but the very lowest-achieving white students—92 percent of whites did better than the median black.

And there is no tendency for the black students to catch up with the whites in the second and third year of law school. A slight drop in the black/white grade gap does occur between the first and third year of law school, but Sander says it is mainly due to the fact that many of the lowest-achieving blacks drop out of law school before completing their final year, thus raising the black average among those who remain enrolled. The black drop-out rate is twice that of whites, with 19.3 percent of blacks failing to graduate after five years, compared with 8.2 percent of whites.

Some may view law school grades as unimportant. But Sander shows that law school grades are in fact closely related to a student's chances of passing the bar exam and becoming a licensed attorney. And the bar failure rate of blacks is very high. In the BPS study 38.6 percent of black law school graduates who took the bar exam failed on their first attempt, and 22.4 percent could not pass even after five tries. These numbers, of course, do not include the 19.3 percent of black law school matriculants who dropped out of law school and never got to the point of taking the bar exam. The black failure rate after five attempts was six times the white rate. And the bar failure rate, Sander found, was substantially higher among blacks at virtually every level of entering academic index scores. For instance, among whites with an index score in the 520–580 range, 26 percent failed to pass the bar exam on their first try. The comparable figure for blacks in this range was 47 percent. At the 460–520 range, 34 percent of whites were first-time failures, but 55 percent of blacks.

One might think that we have another instance here of "underperformance," perhaps one caused by "stereotype threat," "pernicious incentives," or some other race-linked factor. But Sander shows that this is not likely to be the case, since within a given law school the small number of whites with index scores just as low as the blacks have roughly the same chance of failing the bar exam. The real problem, Sander believes, is that of "institutional mismatch." Regardless of their race, law students with very low index scores relative to their peers do worse in terms of bar exam performance than those with similar index scores attending less competitive institutions. The huge difference shown nationally in bar passage rates between blacks and whites who enter law school with the same index score, Sander shows, is entirely a result of the fact that blacks are much more likely to be mismatched than whites. Whites are more likely to attend law schools where others have index scores similar to their own, while the majority of blacks are put in institutions where their index score places them at or near the very bottom of the class.

Sander believes that regardless of a student's race, a student will learn more at an institution where the other students have similar levels of academic aptitude and accomplishment than at one in which almost all of the student's peers are smarter or more intellectually accomplished. He gives as an example of the mismatch process his own encounter with a difficult introductory German course that he took during his freshman year at Harvard. Acknowledging that he does not have great talent for foreign languages, Sander explains that when he got to Harvard, where most of the introductory language students had much more aptitude for the subject than he did, the pace of the course was simply too fast for him to keep up with the others. As a result, he became overwhelmed after only a few weeks, fell behind, learned little German, and almost wound up flunking the course (even though, he says, it is *very* difficult to fail a course at Harvard, which is notorious for its grade inflation policies). Had the students not been as good as Harvard students at language learning, and the pace of the course more consistent with his own more modest level of foreign language ability, he would have learned much more German, he believes.

Sander also gives evidence from his many years as a law school professor, and says that students who begin a course bewildered by some of the initial concepts often do not catch on as the semester advances and make little progress. Mismatching students with their peers is a very harmful pedagogical strategy, Sander believes, which has a severe effect in terms of reducing how much blacks learn in law school, increases their chances of dropping out, lowers the grades they will receive, and substantially decreases their chances of passing the bar exam.

Regardless of race, it is much better, Sander's study shows, for a student to attend a law school where the student is nearer the middle of the class in terms of academic qualifications and where the student can achieve B range grades, rather than one in which a student is at the very bottom of the heap and struggles to get Cs. While more selective institutions offer the allurement of greater prestige, for many students, Sander contends, this prestige is purchased at the price of a severe mismatching penalty. "If one is at academic risk of not doing well at a particular school," Sander writes, "one is better off attending a less elite school and getting decent grades." (p. 176)

Sander sums up the harms of affirmative-action mismatching in the following statement:

> Blacks and whites at the same school with the same grades perform identically on the bar exam; but since racial preferences have the effect of boosting blacks' school quality but sharply lowering their average grades, blacks have much higher failure rates on the bar than do whites with similar LSATs and undergraduate GPAs. Affirmative action thus artificially depresses, quite substantially, the rate at which blacks pass the bar. Combined with the effects of law school attrition [that can also be attributed to affirmative-action policies], many blacks admitted to law school with the aid of racial preferences face long odds against ever becoming lawyers. (p. 107)

The elimination of affirmative-action preferences, says Sander, would actually *increase* the total number of blacks who successfully pass the bar exam each year and go on to become lawyers. Under a race-blind policy of university admissions, 84 percent of current black law school applicants, he calculates, would gain entry to at least some law school, where most would achieve much higher grades and learn more basic law than under the present system of universal upward ratcheting. While the remaining 16 percent would not be admitted to any law school, Sander says that these would mainly be the students whose index scores are so low that they would be unlikely to become successful lawyers under any circumstances and would probably be better off seeking an alternate occupation. Sander estimates that eliminating all racial preferences—and the mismatching penalty that goes with them—would increase the number of blacks who become lawyers by 8 percent.

Sander sees another advantage to this strategy. The higher grades and greater amount of law learned would not only decrease the black drop-out rate and increase black passage rates on state bar exams, but it would also have payoffs in terms of higher income and greater success of black lawyers in securing jobs. Using the results of a more recent database on life after law school that he himself has helped to gather, Sander concludes that law school grades may be more important than law school prestige in determining a law school graduate's desirability to an employer and the amount of income he actually earns as a lawyer. "In all schools outside the top ten," Sander writes, "there is a large market penalty for being in or near the bottom of the class." (p. 190) For example, lawyers in his study who graduated from a third-tier law school with a healthy B average (3.25–3.49) earned $80,000 per year, while those who had attended a more prestigious second-tier school but received C range grades (averages between 2.50–2.74) earned only $49,000 per year. Even at the fourth- and fifth-tier schools those with B averages did much better in terms of income than the typical C student at the second-tier schools, earning, respectively, $65,000 and $57,000 per year. (p. 190)

Sander is unequivocal in his condemnation of affirmative-action policies at America's law schools: "A growing body of evidence suggests that students who attend schools where they are at a significant academic disadvantage suffer a variety of ill effects, from the erosion of aspirations to a simple failure to learn as much as they do in an environment where their credentials match their peers. . . . Blacks are the victims of law school programs of affirmative action, not the beneficiaries. The programs set blacks up for failure in school, aggravate attrition rates, turn the bar exam into a major hurdle, disadvantage most blacks in the job market, and depress the overall production of black lawyers." (pp. 107, 211)

The solution to the problem, Sander believes, is amazingly simple: affirmative action policies at law schools must go, with strict race-blind policies put in their place. "By every means I have been able to quantify," he writes, "blacks as a whole would be unambiguously better off in a system without any racial preferences at all than they are under the current regime." (p. 212) While the proportion of blacks at the most prestigious schools would drop precipitously under a race-blind system to 1 or 2 percent of the student body, many of the schools below the top, Sander says, would benefit greatly by having better qualified black students in numbers not dramatically different from those at present. Even if affirmative-action preferences were not entirely eliminated but substantially reduced—Sander suggests the possibility of top schools reducing their black target goals from the current 6–8 percent range to 4 percent—major benefits would follow, Sander believes, in terms of producing more and better-educated black lawyers.

CONCLUSION

Many years ago, during the acrimonious confrontations over school busing, economist Thomas Sowell observed that for many of its supporters busing had become not so much a policy as a crusade. With a policy, Sowell explained, one asks, "What are the costs?" "What are the benefits?" "Will it achieve its goal?" A crusade, however, is different. With a crusade, said Sowell, the question simply becomes, "Whose side are you on!? The Lord's or his enemies?"

There may be a close parallel here to the affirmative action controversy. For its affluent white supporters—i.e., people like Derek Bok and William Bowen—affirmative action does indeed resemble a moral and religious crusade rather than a rationally considered policy. Its main purpose seems to be the symbolic cleansing of an evil white society from its racist past, whose real logic must be sought in a ritual of sin and redemption rather than an analysis of the actual costs and benefits of the policy. Seen in this light, affirmative action becomes a form of racial penance, a public display of racial virtue, whose emotional center of gravity lies in the expiatory needs of its guilty white supporters more than the real needs of its intended beneficiaries. For its guilt-ridden white supporters affirmative action is a public way of atoning for the past misdeeds of their race. It is a way of proclaiming to black people: We white people are sorry for our past sins and are trying to make amends! The actual effect of the policy in terms of black academic performance, race relations on campus, incentive structures, stigma reinforcement, cascading effects, mismatching penalties, "stereotype threat," "social distancing", failure on the bar exams and in science majors, etc. becomes purely secondary to this overriding symbolic and cathartic purpose. It is for this reason that affirmative action—like a crusade—is often impervious to rational criticism.

One can get a good idea of the deep, existential attachment its affluent white supporters often feel toward the policy from comments by the former career diplomat and Harvard research fellow Lawrence Harrison. Harrison is well aware that affirmative action has huge costs in terms of unintended consequences and widespread hostility on the part of significant segments of the public. Indeed, in a section on the topic in his book *Who Prospers?*, he goes over some of these costs with remarkable candor and in considerable detail.[94] Affirmative action, Harrison acknowledges, "is discrimination against whites, and no euphemism can change that." (p. 213) He sees many other problems with affirmative action and cites several of the criticisms of the policy by Thomas Sowell with apparent approval: Affirmative action has very limited public support; it is deeply resented by many whites; it casts aside the highly worthy principle of merit; it strengthens racial divisions within American society; and in the long run it could lead to the re-segregation of America. (pp. 213–14) In addition, Harrison acknowledges that the policy is not targeted at the worst-off among its black beneficiaries but often helps those least in need of help; it taints the credentials not only of all who benefit from it, but of all who are of the same race as those who benefit from it; it suggests to outsiders that blacks are inferior and cannot make it on their own without racial favoritism; and once in place, the policy is difficult to remove even after it has outlived its usefulness. (p. 213)

Acknowledging all these problems, Harrison proposes that some time limit be set—a kind of sunset law—after which affirmative action will cease and America will embrace once again a meritocratic ideal. The long-range effect of continued affirmative action, Harrison realizes, could be very harmful. Nevertheless, Harrison considers himself to be a loyal supporter of affirmative action, at least during the interim period when it is to remain in place. His reasons for this support are given in two sentences that sum up perhaps more clearly than anything else ever written on this topic the real reasons that many socially and economically privileged whites support what they themselves acknowledge to be a policy so fraught with mischief. "Its costs and inequities notwithstanding," Harrison writes,

---

94. Lawrence Harrison, *Who Prospers? How Cultural Values Shape Economic and Political Success* (New York: Basic Books, 1992).

> I continue to believe in affirmative action, defined as prefer-
> ential treatment in the education system and the workplace.
> I think it has filled a political and psychological need in our
> society: as a catharsis for white guilt about slavery, segrega-
> tion, and acts of racism; and as a concrete demonstration to
> blacks that whites are genuinely committed to the achieve-
> ment of racial equality. (p. 212)

Harrison's remarks are invaluable for the degree of clarity and insight they offer into the motivations of many affirmative-action supporters. It is the need of white people—to expiate their guilt over slavery, segregation, and the racism of the past, and to show black people how much they care—that is the major motivating and sustaining force behind the policy for these supporters. And such supporters are the key to its success. It is the need of the affluent and guilt-ridden among white people that drives affirmative action and keeps the policy in place despite ever-mounting evidence that the policy produces almost all of the harmful effects that its legions of critics predicted it would have more than 40 years ago.

With great trenchancy, essayist Shelby Steele has described the kind of backing given to affirmative action by supporters like Harrison as "iconographic racial reform."[95] Iconographic reforms, Steele explains, are reforms that exist for what they symbolize in the minds of the people who support them more than for what they achieve in the lives of those they are intended to help. "Iconographic programs and policies function as icons of the high and honorable motivations that people want credit for when they support these reforms," he writes. "The announced goals of these programs and policies will be very

95. Shelby Steele, *Second Thoughts about Race in America* (New York: Madison Books, 1991).

grand, the better to represent their high virtuousness, yet vague so that their inevitable failures will not be held against them." (p. 132) The supporters of iconographic programs, says Steele, "are primarily concerned that these policies function as icons of their high motivation, not whether they achieve anything or whether they mire those they claim to help in terrible unintended consequences." (pp. 132–3)

Steele believes that iconographic policies came into prominence in the 1960s as a way for white people to fend off the stigma and shame that came to be associated with being white as a result of the success of the civil rights and black power movements of the period. As a result of the civil rights victories of the 60s, Steele writes, whites "became identified with the shame of white racism that the nation had finally acknowledged, and they fell under a kind of suspicion that amounted to a stigma." (p. 156) Whites underwent during this period a kind of "archetypical Fall," Steele explains, as they "were confronted for more than a decade with their willingness to participate in, or comply with, the oppression of blacks, their indifference to human suffering and denigration, their capacity to abide evil for their own benefit and in the defiance of their own sacred principles." 96 (p. 498) This Fall, says Steele, added a new burden to white life in America—henceforth whites had to prove that they were not racists "in order to establish their human decency."

It was this new burden of guilt and the need to prove their nonracist decency, according to Steele, that marked "the most powerful, yet unspoken, element in America's social-policy making process" of the 1960s and beyond. (p. 498) This guilt-and-expiation-driven policy process, he says, sometimes wound up producing genuine advances for African Americans, among which Steele would include the 1964 Civil Rights Act. But the

---

96. "White Guilt," *American Scholar*, autumn 1990, pp. 497–506. All the subsequent page numbers in the text refer to this article.

process just as often led to harmful public policies, particularly in the form of racial preferences and racial entitlements, which undermined black initiative and reinforced the worst kind of negative stereotypes concerning black competence and character. "White guilt," says Steele, too often had the effect of "bending social policies in the wrong direction." (p. 499) This guilt, which "springs from a knowledge of ill-gotten advantage," helped to shape American social policies with regard to blacks "in ways that may deliver the look of innocence to society and its institutions but that do very little actually to uplift blacks." (p. 498) The effect of whites' hidden need for racial redemption "has been to bend social policy more toward reparation for black oppression than toward the much harder and more mundane work of black uplift and development." (p. 498)

The kind of white guilt that has driven much of American social policy over the last three decades, Steele believes, must be seen not only as socially harmful but also as ultimately narcissistic and self-preoccupied. "Guilt makes us afraid for ourselves," he writes, "and thus generates as much self-preoccupation as concern for others. The nature of this preoccupation is always the redemption of innocence, the reestablishment of good feelings about oneself . . . . and [it] can lead us to put our own need for innocence above our concern for the problem that made us feel guilt in the first place." (pp. 500–1) The moral corruption here is to be seen in the fact that when the selfishly guilty put their own need for a restoration of innocence above the true needs of those they claim to want to help, they often wind up doing great harm while feeling good about what they do. And in their self-preoccupied desire to feel morally cleansed and uplifted, they develop a willful blindness or indifference to the actual consequences of their actions.

The elite universities in America, Steele believes, have been the arenas where this destructive, self-preoccupied white guilt has had some of its worst and most enduring consequences.

"Black student demands," he writes, "pull administrators into the paradigm of self-preoccupied white guilt, whereby they seek a quick redemption by offering special entitlements that go beyond fairness." (p. 503) These special entitlements—above all affirmative-action preferences—are part of a condescending white paternalism, Steele believes, "that makes it difficult for blacks to find their true mettle or to develop a faith in their own capacity to run as fast as others." (p. 505) Such policies encourage in blacks a dependency both on special entitlements and on the white guilt that produces them. An arrangement of this kind is always degrading for all parties involved, though especially for the blacks, Steele believes, since it encourages whites to see blacks "exclusively along the dimension of their victimization." Blacks become "'different' people with whom whites can negotiate entitlements but never fully see as people like themselves." (p. 503) "The selfishly guilty white person," Steele concludes, "is drawn to what blacks least like in themselves—their suffering, victimization, and dependency. This is no good for anyone—black or white." (p. 506)

It is hard to improve on Steele's analysis here.[97] It fails to address, however, the situation with Hispanics. In a curious development, Mexican Americans, and later all the Spanish-language ethic groups, were successfully able to piggyback their way onto the 60s-era black struggle and acquire in the minds of privileged whites a similar status as pity- and guilt-evoking "people of color." Henceforth all people of Spanish heritage,

---

97. The late Irving Kristol levels a charge similar to that of Steele's against many of the middle-class reformers of the 1960s and early 1970s. "The politics of liberal reform in recent years," he wrote in a 1972 *Wall Street Journal* essay, "has been more concerned with the kind of symbolic action that gratifies the passions of the reformer rather than with the efficacy of the reforms themselves. Indeed, the outstanding characteristic of what we call 'the New Politics' is precisely its insistence on the overwhelming importance of revealing in the public realm one's intense feelings—we must 'care,' we must 'be concerned,' we must be 'committed.' Unsurprisingly, this goes along with an immense indifference to consequences, to positive results or the lack thereof." (Irving Kristol, "Symbolic Politics and Liberal Reform," *Wall Street Journal*, 15 Dec. 1972).

including millions of recent immigrants, would be viewed through the lens of the struggle to right the wrongs historically done to African Americans (a fact that many blacks to this day deeply resent). In the eyes of the guilt-ridden whites, Hispanics, while they weren't exactly black, certainly weren't white, and they would go on to acquire a position in the iconography of post-60s white liberalism much like their later position in the academic arena—i.e., between blacks and whites but much closer to blacks. In the eyes of the guilty whites, Hispanics would become a kind of Afro-American Lite.

What happened to the Asians in this post-60s development was even more curious. While they certainly weren't either white or European, and the older generations had certainly endured more than a little white hostility and discrimination, they nevertheless were too successful—too good in school and at making money—to be eligible for special consideration within the white-created preference regime. Hence they would acquire in the minds of the white penitents something of the status of "honorary whites." In view of their newly acquired honorary status, the guilty whites could in good conscience discriminate against Asians in favor of blacks and Hispanics, just as they discriminated against the members of their own guilty race. Asians, however, were accorded one modest consolation. Since their honorary white status did not encompass culpability for the whites' racist past, Asian protests against the preference regime were at least treated with a degree of sympathy and respect by the guilty whites that they would never accord to similar protests from members of their own race. White protests against quotas were often seen to partake of an unseemly lack of shame and contrition (when not motivated by white racism). Similar protests by Asians were seen by the white penitents as at least understandable, though not, of course, justified.

If white guilt really is at the heart of much of the enduring support we see for affirmative action, it suggests that at the elite universities, where white guilt and fear of the R-word are so much in evidence, the policy will be with us for many years to come regardless of the verdict of any social science research. A "catharsis for white guilt about slavery, segregation, and acts of racism" is not likely to be undone by a regression analysis.

For those of us who have long argued against affirmative-action policy, the one hope on the horizon is long term. As generations pass and those whose views on race relations were forged by the upheavals of the 1960s increasingly retire and pass from the academic scene, the experience of the "archetypical Fall" and the white guilt it produced will fade into ever more distant memory. Blacks will increasingly be viewed by a new generation of whites, Asians, Mideasterners, and others simply as people, not as pitiable victims or objects of expiatory atonement for guilty white penitents. As Asians and students from Mideastern backgrounds assume a more prominent place at elite colleges and universities, the pull of the meritocratic ideal will become increasingly strong. And in time affirmative action will come to be viewed as a policy, not a crusade. And as a policy it will be judged by its merits—and found deeply wanting.

IV

DIVERSITY AND ITS DISCONTENTS: THE CONTACT HYPOTHESIS UNDER FIRE

Does racial and ethnic diversity on college campuses further important educational goals? When people of diverse racial and ethnic backgrounds come together—whether in college, on the job, or in local residential communities—are stereotypes broken down? Do horizons broaden? Does greater tolerance and understanding ensue? In this chapter I try to show that the answer to each of these questions is: "It all depends."

Over the past 50 years sociologists and other social scientists have addressed the question of whether bringing together people of diverse racial and ethnic backgrounds is likely to further important social goals. When people of diverse demographic backgrounds are brought together in the same location, is there a marked increase in interpersonal friendships, mutual trust, the formation of reciprocity norms, and the growth of social capital? One theory that used to be popular among reformers of an earlier era and that is still held by many supporters of racial preferences today is called the "contact hypothesis." According to this theory, prejudice of a racial or ethnic kind and the negative stereotyping that promotes it are products of social isolation and ignorance of the alien "other" that such isolation produces. Bring diverse peoples together, it is said, let them encounter one another as they really are, and many of the harmful prejudices and misconceptions people have of those in other groups will substantially diminish. Better contact furthers better understanding, according to this view.

Contact theory, however, at least in its "naïve" or unreconstructed form, is no longer held by knowledgeable researchers—and for good reason. From Central Africa to the Balkans, from multiethnic Indonesia to multiethnic Ceylon, the mere contact around the world of people of diverse racial, ethnic, and religious identity groups seems just as likely to further conflict and discord as peaceful relationships and mutual understandings. Indeed, conflict and hostility are the more typical outcome. One has to close one's eyes to a great deal of what has happened in the world over the past two centuries to believe in the universal truth of contact theory, or in the general claim that greater racial, ethnic, and religious diversity in a population is a source of collective strength.

A "revised contact hypothesis" will show that only under very specific—and not very common—circumstances does the mere bringing together of people of diverse identity groups have the positive social and life-enhancing results that believers in the unreconstructed contact hypothesis claim. I try to show in this chapter just what these circumstances are as they have been described by social researchers—and why they are unlikely to be found in situations where diversity is artificially created by racial-preference policies.

A good deal of the chapter focuses on the research of Harvard political scientist Robert Putnam. Through a survey of over 30,000 Americans scattered across 41 varied communities, Putnam has delivered a stake through the heart of naïve contact theory and the Pollyannaish optimism with which its proponents believe that ethno-racial diversity easily brings about desired social goods. The path to fruitful integration is not easy, Putnam's research suggests, and, we might add, it is hardly likely to be furthered by policies such as racial preferences that large portions of the population openly resent or despise.

The chapter concludes with an explanation of the upward-ratcheting system currently in place across the American college system, whereby black students are placed in institutions more selective than the ones they would have been placed in under a race-neutral system. Such mismatching, it is suggested, undermines whatever positive values racial diversity might achieve.[98]

They see me as an affirmative-action case.
—AFRICAN AMERICAN STUDENT AT UCLA[99]

THE DIVERSITY DODGE

"A farm boy from Idaho can bring something to Harvard College that a Bostonian cannot offer. Similarly, a black student can usually bring something that a white person cannot offer." With these words, Harvard University officials effectively charmed Supreme Court Justice Lewis Powell, who provided the key swing vote in the 1978 Bakke decision[100] upholding the use of race as a "plus-factor" to further educational diversity in university admissions. Ever since Bakke "diversity" has become the watchword of the defenders of racial-preference policies both in the college admissions context and in many other areas of American life. Diversity is said to bring about a host of educational benefits. A more diverse student body, Justice Sandra Day O'Connor declared in the 2003 Grutter[101] decision reaffirming Powell's Bakke holding, helps to promote "cross racial understandings," breaks down "racial stereotypes," and enables people "to better understand persons of different races."

98. This chapter is adapted from my essay "Diversity's Discontents: The Contact Hypothesis Exploded," *Academic Questions*, 21(2008): 409–30.
99. Quoted in Steele, *Second Thoughts*, p. 87.
100. *Regents of the University of California v. Bakke*, 438 U.S. 265 (1978).
101. *Grutter v. Bollinger*, 539 U.S. 306 (2003).

From the very beginning, however, the diversity-produces-educational-benefits rationale has had something of an *ad hoc*—indeed bogus—quality to it. Before Bakke policies of racial preferences in university admissions were rarely defended by their supporters on diversity-enhancement grounds, the rationale of choice usually being either "compensatory justice," or "pressing social needs." African Americans, it was said, deserve special treatment as simple payback for the grave wrongs visited upon them throughout the long and sorry history of American slavery and Jim Crow. Racial preferences were also said to be urgently needed as a means of jump-starting the growth of a stable black middle class—a justification that gained great salience in the late 1960s in the wake of the extensive urban rioting of the period, much of it carried out by disaffected, lower-class black youth.[102]

One can get a good sense of the typical manner of defense of racial preference policies in the pre-Bakke era from a *New York Times* editorial on June 19, 1977. "Reparation, American Style" was how the *Times* titled its long, 3,000-word defense of the racial-preference regime at the U.C. Davis Medical School, where Allan Bakke had unsuccessfully applied for admission. While the *Times* piece spoke at length on the themes of compensatory justice and America's pressing need for more black professionals (the editorial was one of the longest and most detailed in *Times* history), there was almost nothing said in the editorial about the great educational value of diversity within the educational arena itself. The *Times* commentary in this regard was typical of liberal journalism in the mid-1970s.

A year before the *Times* editorial, presidential candidate Jimmy Carter had similarly focused on compensatory justice as the reason he supported racial preferences. "[I believe] in

---

102. See John David Skrentny, *The Ironies of Affirmative Action* (Chicago: University of Chicago Press, 1996).

insuring that all Americans should have not only equal opportunity," Carter remarked at a May, 1976, fund-raising breakfast in Cincinnati, "but should also have compensatory opportunity, if, through my influence or yours, they have been deprived of the opportunity of fully using their talents." Later, at a news conference that day, he added: "You can provide equality of opportunity by law, but quite often that is not adequate."[103] Diversity enhancement was not part of Carter's affirmative-action defense during his 1976 presidential campaign, and his views were emblematic of white liberal thinking at that time.

Only because of Lewis Powell's subsequent declaration that compensatory justice and "social needs" arguments are insufficiently weighty to override the 14th Amendment's color-blind imperative but that educational diversity is of sufficient importance and a "compelling state interest" that can override the requirement of color-blindness, did the diversity-enhancement rationale assume its present dominance among supporters of race-based preferences in college and professional school admissions, as well as in other areas of American life. Before Powell's decision, diversity-enhancement arguments were rare to nonexistent. And they were never at the top of anyone's list of the most important reasons for justifying racial preferences.[104]

"The *raison d'etre* for race-specific affirmative action programs," Harvard Law School professor Alan Dershowitz has trenchantly noted, "has simply never been diversity for the sake of education. The checkered history of 'diversity' demonstrates that it was designed largely as a cover to achieve other legally, morally, and politically controversial goals. In recent years, it has been invoked—especially in the professional schools—as

---

103. *Facts on File* (1976), p. 324.
104. On this topic, see the important study by Peter Wood, *Diversity—The Invention of a Concept* (San Francisco: Encounter Books, 2003).

a clever post facto justification for increasing the number of minority group students in the student body."[105]

Dershowitz's Harvard colleague Randall Kennedy has made similar comments casting doubt on the sincerity, if not the goodwill, of academic administrators who invoke "diversity" as their main reason for increasing the black presence in colleges and professional schools. "Let's be honest," Kennedy writes. "Many who defend affirmative action for the sake of 'diversity' are actually motivated by a concern that is considerably more compelling. They are not so much animated by a commitment to what is, after all, a contingent, pedagogical hypothesis [i.e., that racial diversity promotes a richer, campus-wide learning environment]. Rather, they are animated by a commitment to social justice. They would rightly defend affirmative action even if social science demonstrated uncontrovertibly that diversity has no effect (or even a negative effect) on the learning environment."[106] While Kennedy is generally supportive of racial-preference policies, he agrees with critics that the diversity rationale is a weak foundation on which to base one's defense of such policies, and is at best a secondary concern of many who support and maintain affirmative action policies for other reasons.[107]

While the "diversity defense" clearly emerged late in the game, and while Dershowitz and Kennedy are surely correct about the insincerity of most academics who invoke it, nevertheless many who support racial preferences in college admissions, including influential decision makers like Sandra Day

---

105. See Brian T. Fitzpatrick, "The Diversity Lie," *Harvard Journal of Law and Public Policy*, 27 (2004):395–6.

106. Ibid, p. 396.

107. A similar stance is taken by Peter Schmidt in *Color and Money: How Rich White Kids Are Winning the War over Affirmative Action* (New York: Palgrave Macmillian, 2007). Schmidt speaks of a "diversity dodge" designed to obscure the real, compensatory, and social-justice goals of racial-preference policies—goals that he believes are critically important and not sufficiently furthered by current affirmative-action practices.

O'Connor, are genuinely convinced by the diversity argument and accept at face value what diversity proponents claim. If we just bring together on college campuses or in the workplace people of diverse racial, religious, or national-origins backgrounds, they believe, mutual cultural enrichment will take place, and a better understanding and cooperation between peoples will naturally emerge. Above all, diversity—whether on campus or on the job—is believed by many to be the natural antidote to racial and ethnic prejudice and to the ignorant stereotyping on which it feeds.

THE CONTACT HYPOTHESIS

Social science has had a great deal to say about racial and ethnic diversity, not only in recent years but in research going back more than half a century. The conclusions of this research, however, are not always congenial to those who equate greater diversity with the furtherance of better intergroup understanding, reduced intergroup prejudice, and all the other positive benefits that are supposed to flow from greater exposure to demographically diverse populations. However, Randall Kennedy is correct in his prediction that such research has had little or no effect on the passion with which academic defenders of racial-preference policies have continued to support their positions. Disturbing social science research is simply ignored. This has been particularly true in the case of the large body of research going back to the 1940s dealing with what sociologists call "the contact hypothesis."

The contact hypothesis, which enjoyed its greatest popularity in the years immediately following World War II, views group prejudice and the negative stereotyping of outsider groups as largely the product of ignorance, and believes that the key to dispelling such prejudice and stereotyping is greater contact between people of different racial and ethnic backgrounds.

Increased group contact, the theory claims, brings about more harmonious relations between people of different social-identity groups as they come to realize that their prejudices and negative stereotyping are based on false assumptions and gross overgeneralizations. One proponent of school integration in the 1940s, a prominent educational researcher, put the matter this way: "Where people of various cultures and races freely and genuinely associate, there tensions and difficulties, prejudices and confusions, dissolve; where they do not associate, where they are isolated from one another, there prejudice and conflict grow like a disease."[108]

Supporters of the contact hypothesis in the immediate post-World War II era had two very weighty developments of the period that seemed to lend a certain plausibility to their views. The first was the successful integration of the U.S. armed forces under the leadership of President Harry S. Truman, a white Southerner who as a young man had seriously considered joining the Ku Klux Klan. Truman no doubt had political reasons for his integrationist stance, but he was also swayed by the fact that during the war against Nazi fascism and racism black and white service personnel who shared common tasks and common quarters—such as aboard ships in the Navy and the Merchant Marines—often developed mutual friendships and better understandings despite the existence of formal segregation throughout the U.S. military. Early studies of WWII-era GIs showed that whites with the most contact with blacks during their military service often experienced a reduction in their prejudices.[109] The integration of the military that took place during Truman's

---

108. Theodore Brameld, *Minority Problems in the Public Schools* (New York: Harper and Brothers, 1946), p. 245. Brameld was a professor of educational philosophy at the University of Minnesota and widely respected in his time.

109 H. A. Singer, "The Veteran and Race Relations," *Journal of Educational Sociology*, 212 (1948):397–408; S. A. Stouffer et al., *The American Soldier* (Princeton: Princeton University Press, 1949).

second term in office would prove to be one of the most successful instances of black/white integration in the nation's history.

The second development at this time that contact theorists could point to was the successful integration of professional baseball in the 1940s—"America's Pastime," as it was called in those days—and the rapid acceptance of black ballplayers on formerly all-white teams. Despite initial resistance, sports fans throughout America in 1947 came to appreciate the hitting, fielding, and base-running prowess of Jackie Robinson when he became the first Negro to play in the major leagues and a major reason why the Brooklyn Dodgers won the National League pennant that year. (Robinson himself was named Rookie of the Year in 1947). Following the lead of Dodger owner Branch Rickey, many other major league teams over the next ten years aggressively recruited black ball players for their organizations.

While the successful integration of professional baseball and the military lent a modicum of plausibility to the contact theory, it was clear to more discerning observers from the very start that the contact hypothesis, at least in its unrevised form, was untenable and could only be maintained by a focus on selective and in some ways atypical examples. An obvious and glaring counterexample in the 1940s and 1950s was the racial situation in the American South. While white Southerners generally had much more daily contact with black people than whites in the Northern and Western states, one could hardly argue that their enhanced contact diminished their racial prejudices or outgroup stereotyping. Gunnar Myrdal's *An American Dilemma*, published in the mid-1940s, had clearly demonstrated otherwise, if any demonstration was needed for anyone with the least acquaintance with race relations in the Jim Crow South.

Those knowledgeable of the European scene in the earliest years of the twentieth century had even more reason to doubt—if not ridicule—the contact hypothesis. In multiethnic cities of Eastern Europe before the First World War—cities like

Belgrade, Vienna, and Krakow—people of different racial and ethnic groups often had the opportunity to come into contact with one another on a daily basis, yet the result was hardly one of general ethnic harmony. Enmity, suspicion, and distrust were just as often the result of such ethnic mixing as any positive benefits. The very words "the Balkans" conjured up vivid images of ethnic diversity producing bitter, protracted, often violent ethnic strife. And it was not lost on critics of the contact hypothesis in the immediate aftermath of the Nazi era that Adolf Hitler was a product of multiethnic, multicultural Vienna, a city in Hitler's youth that had elected an openly antisemitic mayor (Karl Lueger) and whose ethnic diversity was more often than not a breeding ground for prejudice against Jews, Poles, Hungarians, Russians, and every other resident minority group.

REVISING THE CONTACT HYPOTHESIS

If the contact hypothesis was to be rescued, it was clear that it was in need of some critical pruning—if not drastic reformulation—that specified under what limited range of circumstances ethnic diversity might be expected to promote rather than diminish intergroup harmony and understanding. Researchers from the 1950s onward eventually identified several conditions that usually had to be met for diversity to have the favorable outcomes that contact theorists sought. Among these conditions were

- Equality of status between those making the contact;
- A noncompetitive environment in which one ethnic group's gain is not seen to be at the expense of another group's welfare;
- The opportunity to encounter sufficient numbers of people who counter the negative stereotype one group holds of the other;

- The challenge of a common goal or common task that requires some collective or cooperative effort to achieve;
- The lack of artificiality or Potemkin-like quality to the interaction; and
- The support of wider community norms and those in authority.[110]

Using these criteria it is easy to see why the integration of a professional sports team like the Brooklyn Dodgers, or of the units of a national military fighting a popular war, were as successful as they were, while the prospects for similar success under many other real-world conditions are much less favorable.

It became clear to the critics of the contact hypothesis that when conditions for successful integration are not favorable, more often than not enhanced social contact spells trouble—often Big Trouble. To the more naïve versions of the contact hypothesis critics sometimes juxtaposed a "conflict hypothesis," which was said to describe more accurately the more typical relationships between people in the real world of demographically diverse populations. According to this more pessimistic view,[111] people of differing racial, ethnic, linguistic, and ethno-religious communities typically, a) harbor innate suspicions and distrust of one another; b) find it more difficult to engage in cooperative ventures with one another than with members of

110. See, for instance, Gordon Allport, *The Nature of Prejudice* (Cambridge, MA: Addison-Wesley, 1954); D. Landis, R. O. Hope, and H. R. Day, "Training for Desegregation in the Military," in N. Miller and M. B. Brewer, eds., *Groups in Conflict: The Psychology of Desegregation* (Orlando, FL: Academic Press, 1984), pp. 257–78; M. B. Brewer and N. Miller, "Beyond the Contact Hypothesis: Theoretical Perspectives on Desegregation," in Miller and Brewer, eds., *Groups in Conflict*, pp. 281–302; D. Chu and D. Griffey, "The Contact Theory of Integration: The Case of Sport," Sociology of *Sport Journal*, 2 (1985):323–33; and J. F. Dovido, S. L. Gaertner, and K. Kawakami, "Intergroup Contact: The Past, Present, and Future," *Group Processes and Intergroup Relations* 6 (2003): 5–21.
111. What is described here, of course, is an "ideal type." Writers on ethnic conflict do not sort themselves so simply into "contact" or "conflict" theorists, and, as explained, "naïve contact theory" is no longer held by anyone.

their own group; c) find it difficult to understand each other's differing customs and folkways; d) tend to see one another more as stereotyped group representatives than as distinct individuals; e) find it difficult to establish ties of friendship or intimacy; f) display less willingness to support government measures to benefit the poor and distressed; and, g) display greater hostility or coldness toward one another if they live close by and regularly interact than if they live more geographically separated lives.[112]

One policy implication frequently drawn from the conflict theory is that identity-group diversity under most circumstances is something to be avoided, that "good fences make good neighbors," and that it is usually best to have people of different racial, ethnic, ethno-religious, or ethno-linguistic groups living in geographic areas separated from one another, whether those separated areas encompass a whole nation-state (Japan, Norway, Iceland), a region of a larger state (the Kurds in Iraq, the Basques in Spain), separate halves of an island (Greeks and Turks on Cyprus), a partitioned territory (India-Pakistan-Bangladesh, Israel-Palestine, Slovakia-Czech Republic), or simply a local neighborhood of the same city (Russian Jewish immigrants in Brooklyn's Brighton Beach, Chinese immigrants in San Francisco's Chinatown). Such arrangements, it is said, reduce

---

112. See, for instance, R. A. LeVine and D. T. Campbell, *Ethnocentrism: Theories of Conflict, Ethnic Attitudes, and Group Behavior* (New York: Wiley and Son,, 1972); M. P. Brewer, "The Psychology of Prejudice: Ingroup Love or Outgroup Hate?" *Journal of Social Issues* 55 (1999): 429–44; Donald Horowitz, *Ethnic Groups in Conflict*, 2nd ed. (Berkeley: University of California Press, 2000); Daniel P. Moynihan, *Pandemonium: Ethnicity in International Politics* (New York: Oxford University Press, 1993); L. Quillian, "Prejudice as a Response to Perceived Group Threat: Population Composition and Anti-Immigrant and Racial Prejudice in Europe," *American Sociological Review* 60 (1995): 586–611; Carol Swain, *The New White Nationalism in America: Its Challenge to Integration* (Cambridge, UK: Cambridge University Press, 2002; and K. Newton and J. Delhey, "Predicting Cross-National Levels of Social Trust: Global Pattern or Nordic Exceptionalism?," *European Sociological Review*, 21 (2005): 311–27.

inter-group hostilities and allow people to associate with those with whom they have most in common and with whom they feel most comfortable. For conflict theorists the contact hypothesis is turned on its head: interethnic contact is seen as a source of suspicion and distrust. Diversity is a harbinger of tension and trouble.

BUT ISN'T THE U.S. DIFFERENT? ROBERT PUTNAM'S RECENT CHALLENGE TO CONTACT-THEORY OPTIMISM

Many readers of this chapter will bristle at the conflict theory and its claims. Aren't we in the U.S the shining example of its disconfirmation? Isn't America the great melting pot where the ancient tribal enmities of the Old World were left behind and a new unity forged out of diverse racial, ethnic, and religious strands? Doesn't *E Pluribus Unum* signify not only a high-minded principle but to some extent an actual reality in America? Outside the Old South hasn't contact between people of diverse racial, ethnic, and religious origins led to mutual enrichment and a general reduction in prejudice as contact theory would predict? Doesn't contact theory, even in its "naïve" or unreconstructed form, provide an accurate description of substantial portions of American racial and ethnic history?

The answers here call for nuance, because the U.S is clearly not the former Yugoslavia or any of the ethnically divided states of post-colonial Africa. Intergroup violence has been much less pronounced and integration far better achieved in America than in almost any other large, diverse, multiethnic, multireligious society. "No other nation has so successfully combined people of different races and nations within a single culture [as the United States]," former British Prime Minister Margaret Thatcher once remarked.[113] Surely, to some extent, America can be described as an integration success story.

Nonetheless, getting people of widely divergent racial and ethnic identities to live together harmoniously and cooperate productively is always a daunting task, and while the U.S. has unquestionably been better at it than many other demographically diverse nations, it should never be forgotten that the process of integration does not flow naturally from mere contact and propinquity and certainly not through the simplistic mechanisms that contact theorists propose. As the history of ethnic and other communal conflicts around the world show, in its naïve or unrevised form the contact hypothesis is mere wishful thinking, and those who implicitly rely on some version of it to defend current racial-preference policies in American universities and elsewhere either delude themselves or knowingly seek to delude others.

Even in a relatively low-ethnic-conflict country like America mere contact between people of diverse racial and ethnic identity groups can hardly be said to reduce prejudice or to increase intercommunal cooperation and understanding. This truth has been confirmed in a powerful way by the outstanding scholarship of Harvard political scientist Robert Putnam. From early on in his professional career Putnam has been interested in the phenomena of interpersonal trust and the social capital and social cooperation that flow from such trust. In an early study of regional differences in modern Italy, Putnam argued that the vastly different levels of civic engagement and social trust displayed by the populations living in the northern and southern parts of Italy were largely responsible for the very different levels of economic development of those two regions. Like Edward Banfield before him, Putnam in his Italian journeys found per-

---

113. Cited in Arthur Schlesinger Jr., *The Disuniting of America* (Knoxville, TN: Whittle Direct Books, 1991), p. 78.

vasive envy and distrust among southern Italians for all those outside one's immediate family and a corresponding inability to network or cooperate with one another to achieve common goals such as economic prosperity or a reduction in government corruption. The low-trust cultures of southern regions like Calabria and Sicily, Putnam argued, were largely responsible for those regions' economic backwardness and their inability to overcome many of the negative political and social elements which Putnam believed were inheritances from their corrupt, feudal-authoritarian past.[114]

In more recent years Putnam has been concerned with the decline in social connectedness and civic engagement in the United States, as manifested in well-documented declines in such organizations as the Red Cross, parent-teachers associations, the Boy Scouts, fraternal groups (like the Lions, Masons, Shriners, and Jaycees), labor unions, the League of Women Voters, as well as organized bowling leagues. This last item inspired the title for his widely read *Bowling Alone: The Collapse and Revival of American Community*, which appeared in 2000. While certain dues-and-newsletter organizations like the American Association of Retired Persons (AARP) and the Sierra Club have experienced huge growth in recent decades, these organizations, says Putnam, act more like paid lobby groups whose members rarely know one another or ever come into contact with one another on a face-to-face basis. They are clearly not organizations, he says, that have positive spill-over effects in fostering social capital, human connectedness, or enhanced human understanding between neighbors and friends. Belonging to them is little different than bowling alone.[115]

---

114. Robert Putnam, *Making Democracy Work: Civic Traditions in Modern Italy* (Princeton: Princeton University Press, 1993).
115. Robert Putnam, *Bowling Alone: The Collapse and Revival of American Community* (New York: Simon and Schuster, 2000).

In his *Bowling Alone* study Putnam drew upon the nationally representative General Social Survey, which indicated an overall decline in the frequency with which Americans spend social evenings with neighbors and friends and a similar decline in the belief that people can generally be trusted. The proportion of Americans agreeing with the statement that "most people" can be trusted, Putnam points out, declined by a third between 1960 and 1993, from 58 percent to 37 percent. These changes are all the more striking, he says, because the educational level of the population was rising over this period, and past research has shown positive relationships between schooling and levels of trust and sociability. While Americans were becoming better educated, they were also becoming more socially isolated and more distrustful of one another.

In his preliminary work on the "bowling alone" phenomenon, Putnam suggested several factors that might be responsible for the loss of social connectedness and the decline in civic engagement. These included the high incidence of divorce and family breakup; the entrance of more women into the workforce (and subsequent decline in organizations like the PTA and the Red Cross, which traditionally relied on the labor of female homemakers); and the radical privatizing and individualizing of entertainment as a result of the growth of television-watching as America's foremost pastime. All of these factors Putnam believed were important in explaining the decline in social connectedness and civic engagement among Americans in the final third of the twentieth century.

In his more recent studies, Putnam has looked at the factor of ethnic diversity and its effects on the formation of social capital ("social capital" being defined simply as the formation of social networks and "the associated norms of reciprocity and trustworthiness" associated with such networks). What Putnam found was arresting, and it certainly presents a challenge to all those who believe that the integration of racially and ethnically diverse peoples into a decent, caring, civic-minded society is anything other than a difficult, long-term task. Ethnic diversity in contemporary America, Putnam found, has few of the present benefits that multiculturalists and contact theorists say it has, and it has some additional disadvantages that even conflict theorists have not generally ascribed to it.

Putnam's study is based on a large nationwide survey, the Social Capital Community Benchmark Survey, that in all sampled approximately 30,000 Americans, including representative samples of populations drawn from 41 highly varied communities across the U.S. These 41 separate community surveys form the heart of Putnam's research, and they range from large urban centers with a million or more residents to smaller cities, suburban areas, and rural towns. Four whole states—Montana, Indiana, Delaware, and New Hampshire—were also among the 41 communities surveyed. Consistent with other studies, but contrary to the view of many enthusiasts for multiculturalism and continuing large-scale immigration, Putnam found that inter-racial trust—that is, the degree to which blacks, whites, Asian Americans, and Latinos said they trusted members of the three broad ethno-racial groups they didn't belong to—varied directly with the degree of ethno-racial *homogeneity*, not diversity, in the area in which they lived. "Inter-racial trust is relatively high in homogeneous South Dakota and relatively low in heterogeneous San Francisco or Los Angeles," Putnam reports. "The more ethnically diverse the people we live around," he says, "the less we trust them."[116]

Those who told researchers that they trusted members of other races "a lot" were much more common in places like Lewiston, Maine, Bismarck, New Hampshire, and the state of Montana, where whites constitute the great majority of the

---

116. Robert Putnam, "E Pluribus Unum: Diversity and Community in the Twenty-first Century," *Scandinavian Political Studies* 30 (2007): 137–74.

population (and nonwhites are not frequently encountered in most community settings) than in places like San Francisco, Los Angeles, North Minneapolis, or East Bay, California, where the populations are much more racially and ethnically diverse. This finding is all the more remarkable—and all the more inconsistent with contact theory—when one considers that the lower levels of interracial trust are often expressed by people living in some of the more politically liberal areas of the country where norms of political correctness and socially-acceptable response patterns might be expected to dampen substantially the level of ethnic distrust to which respondents (particularly whites) would freely admit. The social pressures to affirm publicly one's trust in members of other ethno-racial groups is almost certainly greater in places like San Francisco and Los Angeles than in places like Montana or rural South Dakota, suggesting that the real trust gap is even greater than that indicated by the Community Benchmark Survey data. At least in terms of contemporary America, the data from this survey seem to confirm the view that in interracial and interethnic relations, familiarity breeds distrust.

Having surveyed much of the world literature on these issues, Putnam was not entirely surprised by these findings. They were consistent with many other studies, using many different methodologies, carried out in many different places around the world. People of different racial and ethnic groups have a harder time getting along with one another—and trusting one another—than people who are of the same race or ethnic group. And the more numerous the members of the outsider group, and the more contact people have with them, the greater the interracial suspiciousness and distrust. Putnam's study, however, probed further than most earlier studies in asking a key question rarely posed—i.e., whether increased racial and ethnic diversity has any effect on the degree of solidarity and social capital that exists *within* individual ethno-racial communities.

Although the issue is not often raised, conflict theorists probably assumed that if increased ethnic heterogeneity has any within-group effect it is likely to strengthen in-group bonds of ethnic solidarity and mutual support. Just as populations often pull together when engaged in conflict with an outside enemy, the presence of diverse ethnic groups in the same area, it might be supposed, will increase the level of cooperation and trust within each of the separate groups.

Whether or not such a relationship exists elsewhere, Putnam's study found that the very opposite relationship obtains within the United States. Not only do people in the more diverse communities in the U.S. display lower trust for those who are members of *outsider* ethnic and racial groups, they also display lower trust for members of their *own* group. The distrust engendered by ethnicly and racially diverse communities, Putnam believes, seems to have a strong psychological spillover effect that harms relationships and the formation of social capital even within one's own ethnic group. "In more diverse settings," Putnam writes, "Americans distrust not merely people who do not look like them, but even people who *do*." The distrust engendered by ethnic diversity seems to engender distrust for human beings more generally.

Besides the trust question, respondents in the Community Benchmark Survey were asked a battery of other questions designed to assess the relationship between ethnic diversity and various correlates of social capital, such as participation in community projects, registering to vote, having positive attitudes toward the efficacy of social action, etc. As with the trust question, these other measures of social cooperation and community engagement were found to be negatively correlated with ethnic heterogeneity (i.e., the greater the ethnic heterogeneity the less the cooperation). In areas of the country with greater ethno-racial diversity, Putnam found, respondents tended to display, a) a lower frequency of registering to vote; b) fewer close friends and confidants; c) a lower likelihood of working on a community project; d) less confidence that others would cooperate to solve collective-action problems like water and energy conservation; e) a lower likelihood of giving to charity or doing volunteer work; f) lower confidence in local leaders, local politicians, and the news media; g) greater frequency of participation in protest marches combined with a lower sense of efficacy that one's actions can make a difference; h) lower perceived quality of life; i) lower overall happiness; and, j) more time spent watching television and greater agreement with the statement that "television is my most important form of entertainment."[117]

It's a long list, and while Putnam found some measures of social engagement that were not negatively correlated with ethnic diversity, including the important factor of religious activity, the overall pattern, he says, is unmistakable: People in the more ethnicly diverse communities in America, while they are not at one another's throats, tend to become much more socially isolated and withdrawn than those living in more ethnicly homogeneous communities. There is a decline in social solidarity, community activities, and general neighborliness in such communities as people tend to withdraw into themselves and become more isolated and alienated from others nearby (including members of their own ethnic group). In Putnam's words, people under such circumstances "hunker down" and "pull in like a turtle." Although Putnam believes that in the long run racial and ethnic diversity can have positive benefits in an integration-seeking society, in the short run its effects are overwhelmingly negative. Social isolation, alienation, and anomie are its immediate results.[118]

---

117. Ibid., pp. 149–50.
118. Putnam's empirical results and final conclusions are best summed up in his own words:

> One of the most important challenges facing modern societies, and at the same time one of our most significant opportunities, is the increase in ethnic and social heterogeneity in virtually all advanced countries. Ethnic

Putnam's bleak conclusions about diversity are offset by a number of important qualifications. To begin with, he believes that the problems of ethnic and racial diversity can be mitigated in time presumably as racial and ethnic consciousness gives way, at least in part, to a more encompassing national or universal-human consciousness. To date, however, he has said little about this process. Even in the short run, however, diversity is not all bad, Putnam holds, as it can often be a spur to greater creativity, especially in diverse work groups in educational and business settings when group members work together as a team to solve a common task or problem.

America has been a magnet for many of the most creative and industrious people of the world, and this influx of immigrants from diverse lands, Putnam says, has clearly been of great benefit to the U.S. in many ways. Not only have immigrants been disproportionately represented as winners of such high honors as Nobel prizes, Academy Awards, Kennedy Center awards, and membership in the National Academy of Sciences, but immigrants from diverse lands have taken over many critical low-end jobs for which there are not enough Americans available and have helped to offset the impending fiscal effects of low birth rates among the native population and the retirement of the Baby Boom generation.

---

diversity is increasing in most advanced countries, driven mostly by sharp increases in immigration. In the long run immigration and diversity are likely to have important cultural, economic, fiscal, and developmental benefits. In the short run, however, immigration and ethnic diversity tend to reduce social solidarity and social capital. New evidence from the U.S. suggests that in ethnically diverse neighborhoods residents of all races tend to "hunker down" [i.e., isolate themselves]. . . . Inhabitants of diverse communities tend to withdraw from collective life, to distrust neighbors, regardless of the color of their skin, to withdraw even from close friends, to expect the worst from their community and its leaders, to volunteer less, give less to charity and work on community projects less often, to register to vote less, to agitate for social reform more but have less faith that they can actually make a difference, and to huddle unhappily in front of the television. . . . Diversity, at least in the short run, seems to bring out the turtle in all of us. Ibid., pp. 137, 151.

So immigration and the increase in demographic diversity it brings about are clearly a mixed bag for Putnam. What is so illuminating and refreshing about his work is that he is able to look at the dark side of these developments without blinking and report research that runs counter to the uncritical, celebratory tone of so much of the rhetoric one hears in academic circles about the unalloyed good that increased racial and ethnic diversity is supposed to bring about. His writing is in the best tradition of social realism and brings to light what Max Weber used to call the "inconvenient facts" (*unbequeme Tatsachen*) that social science is duty-bound to investigate. Putnam's research provides the strongest case to date against the more optimistic claims of those who believe that merely getting people of diverse races and ethnicities to live and work in close proximity to one another, or to come together on the same college campus, will automatically provide beneficial social outcomes. The naïve contact theory has never been submitted to a more devastating critique.

RACIAL DIVERSITY IN THE ACADEMY

Although the contact hypothesis, at least in its original, naïve form, has been thoroughly discredited by half a century of research (including more recently Putnam's), and is not currently maintained by any reputable social scientist, it is often the implicit foundation of the defense of current affirmative-action policies in American universities and of the educational-enhancement claims used to justify them. If we just get all those farm boys from Idaho, those Irish kids from Boston, those Mexicans from the barrio, and those black youths from inner-city Detroit to come together on the same college campus, even if it requires a good deal of racial "plus-factoring" by the admissions committee to do so, educational benefits will flow spontaneously and enhance the lives of all concerned. Intergroup contacts will abound, college students will learn from one another, prejudices will diminish, and mutual understanding and good-will will stamp the overall character of campus life.

Alas, things haven't exactly worked out that way. While students of different races and ethnicities coexist peacefully on most college campuses today and treat one another civilly, the ubiquity of self-segregated cafeterias and social groups, the paucity of cross-racial friendships outside of the varsity sports teams and a few other extracurricular activities, and the pervasive suspicion that black and Hispanic students are not as qualified as Asians and whites all clearly indicate that something has gone radically wrong with the integrationist vision propounded by supporters of current preference policies. Things on campus are not the way they are supposed to be or the way defenders of racial preferences told us they would be.

All this, of course, should come as no surprise, as almost none of the factors identified by sociologists as preconditions for beneficial intergroup interactions are met on the contemporary college campuses that indulge in strong affirmative-action preferences. When huge admission preferences are given to black and Hispanic students over whites and Asians, one can hardly speak of members of the ensuing student body as having "equal status." Right from the start entering freshmen begin to think in terms of "regular admits," who were accepted on the basis of their past academic performance, and "the affirmative-action admits," who would not have been accepted but for the huge boost given for their race. Resentments inevitably abound, especially among white and Asian students who remember disappointed high school friends and rejected applicants of their own race, some of whom were much better qualified than many of the black and Hispanic students they meet on campus.

Not only do racial preferences run counter to the widely shared belief that academic merit should be the main criteria for university admissions, but the pervasiveness of huge racial boosts at almost all selective institutions creates an upward ratcheting system in which black and Hispanic students are typically placed at institutions in which the whites and Asians have the clear upper hand in terms of academic talent and abilities. The common stereotype of black and Hispanic students as intellectually inferior to whites, instead of being weakened by actual contact with many group members who counter the stereotype, is more likely than not to be confirmed. When choosing a lab partner in a difficult organic chemistry course, or deciding which study group to join when taking an introductory economics course, it becomes a sensible strategy for incoming freshmen, without further knowledge of individual students, to avoid members of those identity groups that have been admitted under vastly lowered standards. Heightened intergroup tension and self-segregation along racial lines are the inevitable result, with true friendships and understandings across racial divides becoming ever less likely. The terms of the interracial contact on affirmative-action campuses could hardly be less propitious to furthering the integrationist goals that affirmative-action supporters say they favor.

Although empirical research on the topic is limited, we know from what research does exist that all is not well with race relations on college campuses and that racial-preference policies are deeply resented by many white and Asian students whose groups are disfavored by them. In the previous chapter I presented the findings of Douglas Massey and his colleagues in their study of student attitudes at the selective colleges surveyed in *The Source of the River*. White and Asian students expressed a substantial degree of "social distance" between themselves and those black and Hispanic students described as the "beneficiaries of affirmative action," although they expressed no such distance between themselves and blacks and Hispanics "as a group." The admissions processes at the selective universities they surveyed "operate to produce a freshman class composed of two very distinct subpopulations. On one hand are whites and Asians, and on the other are Latinos and blacks." Not surprisingly, students quickly come to understand the racial-preference system and to perceive blacks and Hispanics as academically underqualified, Asians as academically overqualified.[119]

Although the Massey researchers harbor no predisposition against affirmative-action policy, they are forced to conclude that the widespread perception among white and Asian students of substantial social distance between themselves and affirmative-action beneficiaries has had a noxious effect on campus race relations and may undermine the academic self-confidence of those in the lower-achieving groups. The perception of social distance from black and Hispanic affirmative action beneficiaries, they say, has affected the general tone of race relations on college campuses and surely has not contributed to furthering intergroup harmony.

Also in the previous chapter were the reluctant conclusions of linguist John McWhorter about the effects of preferentialist policies at Berkeley: "With it widely known among a student body that most minority students were admitted [to Berkeley] with test scores and GPAs which would have barred white and Asian applicants from consideration, it is difficult for many white students to avoid beginning to question the basic mental competence of black people as a race. . . . This can only leave many young whites with a private suspicion that blacks simply aren't as swift, which will in turn encourage suspicion in black students, and thus perpetuate interracial alienation on campus and undermine the mutual respect that successful integration requires."[120]

119. Douglas Massey et al., *The Source of the River* (Princeton: Princeton University Press, 2003), p. 198.
120. John McWhorter, *Losing the Race: Self-Sabotage in Black America* (New York: The Free Press, 2000), pp. 89, 229–230, 236.

Another study we've seen is that of Stanley Rothman and his colleagues. Recall that the question the Rothman group posed was whether or not enrollment diversity on college campuses under our reigning affirmative-action regime improves the overall educational experience that students feel they receive and furthers interracial understandings and better relations between people of diverse racial backgrounds. And recall too the Rothman group's findings after surveying 140 American colleges and universities: "As the proportion of black students rose, student satisfaction with their university experience dropped, as did their assessments of the quality of their education and the work ethic of their peers. In addition, the higher the enrollment diversity [in terms of blacks], the more likely students were to say that they personally experienced discrimination. The same pattern of negative correlations between educational benefits and increased black enrollment appeared in the responses of faculty and administrators."[121]

But remember that Rothman and his colleagues found a very different outcome when "diversity" was defined in terms of increased Asian enrollment. The increased presence of Asians on campus, but not the increased presence of blacks, seemed to have a number of positive effects in terms of the assessment that students—the majority presumably white—gave of their overall college experience and other outcome variables explored in the study. Rothman et al. explained the difference in terms of affirmative action: "It may be that affirmative action places students in academic environments for which they are unsuited, leading to tension and dissatisfaction all around."[122] What the

---

121 Stanley Rothman, Seymour Martin Lipset, and Neil Nevitte, "Does Enrollment Diversity Improve University Education," *International Journal of Public Opinion Research*, 15:1 (2003), pp. 8–26. A less technical version of this paper appears as "Racial Diversity Reconsidered," in *The Public Interest*, spring 2003 (available online at www.thepublicinterest.com). The quotations in the text are taken from the online version of *The Public Interest* article.
122 Ibid.

Rothman group says is consistent with the highly modified contact hypothesis but not its naïve form, since unlike the latter, the revised form insists that harmonious relationships between different racial and ethnic groups require a sense of equal status, something obviously not achieved when high standards of admission are applied to some groups but not others.

So like McWhorter and the Massey group, Rothman and his colleagues found that all is not well in terms of race relations on college campuses and that at least part of the problem stems from the different admissions standards applied under affirmative-action programs. Once again we find the Pollyannaish optimism of contact theory discredited. Merely getting people of diverse racial and ethnic backgrounds together on the same campus is no guarantee that cross-racial friendships will flourish or that valuable educational and cultural-enrichment outcomes will be realized. Under the wrong circumstances the net effect of such contact is surely harmful. And race-based admissions standards that are resented by large segments of the student body clearly constitute "the wrong circumstances."

Further evidence for the harmful effects of racial preferences at competitive colleges is provided by studies comparing the outcome of blacks at majority-white campuses with those attending the historically black colleges and universities. Sociologist Jacqueline Fleming has studied this issue more extensively than anyone else and finds that black students on the typical majority-white college campus today often face feelings of estrangement and lack of integration into the white social and academic scene. The problem, she says, is most acute for black males. African American males on majority-white campuses, says Fleming, typically experience "feelings of competitive rejection that have consequences for their capacity to muster intellectual motivation."[123] Fleming doesn't blame affirmative-action policies directly for this

---

123 Jacqueline Fleming, *Blacks in College* (San Francisco: Jossey-Bass, 1984), p. 143.

development, but it is hard to imagine that lowering standards for black entrants to competitive colleges doesn't play a supporting role in this.

Fleming's research shows that when comparing blacks with similar background characteristics who attend either predominantly white colleges or an HBCU, those attending the HBCUs typically do better on a host of outcome variables. Summing up much of the research literature on this topic, she writes:

> Previous research makes it clear that Black students adjust better to Black colleges than to predominantly White colleges. Black students who attend predominantly Black schools tend to have higher average grades, a richer learning environment, better relationships with faculty members, exhibit better cognitive development and display greater effort and engage in more academic activities than Black students who attend White schools. In black schools, Black students show better social adjustment, have more extensive social support networks, show greater social involvement, and engage in more organizational activities.[124]

Other researchers have confirmed Fleming's basic findings and conclusions. Sociologist Walter Allen, for instance, did a study comparing the adjustment of blacks on eight predominantly white public universities—most of them highly competitive, where huge affirmative-action preferences are typically given[125]—to those attending eight HBCUs. He found that those at the white institutions often encountered multiple adjustment problems and did much worse on average on a whole host of

---

124 Jacqueline Fleming, "SATs and Black Students," *Review of Higher Education* 25 (2002):281–96, 287.

125 The eight institutions surveyed were the University of Michigan, Ann Arbor; the University of North Carolina, Chapel Hill; the University of California, Los Angeles; Arizona State University, Tempe; Memphis State University; the State University of New York, Stony Brook; the University of Wisconsin, Madison; and Eastern Michigan University, Ypsilanti.

measures than blacks of similar background and abilities who attended the HBCUs. Summarizing the results of his study, Allen writes that the "students in the sample who attend historically Black universities reported better academic performance, greater social involvement, and higher occupational aspirations than black students who attend predominantly White institutions. In short, the college experience was most successful (measured by these outcomes) for African-American students on campuses with Black majority student populations."[126]

These conclusions, says Allen, are supported by the research of many other scholars. Black students today seem to have a very difficult time adjusting to, and feeling welcomed on, college campuses where the majority of students are white (or white and Asian). The problems of social adjustment and alienation for black students on white campuses, says Allen, lead to a host of other problems, including lowered self-confidence, disengagement from challenging academic work, and poor scholastic performance. Summing up both his own and others' research on this topic, he writes:

> The salutary effect of Black students attending a historically Black university speaks volumes about the importance of the social-psychological context for student outcomes. In this respect, previous research demonstrates unequivocally the profound difference that historically Black and predominantly White campuses represent for African-American students. On predominantly White campuses, Black students emphasize feelings of alienation, sense hostility, racial discrimination, and lack of integration. On historically Black campuses, Black students emphasize feelings of engagement, connection, acceptance, and extensive support and encouragement. Consistent with accumulated evidence

---

126 Walter Allen, "The Color of Success: African-American College Student Outcomes at Predominantly White and Historically Black Public Colleges and Universities," *Harvard Educational Review*, 62 (1992): 26–44, 39–40.

on human development, these students, like most human beings, develop best in environments where they feel valued, protected, accepted, and socially connected. The supportive environments of historically Black colleges communicate to Black students that it is safe to take the risks associated with intellectual growth and development. . . . Historically Black universities provide positive social and psychological environments for African-American students that compare to those experienced by White students who attend White universities. In the social aspect, the important ingredients are an extensive network of friends, numerous social outlets, and supportive relationships. In the psychological aspect, the key ingredients are multiple boosts to self-confidence and self-esteem, feelings of psychological comfort and belonging, and a sense of empowerment/ownership—a sense that "this is our campus." When these social-psychological ingredients are present in optimal combination, the chances that a student will be successful in college increase dramatically.[127]

Allen, like Fleming, doesn't speculate on the degree to which racial-preference policies may contribute to the sense of alienation and other negative effects that blacks often experience on campuses that are predominantly white and Asian, but once again it is hard to imagine that the dual-track admissions standards that effectively reign at many of our most competitive colleges and universities (whereby blacks are admitted under much lower standards than those applied to whites and Asians) doesn't contribute mightily to these negative outcomes. It is difficult to see how being a member of a visibly identifiable minority group on a campus in which most of the other students are smarter or more academically accomplished than you are can fail to produce feelings of intellectual self-doubt and estrangement, as well as fear

127. Ibid.

that these other students may be looking down on you. Contacts of this kind lack almost all the ingredients previously discussed that are known to be crucial for breaking down stereotypes and prejudices and promoting greater harmony and understanding between people of different races. It is not surprising that black students on black campuses often do better in terms of the many outcome variables Allen and other researchers have looked at, where, in addition to being among people of one's own race, they are among those with academic abilities and accomplishments that are not significantly different from their own.

SOME FINAL REFLECTIONS ON MISMATCHING AND THE DOWNWARD RAIDING PROBLEM

Our current upward-ratcheting regime in college admissions often places black and Hispanic students in institutions one, two, or three levels of selectivity above the level they would have been placed in without preferences. The system has many harmful consequences that critics have long explored, but one such consequence that is not often mentioned is what might be called the "downward parasitism" or "downward raiding" problem.

The problem can be simply stated: When a Tier-1 school (Harvard, Princeton, Stanford) admits an "underrepresented minority student" who, in the absence of racial preferences, would have attended a Tier-2 school (Tufts, Lehigh, UCLA), or Tier-3 school (Boston University, Rutgers, Tulane), the students at these Tier-2 and Tier-3 schools are denied the diversity-enhancement value that these upwardly ratcheted minority students could have provided. The Tier-2 and Tier-3 schools then feel pressured to engage in similar "downward raiding" by admitting black and Hispanic students through their own preference programs who in the absence of such preferences would have attended less competitive Tier-4 and Tier-5 schools

272 DIVERSITY AND ITS DISCONTENTS

(and could have contributed to a healthy kind of demographic diversity at those schools). One school's diversity gain is always another's diversity loss. Even on its own terms it is not clear how racial diversity is enhanced by the current upward-ratcheting system,[128] which does nothing to alter the "pipeline" of college-eligible blacks and Hispanics coming out of high school (and is likely to constrict the pipeline because of the negative incentives to strive for excellence that college preferences based on race create at the high school level).

One cannot, however, take the diversity-enhancement argument on its own terms because it is implicitly based on a naïve version of the contact hypothesis, which fails to understand the limited sorts of conditions under which racial contact is likely to further rather than inhibit interracial understanding and intergroup harmony. There are good diversities and bad diversities, and diversities brought about artificially through racial preferences—ones that are widely viewed as unfair, that serve to heighten racial tensions on campus, and that reinforce negative stigmas and stereotypes about the mental competence of those in the targeted groups—are clearly in the noxious category. The upward ratcheting and upward mismatching of the affirmative-action system insure that good diversity within the American college system will always be replaced by bad.

Which raises the question of why such destructive policies persist. This topic was breached briefly in the previous chapter, and we can add to what was said there the previously quoted

---

128. It is true that the less selective a college tier, the more colleges there are in it (e.g., there are more Tier-2 schools than Tier-1s, and more Tier-3 schools than Tier-2s), thus downward raiders can probably increase the proportion of black and Hispanic students in their own institutions without reducing by the same proportion the blacks and Hispanics in the lower-tiered institutions that they raid. But the fact still remains that every black and Hispanic student upwardly ratcheted into a more selective college deprives a less selective college of the (more healthy) diversity-enhancement value that that student might have provided to the students at the less selective institution. Bad diversity—stereotype-reinforcing diversity—is always substituted for good.

remarks of Alan Dershowitz and Randall Kennedy to the effect that "diversity" often serves as a cover for more controversial concerns—including "social justice," a perceived need to elevate more blacks to leadership positions, the need of white people to protect themselves against charges of racism, etc.—that cannot be stated publicly either because of Bakke-derived constitutional constraints or fear of public backlash.

What can be said with great certainty, however, is that the terms of the interracial contact on college campuses today are highly unfavorable to achieving the integrationist goals that racial pluralists and diversity advocates claim they support. The upward ratcheting and mismatching of targeted minority students creates a campus-wide racial atmosphere at the most competitive colleges that practically guarantees that the goals of diversity advocates will never be adequately achieved and that racial self-segregation on college campuses will be the order of the day. Those integrationist goals, however, are surely noble and worthy of being pursued.

But if we really want to create a healthy, dignified, equal-status kind of diversity on college campuses today—one that demeans no group, makes no group feel superior, and really does enrich the educational and cultural experience of all parties concerned—we must move to end affirmative-action mismatching and return to the simple idea that college admissions decisions must be race- and ethnicity-neutral. This was the original ideal enshrined in the 1964 Civil Rights Act before college administrators so unwisely abandoned it in the early 1970s, with all the harmful consequences that have since then ensued. Returning to the wisdom that drove the original civil rights movement—including Justice Harlan's ringing cry in the Plessy case that "our Constitution is color-blind"—would have a salutary effect throughout American society and would be of great benefit to all. It would restore the ideal of equal status and provide the context wherein meaningful integration can take place. The greatest beneficiaries would be the rising generation of college students at the more selective colleges and universities.[129]

---

129. Here's a feisty doggerel for a new generation of campus activists:
   Hey, Hey, Ho, Ho,
   Racial Preference Gotta Go!
   So End It, Don't Defend It,
   End It, Don't Defend It!
   We All Gain Superior Traction,
   By Ridding Ourselves of Affirmative Action.
   Merit Can, Merit Must,
   Be the Basis of Our Trust!
   So Hey, Hey, Ho, Ho,
   Racial Preference Gotta Go!

V

SELLING MERIT DOWN
THE RIVER

As previously explained in the introduction to Chapter III, former Princeton president William Bowen and former Harvard president Derek Bok published to much acclaim *The Shape of the River*, the first of three River Books sponsored by the Andrew W. Mellon foundation, which dealt with the fate of black students on some of the nation's most selective college campuses. The Bowen and Bok volume soon became the elite-college establishment's unofficial defense of racial-preference policies and was the subject of extensive commentary in the popular media and elsewhere. In the minds of some, Bowen and Bok had put to rest arguments against racial preferences by their most outspoken critics and showed the great value to American society of taking race into account in assembling a college class.

Using a different data set than *The Shape of the River*, the two subsequent River Books—*The Source of the River* (2003) and *Taming the River* (2009)—provided the initial results of a projected long-term longitudinal study of students at many of the same colleges featured in the Bowen and Bok volume, and they offered a wealth of statistical material about the students at those institutions derived from three separate student questionnaires. Like its two predecessors, it was clear where the authors of River II and River III stood on the hot-button issue of affirmative action. Despite offering much material from their student

surveys that for many would seem to call into question the wisdom of racial-preference policies, all of the River Book authors
were clearly in the camp of affirmative action defenders. "Mend
it, don't end it!" was their collective bottom line.

In this chapter I offer a broadly based critique of the three
River books, with special focus on the last book in the series,
which seems to me to be pervaded by an even greater array of
errors and misunderstandings about the reality of race in America
than either of its two predecessors. The River Pilots, I argue, fail to
grasp the depth and intensity of opposition to racial-preference
policies on the part of large segments of the American public;
they fail to realize the powerful stigma-reinforcement effect of
such policies and their tendency to undermine the incentives of
those in the beneficiary groups to do their best in high school and
college; they fail to come to grips with the reality of dysfunctional
ethnic subcultures in America or to acknowledge their harmful
effects; and they fail to understand the effect preferentialist policies have had in lulling into indifference large segments of the
black and Latino middle class in the face of egregiously poor
academic performance by so many privileged black and Latino
youth at all levels of the American educational system.

In the final section of the chapter, I draw upon the work of
contemporary evolutionary psychology and evolutionary sociology in trying to explain "why race is different" and why ethno-
racial conflicts around the world often engage such highly
charged human emotions that can so easily spin out of control into violence and ethnic riot. The River Pilots, I suggest, are
dangerously ignorant of these forces, draw largely on outdated
60s-era sociological paradigms, and fail to realize the fragility
of national unity in a nation as racially, ethnically, and religiously
diverse as our own.[130]

---

130. This chapter is drawn from a long essay by the same title that first appeared on the
website of the National Association of Scholars (www.nas.org) in the early summer of
2009.

The River Pilots are at it again.[131] Their most recent endeavor, *Taming the River* (River III, 2009), offers a detailed analysis of the results of two sets of questionnaires given to a representative sample of college students at 28 selective colleges and universities who matriculated as freshmen in the fall of 1999. Like their earlier work, *The Source of the River* (River II, 2003), which concerned itself with the achievement of these same students only to the mid-point of their freshman year, this newest installment looks at a blinding complexity of student characteristics and attitudes and the relationship of these to various outcome variables (such as school retention and student grades) traced further on into the students' college life.

This ongoing longitudinal study was inspired by the first River book, *The Shape of the River* (River I, 1998), written by former Princeton President William Bowen and former Harvard President Derek Bok, which used a different database (the College and Beyond Survey), to analyze the progress of students who had attended more than two dozen selective U.S. colleges and universities. River I's main conclusion was that the racial-preference policies the two former Ivy League presidents had done so much to promote were in general a great success and that their critics were mostly wrong in attacking them. All three River books have been sponsored by the Andrew W. Mellon foundation, which William Bowen headed until 2009.

Using a different set of questionnaires to develop a fresh data set—the National Longitudinal Study of Freshmen—the River II and River III books look at the social and academic

131. The three River books dealt with in this chapter are *The Shape of the River: Long-Term Consequences of Considering Race in College and University Admissions*, by William Bowen and Derek Bok, 1998 (designated as River I); *The Source of the River: The Social Origins of Freshmen at America's Selective Colleges and Universities*, by Douglas Massey, Camille Charles, Garvey Lundy, and Mary Fischer, 2003 (River II); and *Taming the River: Negotiating the Academic, Financial, and Social Currents in Selective Colleges and Universities*, by Camille Charles, Mary Fischer, Margarita Mooney, and Douglas Massey, 2009 (River III). All three River books were published by Princeton University Press, Princeton and Oxford.

development of students who in 1999 entered most of the same institutions surveyed in River I and trace their progress through the end of their sophomore year. All three River books, although they have multiple authors and despite the fact that the first River book specifically claimed not to have any policy agenda but to be merely gathering facts relevant to a more informed public debate, are written from the standpoint of those who passionately, even desperately, want to retain current racial-preference policies in American universities and to minimize or refute the claims of the policies' many critics.

The attempt at refutation is particularly aimed at people like Thomas Sowell and Shelby Steele, who argue that current racial-preference policies both stigmatize their intended beneficiaries as intellectually inferior and create a "mismatch" or "bad fit" that often places black and Latino students in academic settings too advanced for their individual talents and needs. Like its two predecessors, however, River III raises issues and underscores problems about current preference policies that readers less committed to racial preferences will find strongly supportive of their own doubts about such policies and sound reason for their immediate termination or gradual phase-out.

But *Taming the River* isn't only about racial-preference policies, and when it is not trying to defend "affirmative action," River III has genuine merit. Among some of the more intriguing findings in *Taming the River* and its predecessors are these:

- Black students at elite colleges come from a much broader range of socio-economic and educational backgrounds than whites or Asians. While most blacks come from what might be considered a broad middle-class sweep of America, and almost 60 percent of their fathers (and 54 percent of their mothers) have at least a four-year college degree, a not-insignificant 17 percent come from a family that some time in the past was on welfare. Much more rarely do white and Asian students come from families that have ever received welfare (4 percent of whites and 9 percent of Asians), and a much greater majority of white and Asian parents have college degrees (84 percent of the white fathers and 80 percent of the Asian fathers) and hold managerial or professional jobs. Twice as many whites as blacks come from households earning over $100,000 annually (51 percent vs. 25 percent). Those from middle- and upper-middle-class households dominate the white and Asian student pool, while both Latinos and blacks are more spread out on the socio-economic continuum, with a more substantial lower-middle and lower-class contingent.[132]

- In their freshman and sophomore years Asians and whites typically achieve around a B average in their college courses, Latinos around a B-, and blacks between a B- and a C+. These differences seem small, but given the grade inflation and grade compaction that characterize the more competitive colleges in America (where C grades are rare and D grades rarer still) the racial difference in GPAs is very substantial.

- Blacks, and to a lesser extent Latinos, "underperform" their entering academic credentials to the extent that they do not do as well in terms of their grades in college as Asians and whites with similar standardized test

132. Although the River Pilots do not acknowledge it, the lower proportion of whites and Asians from low-income households compared with their black and Latinos counterparts is at least partially an artifact of race-conscious admissions policies that accord huge boosts to the black and Latino poor—as well as those from better-off circumstances—but much less of a boost to the white and Asian poor. Poor whites and poor Asians generally do much better on the SAT than poor blacks and poor Latinos do, but they are not what college administrators usually have in mind when they say they want to increase "diversity." Were a "class-based" rather than a "race-based" system of admissions preferences adopted, there would be many more whites and Asians from socioeconomically deprived backgrounds on elite college campuses than exist now, and they would surely overwhelm in number their black and Latino counterparts.

scores and high school grades. This is the opposite of what many people think, especially those who claim that standardized tests are culturally biased. In predictive terms such tests are indeed biased—*in favor* of blacks and to a lesser extent Latinos, overestimating how well they actually do in their college courses.

- Blacks of West Indian or African parentage are greatly overrepresented at the more competitive colleges compared to all blacks. At the Ivy League schools presented in the NLSF survey blacks with parents born abroad—mostly those from West Indian and African backgrounds—constitute 40 percent of all black students, an enormous overrepresentation considering the small percentage (approximately 13 percent) such students represent in the total black student age population in America. Had the definition of immigrant black been expanded to include those with grandparents born abroad—a definition that would include Colin Powell's children—the foreign-origin proportion of blacks would be significantly greater (at the most elite Ivies perhaps 50 percent or more). Immigrant-origin blacks compete with native-origin blacks for affirmative action slots in elite universities, a development some native blacks find objectionable.

- For all ethno-racial groups grades in college are strongly affected by pre-college academic achievement, as reflected in high school grade point average (HS-GPA), scores on the SAT, and self-rated assessment of previous educational quality. The level of parents' education also shows an independent effect on the grades their children earn.

- When a positive self-esteem index is computed by agreement with statements such as "I feel that I am a person of worth equal to others" or "I take a positive attitude toward myself" or by disagreement with statements such as "I wish I could have more respect for myself" or "I feel that I do not have much to be proud of," counterintuitive outcomes result. Using such an index, blacks and Latinos do not reveal lower self-esteem than whites; in fact, they have slightly higher self-esteem, although the index scores of all three groups do not vary much. Black males have the highest self-esteem of any of the ethno-gender groupings. Blacks who have attended all-black or nearly all-black high schools have higher self-esteem than those who have attended mixed-race or predominantly white schools. Asians have by far the lowest self-esteem of the four ethno-racial groups surveyed, showing that the absence of self-esteem—or self-esteem conditioned upon meeting very high academic goals for oneself—may be more conducive to academic success than simply feeling good about oneself regardless of how one performs in the classroom.[133]

- Black women outnumber black men on competitive college campuses by a factor of approximately two to one, whereas for whites and Asians the gender ratio is much less skewed. Since most dating and romantic relationships are intraracial, black women are often left without boyfriends, dates, or potential mates. Asian males are even more likely to be without romantic

---

133. Many other studies have documented the high level of black self-esteem in the face of very poor academic performance. The usual explanation given is that many blacks disidentify or disconnect their sense of self-worth from academic achievement and develop high self-esteem by placing greater emphasis on their success in peer relationships, sports, partying, social life, stylish dressing, displays of "nerve," etc. See for instance Bruce Hare, "Stability and Change in Self-Perception and Achievement among Black Adolescents: A Longitudinal Study," *Journal of Black Psychology*, 11 (1985): 29–42; J. R. Porter and R. W. Washington, "Black Identity and Self-Esteem: A Review of Studies of Black Self-Concept and Identity," *Annual Review of Sociology*, 5 (1979): 53–74; Mary Ann Scheirer and Robert Kraut, "Increasing Educational Achievement via Self-Concept Change," *Review of Educational Research*, 49 (1979): 131–49; and Elijah Anderson, *Code of the Street* (New York: W.W. Norton, 1999).

relationships than black women, but this appears to be due more to their focus on academic pursuits than a lack of opportunity.

- Those who have grown up in violent, chaotic neighborhoods and households are at significant risk of permanent cognitive impairment and difficulty in learning due to the effects that long-term exposure to stress hormones have on the developing brain. Students coming from such backgrounds have a diminished chance of success in college.

- Black and Latino students coming from troubled family circumstances often have intervening "family issues" that interfere with their progress in college. White and Asian students are much less likely to have family problems of this kind to deal with.

While River III, like River II, contains a good deal of interesting material about the characteristics of students at America's more selective colleges, the book is clearly written with two overarching purposes in mind, all the more revealing because they are rarely acknowledged as such. River III wants to convince the reader, 1) that race-based preference programs, although they display at least some of the serious harmful effects that critics ascribe to them, are on balance of great benefit to all parties concerned and should be retained in an improved form; and 2) that the main reason black and Latino youth have such trouble doing well in high school and college is because American society segregates them in ghettos and makes them attend primary and secondary schools in racially isolated neighborhoods from which whites have fled.

In trying to promote their central policy prescription (retention of racial preferences) and major apologetic theme (shifting responsibility and blame for poor black and Latino school performance to the behavior of the dominant white society rather than internal cultural deficiencies or dysfunctional family and neighborhood socialization among the lower-achieving groups themselves), the authors of the River books are forced to engage in mental gymnastics that defy both common experience and common sense. Their main problem, it seems, derives from a cast of mind that filters social reality through a distorting lens of 60s-era left-liberal ideology and the reigning tenets of academic political correctness and from a set of background assumptions about race and ethnicity in America that seem oblivious or indifferent to the many serious challenges posed to their veracity by scholars who do not abide political correctness or share left-liberal assumptions.

Simply stated, the River Pilots display an extreme insularity and parochialism that keeps them ignorant of some of the best writing on race and ethnicity emanating from critics with perspectives different from their own. Insofar as they have read works by critics of the policies and perspectives they favor, they have done so superficially and often missed some of the main challenges presented to their own left-of-center claims. River III in particular seems to be written by and for only those sharing its ideological viewpoint on racial issues, with only the weakest and most half-hearted attempt to come to grips with the challenges to its *Weltanschauung* of those coming from opposing camps. Again and again as I read this book I posed hypothetical questions such as, "What would they say to scholars such as . . . , who against such a view argue that . . . ?" Rarely, if ever, did the River authors provide an answer to such queries or seem to be aware that very weighty and informed arguments against their positions exist.[134]

---

134. Among the names of scholars filling in the first blank were (in no particular order): Donald Horowitz, John McWhorter, John Ogbu, Stephan and Abigail Thernstrom, Pierre van den Berghe, Thomas Sowell, Daniel Moynihan, Margaret Gibson, James Flynn, Dinesh D'Souza, Orlando Patterson, Shelby Steele, Edward Banfield, Curtis Crawford, Amy Wax, Frank Salter, Amy Chua, J. Philippe Rushton, Min Zhou, Michael Levin, Nathan Caplan, John Derbyshire, Myron Magnet, Charles Murray, Myron

They just don't get it! is perhaps the simplest way I can sum up the River Pilots' understanding of the reality of race and ethnicity in America. To be sure, their failing is not due to any lack of intellectual talent—two of the River authors, William Bowen and James Shulman, have displayed outstanding research and critical thinking abilities in their path-breaking study of the corrupting effects on educational values of the professionalization of sports on college campuses.[135] Their failing, rather, is due entirely to the extreme ideological one-sidedness that dominates academic sociology and the other academic disciplines from which they draw and to the general inability of most academic scholars to address issues of race and ethnicity in America with any degree of honesty or candor.

In this chapter I discuss seven important truths about preferential policies and race, which, in my view, all three River books conspicuously fail to understand. While the list is not exhaustive, it addresses what I think are the most salient and most serious of the River Pilots' failings.

THE STIGMA HARM OF RACIAL PREFERENCES

Let's begin with the issue of stigma. For more than four decades now critics of affirmative action—especially black critics—have contended that by placing black students in institutions where white and Asian students have the edge in terms of cognitive development and past performance the image of blacks as intellectually inferior—an image with long-standing cultural resonance in America—is powerfully reinforced. The critics speak of "stigma-creation" or "stigma-reinforcement," a development, they say, that produces a host of problems on college campuses,

---

Weiner, William Kelso, Byron Roth, Jared Taylor, Richard Herrnstein, and James Q. Wilson.
135. James Shulman and William Bowen, *The Game of Life: College Sports and Educational Values* (Princeton: Princeton University Press, 2001).

including a) the creation of feelings of intellectual inferiority and superiority apportioned by racial group membership; b) a diminished sense of collegial camaraderie and closeness; c) diminished academic performance and less intellectual engagement by the stigmatized groups; d) resentment and condescension by the groups (i.e., whites and Asians) not preferentially treated; and, e) tainted credentials for all those in the group receiving the preferential treatment. The list is not exhaustive.

Oddly, in view of their strong support for preferentialist policies, the River Pilots dispute few of these claims. Indeed, their studies document the truth of many of them. Here, for instance, is just a sample of what they say about some of the problems and dilemmas encountered at the various colleges and universities they studied with those institutions' policies of racial preferences:

- "In relative terms we detect a subtle but real tendency [for the students in our survey] to stereotype groups in a manner consistent with racist ideology. African Americans and Latinos, in particular, are more likely to be viewed as having characteristics that are inconsistent with academic success, while the reverse is true for Asians. There is also widely shared rank ordering of groups in terms of traits favorable to academic progress, with Asians on top, followed by whites, Latinos, and blacks. Whites and Asians feel especially distant from blacks and Latinos who 'benefit from affirmative action.' The perception of blacks and Latinos as 'academically underqualified' may be exacerbated by the presence of Asians, who are generally perceived as overqualified." (River II, p. 152)
- "Failure to perform up to institutionally expected academic standards is psychologically distressing because it implies that the stereotype may, in fact, be true: a poor

intellectual performance might convince white observers that black and Latino students indeed *are* intellectually inferior to whites and Asians. . . . . Moreover, if black and Latino students have internalized the negative stereotype themselves, they may adapt psychologically by downplaying the importance of academic success in determining self-worth and put in less effort toward academic achievement, essentially disidentifying from education as a domain of self-evaluation. If they fail, they can always tell themselves that they really did not try hard and that academic success is not that important anyway." (River III, p. 174)

- "Whites and Asians tended to perceive a great deal of [social] distance between themselves and blacks who benefited from affirmative action. . . . Such perceptions of distance from 'affirmative action beneficiaries' carry important implications for the general tone of race relations on campus because one stereotype that emerges . . . is that without affirmative action most black and Latino students would not be admitted. To the extent that such beliefs are widespread among white students at elite institutions, they will not only increase tensions between whites and minorities on campus; they will also increase the risk of stereotype threat by raising anxiety among minority students about confirming these negative suspicions." (River II, pp. 143, 145)

- "If white students believe that many of their black peers would not be there were it not for 'lowering' of standards under affirmative action and, more important, if black students *perceive whites* to believe this, then affirmative action may indeed undermine minorities' academic performance by heightening the social stigma they already experience because of race or ethnicity." (River III, p. 189)

- "At almost every college in our sample, black students are not only performing less well academically than whites but also performing below the levels predicted by their SAT scores. In fact, this underperformance turns out to be even more important than lower test scores in explaining the gap in class rank between blacks and whites. . . . Of the overall black-white gap in average rank in class of 30 points—obtained by subtracting the average rank in class of black students (23rd percentile) from the average rank in class of white students (53rd percentile)—only about half of it (14 points) is accounted for [in our statistical model] by black-white difference in other measurable variables [like SAT scores and high school grades]." (River I, pp. 77, 88)

- "We found that internalization of negative stereotypes has a very strong effect in reducing academic work effort, assessed both subjectively using self-ratings of scholarly effort and objectively using reported hours of study, suggesting a clear process of disidentification. . . . [We also found] that externalization of negative stereotypes is generally associated with a higher subjective performance burden. Minority students who expect others to evaluate them in terms of negative stereotypes feel their performance reflects not just on themselves but on all members of their racial or ethnic group." (River III, p. 186)

- "We . . . find a significant effect of *institutional* affirmative action[136] on the grade performance of black and

---

136. The River Pilots distinguish *institutional affirmative action*, measured by the gap in SAT scores between that of the average black and Latino student at an institution and the institution's SAT average, and *individual affirmative action*, measured by the gap between an individual black or Latino's SAT score and that of higher-scoring blacks and Latinos in the same school who score at the institution's SAT average or above. About individual affirmative action they say: "Black and Latino students with relatively low SAT scores do no better or worse than their counterparts [in terms of college

Latino students . . . The greater the discrepancy in SAT scores between minority students and others on a particular campus, the lower the grades earned by individual black and Latino students at the same campus. Thus a sizable minority-majority test score gap within any insti-

---

grades] who scored at or above the average for their institution" (River III, p. 199). They conclude from this that mismatch theory is wrong. But the SAT measure alone is often an inadequate gauge of affirmative-action preferences in the case of individuals. While the gap between an institution's overall SAT average compared with the mean SAT of all black or Latino students in that school is probably a good indication of how far down admissions committees are reaching academically to enroll more black and Latino students, the SAT score of any individual black or Latino, taken by itself, is *not* a good indication of how far down the institution has reached academically *for that particular student in relation to other black and Latino students in the school*, or how well that student is likely to do in terms of grades. This is because racial preferencing of underrepresented minorities involves considering black and Latino students with *overall* high school academic records lower than whites and Asians, and such records include, besides SAT scores, the high school GPA, the number and scores on AP exams, and the overall rigor of a student's high school preparation. Many lower-SAT-scoring black and Latino students are no doubt admitted to an elite college because of compensating strengths in terms of GPAs, AP course scores, and the greater rigor of the high school program they took, and may have higher scores on such composite indices than many of their higher-SAT-scoring black and Latino college classmates, though with overall performance on such indices still far below the institutional average for whites and Asians. We would not be too surprised, for instance, if a black student with, say, a 580 average on the SATs and a 3.9 HS-GPA does better in college in terms of grades than a black classmate in the same institution who has taken similar high school courses and achieved a 660 average on the SATs but only a 3.3 HS-GPA. For this reason, no matter how much an institution has reached down to admit more underrepresented minorities, one would not necessarily expect to find a strong SAT/college-grades correlation among affirmative-action admits within that institution when SATs are considered alone. Indeed, all of the regressions in the River studies show HS-GPA and reported rigor of high school preparation to be a much better predictor of college grades than the SAT (although the SAT score also counts). Had a composite index been created that included the SAT, the HS-GPA, and the student's reported rigor of preparation, there would almost certainly have been found a strong correlation within an institution between past indicators of cognitive development in high school and the college grades obtained.

What the River I authors in another context say about the graduation rates of the lower-SAT matriculants at the more selective colleges in their survey may be relevant here: "The most selective schools have the best opportunity to 'pick and choose' among applicants within every SAT category. Hence, the high graduation rates of their matriculants in the lower SAT intervals may reflect the success of these schools in identifying and enrolling students with below average [SAT] test scores who had other qualities that gave them excellent prospects of graduating" (River I, p. 63). And, one might add, the lower the SAT interval, the larger the applicant pool will often be from which admissions deans can selectively "pick and choose" high-GPA, or high-maturity, or harder-working students.

tution appears to create a social context that makes it more difficult for minority students to perform academically, thus lowering the grades they earn, an outcome consistent with the social stigma hypothesis. . . . The extensive use of race-sensitive criteria under affirmative action, when it produces a large test score gap between minority and other students on campus, appears to lower minority achievement in two ways. Directly, a large test score gap creates a stigmatizing social context within which black and Latino students find it more difficult to perform, and indirectly a large test score gap heightens the subjective performance burden experienced by minority students because of stereotype threat. We thus confirm both the social stigma hypothesis and the performance burden version of the stereotype threat hypothesis." (River III, pp. 199–200)

- "All students confront common academic, financial, and social challenges in adapting to college . . . but the pressures are generally more intense for minority groups. . . . Most whites . . . are probably blissfully unaware of the racial and ethnic undercurrents that bedevil minority students on campus, and few can likely relate to the onus of stereotype threat or appreciate the stigma of a heightened performance burden from affirmative action programs." (River III, p. 206)
- "Our results show that students who are likely beneficiaries of affirmative action are less satisfied with college than others and that those attending schools that practice more extensive affirmative action earn lower grades." (River III, p. 228)

It's a long and damning list, and the River Pilots at least deserve credit for looking the devil in the eye and not turning away from the fact that "race-sensitive admissions" (their alternative euphemism for racial preferences) has a dark side that cannot be denied. Two strategies are pursued to come to terms with this acknowledged fact that racial-preference policies have many of the serious harmful effects that critics have long attributed to them. The first strategy, which is dominant in River I, is to look at the issue in cost-benefit terms, and while acknowledging considerable stigma and stereotype-threat costs, the authors claim that these are outweighed by the many benefits of having more underrepresented minorities on elite campuses. Among these benefits are said to be the institution's demographic diversity gain and the cultural enrichment said to flow from this diversity for all students on campus. Another important benefit is said to be found in the meeting of pressing social needs. American society, it is argued, needs more black and Latino leaders, and racial preference policies at the elite universities, the argument goes, are a major means of increasing both the number of such leaders and the quality of their education. Without the increased presence of blacks and Latinos at the more competitive institutions of higher learning, America, it is said, would be deprived of many valuable black and Latino leaders.

The second strategy, which is dominant in River III (though not ignored in River I and II), is to propose ways to eliminate or reduce the stigma harm itself. This is to be accomplished, the River Pilots say, by admissions officers, college administrators, and college faculty convincing the specially admitted students that they have not been admitted under lowered standards, but rather, that they have been chosen because of important accomplishments or abilities that may not be captured by such things as high school grades or scores on standardized test. "Institutional efforts to maintain racial and ethnic diversity among students," they write, "should never be presented as involving a lowering of the bar, a bending of rules, a making of exceptions, or a loosening of standards to accommodate students who are somehow lacking, deficient, or challenged on some important dimension. . . . With respect to admissions, institutions should present themselves as looking for manifestations of excellence and achievement in a variety of domains, of which test-taking ability is just one, and a narrow one at that. Framed in this way, each student is presumed to be outstanding and accomplished in some important way." (River III, p. 228)

It is hard to take any of these suggestions seriously, and since the River Pilots are not lacking in normal human intelligence the most charitable interpretation is that they reflect the desperation with which they try to avoid the obvious conclusion that the policies they have long supported do serious harm to race relations on campus—harm that their own studies have abundantly documented. Against the first strategy, it should be remarked that not all diversities are good diversities and that a stigma-reinforcing diversity artificially created by the upward ratcheting of blacks and Latinos into institutions where they are guaranteed to do less well on average than whites and Asians is not a formula for healthy campus race relations. The River Pilots' own surveys show that white and Asian students express a great deal of "social distance" from the black and Latino "beneficiaries of affirmative action," and, as explained in Chapter III, their surveys probably understate the social distances between these groups, since we know from years of polling that the term "affirmative action" for some people means nothing more than outreach programs rather than more controversial preference programs. Had white and Asian students been asked their opinion of black and Latino "beneficiaries of racial preferences," their expressed social distance would no doubt have been much greater. It is difficult to see how more intellectually substandard black and Latino students on college campuses improve race relations, enrich the learning environment for the whites and Asians, or improve the image of blacks and Latinos in the minds of their classmates. Nor is it easy to see how such policies will turn out better educated and more self-confident black and Latino leaders. The studies discussed in Chapter III by Cole and Barber, Smythe and McArdle, Richard Sander, and the research teams of Rogers Elliott and Mitchell Chang certainly suggest otherwise.

The second strategy is even more difficult to take seriously than the first. What could they possibly mean by "[displaying] excellence and achievement in a variety of domains of which test-taking ability is just one"? And regardless of how administrators choose to label such programs, "lowering the bar," "bending the rules," "making exceptions," and "loosening standards" are exactly what virtually everyone—including college administrators themselves, who routinely lie about it— actually believe racial preference programs do. This indeed, is why there has emerged a reticence to talk about them openly, or when they are talked about, only through euphemisms and prettifying obfuscations ("race-sensitive admissions," "affirmative action," "diversity").[137] The River Pilots here apparently want college administrators to give a pep talk to the lower-achieving black and Latino students and explain to them how valued they are for their nonacademic accomplishments, although it isn't stated exactly what these accomplishments are. One supposes the accomplishments imagined are the mere fact of coming from an underrepresented minority group and the educational value to the campus community that a background in such a minority culture is believed to have.

But aside from the harmful effects that a glut of low-achieving black and Latino students will have on the image of their group among the higher-achieving white and Asian students,

---

137. The Germans have a wonderful phrase for this: durch die Blumen sprechen— "to speak through the flowers." College presidents routinely "speak through the flowers"—if they don't outright lie—when talking about racial-preference policies on their campuses since straight talk would often deeply pain preference beneficiaries and encourage acrimonious controversy and discord.

there is the problem of the effect that an emphasis on non-academic qualities will have on the black and Latino students themselves. Imagine, for instance, an admissions dean, inspired by advice given in River III, sending out an acceptance letter something like the following:

Letter of Acceptance

Congratulations Ms. Jones! We are proud to inform you that you have been accepted for admission to prestigious Ivy U. as part of our ongoing commitment to racial diversity and inclusion. We at Ivy are deeply committed to the principles of affirmative action, and we know that you, as an African American, will be able to bring to Ivy a distinct perspective and unique background that will enrich the educational experience and understanding of all our students. At Ivy we seek talent across a variety of domains, and we know that your exceptional life experience will greatly contribute to the rich mosaic of talented students on our campus. We are thrilled to be able to extend our admissions offer to you and we earnestly hope that you will be able to accept our offer and join our entering freshman class in the fall.

Once again, our heartfelt congratulations!

Very truly yours,

Harold Irvington III

Director of Admissions

Admissions deans are not likely to send out such a letter, although it would conform to the prescription the River Pilots offer for making lower-achieving black and Latino students feel welcomed and valued on highly competitive college campuses even though they may not be equal to others in terms of narrow "test-taking ability." People who gain admission to prestigious colleges usually want to think they got accepted on some genuine accomplishment—if not top academic performance then at least some valued nonacademic achievement, as in music or sports. But being told that one is valued because one is an African American or member of an "underrepresented minority group" would be taken by most as both an insult to the group ("Truth be told, Ms. Jones, without special admissions few from your group could make it"), and to the individual given preferential acceptance ("You have a pretty good scholastic record Ms. Jones—for an African American"). Focusing on being valued because of one's race or ethnicity, or for some other nonacademic reason, would seem to be a prescription for enhancing the disidentification—or lukewarm identification—with the realm of learning that the River Pilots themselves believe is partially responsible for underperformance among many black and Latino youth. Such valuation is not likely to lead to greater ease of integration into a white- and Asian-dominated campus and will surely increase protective self-segregation by black and Latino students told that their race or ethnicity is what helped them gain admission to a competitive college.

At one point the authors of River III suggest a comparison between the lowered standards for underrepresented minorities and those for athletes and legacies, and they conclude that just as the latter two groups are not stigmatized by lowered standards and do not display underperformance, so wise policy should enable the minorities to achieve similar results. But they are clearly wrong about the stigma issue regarding recruited athletes, at least those in the higher-profile sports, who are probably even more negatively stigmatized in terms of their intellectual abilities ("dumb jocks") than blacks or Latinos, and the most comprehensive study of the academic performance of recruited athletes finds a pattern of underperformance (achieving grades in college below that predicted by one's SAT scores and high school grades) very similar to that of blacks. Legacies are a different matter, since they usually have entering credentials better than recruited athletes or blacks (i.e., admissions officers do not reach down as far to accept them unless their parents are really big-bucks donors), and not being visibly recognizable as such, legacies are presumably less prone to the debilitating effects of stigma and stereotype threat.[138] And they also do not confront the disincentive effects of an across-the-board system of preferences such as that in place for blacks and Latinos, which reaches well beyond college to professional schools, graduate schools, and jobs in the corporate sector.

The River Pilots are simply wrong to believe that perceptions about racial minorities who receive admissions preferences can be easily manipulated by college administrators and faculty. Their own study in River III shows that it is their *classmates*, not college officials or faculties, who set the general tone and determine the nature of the racial atmosphere on campus. Derogatory comments about race or ethnicity, they report, "were very infrequently reported from professors, staff, or others on campus." "The most frequent source of derogatory comments was other students." About a quarter (23 percent) of black and Latino students reported hearing "derogatory remarks from fellow students" about their group. (River III, p. 141)

At one point in River II the authors do get candid and acknowledge that it may not be in the power of college administrators to do much about negative stigma and the imputation of inferiority to groups receiving special admissions preferences. It is difficult, they say, "to design programs to overcome 'the threat in the air' [of being stigmatized as inferior] that is the hallmark of stereotype vulnerability, for this involves a manipulation of students' deepest feelings, which are often unconscious or unacknowledged" (River II, p. 195). Even if it is possible to improve the grade performance of those admitted under preference programs (the River Pilots cite a successful program along

---

138. On recruited athletes and legacies, see the relevant sections of Shulman and Bowen, *The Game of Life*.

these lines at the University of Michigan), it is still unlikely that there will be much done to change the negative public images that abound, particularly about black intellectual abilities, given the deep roots such images have in the general culture and the continued claim on the part of college administrators and black leaders that racial-preference policies are still needed four decades after their initial introduction. No amount of creative relabeling, pep talks, consciousness-raising sessions, diversity appreciation days, or the like will ever change student perceptions on campus if members of visibly identifiable ethno-racial groups are admitted under different academic standards than apply to others. This is a simple fact that the River Pilots are hesitant to acknowledge.[139]

UPWARD RATCHETING REINFORCES NEGATIVE STEREOTYPES AND REPLACES GOOD DIVERSITY WITH BAD

The River Pilots, particularly in River I, make much of the advantages they believe flow from greater racial diversity on colleges campuses, and suggest that it is "race-sensitive" admissions policies that are responsible for this greater diversity and its many benefits. They arrive at this conclusion largely from

---

139. Preference critic Shelby Steele explains the situation in its simplest terms: "The accusation that black Americans have always lived with is that they are inferior . . . and this accusation has been too uniform, too ingrained in cultural imagery, too enforced by law, custom, and every form of power not to have left a mark. So when today's young black students find themselves on white campuses, surrounded by those who historically have claimed superiority, they are also surrounded by the myth of their inferiority. . . . And today this myth is sadly reinforced for many black students by affirmative action programs, under which blacks may often enter college with lower test scores and high-school grade point averages than whites. 'They see me as an affirmative action case,' one black student told me at UCLA. . . . A black student at Berkeley told me that he felt defensive every time he walked into a class and saw white faces. When I asked why, he said, 'Because I know they're all racists. They think blacks are stupid.'" Shelby Steele, *Second Thoughts about Race in America* (New York: Madison Books, 1991), pp. 87, 97.

responses to two items on their questionnaire for students: 1) how much of their college experience has helped them in their "ability to work effectively and get along well with people of different races/cultures," and 2) how much do they think their institution should emphasize "a racially/ethnically diverse student body." The authors also infer support for racial-preference policies from the many students who said they had gotten to "know well" at college (usually through contacts in their dorms or in class) two or more students of a different race.

The problems with their analysis of this issue, however, are manifold. First, based on several of the comments from students in their survey, much of the racial/ethnic and racial/cultural diversity they seem to prize comes from exposure to students who generally do not receive the kind of admissions preferences enjoyed by many black and Latino students. "My Vietnamese roommate," "a student who was Muslim," "a guy whose family were refugees from the junta in Greece," "[Asians from three] different nationalities," "a third-generation Chinese American," "a Saudi woman," "an orthodox Jew," "a guy who had been at Eton," "people from Tokyo"—these are some of the people cited by their student respondents in praise of the demographic diversity they encountered on campus. None of these people are in categories highly favored by affirmative-action preferences. And surely some of the black and Latino students their respondents would have met and believed to have contributed to a culturally enriching campus environment would not be affirmative-action admits—some portion of the black and Latino students on any competitive college campus would have been admitted on their own achievement without the aid of racial preferences.

The River Pilots falsely assume that a generalized praise of "diversity" by college students means an approval of all elements in that diversity and all ways in which that diversity might be achieved, including overt racial preferences. But what polling data we have about student opinion on these matters indicate that this is not the case. And given the substantial degree of "social distance" expressed by white and Asian students toward black and Latino "beneficiaries of affirmative action" in the River II study, it is almost certain that many students, if asked, would not have agreed that enhancing demographic diversity through racial preferences creates a positive kind of racial and cultural enrichment. Incredible as it seems, in all 92 pages of the four questionnaires that the various students in the River studies were asked to fill out—questionnaires that contain in sum over a *thousand* individual items—there isn't a single item asking students their opinion of the use of racial preferences (or "affirmative action") as a means of enhancing racial diversity on campus, or their view on whether knowledge of the existence of racial-preference policies has any effect on the image of black and Latino intellectual abilities. As I have suggested in Chapter III, the most likely explanation for such blinding omission is the River Pilots' conscious or unconscious fear of what the answers might be.

We know from decades of polling that support for strict meritocratic, race-neutral admissions policies at competitive colleges and universities is widespread and that racial-preference policies enjoy comparatively little support and a great deal of passionate opposition. Recall from Chapter III the June 2003 Gallup question on this issue: "Which comes closer to your view about evaluating students for admission into a college or university?: a) An applicant's racial and ethnic background should be considered to help promote diversity on college campuses, even if that means admitting some minority students who otherwise would not be admitted? Or, b) Applicants should be admitted solely on the basis of merit, even if that results in few minority students being admitted."

It is clear how each of the River Pilots would answer this question as well as most college presidents. The question is excellently worded and gets to the heart of the controversy over racial preferences in college admissions. The choice is simple: strict merit with no racial "plus-factoring" or some degree of special concern for race and ethnicity to promote diversity. Recall, however, the polling results: Of respondents expressing an opinion, whites favored choice "b" (strict merit even if little diversity) over choice "a" by an overwhelming 77 percent to 23 percent, while even among Latinos the merit-only choice was favored 62 percent to 38 percent. Asian responses were not reported (probably because their numbers were too small), but one can assume a response pattern not too far from the whites'. Only blacks preferred choice "a" (special consideration of race to promote diversity), but only by a narrow margin—53 percent to 47 percent.[140] The meritocratic, race- and ethnicity-neutral ideal clearly has widespread support in America, at least among the general public if not among left-leaning sociologists

---

140. An earlier Gallup question, first posed in March 1977 and repeated many times in the following years, tried to gauge support for preference programs as a means of compensatory racial justice. The question asked was this: "Some people say that to make up for past discrimination, women and members of minority groups should be given preferential treatment in getting jobs and places in college. Others say that ability, as determined by test scores, should be the main consideration. Which point comes closest to how you feel on this matter?" Every time the question was asked more than three quarters of those who had an opinion chose the "ability as determined by test scores option" rather than the "give preferential treatment option." The first time the question was posed during the Bakke controversy over racial preferences at a California state medical school, 83 percent of respondents choose the "ability as determined by test scores option," while only 10 percent chose the "preferential treatment option" (7 percent had no opinion). The fact that the question dealt with compensatory justice rather than diversity is illuminating. In the days before Lewis Powell's decision in the Bakke case, which approved of racial preferences only on diversity-enhancement grounds, compensatory justice and the need to create a stable black middle class were the most important justifications given by proponents of racial preferences in university and professional school admissions. Many hold that these are still the most important reasons administrators support racial-preference programs and that their "diversity-enhancement" rationale is merely a façade to please the courts and possibly the general public as well. Others say a fear of being labeled a racist or insensitive to "civil rights" is what drives support among college presidents and admissions deans for the race-based preferences they champion.

or former college presidents who write books defending their past policies.

We don't have data on student views on these issues by the students participating in the River studies (as I suggest, this is most likely a deliberate oversight), but there are at least two national surveys on these matters of student attitudes more generally. One has already been cited: In telephone interviews with a representative sample of students in 140 American colleges carried out by the research firm Angus Reid, overwhelming opposition to racial preferences in employment and college admissions was found.[141] To the statement, "No one should be given special preferences in jobs or college admissions on the basis of their gender or race," 85 percent of students said they either "strongly agreed" (66.7 percent), or "moderately agreed (18.7 percent), with the statement.

In another survey by Zogby International (2000) a representative national sample of American college students was asked to indicate their relative agreement or disagreement with this statement: "Schools should give minority students preference in the admissions process." Although this question for our purposes wasn't as good as the Gallup question (since it didn't state a reason for the minority preference), the results were striking. Over half of the student respondents (51 percent) said they "strongly disagreed," another quarter (26.1 percent) said they "somewhat disagreed," while only 21.3 percent expressed agreement, the vast majority of these saying they agreed only somewhat, not strongly. More than three quarters of the college respondents disapproved of minority-student preferences, with two out of three of these indicating they strongly disapproved. A large portion of college students in America clearly do not support "race-sensitive admissions," and this has to have an

---

141. Cited in Stanley Rothman, Seymour Martin Lipset, and Neil Nevitte, "Racial Diversity Reconsidered," *The Public Interest*, spring 2003, online at www.thepublicinterest.com, p. 4.

effect on the quality of race relations on campuses where such admission policies have long been in place.

In River I, Bowen and Bok seem to adopt a very naïve version of the "contact hypothesis" by which mere contact between people of different races and ethnicities, regardless of the conditions under which it takes place, is presumed to enhance learning and reduce intergroup prejudice and hostility. However, as explained in the previous chapter, the naïve version of the contact hypothesis has been refuted by generations of social science research as well as by the common experience of ethnicly diverse—and ethnicly divided—societies around the world. In many contexts contact greatly enhances prejudice and animosity among groups. The most ethnicly diverse regions of the world are usually among the most unstable and most violent, while the most ethnicly homogeneous regions—places like Denmark, Japan, Barbados, and Norway—are often among the most stable and peaceful.

Bowen and Bok at one point cite Gordon Allport's famous *The Nature of Prejudice*, first published in 1954, as "the classic explanation of 'the contact hypothesis'—i.e., the idea that interpersonal contact breaks down stereotypes and therefore reduces prejudice" (River I, p. 219.n.)—and they seem to imply that Allport adhered to their own version of contact theory. But Allport was no naïve contact theorist. He explicitly states, in fact, that contact reduces prejudice only under very explicit conditions, a key one being that those making the contact are of "equal status." Few whites in America had more contact with blacks than those in towns like Indianola in the Mississippi Delta, which Yale researcher John Dollard studied in the 1930s in his classic *Caste and Class in a Southern Town*.[142] And few whites in America were as prejudiced against blacks as the

---

142. John Dollard, *Caste and Class in a Southern Town* (New Haven: Yale University Press, 1937).

residents of this Delta town. Middle-class whites in Southern towns who encountered blacks mainly as maids, janitors, field hands, shoeshine boys, and prison-release laborers hardly found much reason to overcome their ingrained stereotypical views and prejudices.[143]

In a similar fashion, when whites and Asians matriculate at highly competitive institutions like those in the River I study and the average black at those institutions graduates at the 23rd percentile, or when the whites and Asians go on to competitive law schools or medical schools and the median black has scores on standardized tests that are in the bottom 10 percent of all entering students, one wouldn't expect stereotypical views and prejudices to be diminished. Some stereotypes in fact, especially those involving black intellectual inferiority, will be powerfully reinforced. What racial-preference policies and the upward ratcheting that they involve guarantee is that white and Asians on many college campuses and professional schools will encounter many blacks who clearly are *not* of equal academic status.

Even if one assumed for the sake of argument the truth of the naïve contact hypothesis, none of the River Pilots comes to

---

143. Allport writes on this: "The jobs that most Negroes and members of certain other minority groups hold are at or near the bottom of the occupational ladder. They carry with them poor pay and low status. Negroes are usually servants, not masters; doormen, not executives; laborers, not foremen. Evidence is now accumulating that this differential status in occupation is an active factor in creating and maintaining prejudice." He goes on to explain that "occupational contacts with Negroes of equal status tend to make for lessened prejudice." "It helps also," he continues, "if one knows Negroes of higher occupational status than one's own" (emphasis in original).Gordon Allport, *The Nature of Prejudice* (Reading, MA: Addison-Wesley, 1954), pp. 273, 276. If we translate this status requirement into the world of students accepted to highly selective colleges, we might predict that the more white and Asian students encounter black and Latino students who are equal to or above the academic performance level typical of whites and Asians, the more their prejudices will be reduced; the more they encounter blacks and Latinos below the performance level of whites and Asians the more their prejudices will grow. Yale law professor Stephen Carter makes a similar point in his autobiographical *Reflections of an Affirmative Action Baby* (New York: Basic Books, 1991).

grips with the simple fact that the placement of black and Latino students across the more than 3,000 undergraduate institutions in America is a zero-sum game, whereby one school's diversity gain is always another's diversity loss. This topic was taken up briefly at the end of the previous chapter, but the story is worth retelling. Under our current affirmative-action system, a school like Duke takes black and Latino students away from the student body at places like Vanderbilt and UNC, where the Duke admits would have enrolled absent racial preferences. Similarly Yale and Princeton take black and Latino students away from the students at places like Boston University and Tufts, where the specially admitted black and Latino students would have enrolled had these higher-tiered schools not had racial preference policies.

Tier-1 schools take students who, in the absence of racial preferences, would be attending Tier-2 or Tier-3 schools, while these second and third tier schools, to attain what they consider a "decent" representation of black and Latino students, engage in the same downward raiding vis-à-vis the schools immediately beneath them on the selectivity scale. The effect of this upward-ratcheting/downward-raiding process is to distribute black and Latino students throughout the American college system in such a way that it is guaranteed that on average the members of these groups will be among the lowest academic performers. The very logic of the system guarantees this result. If we take off the kid gloves and stop pretending that the naïve contact hypothesis is valid, what we see is that healthy diversity is always being replaced by a very unhealthy kind—i.e., stereotype-reinforcing diversity is put in the place of racial contacts that might genuinely have weakened negative stigmas and negative stereotypes. Indeed, one can hardly think up a more diabolical system, guaranteed to reinforce among all parties concerned the association of black and Latino students with intellectual inferiority, than our current upward-ratcheting system of racial preferences in undergraduate admissions.[144] Much of the River Pilots' own research confirms this, but they are too ideologically and emotionally committed to their past policies to suggest the obvious remedy—end upward ratcheting and admit all students on a race-neutral basis.[145]

---

144. Many years ago, at the very beginning of the debate over racial preferences, law professor Clyde Summers described a similar upward-ratcheting/downward-raiding process at work in the nation's law schools: "The minority students given [preferences at Harvard and Yale law schools] would meet the normal admissions standards at Illinois, Rutgers or Texas. Similarly, minority students given preference at Pennsylvania would meet normal standards at Pittsburgh; those given preference at Duke would meet normal standards at North Carolina, and those given preference at Vanderbilt would meet normal standards at Kentucky, Mississippi and West Virginia . . . In sum, the policy of preferential admissions has a pervasive shifting effect, causing large numbers of minority students to attend law schools whose normal admissions standards they do not meet, instead of attending other law schools whose normal standards they do meet." Clyde Summers, "Preferential Admissions: An Unreal Solution to a Real Problem," *University of Toledo Law Review,* 1970, p. 384, cited in Stephan and Abigail Thernstrom, "*Reflections on The Shape of the River,*" *U.C.L.A Law Review,* June 1999, pp. 1583 ff, footnote #70.

In this context, I might mention a recent conversation with a law professor at a state law school in the Deep South, who related to me how, in a typical year, no more than one black student in the entire entering class of his law school can meet the normal admissions standards that are applied to every entering white. There are plenty of black law school applicants in his state who could meet the law school's higher "white standard," he explained, but virtually all of them receive acceptances from more prestigious out-of-state schools, both public and private, where they invariably wind up enrolling. Virtually every black law student enters the law school with lower test scores and grades—often substantially lower—than the very lowest-scoring white. He went on to explain that the law school felt it imperative to enroll a substantial number of blacks even though almost none could meet the standards applied to whites because the law school deans feared they would be charged with racism or "turning the clock back on civil rights" if they adopted a uniform standard that no blacks could meet. One wonders in this context how much white contact with the black law students as this school will reduce white prejudice or the negative stereotyping of black lawyers-to-be.

145. Social theorist Alan Wolfe makes an interesting observation here. White students at elite colleges, Wolfe argues, who usually come from more affluent and more liberal households, are usually the least prejudiced against African American students, whereas many working-class whites, who may not be as unprejudiced and who typically attend colleges below the highest tiers, are more often in need of healthy interaction with appropriate blacks to broaden their perspectives and reduce their prejudices. By siphoning off those black students who could serve this role,and placing them in arenas where they will have less of a prejudice-reducing effect, the current racial-preference system does not do a good job of promoting better racial understanding or racial harmony, he believes. The present system "guarantees diversity where it is needed least and detracts from diversity where it is needed most." (Alan Wolfe, "The Rest of the River: A Sociologist's Perspective," *University Business,* Jan.-Feb. 1999, p. 47, cited in

IGNORING THE OBVIOUS: THE DISINCENTIVE
EFFECTS OF THE RACIAL-PREFERENCE SYSTEM

From the very beginning of the affirmative-action debate in the early 1970s, critics have charged that by granting racial preferences in university and professional school admissions those in the beneficiary categories will have less incentive to do their best. Knowing that the bar will be lowered for them, even students attending quality secondary schools and colleges, it was said, will modify their effort, knowing that at the end of the day when they apply to undergraduate schools or graduate programs they will receive a huge admissions boost.

Critics of preference policies have been repeating this claim ever since. Granting racial preferences in college admissions, Abigail and Stephen Thernstrom write, "is not a process likely to encourage its beneficiaries to work hard in high school. The message is clear: color is the equivalent of good grades. If you don't have the latter, the former will often do."[146] Similarly Larry Purdy, an attorney for the plaintiffs in one of the University of Michigan racial-preference cases, writes that "if a black student knows that the level of academic achievement expected from him is demonstrably lower than that demanded from his non-black classmates, there is very little incentive to put in the work necessary to achieve at the same level as his competitors."[147] And long before he became a River Pilot, Derek Bok, in a book published in 1982, accurately summarized the concerns of many critics of racial preferences (without necessarily agreeing with them) when he observed that "some observers believe that leading universities, by awarding a heavy preference to minority applicants, may actually sap the incentive of these students,

---

Thernstrom and Thernstrom, "Reflections on The Shape of the River," pp. 1583ff, n. 165)

146. Thernstrom and Thernstrom, *America in Black and White*, p. 422.

147. Larry Purdy, *Getting Under the Skin of Diversity: Searching for the Color-Blind Ideal* (Minneapolis: Robert Lawrence Press, 2008), p. 57.

since they will know that they do not need to receive the highest grades in order to gain admission to the best graduate and professional schools."[148]

Despite the common-sense appeal of such claims, this issue is taken up in only one of the River books, where the total treatment accorded to it amounts to less than a single page. "Some have argued that black students underperform academically because affirmative action lowers their motivation to do truly outstanding work," the River I authors remark, citing the work of the Thernstroms as an example of this claim. (River I, p. 85) "The willingness of leading graduate and professional schools to admit black candidates who did not rank at the very top of their classes," they go on, "is alleged to reduce the sense among black undergraduates that they must get absolutely top grades to move up academic and professional ladders." The River I authors then say that they "know of no way to test this hypothesis," but they indicate that they do not believe it is true because "there is . . . an abundance of anecdotal information that many black students feel intense pressure to live up to the standards they and their parents have set for themselves," and "it seems unlikely that many of them would suddenly decide to 'coast' academically." (River I, p. 85) At this point the issue of potential disincentive effects of the racial preference system is dropped, never to be taken up again, either in River I or its two successor studies.

One suspects that a "fear of the answer" dynamic is working on this issue, similar to that operative in the (non-)treatment of student opinion on preferential admissions. A crucially important area of inquiry is completely ignored, and the reasons given are suspicious. It is certainly no more difficult to devise questions to test the "preference-system disincentive hypothesis"

---

148. Derek Bok, *Beyond the Ivory Tower* (Cambridge, MA: Harvard University Press, 1982), pp. 101–2.

than to do the same for many other hypotheses the River Pilots test, including stereotype threat, disidentification claims, oppositional culture theory, etc. One could imagine, for instance, a simple question like this:

> On a simple agree/disagree continuum (from 'strongly agree' to 'strongly disagree') evaluate the following statement:
> Since many top graduate and professional schools, and many corporate recruiters, admit black and Latino students who have considerably lower grades and test scores than whites and Asians, black and Latino students have much less reason to strive to get As in their college courses than do their white and Asian classmates.

This would be a question easily comprehended by college students, and the answers would certainly be revealing. Agreement by a substantial number of blacks and Latinos would surely be suggestive of some truth in the claim that there is a disincentive effect to the current across-the-board system of racial preferences, and the degree of agreement with the statement by black and Latino students could be regressed with the degree to which these students "underperform" their entering SAT scores and high school GPAs. A positive correlation would confirm the "preference-system disincentive hypothesis," lack of such a correlation would disconfirm it. Such tests using probing questions are what quantitatively oriented social science is all about, and the failure of the River Pilots even to take up the issue suggests a central failing of their work (and this absence, I repeat, is best explained by a conscious or unconscious fear of the results such an inquiry would produce).

To the claim of the River Pilots that there is anecdotal evidence that black students are often under intense pressure to live up to the high standards they and their parents have set for themselves, one can say this: If the authors are talking about the pressures on blacks who have gotten into elite colleges, it is a sure bet that these students have worked harder than their black high school and black college counterparts who have not gotten into such competitive institutions, and that together with their parents they have put considerable pressure on themselves to achieve. In any within-race comparison, blacks at elite colleges have no doubt been among the harder-working and harder-striving of their race. But when the comparison shifts to blacks vs. whites or blacks vs. Asians, the situation changes—and we don't have to go outside the River studies' universe or rely on anecdotes to see this.

The River II study asked a number of questions intended to gauge how the students in their sample rated members of the four dominant ethno-racial groups on a number of traits, including being "hard-working" or "lazy." What they found was striking. Not only did Asians and whites rate blacks and Latinos as substantially less hard-working than members of their own groups, but in those negative assessments blacks and Latinos clearly agreed with them. "The group that rated blacks as laziest," the River Pilots ruefully report, "was blacks themselves." "The stereotype of black laziness," they explain, "seems to have been substantially internalized by African Americans themselves." All groups, including blacks and Latinos, saw Asians as the least lazy, a result the River Pilots say is consistent with "the stereotype of the 'hard-working Asian.'" (River II, p. 147) Blacks and Latinos were rated least hard-working, with whites in between these two groups and the Asians.

What the River Pilots don't acknowledge is that these laziness stereotypes may have some basis in fact, and that in addition to the harms of internalized feelings of inferiority (stereotype threat), strengthened by the upward ratcheting system,[149] a

---

149. There could perhaps be no more damning indictment of the stigma-reinforcement effect of the current upward-ratcheting system than the self-evaluations offered by blacks and Latinos in the River II study of the intellectual abilities of the members of

"preference-system disincentive factor" may be at work here, diminishing the level of effort blacks and Latinos put into academic achievement. They know they don't have to do as well as the Asians and whites among their classmates to get into the same graduate or professional schools or to get good job offers from large companies. Knowing the psychology of most adolescents, one might predict a drop-off in work effort by many of the members of the specially favored groups. Most adolescents, after all, do not act like Max Weber's restlessly striving, "inner-worldly Puritan ascetics," and they might be more than willing to exchange study time for greater leisure if they do not thereby lose out in the academic competition with many of their harder-working classmates.

Many black critics of racial-preference policies, including ones with long experience with black college students, have been saying this for years. Perhaps the most outspoken critic along these lines is the linguist John McWhorter, who taught for many years at Berkeley. On average, says McWhorter, the black students he taught at Berkeley, at least those who were not of Afro-Caribbean origin, tended to be much less engaged academically than the white and Asian students in his class, and the difference was impossible to miss. McWhorter thinks that much of this has to do with cultural factors, including a diminished commitment by even middle-class African Americans to an ethic of academic achievement. Many blacks too, he says, often play

---

their own group vis-à-vis whites and Asians. Not only did whites and Asians rate blacks and Latinos to be less intelligent than the members of their own group, but once again members of the black and Latino groups agreed with this negative assessment —black and Latino students saw whites and particularly Asians as smarter than the members of their own group (River II, pp. 145–8; note: the mixed-up labels on Table 7.5 must be rearranged to bring them into harmony with the results shown on the next page and in Figure 7.2). There are no doubt many factors that go into such evaluations, including factors completely unconnected with college admissions policies, but it is hard to believe that such policies don't reinforce in a powerful way the image of intellectual inferiority of the groups receiving preferences by joining together on the same college campus students from ethno-racial groups that have made it over a lower entrance standard with those who have made it over a substantially higher one.

a "pitiable victim" game, which does not help their academic progress, and he thinks there is at least some truth in Claude Steele's view of stereotype threat and the harm that internalized feelings of inferiority can sometimes have on black academic confidence and performance. But the racial "plus-factoring" and upward ratcheting of the affirmative action system also has a huge achievement-retarding effect, McWhorter believes, and as we have seen in Chapter III, he offers as Exhibit A his own past behavior in the mixed-race private high school he attended.

Recall McWhorter's own words: "Almost any black child knows from an early age that there is something called affirmative action which means that black students are admitted to schools under lower standards than white; I was aware of this from at least the age of ten. And so I was quite satisfied to make B+'s and A-'s rather than the A's and A+'s I could have made with a little extra time and effort. . . . In general, one could think of few better ways to depress a race's propensity for pushing itself to do its best in school than a policy ensuring that less-than-best efforts will have a disproportionately high yield."[150]

Anecdotal though it may be, McWhorter's account here has the ring of authenticity, at least for anyone with any knowledge of how typical teenagers act in a typical American high school. The knowledge that black students, and to a somewhat lesser

---

150. McWhorter, *Losing the Race*, p. 233. McWhorter continues along these lines: "Imagine telling a Martian who expressed an interest in American educational policy: 'We allow whites in only if they have a GPA of 3.7 or above and an SAT of 1300 or above. We let blacks in with a GPA of 3.0 and an SAT of 900. Now, what we have been pondering for years now is why black students continue to submit higher grades and scores than this so rarely.' Well, mercy me—what a perplexing problem!" (p. 233). The huge gap in scores that McWhorter hypothetically suggests here isn't as exaggerated as one might suppose. Where racial-preference policies have been pursued with the most zeal, gaps of this size actually exist. For instance, data from the University of Virginia obtained under the Freedom of Information Act show that in 2003 a black applicant with a 950–1050 SAT score had a substantially better chance of admission to UVA than a white applicant with a 1350–1450 SAT (See David Armor, "Affirmative Action at Three Universities," paper presented at the Virginia Association of Scholars Annual Meeting, p. 3, obtainable from www.nas.org).

extent Latino students, don't need to perform at the same level as whites and Asians to get into the same colleges as members of these nonpreferred groups is widely disseminated in contemporary America. And while this may have no harmful effect on the work ethic of some students, in more typical cases it probably does. Try to imagine, for instance, how a young, bright black teenager, with an American teenager's typical level of maturity and self-discipline, might react upon hearing, perhaps from an older student or high school guidance counselor, a message like the following (taken from the popular *Princeton Review Student Advantage Guide to College Admissions*): [151]

> Colleges sometimes claim that their admissions departments are "color-blind" . . . but this is never true. The color of your skin . . . can have a big effect on your chances of being admitted to the school of your choice. Sometimes these factors can help you; sometimes they can harm you. . . . Here are some important guidelines . . . Most selective colleges would like to have more African American students than they do, if for no other reason than that they very much want to appear to be unprejudiced. . . . [If you are black] make sure the admissions committee knows you're black (Attach a photograph). Selective colleges generally have less stringent requirements for black applicants. Take advantage of them. Don't be afraid to aim high. . . . You may be able to get into schools that wouldn't accept you if you were white. . . . [If you are Asian, however] pay attention to the following guidelines: If you're given an option, don't attach a photograph to your application and don't answer the optional question about your ethnic background. This is especially important if you don't have an Asian-sounding surname. (By the same token, if you do have an Asian-

---

151. Quoted in Purdy, *Getting Under the Skin of Diversity*, pp. 222–4.

sounding surname but aren't Asian, do attach a photo-
graph.) . . . [Many Asian students] have been extraordinarily
successful academically, to the point where some colleges
now worry that there are "too many" of these students on
their campuses. Being an Asian can now actually be a distinct disadvantage in the admissions processes at some of the
most selective schools in the country.

One can't say for sure, of course, how various individuals will react to the knowledge that they will be given a huge
admissions boost because of their race (just as one can't predict
how students will react to the admissions bar being raised for
their race). Some may see such a bonus the way local governments often view matching grants—i.e., as an incentive to put
in more effort to achieve at their maximum level. Others may
be indifferent to such admissions boosts and not alter their
effort or behavior in any way. But if one considers the typical teenager in America today it is probably safe to say that
racial "plus-factoring" will more likely lead to a slackening
of academic effort—and a correspondingly greater investment
in sports, social life, television watching, and other leisure-
time activities—than to more intense engagement with classroom studies. John McWhorter's response to the knowledge
that he would receive preferential treatment when he applied
to college doesn't seem strange, even though McWhorter, a
self-described "nerd," clearly liked the intellectual challenge
of school better than most other students. Coasting along and
letting the Asians toil away to get the higher grades they need
to get into good colleges may well be a strategy appealing to
many black teenagers even if issues like stereotype threat and
negative cultural forces weren't at work reducing academic
effort still further.

No doubt the way students respond to admissions boosts
(or their opposite) will depend a great deal on their family and

peer cultures. But what we know about black and Latino family and peer culture on this score is not encouraging. Recall from Chapter III the study of nine Wisconsin and California high schools carried out by adolescent development specialist Lawrence Steinberg and his colleagues. The Steinberg team found enormous differences in the degree to which different ethnic cultures support academic achievement, with Asians, as usual, far out ahead of other groups. Dramatic differences were found in both family and peer environments in the degree to which they encouraged mastery of school material. Not only did Asian students encourage high achievement among themselves, but their parents were by far the most demanding of all the groups—blacks and Latinos lay at the opposite end of the spectrum. The "trouble threshold" (lowest grade students could come home with before their parents got angry) averaged A- for Asians, B- for whites, and C- for blacks and Latinos.[152]

Not surprisingly, the Steinberg team found blacks and Latinos to achieve the lowest grades in high school, Asians the highest, with whites in between. This finding is fully consistent with the McWhorter claim that certain features of African American culture interact with the affirmative-action preference system to retard black academic performance. Better to lay back and take it easy, a common black response seems to be; let the Asians and some of the nerdier whites be the hard workers in school and be the ones who miss out on social life, sports, and having fun. Most American teenagers, the Steinberg team found, would greatly prefer to be members of the "popular" crowd, the "partyer" crowd, or the "jock" crowd in their high schools rather than the "brainy" crowd[153]—the latter often have very low status in many American high schools. And if you are black, you can often get into some of the same competitive colleges as the

---

152. Lawrence Steinberg, *Beyond the Classroom* (New York: Simon and Schuster, 1996), p. 161.
153. Ibid., p. 146.

white or Asian "brains" in your school with much lower grades and while still retaining your high-end "jock," "popular" or "partyer" status among your schoolmates.

Not surprisingly, Steinberg and his associates report that while "Asian students were more likely than other students to believe that not doing well in school would have negative consequences for their future," "black and Latino students don't really believe that doing poorly in school will hurt their chances for future success."[154] And the black and Latino students may be right. To some extent at least, given the huge racial and ethnic boosts they often receive in getting into competitive colleges, and given the preferential treatment they are likely to receive after college in graduate schools, professional schools, and the corporate hiring world, the black and Latino students may have correctly gauged how far mediocre grades can take them (just as the Asian students have correctly gauged how much better they must do than the Latinos and blacks to go as far as them in college and beyond). If black and Latino students set their goals on attaining the level of success in their college admittance as that of whites and Asians of similar academic talent and aspirations for college, they will have good reason to spend less time hitting the books and taking their classroom activities seriously than their white and Asian peers. They know, to repeat Shelby Steele once again, that "mediocrity will win for them what only excellence wins for others."[155]

A similar process, of course, will be at work for black and Latino students when they attend college. The authors of the third River book note that black and Latino college students are more likely than whites or Asians to say that they aspire to attain a masters, Ph.D., or professional school degree. The

154. Ibid., pp. 90–1.
155. Shelby Steele, *A Dream Deferred* (New York: HarperCollins Publishers, 1998), p. 126.

River Pilots, however, see this as a very "troubling paradox" because, they say, although blacks and Latinos "are more likely than whites or Asians to aspire to attend graduate or professional school . . . [they] nonetheless earn significantly lower grades." This "probably reduces their odds of admission to top programs." (River III, p. 60)

The River Pilots' concern here may be misplaced, however, for even if black and Latino students do earn substantially lower grades than whites and Asians, they may have just as good a chance as the members of these higher-performing groups of gaining entrance to competitive graduate and professional schools. The admissions boost for being black at many of the most competitive law schools, medical schools, business schools, and graduate programs is often huge—larger even in standard deviation terms than the undergraduate college boost—and black undergraduates all know this. The post-graduate boost for being Latino is less but still substantial. Mediocre grades for a black or Latino student is not the same impediment to getting into a good graduate or professional school as it is for a white or Asian student.

Consider, for example, medical schools. According to the American Association of Medical Colleges, the average college GPA in the pre-med college science courses for all whites who entered an American medical school in 2007 was 3.63, and for Asians a near-identical 3.62. For blacks, however, it was only 3.29. This is by itself a very significant difference, given the grade inflation and grade compaction at many undergraduate institutions, but the spread of the black scores was much wider than that of either the whites or Asians (black SD .43, white and Asian SD each .29), indicating that significant numbers of blacks with science GPAs as low as 2.9 or 3.0 were accepted into medical schools, scores that would virtually preclude whites or Asians. Latino science GPAs were roughly halfway between those of the blacks and the higher-scoring whites and Asians (mean: 3.45).[156]

Scores on the Medical College Admissions Test (MCAT) tell a similar story. The median score on the basic science part of the MCAT for a black admitted to medical school in 2007 was equal to that of a white at only the 14th percentile of white admits, and of an Asian at only the 10th percentile of Asian admits. In other words, 86 percent of whites and 90 percent of Asians entering medical schools did better on the MCAT basic science section than the median black. Once again, Latino scores were roughly halfway between those of the blacks and those of the higher-scoring Asians and whites.

An identical pattern was shown in much earlier studies of MCAT scores. For instance, a Rand Corporation study of admissions policies at ten medical schools in the late 1970s found a black/white gap in MCAT scores well over a standard deviation, and a Chicano/white gap slightly less than one SD. The Rand study calculated that a black or Chicano applicant with a better than 50 percent chance of admission to these ten medical schools, had that applicant been held to the same entrance standards as whites, would have reduced his admissions chances to only about one in twenty, or 5 percent.[157] From a 5 percent admissions chance up to a 50 percent or better chance as the bonus for being black or Chicano—can anyone imagine that this will have no effect on many of those seeking to gain entry into the medical profession?

The law school story is similar. Consider for instance the University of Michigan Law School, one of the ten most prestigious in the nation. Like virtually all competitive law schools,

---

156. "MCAT Scores and GPAs for Applicants and Matriculants to U.S. Medical Schools by Race and Ethnicity, 2007," AAMC:FACTS, Table 19, available at www.aamc.org/data/facts/ 2007mcatgparaceeth07.htm.
157. Albert Williams, Wendy Cooper, and Carolyn Lee, *Factors Affecting Medical School Admissions Decisions for Minority and Majority Applicants: A Comparative Study of Ten Schools* (Santa Monica, CA: Rand Corporation, 1979), p. x.

Michigan places a great emphasis on the LSAT, a test of several kinds of aptitudes needed for the successful completion of a rigorous law school curriculum. Scores on the LSAT range from 120 to 180 (much like the 200 to 800 scoring system on the SAT with the average score of those admitted to the very highest-ranking schools being around 170 (at the lowest-ranked schools admits average around 150). In 2004, a year after the Supreme Court's Grutter decision approving Michigan Law's racial preference program, the median LSAT score for both white and Asian admits was 169, just under the typical score earned by whites at top-rated Harvard and Yale. For black admits, however, the average score was only 160. Now a 160 is certainly a respectable LSAT score, but for a white or Asian such a score might gain an entry ticket to a middle-range law school like Boston University, the University of Washington, or Rutgers, but never to a top-ten school like Michigan. Blacks essentially compete only with one another for entry to the nations' top law schools, all of which practice a system of *de facto* race norming and (slightly flexible) quota admissions (though none of them will admit this publicly). Black LSAT scores need not be, and usually are not, competitive with those of whites and Asians. Indeed, at Michigan in 2004, a 75th percentile black admit had an LSAT score significantly *lower* than that of a 25th percentile white or Asian admit (164 vs. 167). Latino LSAT scores were much better than those of the blacks (mean 166 vs. the black mean of 160) but still significantly behind those of the whites and Asians.[158]

The lowering of the bar for underrepresented minorities in law schools extends to the college GPA as well. A study of Michigan Law School applicants submitted during the litigation over the Grutter case indicated that in 1995 the average GPA

158. The LSAT data come from Althea Nagai, "Racial and Ethnic Admission Preferences at the University of Michigan Law School," Center for Equal Opportunity, Sterling, VA, 2006, p. 10, obtainable at www.ceousa.org.

for white admits was 3.68, that of blacks only 3.33. Of students with college GPAs in the 3.25 to 3.45 range and LSAT scores near the 75th percentile of the national distribution, 51 whites applied to Michigan in 1995, 14 Asians, and 10 blacks. But only *one* of the whites in this credential range was admitted to Michigan's elite law school that year (1 out of 51), while *none* of the Asians were (0 out of 10). Blacks had a much easier time of it: *all* of the blacks in this credential range (10 out of 10) were accepted, although their grades and test scores would have virtually precluded them from admission had they been white or Asian.[159] How reasonable is it to think that knowledge of such lowered standards will not filter down to the black sophomores and juniors at various Michigan colleges who plan on attending Michigan or some other elite law school? And given the knowledge of such lowered standards, how reasonable is it to think that this will not negatively affect the behavior of many of those who know they can get into great law schools like Michigan's without having to match the performance of their white and Asian classmates?[160]

---

159. R. Lawrence Purdy, "Prelude: *Bakke* Revisited," *Texas Review of Law and Politics*, 7 (2003): 323.

160. There is reason to believe that racial preferences at leading graduate and professional schools may even retard the learning of students who have no realistic hope of gaining admission to such schools. Vanderbilt Law School professor Carol Swain offers the following observation about the beliefs of many black students she encountered as an undergraduate in the 1980s. "As an older undergraduate student in the 1980s, I often encountered other black college students struggling with grade point averages at or below a 2.00 on a 4.00 scale who voiced aspirations of wanting to become lawyers and doctors. If I challenged them directly by responding, 'But I thought you needed a 3.0 to get into law or medical school'—almost invariably the student would respond, 'Oh, they have to let us in. They have to let us in, because of affirmative action.' Now, I don't believe that many of those students were actually admitted to professional schools, but the misinformation led some genuinely to believe that traditionally white professional schools were obligated to take them, regardless of their less-than-stellar performance. This perception, I believe, affected how hard these students trained. The knowledge of affirmative action's double standards no doubt caused some to neglect burning the midnight oil. . . . Could such beliefs be a factor in the well-documented fact that black students in college underperform their SAT scores—that is, black students with the same SAT scores as whites exhibit a considerably lower performance in college than white students?" (*Academic Questions*, spring 2006, pp. 48–9)

WHY THE BEST BLACKS UNDERACHIEVE THE MOST

The disincentive effects of the racial preference system to which critics like McWhorter draw attention helps to explain a phenomenon that the River Pilots find utterly baffling. It has long been known, and confirmed by the River studies themselves, that "in highly selective colleges and universities, it is the black undergraduates with the highest [standardized] test scores who tend to perform the furthest below their potential." (River I, p. 89, n.) At least at the most selective schools, the authors of River I write, "underperformance appears to increase as the test scores of black students (who could be admitted even under a race-blind policy, and who have the *least* reason to feel outmatched intellectually) who perform the furthest below their potential." (River I, p. 262) The authors of River I then use this fact to cast doubt on the claim "that *admissions policies* account for underperformance" or have anything to do with increasing the salience of stereotype threat ("it seems likely that such stereotypes are less a product of race-sensitive admissions policies than of deep-seated prejudices that long antedate these policies"). Clueless in answering the puzzle presented, the River I authors are forced to conclude that "no one has yet shown definitely why minority students tend to underperform." (River I, p. 262)

The authors of River II and III will later concede (against the earlier doubts of the River I authors) that admissions policies do have very significant effects on stigma reinforcement and the salience of stereotype threat (in Rivers II and III both are shown to increase at institutions granting the largest racial preferences). But they agree with the River I authors that preferentialist admissions policies cannot explain the disturbing fact that it is those black students at elite universities with the highest SAT scores and high school GPAs—who have the least reason to feel stereotype threat or inferiority to the average white or Asian student—who show the greatest gap in their college grade performance when compared to whites and Asians of similar entering credentials. They are just as clueless as the River I authors in trying to explain this mystery.

The mystery, of course, is not difficult to solve once one considers the effect of *system-wide racial preferences,* including those in grad school, professional schools, and corporate hiring. For preferentialist policies do not end at the undergraduate level but proceed through all levels of the current American educational and occupational system. And the same reasons for expecting harmful effects on the grade performance of the higher-end black high school students (like John McWhorter) apply to their counterparts in college.

Preferentialist policies would seem to have at least two types of grade-depressing effects in highly selective undergraduate schools. First, by bringing together on the same college campus black or Latino students who, however strong within their own group, are less academically accomplished than the average white or Asian student, such policies enhance the effect of stereotype threat (i.e., feelings of intellectual inferiority causing the less prepared members of traditionally stigmatized groups to choke on exams and to disidentify with the realm of academics). But probably more important as a retardant to grade achievement, particularly for the better-prepared blacks and Latinos, is the fact that the pervasive system of preferences beyond the undergraduate college, including that in leading graduate and professional schools, makes it possible for black and Latino students to gain entry to those institutions at much lower grade achievement thresholds than those of their white and Asian classmates. If they can get into institutions beyond college equally prestigious as those of their white and Asian classmates (even those smarter or better prepared than they are) while doing less work and striving less relentlessly, many will surely take this easier path to success. Those internally driven to perform at their maximum, or those who receive intense achievement pressure from home, might behave otherwise, but the more typical black and Latino student will not.[161]

Given this reality, one should not be surprised if the greatest degree of underperformance comes from the best prepared black and Latino students at the most selective undergraduate colleges. This is because as one ascends the selectivity scale in graduate schools, business schools, and various other professional schools, the premium given for being black or Latino rather than white or Asian often increases as the best schools scramble to enroll the highest-achieving blacks regardless of how far they may lag behind the highest-achieving whites or the highest-achieving Asians. The more that Asians and whites tend to outperform blacks and Latinos at the high end, the greater the "plus-factoring" boost that those blacks and Latinos who are better than most of their same-race classmates can count on receiving. For the very highest black and Latino achievers there is another factor—a "ceiling effect"—i.e., those blacks nearer the top of the black national distribution know that even with substantially lower grades and test scores than the highest-scoring whites or Asians, they will still be able to get into top-end institutions, and there is no going beyond the top.

The very best blacks and Latinos at the better undergraduate schools will have these two reasons (more generous "plus-

---

161. In a Working Paper (#11464) of the National Bureau of Economic Research (available at www.nber.org), economists Roland Fryer and Glenn Loury label as a myth the claim that "affirmative action undercuts investment incentives" by students in their schooling (p. 10). But by their own reckoning this statement is unwarranted if by myth one means (as they clearly do mean) falsehood. On the question of how affirmative-action preferences influence the incentives of students to strive to do well in school, the authors correctly note that "economic theory provides little guidance on what is ultimately a subtle and context-dependent empirical question." But if this is true—and it probably is—then calling the preference-disincentive theory a myth is just as unfounded as calling it a truism. If we look at those empirical studies with some relevance to this issue, however, with the extensive study of the Steinberg team surely being among the more important, there is sound reason for asserting the strong likelihood that racial-preference policies diminish the incentives of many black and Latino youth in America today—who receive the least peer-group and home pressures to do well in school—to perform to their maximum.

factoring," "ceiling effects") to feel less pressured to do as well in terms of grades as their white and Asian peers in order to get admitted to those more prestigious schools to which they and their lighter-skinned classmates seek admission. Disincentive factors of this kind will work by themselves or in combination with any black-specific or Latino-specific cultural factors to lower grade achievement.

To add flesh to these speculations I will conclude this section with the story of Annette (not her real name). Annette was a black student in one of my civil liberties precept classes at Princeton a number of years ago; she was clearly the best student in a nearly all-white class. Whenever Annette spoke, her remarks were always intelligent, thoughtful, on-topic, and well-articulated; she was an ideal participant in her student discussion group. Her written work was equally top-shelf, and she received accordingly the highest grade in the class.

A year later when Annette was applying to law schools she asked me if I would write a recommendation letter for her, a request I was more than happy to honor, given her outstanding performance in my class. From the personal resume she handed me, I learned that Annette had scored 1500 on the SAT (combined math and verbal scores)—an impressive feat under any circumstances but doubly impressive for someone who had attended what I knew to be a decent but not top-rated public high school in a lower-middle-income area of Long Island. (Most Princeton students have attended high-end public high schools or quality private schools and typically average about 1450 on the SAT).

But Annette's college GPA, also listed on her resume, was less impressive—only a very mediocre 3.4, which, given the grade inflation and grade compaction over the years at Princeton, was surely not an achievement commensurate with her clearly displayed academic talent. Here was a clear case of what the social scientists were writing about when they talked of "underperformance" by blacks at the high end.

The major theories then fashionable at the time flashed through my mind—was this a case of "stereotype threat"? "Oppositional culture"? "Fear of acting white"? But in Annette's case none of these theories made any sense. Annette was smarter than the average white or Asian student at Princeton—and she knew it, as one could readily discern from her deportment and her self-confidence. There was obviously no stereotype threat here. Annette liked to say smart things in class, she was not anti-intellectual, and she exuded an independent-mindedness that suggested lack of excessive concern with what other students thought of her. I was completely baffled by her GPA situation. The theories of John Ogbu and Signithia Fordham seemed as inapplicable in her case as those of Claude Steele and Joshua Arenson.

It was only after reading John McWhorter's account of the reasons for his more laidback approach to the challenges of his high school classes that it all came together. "Of course!" I said to myself, "that's it! That's Annette!" Annette knew she was among the smartest black students at Princeton, that she would probably do very well on the LSAT, just as she had done outstandingly well on the SAT, and that top law schools look high and low for black students of her intellectual caliber. Even with a 3.4 average, she might reasonably think, she would get into some top law school. She doesn't have to do as well as the white and Asian students at Princeton to achieve this.

And if Annette did think this way, she was hardly proved wrong—Annette was accepted into Harvard Law School, even though a 3.4 GPA would virtually preclude acceptance of a white or Asian student. At last here was a highly plausible theory to explain the underperformance of students like Annette. But the River Pilots aren't interested.

A PERNICIOUS PALLIATIVE: FOSTERING MIDDLE-CLASS BLACK COMPLACENCY

Middle-class black parents, like all parents, enjoy bragging when their sons or daughters get accepted to prestigious colleges such as those studied in the three River books. In none of the River books, however, is the question ever raised about whether substantially lowering the entrance standards for black students or members of other groups might affect the degree to which parents push their children to do well in high school to gain entry to prestigious institutions. Just as the possibility of a "preference-system disincentive effect" operating on college students who want to get into good graduate or professional schools is effectively ignored, so there is no discussion whatever of possible effects on the behavior of the parents and teachers of college-bound high school students—or the high school students themselves—of lowering standards for undergraduate admissions. As will be shown in the next section on *The Game of Life,* this omission is in sharp contrast to what the River Pilots have to say when the topic becomes the professionalization of college sports and the pernicious effects they believe this has on the attitudes and behavior of high school students and the various adults in their lives.

Although River III gives much attention to that minority of black students at elite colleges who come from dangerous urban neighborhoods and suffer from years of exposure to high rates of crime and disorder, the great majority of the black students in both the College and Beyond Survey (River I) and the National Longitudinal Study of Freshmen (River II and III) come from a broad middle class, with many having attended decent integrated schools in relatively safe suburban neighborhoods. Many come from households where at least one parent has a four-year college degree, and significant portions have parents with a graduate or professional degree. "The C&B schools," the authors of River I write, "unquestionably continue to contribute to social mobility. However, they do so today primarily by giving excellent educational opportunities to students from middle-class backgrounds. The academically competitive environment of these schools—both private and public—makes it unrealistic to expect them to serve large numbers of students who come from truly impoverished backgrounds." (River I, p. 50)

But what are the effects of granting huge amounts of racial bonus points to black students who have grown up in communities like Shaker Heights, Ohio, Chapel Hill, North Carolina, Madison, Wisconsin, Mount Airy, Pennsylvania—or similar middle- or upper-middle-class towns from which many of the African Americans attending highly selective colleges in America often come? We can only speculate, but one thing we do know: African American students growing up in such towns are not doing well in high school compared with their white and Asian peers.

Harvard economist Ronald Ferguson has been working since its founding in 1999 with the Minority Student Achievement Network (MSAN), a consortium of 15 public school districts spread across ten states, each of which has a mixed-race, middle-to-upper-middle-class student body. These affluent districts have come together in the MSAN consortium because of their common concern about the uniformly low achievement of black students in their schools in comparison with the whites and Asians. Ferguson has analyzed a good deal of data from these 15 districts, and the results are always depressingly the same: even when black students are matched with whites and Asians for family-background factors like parental education or number of books in the home, black students do considerably worse in terms of their grades in school. And the gap in grades increases as one ascends the socioeconomic (SES) ladder of parental backgrounds.

In a 2001 survey of over 34,000 seventh to eleventh graders in these 15 MSAN districts the black/white gaps in overall grade-point averages were as follows: .14 for the lowest SES group (2.38 vs. 2.52); .26 for the second SES group (2.65 vs. 2.91); .48 for the third SES group (2.88 vs. 3.36); and .50 for the highest SES group (3.18 vs. 3.68). The black/Asian gaps were similar, though greater for the lowest two socioeconomic groups, where Asians substantially outperformed both blacks and whites. (No figures for Latinos were given).[162]

Even at these privileged schools, and even when differences in many important family background characteristics are statistically controlled, black students continue to lag substantially behind whites and Asians in terms of the grades they earn in their high school courses. And Ferguson also found that blacks were much less likely than Asians or whites to be enrolled in honors or Advanced Placement courses. In these affluent, low-crime suburban settings the familiar Asian-white-black hierarchy of academic achievement was still observed.

One of the MSAN school districts—Shaker Heights, Ohio— we have encountered before in John Ogbu's study described in Chapter III. Recall Ogbu's findings: black students at Shaker Heights high school were much less engaged in the academic side of school compared with whites ("low-effort syndrome") and got much lower grades. Whites were not necessarily academic work horses, Ogbu discovered, but they were not nearly as indifferent to their studies as the typical black student. While Ogbu did not find the overt hostility to academic achievement among Shaker Heights blacks that he and Signithia Fordham found in their much-publicized study of an inner-city D.C. high school—where academic striving was dismissed by many as "acting white"—there was a discernable difference, he found, between the white and black school cultures in Shaker Heights,

---

162. Ronald Ferguson, "What Doesn't Meet the Eye: Understanding and Addressing Racial Disparities in High-Achieving Suburban Schools," Wiener Center for Social Policy, John F. Kennedy School of Government, Harvard University, 2002, Table 3b, p. 34.

with the black culture much less supportive of high academic achievement.

In addition to any black-specific historical and cultural factors that are probably at work here,[163] one suspects something like a McWhorter Factor produced by the interaction of the typical fun-loving teenage mentality in America with the generous bonus-granting system that is subscribed to by almost all of the most prestigious colleges in America when it comes to the entrance requirements for blacks. To quote Shelby Steele again: "elite universities in America have offered the license *not* to compete to the most privileged segment of the black youth. Infusing the atmosphere of their education from early childhood is not the idea that they will have to steel themselves to face stiff competition but that they will receive a racial preference."[164]

Steele contrasts this you-needn't-perform-up-to-the-white-standard message—which he considers condescending, insulting, and ultimately self-defeating—with the proud message he received in the pre-affirmative action days of his youth. Steele remembers well the year before he entered college the admonition of Martin Luther King, Jr., in a speech King delivered in Chicago:

> The summer before I left for college, I heard Martin Luther King speak in Chicago, and he laid it on the line for black students everywhere: "When you are behind in a footrace, the only way to get ahead is to run faster than the man in front of you. So when your white roommate says he's tired

163. Besides McWhorter's *Losing the Race*, the most important "culturalist" interpretations of poor black academic performance include Thomas Sowell's *Rednecks and White Liberals* (San Francisco: Encounter Books, 2005); Orlando Patterson, *The Ordeal of Integration* (Washington, D.C.: Civitas/Counterpoint, 1997); Dinesh D'Souza, *The End of Racism* (New York: The Free Press, 1995); John Ogbu, *Minority Education and Caste: The American System in Cross-Cultural Perspective* (New York: Academic Press, 1978; and Abigail and Stephan Thernstrom, *No Excuses: Closing the Racial Gap in Learning* (New York: Simon and Schuster, 2003).
164. Shelby Steele, *A Dream Deferred* (New York: HarperCollins, 1998), pp. 126–7.

and goes to sleep, you stay up and burn the midnight oil." His statement that we were "behind in a footrace" acknowledged that, because of history, of few opportunities, of racism, we were, in a sense, "inferior." But this had to do with what had been done to our parents and their parents, not with inherent inferiority. And because it was acknowledged, it was presented to us as a challenge rather than a mark of shame.[165]

There are a number of other groups like the MSAN consortium that are focused on raising the performance level of the more privileged African American school children, perhaps following W.E.B. DuBois's injunction about the importance to any group of cultivating its Talented Tenth. But it is not clear that they have had any notable success. Part of the problem is surely the lack of any sense of crisis. There is a palpable sense of indifference among the black parents featured in Ogbu's study of Shaker Heights, and one suspects this is an all-too-common phenomenon in a world in which black children do not have to meet the high entrance standards of their white and Asian classmates. Racial-preference policies, Abigail and Stephen Thernstroms trenchantly observe, have served as a "pernicious palliative," promoting complacency and indifference among parents and educators who should be alarmed when even the most privileged black students fail to reach the highest bar.

"For a generation now," the Thernstroms write, "preferences in higher education have served as a pernicious palliative, deflecting our attention from the real problem: the yawning racial gap in educational performance among elementary- and secondary-school pupils. As long as the average black high-school senior reads at the eighth-grade level, efforts to engineer

---

165. Shelby Steele, *The Content of Our Character* (New York: HarperCollins, 1990), p. 138.

parity in college, let alone in the legal and medical professions, are doomed to failure."[166] At the very least, one would like to have seen the River Pilots discuss this issue with some degree of seriousness, even if they were to reach very different conclusions from those of the Thernstroms and other critics of preferentialist policies. Surely it is a topic too important to ignore.

POVERTY AND SEGREGATION OR DYSFUNCTIONAL SUBCULTURES?

One of the more illuminating sections of River III deals with the harmful effects on learning of growing up in a low-income, all-black neighborhood with high rates of crime, disorder, and delinquency. The harm they show has not only a sociological and psychological component but also a powerful biological and endocrinological aspect,which can lead to effects on the brain that permanently damage those who have been exposed long term to violent and chaotic neighborhoods. When "someone is compelled by poverty and discrimination to live in a dangerous and violent neighborhood," they write, the body continues to turn out stress hormones such as adrenaline and cortisol, and this, over time, "has profound effects on cognition, reducing long- and short-term memory, lowering frustration thresholds, limiting attention spans, and interfering with the neural chemistry of learning itself." (River III, p. 152)

In addition to the cognitive impairment that living in such neighborhoods entails, college students from such backgrounds, the authors show, have a much greater than average likelihood of having to deal in their college years with pressing "family issues" that detract from their college studies. The River Pilots on this score make a thoroughly convincing case for the multiple

166. Abigail and Stephan Thernstrom, "Racial Preferences: What We Now Know," Manhattan Institute for Public Policy website, www.manhattan-institute.org, first published February, 1999.

disadvantages those who have grown up in black-ghetto-like circumstances must endure in their college studies, even when such students are on full scholarships and living in idyllic surroundings on safe college campuses. While the River Pilots tend at times to treat such cases as modal for blacks—thus drawing attention away from the much larger contingent of black college students in their study who have not grown up among the crime-ridden, ghetto poor[167]—their discussion of the many impediments to learning that the ghetto-reared black student must endure is most illuminating and should teach us to appreciate all the more the achievements of those who have had to overcome such great adversities.

---

167. In giving the impression at times that impoverished blacks are typical of the black college students surveyed, River III breaks a very wise rule enunciated in River II: "Picking a black student at random . . . one would be hard-pressed to make an accurate guess about his or her background. He or she could be the heir to a sizable fortune, the child of affluent, married professionals, the son or daughter of high-school-educated, working-class parents, or the child of a single welfare mother who dropped out of school in tenth grade. If one were to assume *anything* about a randomly selected black student, one would be wrong most of the time, and if one's behavior toward that student were conditioned on this assumption, it would be very likely to cause offense. To the extent that affluent blacks resent being treated like they are poor and poor blacks resent being treated as if they are rich, all will find plenty of company with whom to share their resentments. . . . The obvious lesson for professors, administrators, and students is to resist making assumptions and attributions about the backgrounds of black or Latino students. Rather, one should suspend judgment until relevant personal facts can be gathered. Assumptions made about the class origins of Latino and black students are very likely to be wrong, creating considerable potential for miscommunication, misunderstanding, and resentment. The wisest course is to resist the natural human tendency to make attributions according to group markers, and to treat Latinos and African Americans as individuals rather than representatives of social categories. Come to think of it, this is not bad advice for navigating social life in general." (River II, p. 200) One might add here, that if we really want "to treat Latinos and African Americans as individuals rather than representatives of social categories" we should stop classifying the student population by race and ethnicity, end affirmative action and all forms of differential treatment according to what ethno-racial categories students fall under, and return to the color-blind ideal that inspired the 50s- and 60s-era civil rights movement and the 1964 Civil Rights Act (see Chapter I). The fact that such a call "to treat everyone as individuals" could be made by the authors of River II suggests how deeply rooted the individualist perspective is in the American psyche, and how, in their more lucid moments, not even left-leaning sociologists are immune to its appeal.

Where the River Pilots go wrong is in defining the black ghetto problem as simply one of "segregation," or "segregation and poverty." For instance, in a chart labeled "The Effects of Racial Segregation on Academic Achievement," they draw simple one-way causal arrows suggesting that "segregation" leads to "exposure to disorder and violence," and this disorder and violence then are seen as producing both "reduced cognitive skills" and various "negative events in family networks" that have a harmful effect on academic achievement—effects that carry over beyond the ghetto into the integrated college campuses where students from such backgrounds must struggle to learn. Although they offer no recommendation for improving the ghetto situation, the fact that the problems are all seen to derive almost entirely from being "segregated" by and from whites, suggests that their real heart may be in a renewal on a grand scale of busing initiatives, aggressive fair-housing policies, and reinvigorated antipoverty programs in order to reduce the racial and class segregation that they believe has such harmful consequences on long-term cognitive development.

"Because of the pervasiveness of segregation in American life," they write, "the interpersonal networks of many African Americans and Latinos inevitably include friends and relatives who attend minority-dominant schools, inhabit racially isolated neighborhoods, and thus continue to experience the risks of life in a poor, segregated setting. . . . Students who come of age in segregated schools and neighborhoods experience higher levels of disorder and violence than those in integrated settings. . . . Even if black and Latino students themselves grew up under conditions of integration, many people within their extended network of friends and relatives will still live in segregated communities. . . . Segregation, in combination with high rates of black and Latino poverty, produces elevated rates of social stress, which undermines academic performance in several ways: by distracting students psychologically from their studies; by compromising their physical and emotional well-being; and by necessitating competing investments of time, money, and energy to attend to family and personal issues. Through no fault of their own, minority students continue to be enmeshed in a web of social relationships that, owing to the pernicious effects of segregation, undermine their academic performance on campus." (River III, pp. 153–4)

The problem with their analysis here, which derives largely from Douglas Massey's ideas in his influential *American Apartheid: Segregation and the Making of the Underclass* (co-authored with Nancy Denton),[168] is that as a matter of historical record racial segregation and the isolation from mainstream American culture that they produce have not always been bad things in

---

168. Douglas Massey and Nancy Denton, *American Apartheid: Segregation and the Making of the Underclass* (Cambridge, MA: Harvard University Press, 1993). The thesis of *American Apartheid* is very simple: the major cause of the many problems among blacks, particularly urban blacks, is a) the white dislike of, discrimination against, and avoidance of African Americans—in a word, white racism; which, b) leads to the social isolation of blacks in geographically confined neighborhoods and ghettos; which, in turn, c) produces all the social pathologies of isolated black communities, including high rates of crime and delinquency, poor school performance, family disintegration, prostitution, drug addiction, etc. There is hardly a hint in *American Apartheid* that the causal arrows go in the other direction as well, i.e., that the high incidence of social pathologies in many urban black communities is mainly responsible for the white (and Asian, and Mideastern, and middle-class black) avoidance of those communities. Nor is there any serious attempt to come to terms with the fact that groups in the past that have been at least as socially and geographically isolated as the most isolated of ghetto blacks today, due to linguistic, cultural, or discriminatory barriers (like the Chinese in the Chinatowns, the Jews on the Lower East Side of New York, or medieval Jews in the European ghettos) have not displayed anything like the pattern of maladjustment to the opportunities of urban life as many urban African Americans in the post-civil rights era. *American Apartheid* is written with a transparent and overriding exculpatory and apologetic purpose that seeks to place the blame for black ghetto pathologies almost entirely on the shoulders of wicked or unfeeling whites and their ongoing racist behavior, while ghetto blacks themselves are seen as passive pawns of hostile outside forces in a game over which they have little if any control. The very terms "segregation" and "apartheid" in the title of the book are designed to evoke images of the white supremacist regime in the Jim Crow South and its equivalent in South Africa and to suggest that in the post-civil rights era little has changed. The black ghetto problem is really a white oppression problem—a problem of white racist malevolence, hostility, and indifference. If change is to come, it is white people who need to do the changing. Ghetto blacks are blameless.

the lives of the segregated and isolated people at least if one is looking at outcomes like group cohesiveness, family stability, avoidance of crime and violent behavior, effective socialization of children, general cognitive development, and academic performance in school. The results of such segregation and isolation clearly depend on the internal strengths and weaknesses of the group involved, something the River Pilots, with their apologetic and exculpatory purpose, refuse to acknowledge. For certain racial and ethnic minorities, segregation and social isolation have helped them pull together as a people and often resist the corrupting effects of a surrounding culture much less self-disciplined and effective in socializing its youth than their own.

The classic examples here are the Chinese and Japanese on the West Coast in the early decades of the twentieth century. Although they were subject to racist white attitudes and discriminatory laws, denied the right to pursue certain professions, excluded for a time from the California public schools, denied the right to testify in court, and made the targets of discriminatory immigration laws, the Chinese and Japanese in their Chinatowns and Japanese neighborhoods in the period before the Second World War nevertheless managed to maintain high levels of group cohesiveness and very low levels of crime and family disruption. Given their linguistic and cultural barriers, their social isolation must have been at least as great as any black in the inner-city ghetto today or any Latino in the barrio. However, the trajectory of their group advancement was very different from that of blacks or Latinos. Indeed, by the latter decades of the twentieth century they would be among the best educated, most law-abiding, least drug-addicted, and most economically successful ethno-racial groups in America.

"The experience of the Chinese and Japanese," write James Q. Wilson and Richard Herrnstein in their classic study, *Crime and Human Nature*, "suggests that social isolation, substandard living conditions, and general poverty are not invariably associated with high rates of crime among racially distinct groups. . . . During the 1960s, one neighborhood in San Francisco had the lowest income, the highest unemployment rate, the highest proportion of families with incomes under $4,000 per year, the least educational attainment, the highest tuberculosis rate, and the highest proportion of substandard housing of any area of the city. That neighborhood was called Chinatown. Yet, in 1965 there were only five persons of Chinese ancestry committed to prison in the entire state of California." [169]

Wilson and Herrnstein go on to explain how "the low rate of crime among Orientals living in the United States was once a frequent topic of social science investigation. The theme of many of the reports that emerged was that crime rates were low not in spite of ghetto life but because of it. Though Orientals were the object of racist opinion and legislation, they were thought to have low crime rates because they lived in cohesive, isolated communities. . . . When crime rates did rise among Orientals, the rise was typically explained as the result of the failure of the familial and cultural heritage of the group combined with 'disorganizing contacts with [white] Americans.' . . . What is striking is that the argument used by social scientists to explain *low* crime rates among Orientals—namely, being separate from the larger society—has been the same as the argument used to explain *high* rates among blacks." [170]

Not only did the Chinese and Japanese in California display low rates of crime and delinquency and high levels of family and group cohesiveness but their children did outstandingly well in school. Indeed in the early decades of the twentieth century the Chinese and Japanese children were often the darlings of their white school teachers, who found them better-behaved and more

169. James Q. Wilson and Richard Herrnstein, *Crime and Human Nature* (New York: Simon and Schuster, 1985), pp. 473–4.
170. Ibid.

eager to learn than their white American counterparts. "The new generations of Chinese children born in America," Thomas Sowell writes, "encountered many of the language difficulties of other immigrants and sometimes attended schools explicitly segregated (as in San Francisco at the turn of the century) or with a concentration of Chinese children due to residential concentration. The Chinese children did equally well in school whether concentrated in all-Chinese schools or scattered among other ethnic groups. Some early studies of Chinese IQs showed them below the national average, but by the 1930s, Chinese youngsters' IQs were at or above the national average—and remained so. Teachers in New York's Chinatown rated the Chinese children 'better behaved, more obedient, and more self-reliant' than their white classmates.'" An identical pattern was seen among the Japanese.[171]

---

171. Thomas Sowell, *Ethnic America* (New York: Basic Books, 1981), p. 147. On the Japanese, Sowell writes: "Japanese children in the public schools were notable for their obedience, politeness, and hard work and were welcomed by their teachers. The schools attended were almost always integrated because of the small number of Japanese children at any given place, and they were typically treated well by their teachers. These children's school achievements were equal to those of white children and so were their IQ scores, despite the fact that they came from homes where English was not spoken and where parents' occupations—and their own occupational prospects, in light of contemporary discrimination—made formal education of little apparent value. It was simply regarded as a matter of honor that they do well. Upholding the honor of the family and the honor of the Japanese people in America were values constantly taught by the Issei [first-generation immigrants] to their children. Strong family control, pressure, and influence were supplemented by that of community organizations and by the informal but pervasive gossip in the small, close-knit Japanese-American communities. Such social controls extended well beyond children. These American communities were notable for their lack of crime, juvenile delinquency, or other forms of social pathology. From the earliest period of immigration, the Japanese-American community had far fewer crimes than other Americans, and the crimes they did commit were less serious. This was true both on the mainland of the United States and in Hawaii. Deviant behavior brought forth pressure not only from the individual's family but also from other relatives, neighbors, and members of the Japanese-American community at large." (pp. 168–9)

Like Sowell, Abigail and Stephan Thernstrom attribute the outstanding school performance of the Chinese and Japanese in early twentieth-century America to a combination of their strong family and cultural traditions coupled with their capacity to maintain those traditions and pass them on to their children because of their social isolation from the general American culture. "Chinese and Japanese were almost

Even the Vietnamese boat people have managed to form cohesive and successful ethnic communities in America, and they are certainly no strangers to violence or stress in their lives (estimates range as high as 50 percent for the number of boat people who perished at sea in their chaotic flight from Vietnam in the late 1970s, and many who survived had to live in squalid refugee camps for long periods before gaining entry into the U.S.). Compared with the whites, the boat-people communities in America have been characterized by low rates of crime, delinquency, drug addiction, and divorce, and, like the Chinese and Japanese, Vietnamese children have often done extraordinarily well in school. They have achieved these results, moreover, often working at the lowest-paying unskilled jobs and living in impoverished sections of inner cities. One study

---

the only Asians who arrived before World War II, and intense prejudice in that era isolated them from the dominant culture in many respects," the Thernstroms write. "That isolation facilitated the transmission of their distinctive cultural attitudes from generation to generation, particularly because intermarriage between Asians and whites was very rare at the time. . . . Asian-American families have successfully transmitted to their children a culture conducive to high academic achievement." (Thernstrom and Thernstrom, *No Excuses*, p. 99)

A similar example to the Chinese in the Chinatowns of the West Coast is provided by the centuries-long ghettoization of Europe's Jews. The word "ghetto" itself comes from an Italian word designating a district of a city—a district in which for many centuries Europe's "Christ killers" were required to live lest they pollute their Christian neighbors and turn them from the true faith. For centuries Jews suffered under all manner of discrimination and oppression, were barred from most professions and often from owning land, were subject to periodic mob violence and the confiscation of their property, and in many of Europe's leading cities had to return at night to a walled ghetto enclave that had many of the features of a day-release prison. They were certainly no strangers to poverty or blocked opportunities. Yet during the time of their ghettoization their sense of solidarity, family cohesiveness, general frugality, sobriety, and sense of group pride was often the envy of Christian observers—including, famously, Blaise Pascal. The Jews themselves, particularly in Eastern Europe and Russia, came to see many of the surrounding Christian population as crude, illiterate, drunken, wife-beating *goyim* whom Jews would do well to avoid or keep at arms length. And when Jews were finally emancipated from the restrictions of the ghetto in the generations following the French Revolution, their children and grandchildren went on to become the carriers of a magnificent intellectual and cultural creativity that in its achievements compares favorably with the best among the achievements of the Elizabethan English, the Italians of the Renaissance, the nineteenth- and early-twentieth-century Germans, and the ancient Greeks of the fourth and fifth centuries B.C.

by University of Michigan researchers during the early 1980s found that despite the fact that the children of Indochinese refugees had only been in the U.S. for a few short years and almost none spoke English at home, the average child was just slightly behind national norms in terms of reading and English language skills (45 percent were above the national median on standardized tests) but substantially above the national norms in both spelling (71 percent above the national median—amazing, since English is insane re spelling) and math (85 percent above the national median).[172]

"We have found the economic and educational achievement of the Indochinese refugees to be stunning in both quantity and quality," the researchers concluded. "These refugees came here with almost no material goods. They arrived with very little English or transferable job skills just as the United States was entering its worst recession since the Great Depression [1980–1982] . . . The refugee children spoke almost no English when they came, and they attend predominantly inner-city schools whose reputations for good education are poor. Yet by 1982, we find that the Indochinese had already begun to move ahead of other minorities on a national basis, and, two years later, their children are already doing very well on national tests. Little in their backgrounds prepared us to anticipate the great leaps in achievement that have given them parity or better with American children in such a brief period. . . . It is important to note that these students attained high academic marks in schools that are in traditionally low-income or inner-city areas. That is, they succeeded in schools generally considered to be both less fortunate in terms of resources and associated with less motivated or more disruptive student bodies."[173]

---

172. Nathan Caplan, John Whitmore, and Marcella Choy, *The Boat People and Achievement in America: A Study of Economic and Educational Success* (Ann Arbor: University of Michigan Press, 1989), pp. 71–4.
173. Ibid., pp. 75, 81–2.

The researchers attributed the boat people's success in school to an ethnic, neighborhood, and family culture that places supreme importance on education, achievement, cohesive families, and hard work. The typical refugee child, they estimate, did three hours of homework each night, with such work being the chief family activity for all children from the completion of after-school chores until bedtime (the average American does between 3–4 hours of homework in a typical school *week*). And the fact that they were often culturally and linguistically isolated from other Americans in their neighborhoods was seen by the researchers as a source of strength, not weakness. Indeed, the Indochinese seemed to engage in active self-segregation not only because linguistic and cultural differences make it difficult to integrate socially with English-speaking American blacks, Latinos, and whites, but also because they wanted to shield their children from what they perceived as the harmful cultural ways of mainstream Americans.

The refugees, the researcher write, "share an apprehension over the possible power and consequences of American cultural influences . . . and in particular the effects on their children." "It has often been assumed," they go on, "that successful adaptation by refugees was, in large measure, the result of their willingness to adopt the ways of their American neighbors. But the successes of these refugees . . . may have occurred for the very opposite reasons. . . . Perhaps the refugees see not only the necessity to rely on their own cultural value system for guidance but also the need to insulate themselves from the behavioral and value standards of their non-refugee neighbors."[174]

Other researchers studying the Vietnamese in New Orleans have found similar patterns of self-segregating behavior and similar patterns of superior performance of refugee school children in the public schools (where the Vietnamese form a conspicu-

---

174. Ibid., pp. 47–8, 131–2.

ous minority among a large majority of inner-city blacks). The social world of the Vietnamese in New Orleans, these researchers explain, "is restricted to the closed and highly interconnected circles of the [Vietnamese] ethnic group. . . . [The group emphasized] obedience, industriousness, and helping others but discouraged egoistic values of independent thinking and popularity, which are most commonly associated with contemporary American society. . . . [The Vietnamese children] are pressured to avoid hanging out too much with non-Vietnamese children in the neighborhood, dating non-Vietnamese, and becoming too 'American.' These Vietnamese family values constitute a source of direction to guide children to adapt to American society the Vietnamese way."[175]

While the Vietnamese are eager to see their children advance educationally and occupationally, and thus to become in a sense "middle-class Americans," the best way to do this, they believe, is to rely on their own Buddhist and Confucian values while keeping their social distance from mainstream Americans and their values. Rather than being seen as role models or people to emulate, white Americans are often seen as lazy, undisciplined people, with disrespectful children whom Vietnamese children should not try to emulate. Black Americans are held in even lower regard.

Such self-segregated patterns of achievement, it should be stressed, are not confined to East Asians or those influenced by Buddhist or Confucian values. Many immigrant groups from different cultures have displayed similar patterns. In her study of Punjabi Sikhs in an agricultural region of California, for instance, anthropologist Margaret Gibson found the Sikhs displaying a nearly identical pattern to earlier Chinese and Japanese immigrants. The Sikh children, whose parents were

175. Min Zhou and Carl Bankston III, "Social Capital and the Adaptations of the Second Generation: The Case of Vietnamese Youth in New Orleans," *International Migration Review*, 28 (1994): 821–45, 831.

usually uneducated laborers, did outstandingly well in the predominantly white schools they attended, Gibson shows, largely because of the close parental monitoring of their school progress and the focus placed on educational achievement by almost all the adults in the tight-knit Punjabi community. An important part of the successful school strategy of the Punjabis involved avoiding too intimate social integration with whites and maintaining their social and cultural distance from more mainstream Americans.

"Punjabi children [were] advised against too much social contact with non-Punjabi peers," Gibson explains, and "Americanize" was not a term of approbation among Punjabi parents. "Punjabi parents defined 'becoming Americanized' as forgetting one's roots and adopting the most disparaged traits of the [white] majority group. . . . For the Punjabi Sikh students and their parents, 'acting white' meant doing little homework, spending a lot of time socializing with friends (especially if of the opposite sex), dancing, dating, working long hours at an outside job, being indifferent to school work, cutting up in class, and rejecting the authority of parents and teachers."[176]

THE SALIENCE OF CULTURAL FACTORS
The conclusion to be drawn from facts such as these is that the River Pilots err when they suggest that the poor school performance of black and Latino youth can be adequately explained by their degree of "segregation" or "racial isolation." Under varying circumstances such factors can work to retard educational progress, but there is no *a priori* reason for believing that the effects will be negative or uniform. Family and ethnic group cohesiveness and the values and cultural patterns of the group

---

176. Margaret Gibson, "The School Performance of Immigrant Minorities: A Comparative View," *Anthropology and Education Quarterly*, 18 (1987): 262–75, 267, 269.

involved seem to be the real movers and shakers in terms of differential academic performance among groups. But the River Pilots—like left-oriented sociologists in general—are loath to admit this.

Things weren't always this way. In the 1950s and early 1960s, for instance, social scientists like Lee Rainwater and Kenneth Clark could candidly describe certain features of ghetto culture that were inhibiting to black educational and occupational advancement without fear of recrimination and with the belief that the problems they found needed to be confronted honestly and openly. But all this changed very abruptly between 1965 and 1967 in the wake of the near hysterical response in left-oriented social science circles to Daniel Patrick Moynihan's study of the black family, when Moynihan was accused of "blaming the victim." As a result of the acrimonious controversy that surrounded Moynihan's report,[177] there developed from the late 1960s onward what Moynihan tellingly described as "a near-obsessive concern to locate the 'blame' for poverty, especially Negro poverty, on forces and institutions outside the community concerned."[178]

Interpretations of poverty, inferior school performance, and many other social ills in the black community that drew upon cultural factors and factors rooted in family structure were effectively placed off limits as scholars desperately sought ideologically safe alternative explanations, the most common being ongoing racial discrimination, structural changes in the domestic economy, and segregation from whites. And when Latino groups effectively "piggybacked" their own drive for solicitous concern on the previous black struggle, the same taboo against "blaming the victim" was extended to Latino culture and community values as well.

---

177. This topic is discussed in much greater detail in the next chapter.
178. Daniel Patrick Moynihan, "The Professors and the Poor," in Moynihan, ed., *On Understanding Poverty* (New York: Basic Books, 1969), p. 31.

It is within this context that all three River Books were written, and it explains why they avoid any serious discussion of cultural, familial, or group norms as a source of the huge divergence in educational performance between the black and Latino students and the higher-achieving Asians. When comparisons between these groups are made, they are invariably cursory and superficial—usually restricted to noting that Asian college students often come from wealthier, better educated, and more intact families that can afford to live in racially integrated suburbs (with no acknowledgment that cultural and family factors may be at least partially responsible for why so many Asians got wealthy so fast and could afford to live in the more affluent suburbs, and for why whites feel less threatened, and less prone to move, by an Asian presence in their neighborhoods than an African American presence).[179] A culture phobia and culture blindness permeate all three River Books.

As the East Indian-born conservative scholar Dinesh D'Souza explains, "The incredible economic and intellectual achievements within a single generation not just of middle-class and professional Japanese and East Indians, but also of poor immigrants from Vietnam, Cambodia, Thailand, and Korea have called into question the claim that in America one has to be white and preferably male in order to succeed. By proving that upward mobility and social acceptance do not depend on the absence of racially distinguishing features, Asians have unwittingly yet powerfully challenged the attribution of minority failure to discrimination by the majority. Many liberals are having

---

179. River III indicates that about 9 percent of Asian students come from households that have at some time received government assistance payments (welfare), while the figure for blacks is almost twice as large, at 17 percent. A comparison between the students in these two subcategories would be illuminating, but it hasn't been undertaken. A similarly illuminating comparison might be between Asians and blacks with very well educated parents living in integrated, low-crime-rate neighborhoods. A showing of "black underperformance" by students from such backgrounds with comparable HS-GPAs and SATs would suggest the salience of McWhorter's "preference system disincentive factor."

trouble providing a full answer to the awkward question, 'Why can't an African American be more like an Asian?'"[180] For the River Pilots the awkward question is not awkwardly answered but more often than not simply ignored.

Again and again in River III and its predecessors the talk is of "minority students"—or simply "minorities"—when what the River Pilots really mean is "African Americans and certain Latino groups." The choice of locution is revealing. The authors clearly want to gain sympathy for American blacks and many Latino groups by contrasting them with the more privileged "white majority" while avoiding comparison with the "model minority" Asians. The Asian comparison would be not only unflattering to members of the lower-achieving minority groups but also subversive to the implicit underlying theme of River III that racial minority status and white segregating behavior, rather than any negative features of American black or Latino culture itself, are the main reasons for the deficient academic performance of the lower-achieving ethno-racial groups.

The awkwardness of this terminology becomes apparent when one considers that on many of the college campuses the River Pilots survey Asians greatly outnumber both blacks and Latinos and are by far the demographically dominant minority group. There is a clear reluctance to acknowledge that Asians, who have adapted so well to the educational opportunities offered in America,[181] are a racial minority. Most commonly they

180. Dinesh D'Souza, *The End of Racism* (New York: The Free Press, 1995), p. 436. D'Souza's "culturalist" perspective is well captured in the following statement: "The main contemporary obstacle facing African Americans is neither white racism . . . nor black genetic deficiency . . . Rather it involves destructive and pathological cultural patterns of behavior: excessive reliance on government, conspiratorial paranoia about racism, a resistance to academic achievement as 'acting white,' a celebration of the criminal and outlaw as authentically black, and the normalization of illegitimacy and dependency. These group patterns arose as a response to past oppression, but they are now dysfunctional and must be modified." (Ibid., p. 24.)
181. By the year 2000, 55 percent of Asians aged 18–24 were attending college or other institution of higher learning compared with only 36 percent of whites in that age category, 30 percent of African Americans, and 22 percent of Latinos. This "model

are lumped together with the whites, with their racial minority status obscured and the remaining black and Latino students simply referred to as "minority students," never as "non-Asian minorities" or "members of lower-achieving minorities" (locutions that almost never appear in any of the River books). Better to contrast the lower-scoring minorities with the racially privileged whites, the strategy seems to be, rather than make them look bad by contrasting them with the higher-scoring minorities and thus perhaps suggest that their own group attitudes and group behaviors, not simply white racism or minority status itself, may have something to do with their poor academic performance.

What the River Pilots clearly want to avoid acknowledging is the simple fact that racial segregation, isolation, and geographic concentration constitute an educational and crime-control problem only when the group in question has the internal characteristics of a "problem minority" (like the Irish in the nineteenth century)—with weak internal control mechanisms, diminished social support networks, low levels of family cohesiveness, high levels of present-time orientation, high levels of substance abuse, inability to delay gratifications, poor capacity to respond to urban challenges, lack of entrepreneurial initiative, etc. When the group in question is internally stronger and lacks these negative characteristics, it often displays patterns of adjustment to the challenges of schooling and occupational advancement in America superior to those of U.S. whites. Such people do not need to be socially integrated with native whites in order to advance. And they know how to rear their children for achievement without having to take lessons from wealthier

minority" was also the model of "overachievers," with many Asians pushing their brains to the limit and successfully pursuing careers as professionals and managers at very modest IQ levels where many whites would have concluded that they didn't have the aptitude for such occupations and would have chosen less cognitively demanding pursuits. See James Flynn, *Asian Americans: Achievement beyond IQ* (Hillsdale, NJ: Erlbaum, 1991).

and more assimilated WASP neighbors. The River Pilots avoid such awkward facts and comparisons, I have suggested, because they would detract from the overarching apologetic theme of their work.

In my own experience I have found that the only way to get left-oriented sociologists to acknowledge the possible salience of cultural factors in explaining the poor academic performance of so many black and Latino youth is to bring up the alternative explanation of genes. "So if it isn't culture, do you think the problem is related to genes?" I once impishly asked a distinguished left-liberal sociologist in the question-and-answer period to a talk she had just delivered at Princeton pooh-poohing culture-based explanations for racial differences in academic achievement. Instantly under such prodding leftist sociologists become born-again culturalists and eagerly embrace the theories of people like John Ogbu and Thomas Sowell, whom they normally would ignore or spend considerable effort trying to refute.[182] Cultural explanations within such circles are accept-

---

182. On the instant embrace by leftist sociologists of the theories of Ogbu and Sowell, see the anti-Bell Curve writing of Claude Fischer and his Berkeley colleagues, *Inequality by Design: Cracking the Bell Curve Myth* (Princeton: Princeton University Press, 1996). Sowell's and Ogbu's theories are offered in this work as the major alternative to the emphasis in Murray and Herrnstein's writings on IQ differences as a major source of black and Latino achievement gaps in school. Harvard sociologist Orlando Patterson sums up the situation nicely: Statements by Richard Nisbett and Howard Gardner pointing to deficiencies in black culture as an alternative to genetic-based theories of black educational difficulties, says Patterson, are "warmly approved by Afro-American intellectuals and other liberal 'racial' advocates. However, had they been made in the context of a discussion of the educational problems of Afro-American youth, both men would almost certainly have been angrily corrected and dismissed as hopeless racists. . . . While Afro-American intellectual leaders, and all those who take a sympathetic interest in the plight of Afro-Americans, are quick to point to cultural actors in the defense of Afro-Americans against the onslaught of hereditarians . . . these very same leaders are equally quick to traduce, in other contexts, anyone who dares to point to the subcultural problems of the group in trying to explain their condition. It is now wholly incorrect politically even to utter the word culture as an explanation in any context other than counterattacks against hereditarians." Orlando Patterson, *The Ordeal of Integration* (Washington, D.C.: Civitas/Counterpoint, 1997), pp. 144–5.

The issue of genetic explanations of racial differences in cognitive achievement is too big to take up in a discussion of this kind. The strongest case for a genetic

able only as alternatives to genetic-based theories, and even then they are embraced only with great reluctance for fear of appearing to "blame the victim." Needless to say, this all has little to do with honest scholarship, honest social science, or a sincere effort to find out what is wrong and how to fix it. In perhaps no other area of American life are strictures of political correctness and ideology-based impediments to honest discussion more formidable than on the issue of academic achievement and race. And such impediments characterize almost everything the River Pilots write.

RECRUITED ATHLETES, RECRUITED LATINOS, RECRUITED BLACKS: THE CORRUPTION OF EDUCATIONAL STANDARDS

The River Pilots have produced one outstanding book—*The Game of Life: College Sports and Educational Values*.[183] That this (non-River) book should be produced by two of the authors (William Bowen and James Shulman) who collaborated in producing River I (*The Shape of the River*) tells us something about how otherwise talented, intelligent, and perceptive researchers,

---

component to differential academic performance among racial groups is made by Arthur Jensen, *The g Factor: The Science of Mental Ability* (Westport, CT: Praeger, 1998); J. Philippe Rushton, *Race, Evolution and Behavior*, 3rd ed. (New Brunswick, NJ: Transaction Publishers, 2000); Richard Lynn, *The Global Bell Curve* (Augusta, GA: Washington Summit Publishers, 2008); and Michael Levin, *Why Race Matters* (Westport, CT: Praeger, 1997). The strongest case against these genetic-based theories are to be found in Richard Nisbett, *Intelligence and How to Get It* (New York: W.W. Norton & Company, 2009); James Flynn, *What is Intelligence: Beyond the Flynn Effect* (Cambridge, UK: Cambridge University Press, 2007); Ulric Neisser, ed., *The Rising Curve: Long-Term Gains in IQ and Related Measures* (Washington, D.C.: American Psychological Association, 1998); and more generally the many works of Thomas Sowell.

183. James Shulman and William Bowen, *The Game of Life: College Sports and Educational Values* (Princeton: Princeton University Press, 2001). Though not listed as one of the two main authors, Shulman was a major researcher and consultant for the first River project, *The Shape of the River*, hence his inclusion as a River Pilot.

who are capable of first-rate scholarship and thoughtful policy analysis, can have their common sense weakened and judgment distorted when the issue becomes academic admissions and race.

The Game of Life focuses on the many changes that have occurred over the past 50 years in college sports programs. It explains how these programs have greatly expanded in scope, involving ever larger numbers of individual sports, how even low-profile sports have become increasingly competitive and professionalized, and how these changes have negatively affected the core academic mission of institutions of higher learning. The more intense recruitment of high school athletes with substandard academic records and their subsequent participation in competitions that have become more like professional athletics than the amateur college sports of old are developments deeply disturbing to the authors, who sound the alarm in a work that is a model of engaged but fair-minded advocacy scholarship.

The authors document many of the harmful effects of current sports recruitment policies on college campuses and conclude that such policies negatively impact the athletes themselves, the institutions that recruit them, and the wider social matrix in which professionalized college sports have become accepted and affirmed. Here are a few of their more salient findings and conclusions:

- High school athletes are heavily recruited and admitted to even the most academically selective colleges with substandard academic records that would preclude the admission of most nonathletes.
- There is "a consistent tendency for athletes to do less well academically than their classmates—and, even more troubling, a consistent tendency for athletes to underperform academically not just relative to other students, but relative to how they themselves might

have been expected to perform [given their entering SAT scores and high school grades]." (GOL, p. 271)

- These underperformance tendencies have become more pervasive over time: "academic underperformance is now found among women athletes as well as men, among those who play the Lower Profile sports as well as those on football and basketball teams, and among athletes playing at the Division III level of competition as well as those playing in bowl games and competing for national championships." (GOL, p. 271)

- "Stereotype vulnerability" may be part of the reason for this underperformance. There is a widespread stereotype of recruited athletes as "dumb jocks," and this stereotype may lead to a weakening of self-confidence in the academic arena, a disidentification with the goals of academic excellence, and a focusing on the one arena (i.e., sports) where the recruited athletes can excel.

- Whatever the reason, it is clear that recruited athletes on many campuses have formed their own "culture of sports" (some would say "jock culture"), which places less emphasis on the academic side of college life, focuses on a few (usually easier) majors, and is concerned mainly with getting by academically and just graduating rather than pursuing more ambitious academic goals. There are often team-specific effects that influence how recruited athletes think and act depending on the sports team they're a part of.

- The poor academic performance of recruited athletes cannot be ascribed to the heavy time commitments in their sports—musicians and college newspaper editors with similarly burdensome extracurricular commitments do not underperform their SAT scores or high school GPAs, and recruited athletes display the same level of underperformance in the off-season as during the regular season.

- When schools admit large numbers of people like recruited athletes with substandard academic records, and when these people form distinct subcultures within a college or university that place lesser value on academic excellence, there occurs a significant change in the whole ethos of an institution that compromises its basic educational and intellectual mission.

- When the most academically prestigious institutions in America dramatically lower their entrance standards to recruit high school athletes, a message is sent to students, their parents, and teachers about what is most valued in a high school student. This has a corrupting effect on the intellectual atmosphere of American high schools, and to many the message it conveys is that it is better to excel at a sport and be recruited by a college coach than to do outstanding academic work.

- This corrupting message probably has its greatest impact among black high school students, who see so many black athletes on college basketball and football teams. The message many receive is: If you want to get into a good college, "Hit the hoops, not the books!"

- "High school students, their parents, and their schools watch attentively for the signals that colleges and universities send. . . . When a school makes an admissions decision, it not only offers an opportunity to an individual, it also sends a signal to others, including students who have not even applied. Through this signaling effect, the school is saying, in effect, 'here is what we value.'" (GOL, pp. 52, 278) And when colleges and universities admit substandard athletes coming from high schools in which they have turned down students with far superior academic records, a message is sent to all the students in the school about what institutions of higher learning in America value the most.

- "If we take seriously the notion that students should take full advantage of what are very scarce educational opportunities, evidence of high graduation rates [among recruited athletes at selective institutions] should not end the conversation. It is not good enough, we believe, just to get by. Respect for core academic values and the educational mission of these schools requires more than that. Otherwise, colleges and universities are failing to put their most valuable resources—their faculty and their academic offerings—to their highest and best use. . . . They are not focused on fulfilling their educational missions. . . . We most emphatically do not mean to suggest that the athletes who are admitted are bad people, that they will not benefit from attending these schools, or that attending one of these institutions will fail to help them achieve their personal goals. The more difficult, and more relevant, question is whether admitting other students in their place might not have done even more to fulfill the educational mission of the school." (GOL, pp. 270–1)

In surveying these points, the discerning reader will no doubt have noticed an eerie parallel between lowering entrance standards for athletes and lowering standards for members of underrepresented minority groups. Indeed, substituting for "recruited athletes" in the above statements "recruited minorities," for "dumb jocks" "dumb affirmative-action students," and for "culture of sports" "culture of stereotype threat and racial entitlements," there are disturbing parallels to be observed between the racial-preference policies at American universities and the recruited-athlete policies at those same institutions.

Such parallels have not gone unnoticed by the authors of *The Game of Life*. Indeed, the parallels are so obvious and so close that the River Pilots devote a whole section in their study to exploring them. Here are some of the things they say:

> Earlier research using the [College and Beyond] database found that African American students at these academically selective schools exhibited many of the same patterns as the athletes we have been studying [in *The Game of Life*]. . . . We know that the two groups (which of course overlap, but only slightly) share an important initial characteristic: both have been recruited actively and have enjoyed an "admission advantage." . . . On average, African Americans (like athletes) came to campus with less impressive precollegiate academic credentials than their peers. Then, once on campus, they earned lower grades than their classmates. Moreover, the average rank in class of African Americans, like that of the athletes, was lower than the rank that would have been predicted for them on the basis of test scores and high school grades—which is what we mean by "underperformance."[184] (GOL, pp. 83–4)

---

184. The River III authors claim that recruited athletes experience no "underperformance," and they hold out hope that black and Latino affirmative-action students may some day display similar positive outcomes. But the more comprehensive treatment of this issue in *The Game of Life* shows that recruited athletes at a variety of colleges and universities very definitely do display "underperformance," and it is of a kind very similar to that experienced by the black students showcased in River I. River III also contends that legacy students do not experience underperformance of their entering academic credentials, and this may be correct (*The Game of Life* found this to be true of the legacies in their database). But legacies are unlike recruited athletes or blacks in that a) they have entering academic credentials often closer to the institutional norm than athletes or affirmative-action blacks (and thus have less reason to feel academically inferior); b) they are not clearly visible as a group that has been admitted under lowered standards, as black students are; and c) unlike both black students and the recruited athletes on various sports teams, they do not spend a lot of their time together or form a distinct subculture on most college campuses. And unlike blacks, they do not face the disincentive effects of having most graduate and professional schools admit them under much lower standards than others are admitted.

In both cases [i.e., African Americans and recruited athletes] part of the explanation [for underperformance] may be found in what social psychologist Claude Steele has called "stereotype vulnerability": the assumption (or collective societal expectation) that a group of students will not do well academically can cause even high achievers to experience performance anxiety. . . . Although Steele did not conduct similar experiments with athletes, there is certainly a widespread impression on many campuses that athletes . . . are "dumb jocks," and there is no reason to doubt that such stereotyping could have similar negative effects on classroom performance. . . . (GOL, p. 84)

Peer group pressures can also afflict both groups. Anthropologist John Ogbu has suggested that black students sometimes exert pressure on their peers not to "act white" and not to identify with "white" academic values. We saw [in an earlier chapter] that the athletic culture has its own values, and that team-specific effects can harm the academic performance of athletes. (GOL, p. 84)

For the recruited-athlete situation the authors of *The Game of Life* have a simple solution—one they acknowledge may not be easy to implement, given the reality of campus politics, but conceptually very simple: stop recruiting academically substandard athletes. The model they sometimes look toward is MIT, which has extensive athletic programs and considerable student participation in these programs but makes no distinction in admissions between athletes and nonathletes. The jocks at MIT are not dumb, and one cannot conclude from seeing on campus a 260-pound male with a highly muscled body build or an athletic-looking 6' 3" female that they are intellectually any less capable than the average MIT student.

Acknowledging the close parallels between the harmful effects of recruiting academically substandard athletes and recruiting equally substandard blacks or Latinos, *The Game of Life* authors try valiantly to distinguish the two cases. For many the obvious response would be, "Well, if the harmful effects are so palpable, let's end recruitment of the academically substandard in all its guises and have one uniformly high entrance standard that encompasses everyone, including athletes as well as 'underrepresented minorities.' In that way we will do away with stereotype threat, stigma reinforcement, underperformance, the formation of peer groups that direct attention away from learning, the corruption of academic standards, and the sending out of bad messages to high school students and their parents as to what admissions officers are looking for in America's most prestigious colleges. Elite colleges and universities will thereby make the best use of their top-flight faculties and other scarce academic resources and will be true to their noble educational mission."

If one wanted to add meat to the bones of such a recommendation one might look to MIT's smaller West Coast sibling, Caltech, which appears to apply the same high academic standards to all its applicants, including athletes, blacks, and Latinos, as it focuses on assembling the very best and brightest in terms of the likelihood that its graduates will become world-class leaders in science, technology, mathematics, and engineering. (The fact that Asians are grossly "overrepresented" at Caltech, while blacks and Latinos are grossly "underrepresented," doesn't seem to phase its merit-focused administration very much.)[185]

---

185. One suspects that Caltech takes as its model the early National Aeronautics and Space Administration, which put a man on the moon; the Manhattan Project, which built the atomic bomb; and Britain's Bletchley Park, which cracked the super-secret Nazi Enigma Code. Each of these successful organizations recruited large numbers of "the best and the brightest" from a diversity of disciplines, and although in each case there was great ethnic and national-origins diversity, it was the diversity produced by a strict merit system, not one produced by any socially engineered "affirmative action" or "race-sensitive" admissions program. And no one kept tabs on how many of this or that group were employed. No doubt some groups—like the Jews on the Manhattan

Alas, this is not how Shulman and Bowen view the matter. They readily acknowledge that there are grave problems involved in lowering the admissions bar both for recruited athletes and for underachieving minorities and that many of these problems are driven by a similar dynamic. However, as in River I, they say the benefits of having more blacks and Latinos on elite college campuses, even if many are underqualified by the high standards of the institutions, overshadow the very real costs of racial-preference policies. Diversity enhancement and the need to turn out more black and Latino leaders are the main benefits they claim in this context, although little is said to address the downward-parasitism problem (i.e., "Duke's diversity gain is UNC's diversity loss"), the stigma reinforcement issue, the problem of disincentives and "pernicious palliatives," the mismatch problems, the necessity of lying, or the myriad other arguments brought against race-based admissions by critics.

Where *The Game of Life* authors really missed an opportunity to contribute to the affirmative-action debate was in comparing black students at selective colleges under our current preferences regime and black students in the pre-affirmative action era. The authors of *The Game of Life* have access to a database collected by the Mellon Foundation that contains information on college students who graduated from several competitive colleges in 1951. This was long before there was any special preference program for either blacks or athletes, and, indeed, the authors report that the athletes from the college class of 1951 actually did *better* academically in terms of college grades than the average student of their day, with half graduating in the top third of their class. It would be instructive to see what the record was for the black students of that era.

Project—were greatly overrepresented, other groups greatly underrepresented. But to speak more properly, no groups were "represented" at all, because individual excellence rather than the representation of groups was the only criteria of selection.

If I had to make a guess, I would say that they displayed no underperformance, as today's athletes and affirmative-action students do, and I wouldn't be surprised if they actually over-performed their entering high school grades and test scores, perhaps heeding the message delivered to Colin Powell's generation of ambitious black men by black leaders of the day that if they wanted to succeed in a white world they would have to work harder and do better than the whites to prove themselves.[186] The message today, that if you are black you don't have to prove yourself, that you will be pitied and patronized and given a huge admissions boost over the whites and Asians in your class, may be more comforting to some blacks and surely reflects a decline in overt white racial hostility. But it is an unhealthy message nevertheless, which carries with it substantial psychological and pragmatic harm to all parties concerned. It would be interesting to see how black graduates of selective colleges did in the 1950s—a time (to quote the black economist and affirmative-action critic Walter Williams), "when it was not yet fashionable for white people to like black people." We are not likely to find out, however, because the Mellon Foundation restricts access to its college databases, and no doubt it fears further evidence that

186. "All army men who rise to the top are disciplined, but some seem to be more disciplined than others. That was especially true of the generation of young black officers to which Powell belonged, who entered the officer corps when prejudices were stronger than they would be fifteen years later when he was in midcareer. . . . These young black officers . . . were bonded together by two powerful forces. First, they were black in a white man's world, but a white man's world that seemed to be getting better. Second, they all had had it drummed into them by their parents that if they intended to succeed, they had to be better, much better, than any white person. Powell was very good, always at his best, because the price for not being good, if you were black, was severe; not only did you not rise quickly, you descended quickly. . . . As a military man working with civilians, [Powell] had no peer. . . . Powerful civilians in the bureaucracy, men at the cabinet and immediate subcabinet levels, fought for his services, but not because they wanted a token black man sitting in their outer office. They did it because he was very, very good and, they soon began to realize, his talents served to make them look good." David Halberstam, *War in a Time of Peace: Bush, Clinton, and the Generals* (New York: Simon and Schuster, 2001), p. 235.

affirmative-action policies have many of the harmful effects critics have long attributed to them.

PLAYING WITH FIRE: TRIBAL LOYALTIES, TRIBAL ENMITIES, AND INTERGROUP NORMS OF RECIPROCITY AND FAIRNESS

A number of years ago a Korean American student in one of my politics precept classes at Princeton described to me with great passion the hostility and ill-will felt by the Asian and white students in the California prep school he attended when the college acceptance and rejection letters arrived in the spring of their senior year. A female black student, he explained, had applied to more than half a dozen of the most prestigious colleges and universities in the nation and got accepted to every one of them, deciding eventually to enroll at Stanford.

Why was there such hostility and ill-will among his classmates, I wanted to know. "Were there better-qualified Asian and white students with higher SAT scores than the black student?" I asked. "*Better qualified*?" he asked. "There were *loads* of Asian and white students who were *much* better qualified, with *much* higher SAT scores, *much* higher grade-point averages, and who were more active in student government and a host of other extracurricular activities than this black student." To add further fuel to his classmates' anger, he went on, this particular black student had a cold, off-putting, self-centered personality, which hardly endeared her to her classmates. "She didn't make it on charm" was the gist of his further remarks.

Although the quality of her academic performance was not in the same league as the highest-achieving Asian and white students, this black student had apparently received such favorable treatment from elite colleges and universities because she had received a quality education from a first-rate prep school and was probably able to score substantially above average in terms of national black norms on standardized tests like the SAT even if her scores were substantially below those of many of her white and Asian classmates. It's what Yale law professor Stephen Carter has called the "best black" syndrome. Her classmates' anger was no doubt triggered by the fact that they were all in the same boat as she was in terms of opportunity, all enjoying the benefits of a quality private school education, yet she, with her less than stellar performance, got acceptance letters to a host of the most prestigious colleges in America while many far superior students in the same school had to settle for second-tier institutions because they were of a different race. Whatever justification admissions officers might give for racial preferences of this kind, they seemed terribly unfair to the Asian and white students in this particular high school.

A short time after I heard this story, another student of mine, this time an Ashkenazic Jew, related in a term paper a similar situation in the high school he attended. A black female in his graduating class, he said, was accepted by Princeton despite much lower grades and SAT scores than many of the "non-minority" students in his class whom Princeton rejected. "I knew that countless students had worked much harder than the minority student," he wrote, "but they had not been admitted only because they were not black." Although this Jewish student himself did well in the admissions process and was grateful for that fact, he harbored a deep sense of grievance and injustice for many of his less fortunate high school friends, who were judged by a different standard from that apparently applied to black students.

Stories of this kind could be multiplied endlessly. One of the more recent cases that received a fair amount of media coverage is that of Jian Li, a New Jersey high school graduate who lodged a racial-discrimination complaint with the Department of Education against Princeton University on behalf of himself and similarly situated Asians. Though gaining admission to

Yale, Li was rejected at Princeton and four other elite universities (Harvard, MIT, Stanford, and Penn) despite the fact that his academic and general performance in the competitive suburban high school he attended can only be described as stellar. Li had a perfect 2400 on the newer version of the SAT (i.e., three 800s), achieved near-perfect scores on several of the SAT achievement tests (SAT IIs), took nine Advanced Placement courses, and had a near-perfect grade-point-average that placed him in the 99th percentile of his graduating class. In addition to his top-of-the line academic performance, Li was active in a number of extra-curricular activities and was a delegate to the prestigious Boys State. All these accomplishments would be impressive under any circumstances, but Li was the son of Chinese immigrants, his first language was Chinese, and English was not spoken in his home. Li's academic achievement was a truly remarkable and inspiring story of talent, persistence, and the immigrant work ethic in pursuit of the American Dream.

Li was happy at Yale and lodged his complaint not because of any animus against Princeton or the other four schools that rejected his application but because of a general sense that Asian applicants to elite colleges were being unjustly disfavored in comparison with the members of other minority groups, especially blacks and Latinos. They were not, he believed, being evaluated fairly under the same set of academic standards as these other groups. And Li's perceptions were clearly correct. The simple fact is that a black or Latino student with Li's credentials would almost certainly have gained admission to *every* elite institution he or she applied to. Indeed, an "underrepresented minority student" would have stood a decent chance of gaining admission to some of the schools Li was rejected at with test scores as much as 200 points below each of his 800 scores on the three-part SAT exam and substantially lower grade-point averages and rank-in-class standings in high school. Li clearly felt aggrieved, not just for himself but for the countless Chinese and other high-achieving Asians who are not blacks or Latinos but members of less favored racial and ethnic groups.

Why do students like Jian Li, the Korean-American, and the Ashkenazic Jew perceive racial-preference policy to be so unfair? And what is the basis of the obvious passion animating their sense of injury and injustice? The River Pilots, particularly the authors of River III, clearly want to suggest that such a sense of grievance is unwarranted, that the use of racial preferences is in no way unjust, and they deliberately use the provocative phrase "affirmative action for athletes and legacies" to suggest that there is no more harm or injustice in abandoning the academic-merit criteria in admitting more black and Latino students to elite colleges and universities than in abandoning it to admit more athletes or legacies. Since people generally seem to get much less incensed over the latter types of preference (even those who disapprove of them), they have little reason, the River III authors seem to suggest, to get overly upset by racial preferences. The River Pilots are diplomatic enough—and sufficiently measured in their prose—not to accuse affirmative-action opponents of racism or hostility to blacks or other racial minorities (as leftist scholars often do), although their general impatience with affirmative-action critics faintly suggests this may be their hidden belief.

It is clear that in terms of their capacity to provoke impassioned protest, taking race into account and preferencing one ethno-racial group over another really is different from athlete or legacy preferences, although the River Pilots fail to grasp the source of this difference. Though corrupting to intellectual standards, athletic preferences can at least be defended on the grounds that there are other forms of merit a college might acknowledge besides the strictly academic kind and that these might include, in addition to special musical or dance talent, the ability of an accomplished athlete. Whether or not one accepts this rationale, it is hard to see mere membership in an "underrepresented minority group" as a form of nonacademic talent comparable to that of being an accomplished athlete or musician—although some have tried valiantly to defend this claim.[187]

Legacy admissions are more problematic. Like race, being a legacy or a child of a wealthy donor can't be justified as a special form of either academic or nonacademic merit, which is why so many people see something untoward about preferences based on these factors. But legacy and wealthy-donor preferences, even if considered unfair, are rarely opposed with the vehemence of racial preferences, in part because most people realize that private colleges and universities are dependent on private funding to survive and that loyal alumni donors (and generous nonalumni donors) are often important sources of such funding. College administrators will often defend donor and alumni preferences on the grounds that the money they get through such policies, however questionable in other ways, is often used for unquestionably worthy purposes, including the provision of more scholarship aid to students in financial need. Partially for this reason they do not provoke the visceral hostility of race-based preferences.

If the black students described by the Korean and Ashkenazic Jewish students had come from wealthy families that had donated millions to the elite institutions to which their daughters applied, or if the black students had parents, grandparents, or other close relatives who were graduates of these elite institutions, it is doubtful that the level of hostility to their admissions success would have been as intense as it actually was. Surely the

---

187. Although he seems to have changed his position in recent years, Harvard Law School professor Randall Kennedy once suggested that merit is "a malleable concept, determined not by immanent, preexisting standards but rather by the perceived needs of society. In as much as the elevation of blacks addresses pressing social needs, [supporters of race-conscious admissions] rightly insist that considering a black's race as part of the bundle of traits that constitute merit is entirely appropriate." (Randall Kennedy, "Persuasion and Distrust: A Comment on the Affirmative Action Debate," *Harvard Law Review*, Apr. 1986, p. 1327)

parents of the Korean and Jewish students would have understood, if not the students themselves. As the old *Cabaret* tune has it, "money makes the world go around"—and pragmatically minded people understand this, regrettable though some of its implications may be.

It is also doubtful that the admissions of either of the two black students to an elite college would have been the occasion for the level of anger and sense of injustice provoked among the whites and Asians had the black students been from poor families with uneducated or non-English speaking parents and the students had distinguished themselves by being among the hardest workers in their school. Even if the black students under such circumstances received grades that were somewhat lower than those of the highest-scoring students, it is unlikely that there would have been such a strong sense of grievance among their classmates since it has always been considered legitimate for colleges to evaluate high school grades and SAT scores in view of the hurdles a student has had to overcome in life. Overcoming obstacles legitimately counts as merit. Nor is it likely that the admissions success of either of the two black students would have provoked much hostility if the students had been high school sports stars and actively recruited by college coaches.

WHY RACE IS DIFFERENT

There remains something about giving unmerited preference to ethno-racial status—though not to legacy status, athletic-performance status, wealthy-donor status, or underprivileged-family status—that calls out for explanation. On this matter the River Pilots are clueless—and dangerously so. I will argue here that the reason racial preferences evoke such passionate hostility must be sought in an understanding of our basically tribal nature as human beings and the ways in which the potentially destructive tendencies of this tribal nature are mitigated in multiracial, multiethnic societies like the U.S. Most people of common sense and worldly experience, I believe, have long understood these things—at least in a vague sort of way—although much light has been cast on these issues in recent years by the burgeoning disciplines of evolutionary biology, evolutionary psychology, and related social science disciplines drawing on Darwin's path-breaking insights. I will try to explain why race and ethnicity are different, and why in supporting racial preferences the River Pilots are playing with a dangerously explosive sorcerer's brew whose nature they do not understand and which continues to exert a corroding effect on the fragile bonds that hold racially and ethnicly diverse societies together.

Evolutionary thinkers begin with the assumption that, like all living organisms, modern humans, *Homo sapiens*, evolved over long stretches of time from earlier organic life. Anatomically modern humans first appeared in Africa, the archeological evidence suggests, approximately 200,000 years ago, with the hominid line that preceded them stretching back several million years. For 95 percent of the time that modern humans have existed on this planet, human beings lived almost exclusively as hunter-gatherers in relatively small, intimate, face-to-face aggregations of clans or tribes confronting overwhelming problems of survival. Besides the necessities of hunting and gathering food to avoid starvation, providing shelter against the elements, and providing defense against animal predators and parasites, early humans, like their modern counterparts, faced the daunting task of defending themselves against hostile forces of their own kind. We humans, like our nearest relatives the chimpanzees, are among the very few animals on earth that engage in coalition warfare against members of our own species. The ancient saying, *homo homini lupus*—"man is a wolf to man"—well captures this reality. Wolves hunt in packs against members of other species; humans fight in highly organized coalitions against coalitions of other human beings.

With the greater ability of humans than chimpanzees to make and use weapons (spears, clubs, darts, etc.), to move over great distances (bipedalism), to effectively use vocal communication and language in order to develop successful war-fighting strategies and counter-strategies, and to organize males into effective warrior bands, the survival danger of group-against-group warfare in humans was exponentially raised over that in chimpanzees. Failure to meet the challenges posed by murderously rival human groups could mean death to many of the members of one's clan or tribe as well as the abduction of fertile women and their incorporation into rival tribes for the use of their men as secondary wives or concubines.[188] Some evolutionary thinkers believe that the enormously larger brains that we humans have compared to those of chimpanzees evolved in part in response to the intense selective pressure created by coalition violence, whereby the need arose for ever greater mental capacities to discern and outwit group rivals in a high-stakes Darwinian game of intertribal warfare and intertribal wife capture. The fact that an estimated 25 percent of males in hunter-gather societies die violent deaths, usually through tribal raids or other

---

188. The description given in the Hebrew Bible of the conquest of Canaan by the ancient Hebrew tribes might be seen as paradigmatic of ancient tribal warfare in the early herding and primitive agricultural stages of human development (warfare in hunter-gather times was less organized but its aims quite similar): "When you advance to the attack on any [far distant] town, first offer it terms of peace. If it accepts these and opens its gates to you, all the people to be found in it shall do forced labour for you and be subject to you. But if it refuse peace and offers resistance, you must lay siege to it. [The Lord] your God shall deliver it into your power and you are to put all its menfolk to the sword. But the women, the children, the livestock and all that the town contains, all its spoil, you may take for yourselves as booty. You will devour the spoil of your enemies which [the Lord] your God has delivered to you. . . . When you go to war against your enemies and [the Lord] your God delivers them into your power and you take prisoners, if you see a beautiful women among the prisoners and find her desirable, you may make her your wife and bring her to your home. . . . She is to stay inside your house and must mourn her father and mother for a full month. Then you may go to her and be a husband to her, and she shall be your wife." (Deuteronomy 20:10–14; 21:10–13; JB) Many similar descriptions can be found in the Book of Joshua, where women, children, and even livestock are sometimes not spared the murderous rage of the victors in tribal warfare.

hostile action by tribal competitors, lends support to such an interpretation.[189]

Evolutionary psychologists speak of the 95 percent of the time that humans lived in hunter-gatherer circumstances as the Environment of Evolutionary Adaptedness (EEA), and they stress that we carry within our genome many adaptive tendencies that evolved during that long period. But adaptive tendencies that may have been useful in Paleolithic hunter-gatherer societies, these psychologists stress, may not be useful in the very different material and social environments that we live in today. One example evolutionary thinkers often give is the development of our human food-intake instincts. In the EEA virtually all of the sweet foods available (mainly berries, fruits, and honey), as well as most of the high-fat-content foods (wild game, fish, nuts), had the properties of being both scarce and highly nutritious. Much of it, too, was perishable, and lacking modern means of refrigeration and preservation it spoiled and became inedible very quickly. Under such circumstances, the evolutionists say, our hunter-gather forebears evolved food-intake instincts that said in effect, "When in the presence of sweet and high-fat-content foods indulge yourself—eat while the eating is good!"

---

189. See Lawrence Keeley, *War Before Civilization* (New York: Oxford University Press, 1996). For males, bigger brains would not only enhance war-fighting and war-strategizing capacities that would aid in violent conflicts with hostile outside groups but also confer considerable within-group advantage for the man with superior "Machiavellian intelligence" in the struggle for status and power within his own tribe. Since the Big Man and other tribal leaders in prestate societies often enjoy the reproductive benefits of having the most wives and the most resources to see to it that they and their offspring survive, the Darwinian gain to greater intelligence and the larger brains to support it would thus have both inter-tribal and intra-tribal advantages. That women have brains that in proportion to body weight are almost as large as men's may be a development similar to the existence of nipples in males and would explain the protest from Plato to modern feminism that women have much greater mental capacity than that reflected in their traditional evolved social roles. On Machiavellian intelligence, see Richard Byrne and Andrew Whiten, eds., *Machiavellian Intelligence: Social Expertise and the Evolution of Intelligence in Monkeys, Apes, and Humans* (New York: Oxford University Press, 1981).

Those possessing genes predisposing them to adopt this eating strategy were more likely to survive and pass on their food-intake proclivities to succeeding generations than those lacking these genetic tendencies. In hunter-gather days, ravenous and ungoverned appetites in the presence of sweet and fatty foods conferred a substantial survival and reproductive payoff. In modern, fast-food America, however, our problems are very different, evolutionary psychologists say, insofar as our food availability environment is radically out of sync with our inherited food-intake instincts, which were adapted to an environment of scarcity when the few sweet and fatty foods available were generally healthy and nutritious. If we follow the "whispering within," which tells us that we should indulge ourselves and eat as much as we can when in the presence of sweet and fatty foods, we will not only wind up eating a lot of non-nutritious junk-food but will also clog our arteries, get diabetes, and become one of the growing statistics of the morbidly obese.

The lesson learned here is that our evolved tendencies may be maladaptive under changed circumstances. Perhaps nowhere in the modern world is the maladaptive nature of our evolved human propensities more striking, some evolutionary psychologists believe, than in the all-but-universal human tendency toward ethnocentrism, xenophobia, clannishness, and racism. The tendency to divide the human world into an "us" of our own kin and clan and a "them" of everyone else, to ascribe a fundamental importance and positive evaluation to the "us" and a more negative, out-group status to those in the "them," appears to be present in almost all hunter-gatherer societies, and in all modern societies as well. "For millennia," writes the evolutionary psychologist J. Philippe Rushton, "racism was not a word, it was a way of life." "The most fundamental relationship recognized by tribal man," he explains, "is that of blood, or descent; in many cases anyone not made a relative becomes an enemy. Primitive society often seems to be organized on two major principles: that the only effective bond is a bond of blood, and that the purpose of society is to unite for wars of offense and defense."[190]

The late-nineteenth-century sociologist William Graham Sumner first coined the term "ethnocentrism" and defined it as the "view of things in which one's own group is the center of everything, and all others are scaled and rated with reference to it."[191] Closely tied to the ethnocentric attitude that Sumner describes is "xenophobia," the fear or suspicion of strangers—of outsiders to one's own family, kin, and clan—which, according to the learned European ethologist Irenäus Eibl-Ebesfeldt, "manifests itself in all cultures we have so far studied."[192] Some ethologists and followers of Sumner speak of a universal human tendency toward "in-group amity" and "out-group enmity." And this tendency seems to begin at the earliest ages. As two *Newsweek* science writers reported in summing up recent studies of infant behavior, "Kids as young as 6 months judge others based on skin color"—and those with different skin color than that of their parents and nurturers are usually judged negatively.[193]

The tendencies toward ethnocentrism and xenophobia can be greatly enhanced culturally through ideological indoctrination, the deliberate use of self-segregating ethnic markers, participation in distinct ethnic or ethno-religious rituals and initiations, and the like. But a tendency toward ethnocentrism and xenophobia, many evolutionary biologists now argue, seems

---

190. Rushton, Race, Evolution and Behavior, p. 91.
191. William Graham Sumner, *Folkways* (New York: Ginn, 1906), Section 15; cited in Joseph Lopreato and Timothy Crippen, *Crisis in Sociology: The Need for Darwin* (New Brusnwick, NJ: Transaction Publishers, 1999), p. 253.
192. I. Eibl-Ebesfeldt, "Familiality, Xenophobia, and Group Selection," *Behavioral and Brain Sciences*, 12 (1989): 523.
193. Po Bronson and Ashley Merryman, "See Baby Discriminate," *Newsweek*, Sept. 5, 2009.

clearly hard-wired in our brains and can be observed in infants who have spent less than a year with their nurturing mothers. Studies have shown that infants and young children react with greater fear, suspicion, and disdain when in the presence of adults or other children who look different, dress differently, and perhaps smell different than their nurturing parents and the siblings and close relatives with whom they have been raised.[194] A natural imprinting process seems to be at work in which we are born with a tendency to respond negatively toward people who do not resemble those with whom we were reared in our earliest formative years.[195]

As infants, write the evolutionary sociologists Joseph Lopreato and Timothy Crippen, we develop "a close attachment to those who provide comfort and sustenance." But the other side of this coin is that "we are born with an aversion toward people who will not readily remind us of those with whom we spent our earliest years."[196] In other words, to some extent we are all predisposed to be ethnocentrists and xenophobes; we all have (in Lopreato and Crippen's words) a genetically based "inclination to favor alliances . . . with others in direct proportion to [our] degree of kinship and/or phenotypical similarity to these," and a "biologically based predisposition to have negative attitudes toward others on the basis of real or perceived differences that are typically, though not exclusively, of an ethnic nature." "The more phenotypically dissimilar [we] are, the more [we] tend to avoid each other and, as occasion arises, oppose each other's aims, moral standards, and the like. The more phenotypically (and, by implication, genotypically) similar [we] are

---

194. See F. Abound, *Children and Prejudice* (Oxford, UK: Blackwell, 1988); D.G. Freedman, *Human Infancy: An Evolutionary Perspective* (Hillsdale, NJ: Lawrence Erlbaum, 1974); and S. Feinman, "Infant Response to Race, Size, Proximity, and Movement of Strangers," *Infant Behavior and Development*, 3 (1980): 187–204.
195. Lopreato and Crippen, *Crisis in Sociology*, p. 264.
196. Ibid.

to each other, the more [we] tend to attract each other and to practice mutual favoritism."[197]

In the EEA all this probably made good sense, since those outside one's immediate clan or tribe were real potential threats, there were no organized states or law enforcement agencies to keep the peace between rival groups, and one had to close ranks with one's extended kin to survive against a hostile world. Groups whose members had a strong sense of in-group loyalty and ethnocentric favoritism, combined with a willingness to respond with lethal violence and rage against members of any outsider group that threatened the group's well-being or survival, would be the ones that survived in a universe where group-against-group rivalry and violence were the order of the day. Members of successful groups would thus pass on their genetic predisposition for in-group loyalty and out-group enmity to succeeding generations. We today are the descendants of those groups able to hold their own in this clan-against-clan struggle for dominance and survival. Groups whose members lacked a genetic predisposition toward in-group favoritism or out-group suspiciousness and who allowed their kinsmen to be picked on or exploited by members of rival groups without violent retaliation would soon die out and their more pacifist genetic predispositions along with them. We today are not the descendants of such people.

As Lopreato and Crippen write further on this: "Human beings are ethnocentric ultimately because they are the descendants of organisms whose natural selection within a context of inter-group competition favored the installation of intense nepotistic favoritism. . . . In-group solidarity, [while it] was rooted in familistic psychological adaptations, was reinforced by the ever-present threat coming from without. This is another way of saying that in general the greater the ethnocentrism the greater

---

197. Ibid, p. 267.

the probability of survival, reproduction, and genetic representation in subsequent generations. . . . Equipped with these primeval adaptations, our clan progenitors entered the historical era and the megasociety with zealous conceptions of 'us' and 'them'. Paleogenetic evidence shows, however, that while societal organization has changed dramatically, our neurobiology is still back in the clan. In the continuing struggle for existence, we are still driven to make common cause with some and to suspect evil intentions in others."[198]

The bottom line for many evolutionary psychologists and sociologists is that racial, ethnic, and linguistic tensions and disorders will be a constant presence in the modern world wherever people of different racial and ethnic groups intermingle, and that ways must be developed to deal with the inevitable tensions and problems created by this fact. Expanding the scope of human collectivities beyond the hunter-gather tribe, these social scientists say, has many advantages, especially scientific and economic, but it is a source of great friction and discord inevitably arising from our clannish brains, and it must be properly managed.

One form of proper management, of course, is that imposed by a centralized, authoritarian state like the former Soviet Union, the Austro-Hungarian monarchy, the Yugoslav state under Tito, or the Iraqi state under Saddam Hussein. However undesirable in other ways, a strong, centralized, authoritarian state can often mitigate ethno-racial, ethno-religious, and ethno-linguistic conflicts through an iron-fist policy of intimida-

---

198. Ibid., pp. 266, 276. Besides outward physical appearance, deportment, and dress, the most salient ethnic marker has always been dialect and language, and the fact that humans generally lose the ability after their childhood to learn to speak correctly the sounds of any given language insures that one's "mother tongue" will forever be a powerful in-group marker that usually cannot be mistaken by members of one's own clan or tribe or counterfeited by outsiders. It is no surprise that conflicts over ethnicity and language are so often two aspects of the same identity problem and elicit similarly high-charged emotional responses.

tion and coercive "law and order" measures that maintain at least an outward semblance of interethnic harmony and peace. As long as the authoritarian regime is maintained in power, this outward peace can persist.

We know from recent history, however, that when the authoritarian state begins to lose its grip on things, ethnic fragmentation and Balkanization, sometimes preceded by bloody ethnic civil wars, are the inevitable outcome. In his book *Blood and Belonging*, written shortly after the breakup of the Soviet Union, Canadian writer Michael Ignatieff observed that at the close of the twentieth century "multinational, multi-ethnic nation-states are discovering that their populations are often more loyal to the ethnic units that compose them than to the federation and the laws that hold the state together." Although liberal reformers and multiculturalists often obscure these facts, it is difficult to deny Ignatieff's observations here. Belonging attaches to blood and can fragment multiethnic nations.[199]

More democratic societies seek less brutal means than those of dictatorships to create harmony between rivalrous ethnic groups, and among the more successful attempts have been structural arrangements that produce long-range benefits for all groups concerned. A characteristic feature of such arrangements is that they replace the zero-sum, win-lose games played out between warring ethnic groups with the potential for positive-sum, pie-expanding, cooperative outcomes from which, in the long run, most people or their immediate descendants can benefit.

In the international arena the model for such long-run, win-win arrangements is the reciprocal trade agreement. Although many free-market economists believe that even the unilateral reduction of import barriers is good for the health of a domestic

---

199. Michael Ignatieff, *Blood and Belonging: Journeys into the New Nationalism* (New York: Farrar, Straus, Giroux, 1993), p. 13.

economy, most noneconomists (especially people employed in industries facing foreign competition) believe that it would be best for the economic health of their country to restrict imports of foreign-made goods while foreign markets remained opened to the exported products of their own manufacturers. Realizing, however, that erecting tariff barriers to foreign goods will encourage retaliatory barriers by foreign countries, and that such a situation is much worse for their home economies than a free-trade regime, manufacturing countries often come together to cooperate with one another through reciprocal trade agreements. These agreements say in effect, "We will give up our natural inclination to favor our home manufacturers through protective tariffs if you do the same vis-à-vis your home manufacturers." Experience shows that insofar as international free trade is a win-win, positive-sum game, many more people in the long run will experience benefits from such an arrangement than from a regime of beggar-thy-neighbor protective tariffs and trade wars.

I believe there is a similar logic at work domestically in the plea for a merit-based system of allocating positions in competitive universities as well as in public- and private-sector jobs. A best-qualified-applicant system for allocating scarce educational resources and jobs has many of the same benefits—in terms of competence, efficiency, noncorruption, and technological advance—as a tariff-free, open-market economic system. And it also has the great advantage of being a system to which members of different ethnic groups can be welcomed on board knowing that the sacrifices they are being asked to make in terms of abandoning their natural tendency toward ethnic favoritism are being reciprocated by other ethnic groups.

The logic involved in a merit-based system mitigates the potential harm posed by our clannish brains by an implicit reciprocity agreement that if put into words would say something like this: "In order to achieve greater social harmony among ethnic groups and to establish a more progressive system of resource allocation that in the long run will have major benefits for all of us, I will give up acting on the natural human partiality that I feel toward my kin and clan if you are willing to give up acting on the natural partiality you feel toward your kin and clan. My ethnic identity group will not use political power or other influences to promote ethnic favoritism on behalf of our people; your ethnic identity group must not use political power or other influences to further ethnic favoritism on behalf of your people. At least in the public realm, including admissions to universities heavily subsidized by the government, we will all be just Americans, not representatives of contending tribes. Merit, defined in a race-neutral manner, will be our guiding light, which will ensure that jobs and positions in our nation's best educational institutions are staffed by the objectively best-qualified applicants regardless of racial, ethnic, religious, or other tribal affiliations. The more successful we are in achieving these goals, the healthier and more prosperous we will be as a people, and the greater we will be able to expand our horizon of empathy and identity so that 'your people' and 'my people' will become, for many public purposes, 'our people.'"

This is the kind of logic—the kind of interethnic reciprocity norm and empathy-expansion formula—that I believe is at least implicitly embodied in many of the most progressive developments that have occurred in America over the past 125 years. It is embodied in the civil-service exam system of government hiring that began to replace the earlier systems of ethnic nepotism and political spoils in the waning years of the nineteenth century. It is embodied even more clearly in the many state Fair Employment Practice Laws (FEP) passed in the 1940s and 1950s, which prohibited racial and ethnic discrimination in the jobs market. It is seen in the Civil Rights Act of 1964, which prohibited race-based decision-making in a host of areas, including federally financed education, corporate employment, and public accommodations; in the 1968 Fair Housing Law, which extended the nonpreferential and nondiscrimination regimes to the sale or rental of private housing; in Lyndon Johnson's two executive orders (Nos. 11246 and 11375)[200] barring many different types of discrimination by government contractors; and, of course, in Justice Harlan's ringing dissent in the Plessy case declaring that "our Constitution is color-blind." In more recent times this logic has found perhaps its pithiest formulation in Justice Scalia's concurrence in the Adarand case striking down race-based set-asides in government contracting: "In the eyes of government, we are just one race here. It is American." (*Adarand Constructors, Inc. v. Pena*, 1995)

When the interethnic reciprocity norm is breached, a sense of outrage and moral injustice follows that stirs the deepest passions of our clannish brains, provoking primordial feelings of in-group solidarity and out-group enmity and a general "circling of the wagons" response that gets ready to do battle. In the face of reciprocity defaults and assaults by rival tribes, there is a triggering of our evolved rage-and-retaliation response that natural selection has imprinted in our brains. Under such circumstances, the range of human empathy dramatically contracts and the forces of win-win, positive-sum outcomes that had provided a counterweight to clannish parochialisms give way to

---

200. The wording of Executive Order 11375, issued by Lyndon Johnson in 1967, is most explicit in understanding itself as part of a legal regime seeking to substitute merit for a system of employment based on racial, ethnic, religious, or national origins favoritism or discrimination, or for differential treatment based on sex: "It is the policy of the United States Government to provide equal opportunity in federal employment and in employment by federal contractors on the basis of merit and without discrimination because of race, color, religion, sex or national origin. The Congress, by enacting Title VII of the Civil Rights Act of 1964, enunciated a national policy of equal employment opportunity in private employment, without discrimination because of race, color religion, sex, or national origin. Executive Order 11246 of September 24, 1965, carried forward a program of equal employment opportunity in government employment, employment by federal contractors and subcontractors, and employment under federally assisted construction contracts regardless of race, creed, color, or national origin. It is desirable that the equal employment opportunity programs provided for in Executive Order 11246 expressly embrace discrimination on account of sex."

bitter, zero-sum conflicts over racial entitlements, ethnic quotas, and tribal turf. The promptings of the clannish brain reassert themselves, and the outcome is usually increased racial hostilities and vastly diminished cooperation between rival clannish groups.

In many developing countries, including India and Sri Lanka, this process has often culminated in spontaneous violence and lethal ethnic riots. Scholars of ethnic conflict, including Donald Horowitz, Thomas Sowell, Myron Weiner, and Mary Katzenstein, have shown on a global scale how frequently preference policies produce a profound sense of ethnic grievance and ethnic outage, especially among the less privileged members of the nonbeneficiary groups.[201] In America the latter would include poor whites and poor Asians, and it is no surprise that they are often among the most hostile to policies that favor blacks and Latinos while disfavoring members of their own kin and clan.

On American college campuses the racial enmity unleashed by preference programs rarely results in violence or other acts of racial hostility. But self-segregation and racial color barriers have become a near universal phenomenon on most college campuses despite the wishes of college administrators, and as one keen observer of the campus scene (the previously cited Dinesh D'Souza) explains, "From the moment students arrive on campus, they know that the rules have somehow been politically rigged, and their fate as individuals depends on whether they belong to the favored group or the unfavored group." "[The students] think of themselves as ethnic platoons engaged in a silent struggle in which the gains of one necessarily entail

---

201. Donald Horowitz, *Ethnic Groups in Conflict* (Berkeley: University of California Press, 1985); Myron Weiner and Mary Katzenstein, *India's Preferential Policies* (Chicago: University of Chicago Press, 1981); Thomas Sowell, *Preferential Policies: An International Perspective* (New York: Basic Books, 1991).

the losses of the other." And with considerable understatement, D'Souza adds, "This is not a formula for racial harmony."[202]

The River Pilots don't seem to understand that in dealing with racial preferences and racial favoritism, they are dealing with fire, and that the sense of grievance and injustice sometimes felt over legacy preferences, athletic preferences, or wealthy-donor preferences pales in comparison with that felt over preferences based on race and ethnicity. When my kin and clan are disfavored and yours favored, deep feelings of primordial solidarity and protectiveness are evoked that produce a rage against any policy that would hold members of your racial and ethnic group to be worthier of concern than members of mine—and my group thus less valued than yours. Such favoritism is experienced by many in the disfavored groups as an outright ethnic assault, which dangerously provokes our evolved tribal instincts for within-group loyalty and between-group warfare. People of common sense and worldly experience, as I have said, have vaguely understood all this, and contemporary evolutionary social science helps us to understand these primordial feelings much better.

To state the bottom line once again: Racial-preference policies provoke among the groups not favored a self-protective ethnic solidarity and defensive rage that tap into our primordial instincts of ethnocentrism and xenophobia derived from our evolutionary past—instincts hard-wired in our brains. They transform the kind of thinking that says "we're all just Americans" into a "your people vs. my people" kind of hostile group rivalry that is thoroughly destructive to the American commonweal. They are almost always perceived by the disfavored groups as an injustice and a breach of the interethnic social contract calling for reciprocity and fairness. Whatever

---

202. Dinesh D'Souza, *Illiberal Education: The Politics of Race and Sex on Campus* (New York: The Free Press, 1991), pp. 50–1.

sense of grievance may be provoked by other nonmeritocratic forms of selection, they pale in comparison to the deep sense of ethnic insult and ethnic grievance that racial-preference policies provoke.

Even if America is spared the fate of those Third World countries where preference policies have produced violence and ethnic riot, they are surely a major vehicle promoting what Arthur Schlesinger, Jr., correctly called *The Disuniting of America*.[203] And if the evolutionary thinkers are correct, the fact that the beneficiaries of racial preferences are phenotypically and genotypically widely divergent from the nonbeneficiaries makes the breakdown in comity particularly severe. If it is true that there is an imprinting process that dictates that the less other people look like the people we've been raised with the more difficult it is to have feelings of empathy and solidarity with them, then our current policies of racial preferences will have even more serious long-term consequences for our continued unity as a people than even the critics of those policies contend.

MAKING WHITES HATE BLACKS: SNIDERMAN AND PIAZZA'S "MERE MENTION" EXPERIMENT

One of the best indicators of the potential of preferentialist policies to increase racial discord in America was provided by political scientists Paul Sniderman and Thomas Piazza in a clever experiment they did a number of years ago using a simple technique of survey research.[204] Sniderman and Piazza were initially struck by "the intensity of many people's feelings about affirmative action," which in the case of whites, they discovered, was overwhelmingly hostile. To see if these nega-

---

203. Arthur Schlesinger, Jr., *The Disuniting of America*.
204. Paul Sniderman and Thomas Piazza, *The Scar of Race* (Cambridge, MA: Harvard University Press, 1993), pp. 102–9.

tive feelings might have some harmful effects on race relations or the way whites perceive blacks, they devised an ingenious way of tapping into white thought processes. In a representative national sample, respondents were given a list of character traits—both positive and negative—and asked to what extent they accurately characterized "blacks as a group." The respondents were also presented with a made-up story about the government in a neighboring state that, in order to increase the number of blacks in government jobs, accorded preferential hiring treatment to blacks who had scored lower than whites on merit-based employment exams. For half of the respondents the preferentialist hiring story was presented before asking the question about black character traits, while for the other half the hiring story was presented only after asking the character trait question. The hiring story was worded as follows:

> In a nearby state, an effort is being made to increase dramatically the number of blacks working in state government. This means that a large number of jobs will be reserved for blacks, even if their scores on merit exams are lower than those of whites who are turned down for the job. Do you favor or oppose this policy?

Sniderman and Piazza found that in just bringing up ("mere mentioning") the hiring preference story, white respondents were much more likely to rate blacks as "lazy" and "irresponsible." While only 26 percent of those presented with the preferentialist hiring story after they had already given their assessment of black character traits rated blacks as "irresponsible," 46 percent of those given the hiring story before their opinions about black character traits were asked rated blacks in this manner. And the results were similar for "lazy": the proportion of whites considering blacks lazy rises from 20 to 31 percent depending on whether the preferentialist hiring story was given after or before the character trait question.[205]

Sniderman and Piazza conclude that racial-preference policies are so hated by whites that they cause whites to dislike blacks (or dislike them more intensely) and have a thoroughly negative effect on American race relations. Their conclusions are consistent with what has been outlined here about the "clannish brain" imperative and the importance of establishing race-neutral fairness and reciprocity as a means of overcoming its potentially hateful and destructive possibilities. Here are Sniderman and Piazza in their own words:

> What we found was that merely asking whites to respond to the issue of affirmative action increased significantly the likelihood that they will perceive blacks as irresponsible and lazy. . . . Affirmative action, defined to mean preferential treatment . . . produces resentment and disaffection not because it assists blacks—substantial numbers of whites are prepared to support a range of policies to see blacks better off [e.g., spending more on job-training programs]—but because it is judged to be unfair. . . .
>
> Affirmative action did not create the problem of prejudice. But it can aggravate it. Indeed, in reviewing the results of the "mere mention" experiment and in particular in gauging the size of the effects, the point to underline is that any effect at all was observed. The whole of the experimental manipulation, after all, consisted in asking a question in an interview—only one question, in a standard form, in an interview made up of a hundred questions. No effort was

---

205. It would have been interesting to see what the effects would have been of doing a similar experiment on white and Asian perceptions of black intelligence with a story involving preferential admissions to elite colleges and universities. One suspects that a similar effect would have been shown as in the case of the jobs-preference story with whites and Asians being much more likely to rate blacks as lacking in intelligence after hearing a story about preferences in college admissions.

made to whip up feelings about affirmative action. Respondents were not shown the equivalent of a "Willie Horton" type advertisement. They were not even subjected to a lengthy discussion of racial quotas or preferential treatment to arouse latent feelings they might harbor. All that was done was to ask them a single question about affirmative action "in a nearby state." And that was sufficient to excite a statistically significant response, demonstrating that dislike of particular racial policies can provoke dislike of blacks, as well as the other way around. . . .

Politics shapes as well as reflects public opinion, as the politics of affirmative action painfully demonstrate: whites have come to think less of blacks, to be more likely to perceive them as irresponsible and lazy merely in consequence of the issue of affirmative action being brought up. With the battle to persuade whites that blacks should be treated the same as whites only partly won, the political agenda raced on, fashioning a set of policies demanding, as a matter of principle, that blacks should be treated better than whites— that a black should be admitted to a school or get a job in preference to a white even if the white has higher grades or superior work skills. The new race-conscious agenda has provoked broad outrage and resentment. Affirmative action is so intensely disliked that it has led some whites to dislike blacks—an ironic example of a policy meant to put the divide of race behind us in fact further widening it.[206]

CONCLUSION

As I have tried to explain in this chapter, the intense opposition to racial preferences by disfavored groups derives less from intrinsic or ineradicable racial hostility than from the breach

---

206. Ibid., pp. 103, 109, 177.

they represent in the norm of interethnic fairness and reciproc-ity—a norm that is the linchpin holding together nonauthori-tarian, multiethnic, multiracial societies like the United States. The River Pilots have never understood these forces and remain dangerously naïve. They are mostly caught up in 60s-era socio-logical paradigms, with white guilt much in evidence (especially in River I and II), and they have a barely concealed exculpatory agenda that tries to absolve the lower-achieving minorities of any co-responsibility for their current plight (this is especially true in River III). They display virtually no interest in the newer, expanding fields of evolutionary biology, evolutionary psychol-ogy, or evolutionary sociology and can hardly be said to have advanced the public conversation.

The River Pilots began their journey almost 15 years ago and told us then that their goal was to learn more about the twists and turns in the flow of black students as they moved from high school to college and beyond. Their goal was to describe "the shape of the river." Their more overriding objective, how-ever, was to defend the admissions policies the two senior River Pilots (Derek Bok and William Bowen) had previously cham-pioned as presidents of Harvard and Princeton. Much of their own research, however, shows just how questionable such poli-cies have been and the harm they have done in creating social distance and social discord between the favored and disfavored groups.

The lessons to be learned here are clear: Racial and eth-nic preferences have no place in contemporary America, and regardless of how benign the motives of their supporters, such policies have proven to be seductive impediments to the quest of those targeted for the preferences to achieve at high levels and to obtain the honor and respect of their nonfavored peers. They have provoked ethnic outrage and a deep sense of personal and collective grievance among members of the nonpreferred groups, and they are a bane to healthy and harmonious group relations on college campuses. Both wisdom and justice—now supported by a growing body of social science research—cry out for their repeal.

VI

STILL AMERICA'S
CONTINUING DILEMMA

In the introduction to the first chapter of this book I explained the sense of betrayal and outrage that so many of us felt when the color-blind principle of equal justice for all—the principle that had energized the earlier civil rights movement—was cast aside to make room for the post-60s era regime of race-based preferences and quotas. That dramatic transition, I explained, was driven largely by the urban riots of the late 1960s and by the overriding concern of important policy-planning elites with the plight of the inner-city black poor. The latter were seen as victims of grave social injustices that called out for immediate public redress.

Lost in the ensuing decades in the never-ending controversy over racial preferences were those whose plight had provided the initial impetus for special action and concern. While the first of the national "affirmative-action" initiatives—Richard Nixon's Philadelphia Plan for opening up jobs in the urban construction industry—did focus on the black inner-city poor, it proved to be the exception as recipients of racial preferences quickly came to be the better-off, not the truly needy, among the targeted ethno-racial groups. Those who once occupied the preeminent place in public policy concern—those "hobbled by chains," as Lyndon Johnson called them in his Howard University address, or the "truly disadvantaged," as William Julius Wilson later described them—fell off the national radar screen. And while there was considerable academic interest in "the black underclass" in the 1980s and early 1990s, especially in the wake of Charles Murray's controversial book indicting Great Society welfare programs for much of the underclass problem, this interest quickly faded, and today it has reached a low ebb.

Considerable changes have taken place since the early 90s in policies directed at the urban poor, the most salient of which involved the ending of unlimited welfare payments under the older AFDC program, and a get-tough policy of law enforcement that is at least partially responsible for making lower-class urban neighborhoods much safer places than they once were. But some things haven't changed. And, yes, the urban black underclass is still with us, and while there are surely great hopes and points of light on the horizon—Geoffrey Canada's Harlem Children's Zone deserves special mention in this context—the urban black poor who were the concern of Daniel Moynihan and Kenneth Clark in 1965 still suffer from many of the same problems they did back then (including educational failures, failure to form stable two-parent families, drug and alcohol addiction, and many more).

In the following chapter, which reworks an essay originally written in the early 1990s, I try to explain the historical and demographic circumstances that contributed to the explosive growth of a downwardly mobile inner-city black underclass in the period following the mechanization of Southern agriculture in the 1950s and 1960s. Part of the answer to the underclass enigma is explained by the valuable contributions of influential scholars such as William Julius Wilson, Charles Murray, and Christopher Jencks. But missing from each of their discussions is what an older social science literature called "the problem of second-generation maladaption and delinquency." I take up this latter issue at great length. Displaced rural peasants, set adrift in a bewildering new world, have difficulty adjusting to the challenges and rewards of an urban environment. But it is their children and grandchildren—the second and subsequent generations—who suffer the most, and without proper parental guidance and correction, often wind up in the ranks of the drop-outs, drug addicts, jailbirds, and delinquents. A better understanding of a problem, of course, doesn't solve it, but at least it should awaken us to the human tragedy involved. The "affirmative-action response," focused mainly on the black middle class, has diverted our gaze from the place it really belongs and done much to undermine interracial sympathy and goodwill. The sorry plight of a black underclass in our inner cities is the second major wound that will not heal and cries out for a renewed private and public policy response. [207]

Perhaps never in history has a more utterly unprepared folk wanted to go to the city.

—RICHARD WRIGHT

[Some Negro families] found their way to the North in a movement [sociologist E. Franklin Frazier] aptly describes as "into the city of destruction." Illiterate, undisciplined, afraid, and crushed by want, they were herded into slums. City life then, as now for migrant groups, has been ruinous for peasant people. The bewilderment of the complex city undermined the confidence of fathers and mothers, causing them to lose control of their children whose bewilderment was even more acute.

—MARTIN LUTHER KING, JR.

I guess I had an arrogant attitude toward the family. I saw them all as farmers.

—CLAUDE BROWN (FROM *MANCHILD IN THE PROMISED LAND*)

---

207. This chapter is derived from the essay "The Disintegration of the Black Lower Class Family," that appeared in *Political Science Reviewer*, 22 (1991): 44–100.

The full impact of Northern life upon Negro ambitions did not come until the second and third generations. Although some migrants became disillusioned with the North . . . apparently most experienced some relief from the more direct and humiliating forms of white domination. Although Negroes were at the bottom of the Northern economy, most of them enjoyed higher incomes and better living conditions than they had in the South. Since they measured their situation against their Southern past, they were fairly well satisfied. In contrast, their children and grandchildren with little or no experience in the South measure their situation against the standard of equality and the condition of Northern whites.

—LEONARD BROOM AND NORVAL GLENN

The period from 1961 to 1965, that is, the period spanning the entire Kennedy administration and the first two years of Lyndon Johnson's presidency, was in many ways a period of great hope in America with regard to the resolution of what at the time was called "the Negro problem." A generation of liberal reformers who had grown up on Gunnar Myrdal's *An American Dilemma,* and who had witnessed first hand the murderously destructive effect that racial hatred and theories of racial superiority had recently visited on European civilization, was determined to eradicate the system of racial subordination and segregation that had successfully kept the black man "in his place" since the end of the nineteenth century. The can-do optimism of the New Frontier and early Great Society periods found expression in the widespread belief that the vast bulk of the black population in America would be able to advance socioeconomically and integrate into middle-class life once all artificial barriers to advancement had been removed. Black progress, it was hoped, would be sped along not only by the elimination of discrimination but also by aggressive antipoverty programs that would provide free education, job training, health care, business loans, and decent housing to all poor Americans.

With the aid of the federal government, strong leadership at the presidential level, and the general goodwill of the American people, the black population of America, it was said at this time, would be able to advance into mainstream society much the way the Germans, Italians, Jews, Poles, Hungarians, Chinese, Japanese, and other immigrant groups had done previously. This optimism was buoyed by the unprecedented legislative successes of the period, which, in the form of the 1964 Civil Rights Act and the 1965 Voting Rights Act, together with President Kennedy's Executive Order 10925 and President Johnson's Executive Order 11246 (both of which banned discrimination from firms doing business with the federal government), constituted the most comprehensive legal attack on racial discrimination and segregation since the era of Reconstruction. The optimism of the period is well reflected in the title of an article by Irving Kristol that appeared in the September 11, 1966, issue of the *New York Times Magazine*, "The Negro Today Is Like the Immigrant Yesterday."

Not everyone at this time, of course, was optimistic. The journalist Charles Silberman, for instance, had written a series of influential articles for *Fortune* magazine in the early 1960s, which were later expanded into his best-selling book, *Crisis in Black and White*,[208] which questioned the ability of Southern black migrants to the northern cities to assimilate unaided into a middle-class white society. Black leaders in general were also not as sanguine as many of the early Great Society enthusiasts. The National Urban League Director Whitney M. Young, Jr., for instance, spoke for many black leaders when he stated in his impassioned manifesto *To Be Equal* that nothing short of an all-out Marshall Plan for America's black poor would enable the

---

208. Charles Silberman, *Crisis in Black and White* (New York: Random House, 1964).

Negro to attain full equality and full participation in the rewards of American citizenship.[209] The optimists, however, were clearly dominant among the white liberal elite of the country throughout 1964 and 1965, especially after the landslide victory of Lyndon Johnson and his liberal running mate Hubert Humphrey in November 1964 over the laissez-faire-oriented Barry Goldwater seemed to establish a strong national consensus behind liberal-activist civil rights policies. White liberals at this time generally believed that a great turning point in American history had occurred as a result of the successes of the nonviolent black protest movement—a movement that had progressively gained in strength since the days of the Montgomery bus boycott of the mid-1950s—and it is probably safe to say that most white Americans at this time, regardless of their political or ideological persuasion, thought the future for blacks in America looked very promising.

It was during this period that Daniel Patrick Moynihan, a little-known assistant secretary in the Department of Labor, began to have grave misgivings about certain disturbing trends that were taking place at the time in the inner-city black ghettos of the larger metropolitan areas. Within weeks after Johnson's landslide victory, Moynihan had come to the conclusion that the great battles against segregation and discrimination were now largely won, and that a new emphasis would be required on the part of public policy to help reverse the trend toward black family dissolution, which he saw occurring in central Harlem and other black urban ghettos throughout America. The result of Moynihan's studies and reflections in late 1964 and early 1965 was a 78-page internal DOL memorandum, first completed in March of 1965, bearing the title *The Negro Family: The Case for National Action*.[210] It is no exaggeration to say

209. Whitney M. Young, Jr., *To Be Equal* (New York: McGraw Hill, 1964).
210. The Moynihan Report itself (MR), together with an extensive monograph describing the controversy it provoked, is photographically reproduced in Lee

that this modest report, which combined insights culled from the disciplines of economics, history, sociology, and psychology and represented a distillation of more than 40 years of scholarly research on America's greatest domestic "dilemma," proved to be one of the most prescient pieces of social science analysis ever written. In it Moynihan sought to strike a tone of urgency in order to convince policy planners in the executive branch in Washington that the situation in the inner-city ghettos had been deteriorating rapidly since the Second World War and that it had now reached a crisis stage and would continue to decline unless the federal government committed itself to a national policy that sought to stabilize the disintegrating black family structure.

"The United States is approaching a new crisis in race relations," the report began. Although the old style of segregation and discrimination was doomed, great new challenges now posed themselves, the report continued, if Negroes were to compete successfully with other ethnic groups for the desired benefits of American society. "Three centuries of sometimes unimaginable mistreatment have taken their toll on the Negro people," Moynihan explained, and the result was that without special efforts on the part of government many Negroes would not be able to compete on equal terms with the members of other racial and ethnic groups in America:

> The harsh fact is that as a group, at the present time, in
> terms of ability to win out in the competitions of American
> life, [Negroes] are not equal to most of those groups with
> which they will be competing. Individually, Negro Americans
> reach the highest peaks of achievement. But collectively, in
> the spectrum of American ethnic and religious groups, where

Rainwater and William Yancey, *The Moynihan Report and the Politics of Controversy* (Cambridge, MA: MIT Press, 1967).

some get plenty and some get none, where some send eighty percent of their children to college and others pull them out of school at the 8th grade, Negroes are among the weakest. (Moynihan Report, Introduction)

Moynihan then went on to explain how the situation was actually getting worse in the urban ghettos and that in terms of social mobility the Negro population was polarizing into a middle-class group that was becoming increasingly successful and a disorganized lower class that was becoming ever more dysfunctional and pathological:

> The most difficult fact for white Americans to understand is that . . . the circumstances of the Negro American commu-nity in recent years has probably been getting worse, not bet-ter. . . . The gap between the Negro and most other groups in American society is widening. The fundamental problem, in which this is most clearly the case, is that of family struc-ture. The evidence—not final, but powerfully persuasive—is that the Negro family in the urban ghettos is crumbling. A middle-class group has managed to save itself, but for vast numbers of the unskilled, poorly educated city working class the fabric of conventional social relations has all but disin-tegrated. There are indications that the situation may have been arrested in the past few years, but the general post-war trend is unmistakable. (MR, Introduction)

The report went on to establish its case through an array of charts and statistics which highlighted the high incidence of black divorce and spousal abandonment; the high rates of black illegitimacy, welfare dependency, unemployment, delin-quency, crime, and narcotics addiction; as well as the low scores of black students on standardized tests and other measures of academic performance. The report also offered an elaborate historical explanation for how this "tangle of pathologies" had come about, with the emphasis on the various ways that slavery and the brutal Southern system of caste subordination had undermined the traditional male role of breadwinner and dominant force in the family. The lower-class black family, Moynihan said, had a matriarchal structure that was not only out of line with the patriarchal structure dominant in the rest of the society, but was dysfunctional in terms of providing the young with the means for acquiring discipline, respect for authority, and the products of socialization needed for success in a competitive environment. In one of the more memorable passages of the report Moynihan wrote:

> Segregation and the submissiveness it exacts is surely more destructive to the male than to the female personality. Keeping the Negro "in his place" can be translated as keeping the Negro male in his place; the female was not a threat to anyone. Unquestionably, these events worked against the emergence of a strong father figure. The very essence of the male animal, from the bantam rooster to the four-star general, is to strut. (MR, p. 16)

In addition to the legacy of slavery and segregation, Moynihan also saw the black male's dominant role in the family being undermined by the often bewildering transition from the rural Southern farm to the large Northern city, and by the lack of well-paying jobs for black men, especially during downturns in the business cycle. On this latter topic he offered a trenchant quotation from Whitney Young's *To Be Equal*:

> The effect on family functioning and role performance of this historical experience [of economic deprivation] is what you might predict. Both as a husband and as a father the Negro male is made to feel inadequate, not because he is

unlovable or unaffectionate, lacks intelligence or even a gray flannel suit. But in a society that measures a man by the size of his pay check, he doesn't stand very tall in a comparison with his white counterpart. To this situation he may react with withdrawl, bitterness toward society, aggression both within the family and racial group, self-hatred, or crime. (MR, p. 34)

Another quotation from the sociologist Robin M. Williams, Jr., reporting on a study conducted among the black population of Elmira, New York, described the alarming incidence of fragmentation in black families compared with the families of other ethnic groups:

Only 57 percent of Negro adults reported themselves as married [with] spouse present, as compared with 78 percent of native white American gentiles, 91 percent of Italian-Americans, and 96 percent of Jewish informants. Of the 93 unmarried Negro youths interviewed, 22 percent did not have their mother living in the home with them, and 42 percent reported that their father was not living in their home. One third of the youths did not know their father's present occupation, and two thirds of a sample of 150 Negro adults did not know what the occupation of their father's father had been. Forty percent of the youths said that they had brothers and sisters living in other communities. (MR, p. 34)

Moynihan did not in his report offer specific policy proposals, in part, it would seem, because he did not want to distract from the report's main purpose, which was to draw official attention to the seriousness of the problems in the inner-city ghettos and to focus on the stability of the black family as the central means of addressing those problems. Moynihan left no doubt, however, that to deal with the deteriorating situation, a national effort would be required beyond anything previously contemplated by public officials. Toward the end of the report he wrote:

> Three centuries of injustice have brought about deep-seated structural distortions in the life of the Negro American. At this point, the present tangle of pathology is capable of perpetuating itself without assistance from the white world. The cycle can be broken only if these distortions are set right.
>
> In a word, a national effort towards the problems of Negro Americans must be directed towards the question of family structure. (MR, p. 47)

RESPONSE TO THE MOYNIHAN REPORT

The Moynihan Report was intended as a confidential internal Labor Department memorandum, but in the late summer of 1965 a decision was made at the White House to release it to the general public. While some prominent liberals greeted the report with considerable enthusiasm, the more general response among left-leaning intellectuals, both black and white alike, was one of impassioned outrage and vituperation, which, even with the advantage of hindsight, is difficult to comprehend. Moynihan was frequently attacked, usually in bitter or sarcastic terms, for placing the blame for the dissolution of the inner-city black family on the black population itself rather than on the racist practices of the larger white society, and it was not infrequently suggested or hinted that Moynihan himself was a racist. Despite the fact that the charges were complete fabrications, with no foundation whatever in reality—the Moynihan Report had placed the blame for the disintegration of the lower-class urban black family on a combination of economic, sociological, and historical forces, with white oppression being seen as dominant among the latter—the view that the report perversely "blamed the victim" came to dominate liberal intellectual discussion of the matter especially after a particularly virulent review appeared in *The Nation* magazine (November 22, 1965) by psychologist William Ryan. (It was Ryan who popularized the phrase "blaming the victim" in a subsequent book by that title).

Why the contents of the report were so distorted is difficult to say. In part the distortions seem to have resulted from the intrinsically sensitive nature of the material itself, since the candid discussions of illegitimacy, male joblessness, and poor academic performance among blacks addressed issues about which powerful antiblack stereotypes existed, which some might see only confirmed by the report's findings. A more important factor, however, seems to have been the coincidence that the report was released during the violent riot in the Watts section of Los Angeles. The riot produced a major change among important black intellectuals and civil rights leaders, many of whom came to feel that in their preoccupation with dismantling the Jim Crow system and guaranteeing voting rights in the Deep South they had ignored the deteriorating plight of the black poor in the inner-city northern and western ghettos. Moynihan's characterization of much of ghetto behavior as "pathological"—a term he had borrowed from Dr. Kenneth Clark, whose book *Dark Ghetto*,[211] published in the same year as the Moynihan Report, had conclusions about inner-city blacks that harmonized well with Moynihan's own analysis—produced a new defensiveness among many black leaders regarding the inner-city black poor that would subsequently preclude any candid assessment of the disordered lives that so many ghetto residents led. A new black pride move-

---

211. Kenneth Clark, *Dark Ghetto* (New York: Harper and Row, 1965).

WOUNDS THAT WILL NOT HEAL **395**

ment was also beginning to gain momentum at this time, and Moynihan's report, in its honest though unflattering depiction of the illegitimacy, delinquency, and black-on-black crime in the inner-city ghetto, could only appear to many to undermine the basis of this pride and to provide ammunition for anti-black racists. Years later Moynihan would explain the hostile reception his report received:

> Hours after the [1965] Voting Rights Act was signed, the riot broke out in Watts. . . . In the midst of the crisis, the White House made public my report. Suddenly the subject of family structure came to be associated with this painful new circumstance, which is to say, riotous and self-destructive behavior on the part of a group previously (and accurately) depicted as singularly victimized. With the onset of rioting, black spokesmen were in a defensive position in America, no matter how much whites were blamed for having made it possible or inevitable. These spokesmen made it impossible to face up to what was really happening in the ghettos. . . . Black leaders took every such effort at discussion as a white, racist attempt at self-exculpation, and evasion of responsibility for the black condition. . . .
>
> It is now about a decade since my policy paper and its analysis. As forecasting goes, it would seem to have held up. There has been a pronounced "up-and-down" experience among urban blacks. That is to say, the measures of social well-being then employed have moved in the two contrary directions I forecast [i.e., some ascend into the middle class while others descend into the underclass]. This has been accompanied by a psychological reaction which I did not foresee, and for which I may in part be to blame. Allow equivocation here. I did not know I would prove to be so correct. Had I known, I might have said nothing, realizing

that the subject would become unbearable, and rational discussion close to impossible.[212]

One of the results of the controversy over the Moynihan Report was that serious research into the problems of family disorganization in the inner-city ghetto was effectively terminated. While a few studies that had been underway at the time the controversy broke were eventually completed and published (the most important of these were Elliot Liebow's *Tally's Corner*,[213] David Schultz's *Coming Up Black*,[214] Ulf Hannerz's *Soulside*,[215] and Lee Rainwater's *Behind Ghetto Walls*),[216] for the most part white social scientists avoided research into the problems of black families out of fear of provoking the sorts of reactions that the Moynihan Report had encountered. From the late 60s onward the only type of research into lower-class black families that was generally acceptable in mainline liberal intellectual circles was research focusing on the strengths and positive qualities of these families. While some of the works produced under these circumstances managed to highlight important adaptive features of the female-headed black household, at the same time they tended just as often to romanticize ghetto family life and to downplay the degree of suffering, disorganization, and violence that afflicted so many ghetto families.

The most influential works of this latter type were Carol Stack's *All Our Kin*,[217] Andrew Billingsly's *Black Families in White America*,[218] and Joyce Ladner's *Tomorrow's Tomor-*

---

212. Daniel Patrick Moynihan, "The Schism in Black America," *The Public Interest*, spring 1972, pp. 7, 15.

213. Elliot Liebow, *Tally's Corner* (Boston: Little Brown and Company, 1967).

214. David Schultz, *Coming Up Black* (Englewood Cliffs, NJ: Prentice Hall, 1969).

215. Ulf Hannerz, *Soulside* (New York: Columbia University Press, 1969).

216. Lee Rainwater, *Behind Ghetto Walls* (Chicago: Alding, 1970).

217. Carol Stack, *All Our Kin* (New York: Harper and Row, 1974).

218. Andrew Billingsly, *Black Families in White America* (Englewood Cliffs, NJ: Prentice Hall, 1968).

row.[219] In these works the authors rejected the characterization of the mother-only black family of the inner city as broken or disorganized and claimed instead that the matriarchal black family form was a creative adaptation to poverty and discrimination that in many ways was a superior kind of organization to the two-parent white middle-class family. Lower-class black families, it was said, had a highly developed communal kinship network that engendered a spirit of mutual cooperation and mutual aid in stark contrast to the destructive individualism and competitiveness that white bourgeois families were said to produce. To judge the ghetto family by white standards was seen as a form of cultural myopia if not cultural imperialism. The black family, Andrew Billingsly contended, was "an absorbing, adaptive, and amazingly resilient mechanism for the socialization of its children and the civilization of its society." (BFWA, p. 33)

FROM CRISIS TO CATASTROPHE

The intellectual fallout from the Moynihan Report controversy persisted more than 15 years. During this time scholars as well as journalists scrupulously avoided drawing attention to aspects of inner-city ghetto life that might prove stigmatizing or stereotyping to the black population that lived there. By the early 1980s, however, the intellectual climate began to change very rapidly, and by the latter part of the decade the black urban underclass had become a major focus of public concern, both in scholarly and intellectual circles and in the popular press. Part of the reason for this shift in focus seems to have been the emergence of a new conservative mood in the electorate following the two victories of Ronald Reagan and the rise of a self-confident conservative intelligentsia that was much less concerned about the sensitivities of liberal black leaders than their white

219. Joyce Ladner, *Tomorrow's Tomorrow* (Garden City, NY: Doubleday, 1971).

liberal counterparts were. Another reason for the shift seems to have been the popularization of the works of a number of black feminist writers, who often painted a picture of the violence in many lower-class black households and the irresponsibility of many lower-class black males that was more candid—and more shocking—than anything white liberal scholars would ever have done. Alice Walker's *The Color Purple*,[220] which was made into a hit movie, and Gloria Naylor's *The Women of Brewster Place*,[221] which provided the basis of a nationally broadcast TV drama, were among the more influential of these feminist works.

Clearly, however, what lifted the taboo on candid assessments of black ghetto life were the deteriorating conditions found in the ghetto itself. When Daniel Patrick Moynihan wrote his report, the conditions of black families living in inner-city ghettos had reached crisis proportions, with the dimensions of the problem perhaps best indicated by the 43 percent out-of-wedlock birth rate that Moynihan reported for Central Harlem. By 1980 the stable two-parent black family in the inner-city ghettos had all but disappeared: A 1979 survey of births in Harlem Hospital found that almost 80 percent were out of wedlock, and a similar pattern was found in the inner cities of most other large metropolitan areas. The statistics that gradually accumulated from the late 60s onward tell a tale of family disorganization, personal suffering, and a climate of violence in poor black neighborhoods that is difficult for outsiders to imagine.

To give just a sampling of those statistics: By the mid-1980s a majority of black children were living in single-parent families, and of these almost 60 percent were living below the official government poverty level. Moreover, whereas most whites who are poor remain poor only for a relatively short period of time,

---

220. Alice Walker, *The Color Purple* (New York: Harcourt Brace Jovanovich, 1982).
221. Gloria Naylor, *The Women of Brewster Place* (New York: Viking Press, 1982).

the average poor black child according to an important 1983 study was found to be in the midst of a poverty spell that would last two whole decades. Black women who give birth to children out of wedlock are rarely able to marry, and those who do manage to find mates will face a high incidence of divorce and separation. According to one widely quoted estimate by Larry Bumpass, if the rates of divorce, separation, and out-of-wedlock births that were registered in the 1980s remain unchanged, 86 percent of black children would spend at least part of their childhood in a single-parent family. Among black children living in the worst areas of the inner-city ghetto the figure would probably be close to 100 percent. What this means, of course, is that black children in the inner city not only grow up without a working father present in the home but also live in a neighborhood where most other children grow up under similar circumstances and the influence of the stable two-parent family is all but unknown.

Criminal justice statistics revealed an equally depressing picture. According to one widely publicized estimate, by the mid-1980s a quarter of all black males between the ages of 20 and 29 were either in jail, out on bail, on probation, on parole, or awaiting sentencing by the courts. Estimates indicating that there were more young black males under supervision of the criminal justice system than in college received widespread media attention. According to a study by the National Bureau of Economic Research, one quarter of all the income reported by inner-city black youth in the immediate post-civil rights era was from crime. In the years following the ghetto riots of the 1960s, virtually all black families became the victims of one or another type of serious crime in the inner cities, and violent crime in particular produced a mood of fear and suspicion that pervaded all of black ghetto life. Blacks nationally were six to seven times as likely as whites to be murder victims, with homicide being the leading cause of death for young black males. According to one estimate by an MIT researcher and his associates, if the high murder rates of the immediate post-60s era persisted, the chances of an inner-city black male being murdered if he were to spend his entire life in the ghetto were many times greater than the chances of an American soldier being killed during World War II.

The situation was most frightful in government-subsidized urban housing projects. To give one example: In Chicago's Cabrini Green housing complex during the winter of 1981, 10 people were killed and 35 wounded by gunfire in just one particularly violent nine-week period. Over the same period, more than 50 illegal firearms were confiscated in the project, as residents were subjected to an onslaught of violence led by four major teenage gangs. The streets and housing projects of many inner-city neighborhoods became virtual war zones in the years following the late-60s riots, with daily life resembling more that in a Third World failed state than in a modern democratic nation, as rival teenage gangs fought over turf and drug dealers shot and killed not only one another but also innocent bystanders. Along with the drug dealers and gang members, ghetto residents had to contend with neighborhoods that were often overrun by pimps, prostitutes, winos, muggers, and a wide assortment of deranged and pathetic street people who made safe and wholesome community life in black neighborhoods all but impossible. By the late 1970s and early 1980s, even the most casual observer of the ghetto scene sensed that in some fundamental way civilization had broken down.

ENTER CHARLES MURRAY

What caused the ghetto implosion in the years immediately following the reforms of the civil rights era? By the mid-1980s this question became ever more pressing, and the most controversial and widely discussed answer came in the form of a sensitive and cogently argued book by social scientist Charles

Murray, *Losing Ground: American Social Policy 1950–1980.*[222] Unfortunately, Murray's book immediately got caught up in the ideological wars of the middle Reagan years, and as is often the case in such circumstances, both supporters and opponents of Murray often failed to appreciate the subtlety and complexity of the arguments that Murray's book presented. Murray, a former member of the Peace Corps who had spent his undergraduate years at Harvard College and received his Ph.D. from MIT, wrote *Losing Ground* as a disillusioned New Frontiersman whose work in the late 1970s as a professional evaluator of federal antipoverty programs convinced him that many of the dramatic policy changes of the mid- and late 1960s in regard to America's poorest citizens had seriously backfired and greatly exacerbated the conditions they were intended to alleviate. The idea of unintended consequences is certainly nothing new to social scientists, but what made Murray's book so valuable was its ability to combine a quantitative approach to analyzing the problems of the black poor with a psychological sophistication and keen understanding of the motivations and thought processes of lower-class people, that is rarely to be found among quantitatively-oriented social scientists, especially those from middle- and upper-middle-class backgrounds. What made Murray's book so unique was its ability to combine extensive data analysis with insights into the world of poor people that one generally encounters only in the work of cultural anthropologists.

Like all observers of the black ghetto, Murray asks in *Losing Ground* how it could have come about in the late 1960s that so many young blacks seemed to give up on getting ahead in the world at the very moment when other blacks were demonstrating that it was now possible to do so. "If in the early 1960s," Murray wrote in an early article anticipating much of the more

---

222. Charles Murray, *Losing Ground* (New York: Basic Books, 1984).

detailed analysis of *Losing Ground,* "one had foreseen the coming decade of sweeping civil rights legislation, an upsurge in black identity and pride, and a booming economy in which blacks had more opportunities than ever before, one would not have predicted massive family breakup as a result. The revolutionary change in black family composition went *against* the grain of many contemporaneous forces."[223] In *Losing Ground* Murray shows that from the turn of the century until the early 1960s, young black males participated in the labor force at rates roughly equal to, or even higher than, those of their white counterparts. But by the early 1970s a gap began to open up between the labor-force participation rates of the two populations as many young black males seemed to be giving up on the idea of steady work. At the same time that young black males were dropping out of the labor force, Murray shows, young black females in ever-increasing numbers were having babies out of wedlock, with the fathers of their children showing ever less inclination either to marry them or to provide long-term support.

Murray rejects the view explaining the increase in black male unemployment and black out-of-wedlock births primarily as a result of the decreased demand for unskilled labor in an increasingly high-tech-oriented economy. Unskilled older black males in the late 60s did not encounter the same sorts of problems finding and keeping a low-skilled job as young black males, Murray points out, and the rise in irregular employment among the latter group, together with the rise in both out-of-wedlock births and welfare dependency among young black females, was too precipitous, occurring over too short a period of time, Murray argues, to be explained by long-term structural economic forces. The major source of the weakening of inner-city black

---

223 Charles Murray, "The Two Wars against Poverty: Economic Growth and the Great Society," *The Public Interest,* Fall 1982, p. 15.

families, Murray says, is to be sought in counterproductive public policies instituted during the "generous revolution" of the Great Society period. Although most of the reviewers of *Losing Ground* paid heed only to what Murray had to say about changes in welfare policy, *Losing Ground* criticizes not only Great Society welfare policies but also policies in education, crime control, and what Murray calls the allocation of "status rewards." The policy changes in each of these four areas, Murray argues, while instituted for the noblest of reasons, had the effect of radically altering the status and incentive structures of the world in which poor black people lived and did so in such a way that made it rational for the poor of any race to act in the short run in a manner that was detrimental to their long-term interests. Murray writes in this regard:

> It is not necessary to invoke the *Zeitgeist* of the 1960s, or changes in the work ethic, or racial differences, or the complexities of post-industrial economies, in order to explain increasing unemployment among the young, increased dropout from the labor force, or higher rates of illegitimacy and welfare dependency. All were results that could have been predicted (indeed, in some instances were predicted) from the changes that social policy made in the rewards and penalties, carrots and sticks, that govern human behavior. All were rational responses to changes in the rules of the game of surviving and getting ahead. (LG, pp. 154–5)
>
> The most compelling explanation for the marked shift in the fortunes of the poor is that they continued to respond, as they always had, to the world as they found it, but that we— meaning the not-poor and undisadvantaged—had changed the rules of their world. Not of our world, just of theirs. The first effect of the new rules was to make it profitable for the poor to behave in the short term in ways that were destructive in the long term. . . . We tried to provide more for the

poor and produced more poor instead. We tried to remove
the barriers to escape from poverty, and inadvertently built a
trap. (LG, p. 9)

In the area of welfare policy, Murray singles out no less
than eight important changes that occurred between 1965 and
1970, all of which, he contends, tended to undermine the lower-
class male provider role and make it rational for poor women
to have children out of wedlock and rely on the welfare system for their support. These changes included the following:
a) more generous public assistance payments to single mothers with dependent children under the Federal Aid to Families
with Dependent Children program (AFDC); b) a vast expansion
in the federal Food Stamp program; c) the introduction of the
Medicaid program, which provided free medical benefits for the
poor; d) increases in public-housing assistance; e) changes in
HEW guidelines that eliminated intrusive at-home welfare eligibility checks; f) the 1968 Supreme Court decision in *King v.
Smith*, which struck down the man-in-the-house restriction that
tried to limit AFDC payments to single women not living with
a male companion; g) the 1969 Supreme Court ruling overturn-
ing local residency requirements for welfare eligibility; and h)
the Congressional thirty-and-a-third rule, which allowed welfare recipients to supplement their welfare-benefit package with
their own part-time earnings (the first $30 could be kept in its
entirety, after which $1 could be kept out of every $3 earned).

These changes, Murray contends, together with a much
more tolerant and supportive attitude on the part of the white
cultural elite toward welfare recipiency itself (even among the
young and able-bodied), radically transformed the benefit and
incentive structures in which the lower-class poor operated.
These changes, Murray argues, had the effect of making the
welfare system a more attractive option for many poor women
than reliance on the low wages of a young unskilled male worker

who had little immediate chance of securing a job that paid a middle-class wage.

It was these multifarious changes in the welfare system, according to Murray, that were largely responsible for the fact that the AFDC caseload, which had increased a mere 7 percent during the entire decade of the 1950s and 24 percent during the period 1960–1965, increased an astounding 125 percent during the period 1965–1970 (the rise leveled off after this time, with the caseload increasing 29 percent between 1970 and 1975 and only 3 percent between 1975 and 1980). These changes also contributed, according to Murray, to the tremendous increase in black out-of-wedlock births and to the dramatic decline in two-parent households.

To illustrate the disincentives to marriage and stable two-parent family life that such changes produced, Murray offered the reader a thought experiment involving a hypothetical unmarried couple, Harold and Phyllis, who had just graduated from high school and were expecting a child. The couple, who had no intention of going to college, had to decide in the experiment whether they would marry and live off the earnings of Harold's minimum-wage job, or not get married and try to live, either in whole or in part, off of the benefits of the welfare system. Murray tries to show, using the level of welfare benefits available in Pennsylvania (an industrial state that Murray says is typical of the states in which the majority of welfare recipients live), that in 1960 it would not have been a rational choice, at least not from a purely economic standpoint, for Phyllis to have remained unmarried and to have tried to live off public assistance rather than marrying Harold and living off his minimum-wage job. If she had gone on welfare in 1960, moreover, not only would she have done worse in purely economic terms than she would have done had she married Harold, but she would not have been able to have Harold around as a live-in companion without jeopardizing what meager welfare benefits she might receive.

By 1970, however, changes in welfare policy, Murray tries to show, had produced a very different set of options. With the expansion in the Food Stamp program, more generous AFDC payments, the additional Medicaid and various housing subsidies, as well as the possibility of supplementing government payments with part-time work, someone in Phyllis's position, Murray contends, would have been better off in several ways by not marrying Harold and allowing herself and her child to be supported by the welfare system.

Since Murray assumes in the thought experiment that Harold and Phyllis desire to remain together, at least for the immediate future, the best option for both to have taken in 1970, Murray says, was for the couple to live together unmarried, supporting themselves with Phyllis's welfare check as well as with any additional income that Harold may have been able to bring in from outside work. The welfare system provided a more generous (and more secure) package of benefits in 1970 than a woman could get from a minimum-wage-earning husband, Murray shows, and after the invalidation of the man-in-the-house rule in 1968, a live-in lover who worked, unlike a live-in husband who worked, was no threat to a mother's receipt of AFDC benefits. Under such circumstances, says Murray, it would be a better option for Phyllis to live with Harold unmarried since she would get companionship and certain other benefits of marriage without its financial disabilities and risks. Moving in with Phyllis without marrying her would also be the best option from Harold's perspective, according to Murray, since he would be able to supplement her welfare check with his own earnings but would not be under any obligation to stay with her or the child should he get tired of either.

An important theme in Murray's treatment of welfare policy in *Losing Ground* is the difficulty—if not the impossibility—of designing a system that provides an incentive for people to get off welfare without at the same time giving other people who are not on welfare a greater incentive to come onboard. To illustrate his point, Murray offers another thought experiment of a hypothetical government program designed to reduce cigarette smoking by offering bonuses to people who quit. No matter how such a program is designed, Murray says, it is likely to have either no net beneficial results or very possibly negative results, since there will always be some people who engage in the unwanted behavior in order to become eligible for the rewards of the program, and the harmful effects thus brought about will probably offset any good that is done. In the context of late-60s welfare policy, Murray points to the thirty-and-a-third rule as an illustration of his point. This rule was intended to give people already on welfare an incentive to seek outside work so that they might eventually become independent, but it had the unintended effect of making welfare a much more attractive option for those who were not yet receiving it. Murray acknowledges that some people have absolutely no choice in terms of being in the negative condition for which government programs offer some type of relief. "Paraplegics receiving Medicaid cannot easily be seen as 'rewarded' for becoming paraplegics by the existence of free medical care." (LG, p. 213) But while some people are involuntarily in an undesirable situation, in most instances, Murray contends, voluntary action will play some role, whether large or small, in shaping the situations people are in, and in such cases changes in incentive structures will often have a considerable impact on what people do.

Besides changes in welfare policy, the quality of life in the inner-city ghetto was adversely affected in the late 1960s, Murray says, by a number of important changes in the areas of educational policy and crime control. In educational policy, *Losing Ground* focuses on the increasing reluctance on the part of school administrators during this period to suspend disruptive students or to use the sanctions schools had traditionally used to maintain classroom discipline and to provide for a healthy learning environment. Since they often lack the backing of strong achievement pressure from their homes and peer groups, inner-city students, says Murray, need the support of dedicated teachers who will demand from them regular attendance, punctuality, and the regular completion of homework assignments. In the past, to be effective, these demands had to be backed up by the threat of various sanctions, including in-school disciplinary measures, failure to promote a student to the next grade, or outright suspension or expulsion. But in the late 1960s, says Murray, these sanctions came into increasing disuse as more and more schools adopted a policy of demanding very little from their students academically, of tolerating greater degrees of disruption, and of automatically promoting students to the grade level commensurate with their chronological age. The effect of these new policies in the classroom, Murray believes, was disastrous, as teachers became demoralized over their inability to get students to work, and many of the ablest and most ambitious students left the public-school system in order to enroll in private or parochial schools that offered a better environment in which to learn.

Murray attributes the changes in educational policies during this period to a number of factors. One, he suggests, was simply ideological. The idea began to gain ground during the late 60s, Murray says, that inner-city black culture had a dignity and uniqueness of its own and that it was wrong to try to force inner-city youth to master standard English and the sorts of skills typically taught in white middle-class suburban schools. Radical critics of the period often viewed the imposition of the traditional American school curriculum on lower-class blacks as a form of cultural imperialism that helped to undermine black self-esteem. The idea also gained ground at this time that schools in general were too authoritarian and should be more flexible in allowing students to develop according to their own inclinations and desires. Murray mentions in this context an influential book in the late 60s by Jonathan Kozol, *Death at an Early Age*, which called for a much more loosely structured curriculum in the public schools.

Besides ideological factors, educational policies during this period, Murray says, were influenced by important changes in judicial interpretations of constitutional rights. The Supreme Court decision in *Gault v. Arizona* (1967), Murray explains, was the key factor here, since its effect was to extend new due process rights to students facing disciplinary suspension, something that had not existed previously. While this new concern with student rights prevented certain abuses of disciplinary authority, Murray concedes, one of the effects of this new emphasis on student rights, he says, was to make it much more difficult for teachers and school officials to deal with disruptive students. "Teachers and administrators became vulnerable to lawsuits or professional set-backs for using the discretion that had been taken for granted in 1960," Murray writes. "The rebellious students could make life considerably more miserable for the teacher than the teacher could for the students—through their disruptive behavior in class, through physical threats, or even through official channels, complaining to the administration that the teacher was unreasonable, harsh, or otherwise failing to observe their rights." (LG, p. 173) The result of all this, says Murray, is that by 1970 very little learning went on in inner-city schools.

Changes in crime-control policy also adversely affected the quality of life in the inner-city ghetto, according to Murray's analysis. Applying a rational-choice model to crime, Murray says that whatever other factors may be involved, the easier it is to get away with a crime without being caught or, if caught, without being punished by a jail term, the more likely it will be that people will engage in criminal behavior. *Losing Ground* applies the insight of this simple proposition to the observed declines in apprehension and incarceration rates and to the new protection of the rights of the criminally accused that came about during the 1960s and 1970s. Regarding the latter development, Murray acknowledges that increased concern over the rights of the criminally accused had the positive effect of extending equal justice to the poor, but it also had the negative effect, he says, of making it less risky for criminally inclined people to indulge their criminal propensities, with the result that ghetto neighborhoods became much less safe.

One of the most important changes in criminal-justice practices that occurred during this period, Murray demonstrates, was a dramatic decrease in the punishment of juvenile offenders. Juvenile delinquents in the 1960s were increasingly put on probation rather than sent to reform school or jail, Murray shows in *Losing Ground*, and even if juvenile offenders did do time in a penal institution, it became the practice of the time to seal their official records so that having a police record in the 1960s and 1970s was a much less serious matter for a juvenile than it had been a decade before. Murray uses juvenile-incarceration statistics from Cook County, Illinois (which includes Chicago), to illustrate his general point of how easy it was for young people to get away with crime following the 60s-era changes: Despite soaring increases in juvenile crimes over the previous ten years, by the mid-70s Cook County juvenile offenders had on average to be arrested an incredible 13.6 times before they were first committed to a reform school. Murray also offers national statistics showing a steep drop in the odds of being apprehended for a burglary or robbery during this period, and when this declining apprehension rate is seen in conjunction with the declining risk of being sent to prison after one has been apprehended and convicted, the true decline in the deterrent value of the criminal justice system in the immediate post-60s era is made abundantly clear.

The three factors of a) changes in welfare policy, b) changes in educational policy, and c) changes in criminal-justice practices, Murray says, not only acted individually to bring about the destruction of the inner-city ghetto, but also displayed a certain interactive or synergistic effect in which each factor served to reinforce the destructive potentials of the other. Summarizing a good deal of the argument of *Losing Ground*, Murray writes:

> My proposition is that the environment in which a young person grew up changed in several mutually consistent and interacting ways during the 1960s. The changes in welfare *and* changes in the risks attached to crime *and* changes in the educational environment reinforced each other. . . .
>
> None of the individual links is nearly as important as the aggregate change between the world in which a poor youngster grew up in the 1950s and the one in which he or she grew up in the 1970s. All the changes in the incentives pointed in the same direction. It was easier to get along without a job. It was easier for a man to have a baby without being responsible for it, for a woman to have a baby without having a husband. It was easier to get away with crime. . . . Because it was easier to get away with crime, it was easier to support a drug habit. Because it was easier to get along without a job, it was easier to ignore education. Because it was easier to get along without a job, it was easier to walk away from a job, and thereby accumulate a record as an unreliable employee. (LG, pp. 165, 167)

STATUS REWARDS

In many ways what Murray has to say about the shift in "status rewards" that occurred during the Great Society period is the most valuable part of *Losing Ground*, although it is a part that critics and reviewers generally ignored. While the very term "status rewards" is intended to link the ideas subsumed under this label to an economic type of rational choice or utility-maximization

model in actuality Murray treats under this theory certain fundamental changes in social attitudes and cultural values occurring
during the late 1960s that are not normally thought of within
the context of an economic or utility-maximizing theory. One of
the problems with *Losing Ground*, in fact, is that it is a much
richer book, with a much more subtle and complex understanding of what occurred in poor inner-city neighborhoods in the late
1960s, than is sometimes suggested by Murray's own description
of what he is trying to do in the book. Murray's theory is much
less parsimonious than he would lead us to believe, although,
given the complexity of the problem, lack of simplicity or parsi-
mony is hardly a fault. The changes in cultural values with which
Murray deals occurred, he says, primarily among the intellectual
and cultural elite rather than among blue-collar workers or more
traditionally minded white-collar conservatives, although their
effect was still enormous, he believes, as they helped to destroy
the basis of independence and personal dignity among the working poor.

Before the late 1960s, Murray says in this context, it was
almost universally accepted in American culture that healthy
people of working age should get jobs to support themselves,
should care and provide for their families, and in general should
carry their own weight and get by in the world without being
a burden on others. Financial independence and self-reliance
were considered very important American values, and, barring great depressions, the death of a working spouse, or other
extreme circumstances beyond a person's control, able-bodied
people were not supposed to seek outside aid from government
or from public charities. Irresponsible or improvident people
who neglected their families or had children out of wedlock and
as a result became burdens on the public treasury were severely
condemned by the mores of the general community, Murray
points out, with the sharpest condemnation often coming from
the ranks of the working poor and working lower-middle class,

who often prided themselves on their own hard work and independence and on the fact that they had never taken a penny of public assistance. Before the late 60s, Murray explains, "a person who was chronically unable to hold onto a job, who neglected children and spouse, was a bum and a no-good, consigned to the lowest circle of status." (LG, p. 180)

Until the Great Society reform period, Murray says, the thinking among America's intellectual and cultural elite tended to agree with this general American view of the value of self-reliance and the universal requirement that all healthy adults should seek economic self-sufficiency within the context of a stable family structure. Elite opinion also agreed with the important and commonly drawn distinction between the deserving and the undeserving poor. In the late 60s, however, there was a radical shift in opinion on these matters, Murray explains, as a new wisdom emerged among the cultural and policymaking elite, one that sought to obliterate the distinction between the worthy and unworthy poor by suggesting that all poverty was the result of outside forces largely beyond the control of individual poor people. The poor, says Murray, were "homogenized," as poverty was no longer associated with indolence or vice but with faults inherent in the American social and economic order itself. If a person was poor, if a young woman gave birth to a child out of wedlock whom neither she nor her family could support, if a man neglected his spouse or family the system was to blame, said this new wisdom. Under this new elite wisdom, Murray says, welfare dependency, even by the young and healthy, was radically destigmatized, and public financial assistance for all who were below a certain level of income came to be seen as a fundamental human right or entitlement that the taxpayers were obligated to honor. The older middle-class and working-class norms of self-reliance and self-sufficiency, Murray says, were attacked most vehemently by the welfare rights advocates of the late 60s, who were vocal in their insistence that all who were on the dole should consider their assistance a right, not a charity. Within elite circles, adherence to the older distinction between the deserving and the undeserving poor came to be looked on as callous and reactionary.

The effect of treating all welfare-dependent people as victims, however, is not without consequences for the lives of poor people, Murray says. Telling people that they are not responsible for their behavior because "the system is to blame" and encouraging people to believe that they have little control over their lives engenders, says Murray, a sense of fatalism and helplessness, as well as a tendency toward irresponsible excuse-making, that seriously undermines upward mobility and the capacity of the poor to cope with their day-to-day problems. Writing more as a pragmatist than a moralist, Murray says that "by taking away responsibility—by saying, 'Because the system is to blame, it's not your fault . . . ' society also takes away the credit that is an essential part of the reward structure that has fostered social and economic mobility in the U.S." (LG, p. 186) If society can't blame individuals for bad behavior, Murray argues, it can't very credibly praise them for good behavior either. It's like the teacher who gives all his students As. The grading system under such circumstances ceases to serve as an incentive system, and many of the students will not work very hard as a result. In an article in *Political Science Quarterly* defending the argument of *Losing Ground*, Murray says that the message that the elite was transmitting to struggling poor people in the late 1960s was this: "When things go wrong, there are ready excuses; when things go well, it is luck."[224]

Among poor people, blacks in the late 60s, says Murray, were singled out for special consideration by elite opinion makers, and the effect was even more devastating than the opinion

---

224. Charles Murray, "Have the Poor Been Losing Ground?" *Political Science Quarterly*, Fall 1985, p. 11.

shift with regard to the poor in general. The new white elite attitude was driven, Murray says, by white guilt and white confusion over the mid-60s ghetto riots, which produced, he believes, the general conviction among the white intelligentsia and the white policymaking elite that blacks were owed a special debt for their past victimization, and that because of this victimization blacks should not be held accountable for what they do. This attitude Murray characterizes as a form of condescension that undermines not only the kind of status reward system that leads to upward mobility but also the capacity of a people to achieve a sense of personal dignity and self-respect. Murray writes in this regard:

> It was a very small step from [the premise that it was not the fault of the poor that they are poor] to the conclusion that it is not the fault of the poor that they fail to pull themselves up when we offer them a helping hand. White moral confusion about the course of the civil rights movement in general and the riots in particular created powerful reasons to look for excuses. It was the system's fault. It was history's fault. (LG, p. 39)
>
> Whites began to tolerate and make excuses for behavior among blacks that whites would disdain in themselves or their children. (LG, p. 223)
>
> The white elite could not at one time cope with two reactions. They could not simultaneously feel compelled to make restitution for past wrongs to blacks and blame blacks for not taking advantage of their new opportunities. The system *had* to be blamed, and any deficiencies demonstrated by blacks had to be overlooked or covered up—by whites. A central theme of this book has been that the consequences were disastrous for poor people of all races, but for poor blacks especially, and most emphatically for poor blacks in all-black communities—precisely that population that was object of the most unremitting sympathy. (LG, p. 223)

The moral agonizing among whites was strikingly
white-centered. *Whites* had created the problem, it was up to
whites to fix it, and there was very little in the dialogue that
treated blacks as responsible actors. Until July 1964 most
whites (and most blacks) thought in terms of equal access
to opportunity. Blacks who failed to take advantage were
in the same boat with whites who failed to take advantage.
By 1967 this was not an intellectually acceptable way to
conceive of the issue. Blacks were exempted. Once more, in
a new and curious fashion, whites had put up the "Whites
Only" sign. (LG, p. 33)

Besides discouraging upward mobility, personal dignity, and
economic independence, the shift in elite opinion during the late
1960s, Murray contends, had the effect of dramatically worsen-
ing the quality of life and sense of personal well-being among
the working poor. These were the people who often did not live
much above the living standard of the welfare poor but who had
always enjoyed a much higher status in society because of the
appreciation others felt for the sacrifices they made in remaining
self-sufficient and not burdening anyone outside their extended
family. But one of the inevitable consequences of "homogeniz-
ing" the poor, Murray says, was to withdraw status and praise
from those who struggled to remain off welfare. And as status
and praise were withdrawn from the working poor, the quality of life for such people, Murray says, dramatically declined.
Their situation, moreover, was made even less tolerable by the
tendency of the white elite to treat certain menial jobs as too
demeaning to ask welfare recipients to perform. "When social
policy reinforces the ethic that certain jobs are too demeaning
to ask people to do," says Murray, "it was those who preferred
such jobs to welfare whose basis for self-respect was stripped
from them." (LG, p. 201)

Although Murray does not mention the fact, it was the very working poor that he describes who protested in anger in the late 60s against the withdrawl of public recognition of their efforts with the popular bumper sticker of the period: I FIGHT POVERTY—I WORK! When the working poor receive no greater status in society than the welfare-dependent poor, there will be little incentive for poor people to work. Indeed, Murray suggests that when working provides no greater benefits in terms of standard of living or social status than remaining idle, the person who works at a menial job may come to see himself as a chump or a fool.

ASSESSMENT OF MURRAY

Losing Ground was widely reviewed in scholarly journals and popular magazines and created a sensation in Washington, where Murray's final thought experiment, suggesting that America's poor would be much better off if most of the reforms of the Great Society were scrapped, was enthusiastically embraced by many conservative supporters of the Reagan administration. Not since the publication of Friedrich Hayek's *The Road to Serfdom* in the mid-1940s had a public-policy-oriented book provoked such strong reactions from both the left and the right, although, as previously suggested, this situation did not always contribute to a conscientious understanding of Murray's often complex arguments. The attack on *Losing Ground* from the left side of the political spectrum was often fierce, with Robert Greenstein's widely read article in *The New Republic*, "Losing Faith in *Losing Ground*," setting the tone for a good deal of the subsequent discussion and debate.[225]

---

225. Robert Greenstein, "Losing Faith in *Losing Ground*," *The New Republic*, Mar. 25, 1985, pp. 12–17.

Critics of Murray tended to present two sets of data, which, they contended, called into question *Losing Ground's* basic contention that increases in welfare expenditures between 1965 and 1970 caused an increase in the rate of out-of-wedlock births, female-headed households, welfare dependency, and marital instability among the black poor. If the level of welfare generosity had all these bad effects, critics argued, then one would expect to find much higher incidence of such conditions in states with generous benefits as compared with states that offered more meager welfare aid. The gap between generous and stingy states was enormous, critics pointed out—in 1975, for instance, Mississippi offered a family of four only $60 monthly in AFDC funds, while California offered more than $400—and even when one added in the value of food stamps, which were more uniform across states, the gap between states was still very wide. Moreover, if generous welfare expenditures were responsible for the rising illegitimacy and other negative trends of the late 1960s that Murray listed, one would expect these trends to have reversed themselves in the 1970s, Murray's critics argued, since the real value of AFDC benefits declined sharply over this decade as states failed to adjust their benefit levels to the inflationary rise in the cost of living. Yet neither of these two conditions obtained. The most exhaustive series of regression analyses of the available data on births to unmarried women across states could find no evidence that AFDC levels affected the decisions of young unmarried women to bear children, and the authors of the study concluded that AFDC, though having considerable influence on the ability of a young unmarried women to form her own separate household, had no effect on rates of illegitimacy.[226] Given the fact that the rate of illegitimacy and of female-headed households continued to rise

---

226. David Ellwood and Mary Jo Bane, "The Impact of AFDC on Family Structure," in Ronald Ehrenbert, ed., *Research in Labor Economics*, vol. 7 (Greenwich, CT: JAI Press, 1985).

throughout the 1970s despite declining real values of AFDC and food stamps, the thesis of *Losing Ground*, critics concluded, must be wrong.

Murray responded to such criticisms on at least three occasions,[227] and the counter-arguments he offered were strong. Many of the critics of *Losing Ground*, Murray rightly charged, attacked a stick-figure caricature of what is actually argued in the book. To begin with, most critics zeroed in almost exclusively on what was said about Great Society welfare policies, ignoring all that was said in *Losing Ground* about changes in criminal-justice procedures, changes in educational policy, the destigma-tization of welfare recipiency, the changes in status rewards for the working poor, and the mutual-enhancing effect of all the late 60s changes taken together. Moreover, even with regard to welfare policy, his critics, Murray charged, acted as if he had treated AFDC alone, or AFDC augmented by food stamps, as responsible for the disintegration of the black lower-class family, completely ignoring all that is said in *Losing Ground* about the other six or seven significant changes in welfare policy enacted during this period.

To his critics' charge that rates of out-of-wedlock births and female-headed households should show some positive correla-tion with the vast differences across states in AFDC levels if the basic thesis of *Losing Ground* is correct, Murray countered that the true differences in the total welfare benefit package across states were really quite small once one added in the value not only of AFDC but also of food stamps, Medicaid, housing allowances, and other available benefits. In addition, Murray contended, when one views the total benefit packages in terms of local costs of living as well as local standards of living, they

---

227. Along with the two previously cited articles by Murray ("Have the Poor Been Losing Ground?" and "The Two Wars against Poverty: Economic Growth and the Great Society"), Murray has responded to arguments of critics in "How to Lie with Statistics," *National Review*, Feb. 28, 1986, pp. 39–41.

begin to look very similar. Murray offered in this context figures from a General Accounting Office study which indicated that during the late 1970s the total monthly benefit package available to a poor unmarried mother in the low-benefit area of New Orleans was $654 if housing benefits were obtained ($511 if they were not); in the very high-benefit area of San Francisco, by contrast, with housing benefits the value of the total package was $867 ($734 without housing benefits). Even as they stand, these figures do not indicate a tremendous difference across states, Murray said, and what difference there is, he showed, almost disappears when the standard of living in each area is taken into account. The total welfare benefit package in San Francisco (with housing benefits) represented 65.6 percent of the median household income for that area, while the comparable figure for New Orleans was 66.4 percent (without housing benefits the figures were 55.5 percent and 51.9 percent, respectively).

Murray disavowed the view, however, that poor women micro-manage their fertility rates in response to incremental changes in welfare benefit packages. Poor women, he says, often want to have a baby to have someone to love, and if they do not have much of a prospect for an interesting job or for marrying a high-wage-earning husband, they may well decide to have a child out of wedlock *if* the welfare system will allow them to live at what they consider a minimally decent level. What level this is will vary from person to person, but the individual threshold points, Murray says, will tend to cluster together so that there will be a great jump in the number of people availing themselves of the welfare option once the total welfare benefit package reaches the minimum level of acceptability at which many young married women are clustered.

In addition to the size of the total benefit package itself, the attractiveness of the welfare option, Murray claimed, was enhanced by such changes in welfare regulations as the thirty-

and-a-third rule and the elimination of the man-in-the-house restriction. These changes were not repealed by the inflation of the 1970s, and the welfare benefit package, according to Murray, still remained high enough throughout this period to enable poor young women to have a child out of wedlock, which they otherwise would have avoided, either through sexual abstinence, contraception, marriage, adoption, or abortion. In addition, as a result of the total ensemble of policy changes in the late 60s, Murray says, the destructive trends that developed in the inner cities began to take on a life of their own, as community standards broke down, two-parent stable families disappeared, crime and the benefits to be gained from crime increased, and schools ceased to be a means of upward mobility. Under such circumstances, according to Murray, it is not surprising that a decline in the real value of AFDC and food stamp benefits in the late 1970s and beyond failed to produce a return to lower levels of illegitimacy and single-parent families. Once older patterns of discipline and responsibility break down, Murray says, it is not easy to bring them back, even when incentive structures become less antagonistic to them.[228]

If one surveys the whole range of policy changes during the late 1960s that Murray focuses on in *Losing Ground*, the contention seems unassailable that their overall effect on the stability of the inner-city black family was negative. To use Murray's own instrument of the thought experiment, one might ask what would have happened in the late 1960s if most of the Great Society reforms Murray excoriates had never been enacted and the country instead had moved in the opposite direction in terms of both public policy and public philosophy. What would have happened, for instance, if Senator Goldwater had

---

228. This would also be a good explanation for why out-of-wedlock birth rates among the black poor did not drop precipitously after the 1995 welfare reforms, when welfare benefits were time-limited and the older AFDC program replaced by the Temporary Assistance to Needy Families (TANF) program.

won a landslide victory in 1964 comparable to that of Lyndon Johnson, and with the backing of a Congress overwhelmingly Republican and viscerally anti-welfare, his administration had successfully proceeded a) to pressure states to reduce their AFDC benefits to two thirds of their 1950 levels; b) to eliminate the food stamp program for all but the elderly and disabled; c) to defeat all attempts to pass a Medicaid bill; d) to require six or more unannounced at-home eligibility checks per year for AFDC recipients; e) to make any attempt to supplement welfare benefits through unreported outside earnings a serious felony crime and provide for rigorous enforcement of such a law; f) to appoint judges to the Supreme Court who would find nothing constitutionally suspect about a rigorously enforced man-in-the-house restriction; g) to limit welfare recipiency to a maximum of five years over a lifetime; and h) to require all able-bodied welfare recipients not caring for very young children to work at least 20 hours per week in workfare-type programs, if need be, at government-sponsored WPA-type jobs?

While Murray's critics claimed that "welfare" had no effect on the rise in the rate of out-of-wedlock births and female-headed households among urban blacks, it is simply inconceivable to anyone with the least bit of common sense or intuitive understanding of human nature that such a scenario as that described would have been consistent with the actual experienced rise in out-of-wedlock birth rates among inner-city black residents from the 40 percent range that Moynihan reported for central Harlem in the early 1960s to the 80+ percent range of the early 1980s. Whatever other factors may have been at work in bringing about such developments, the fact remains that a kinder and more generous welfare system enabled significant numbers of people to engage in types of behavior regarding childbirth and employment that they would not have engaged in otherwise (either because they themselves had thought of the negative consequences or because one of more of their parents or guardians had).

The paradoxes and unanticipated consequences of a generous system of poor relief is one that has been recognized by perceptive observers for two centuries or more, and is certainly not the discovery of Charles Murray. In the nineteenth century, it was well recognized by philanthropists and Social Darwinists alike. One of the clearest statements on the subject is to be found in Alexis de Tocqueville's "Memoir on Pauperism," which he published in 1835 based on his own observations of the effects of the English poor laws. "Almost two and a half centuries have passed since the principle of legal charity was fully embraced by our neighbors [in England]," Tocqueville wrote,

> and one may now judge the fatal consequences which flowed from the adoption of this principle. . . . Man, like all socially organized beings, has a natural passion for idleness. There are, however, two incentives to work: the need to live and the desire to improve the conditions of life. Experience has proven that the majority of men can be sufficiently motivated to work only by the first of these. The second is only effective with a small minority. Well, a charitable institution indiscriminately open to all those in need, or a law which gives all the poor a right to public aid whatever the origin of their poverty, weakens or destroys the first stimulant and leaves only the second intact. . . . I recognize not only the utility but the necessity of public charity applied to inevitable evils such as the helplessness of infancy, the decrepitude of old age, sickness, insanity. I even admit its temporary usefulness in times of public calamities which God sometimes allows to slip from his hand. . . . But I am deeply convinced that any permanent, regular, administrative system whose aim will be to provide for the needs of the poor, will breed

more miseries than it can cure, will deprave the population that it wants to help and comfort.[229]

One can view much of Murray's argument in *Losing Ground* as a sustained attempt to demonstrate the truth of Tocqueville's insight, although it must be kept in mind that the number of people who become "trapped" by the welfare system represent only a small minority of the people who have actually used it. As a number of Murray's critics correctly pointed out, most users of welfare do not become permanently dependent, a fact the reader of *Losing Ground* could easily lose sight of.

Even more unassailable than *Losing Ground's* analysis of the disincentives created by Great Society welfare policies is its analysis of the effects of destigmatizing welfare recipiency among the able-bodied and diminishing the social status of the working poor. Many blacks of an earlier generation tell of the disgrace it was to be on welfare even during the Great Depression of the 1930s, when honest work was hard to come by even for the most eager and ambitious. The *Ebony* publisher John H. Johnson, for instance, relates his own family's experience of being on welfare in the city of Chicago between 1934 and 1936: "What I remember most about my days on welfare," Johnson recalls in his autobiography, "was the shame." "I used to sit on a stoop with a group of young men and watch the welfare trucks cruising the neighborhood. The trucks would drive up to my house, and someone would say, 'They're going to *your* house.' And I would say, 'That's not my house.' We knew the trucks were going to our houses; we were just too ashamed to admit it."[230]

229. Alexis de Tocqueville, *Tocqueville and Beaumont on Social Reform*, ed. Seymour Drescher (New York: Harper and Row, 1968), pp. 14, 24–5.
230. John H. Johnson, *Succeeding Against the Odds* (New York: Warner Books, 1989), pp. 74–5.

However one may criticize the social norms that encouraged young men such as Johnson to feel as they did, such norms certainly had the positive effect of encouraging all self-respecting people to get off welfare and become economically self-sufficient as soon as they possibly could. The effects of destigmatizing welfare recipiency are perceptively analyzed by another black writer, Bernard Gifford, a former deputy chancellor of the New York City Board of Education:

> In many ways the kids today are victims of liberal victories. One of the battles we fought in the 1960s was to take the stigma away from people who are poor and place it on society; to emphasize the structural barriers to poverty. That needed to be done. We were successful in saying to society: there are real structural impediments. . . . The problem was that we shifted the focus of attention from local institutions—family, church, neighborhood organization—to government. We undermined those institutions and made it possible for people to accept welfare.
>
> My mother was always ashamed to be on welfare. My brother was ashamed. I was ashamed. And though we grew up in a neighborhood where it was prevalent, we never accepted it. And what is different now is that I see lots of people accepting dependency. No one ought to be ashamed to be poor. Yet I'm convinced that the shame we felt being on welfare made us get away and escape repeating this cycle.[231]

What Gifford has to say here, of course, fully confirms Murray's analysis in *Losing Ground*.

---

231. Bernard Gifford, quoted in Ken Auletta, *The Underclass* (New York: Random House, 1982), p. 301.

BUT IT DIDN'T START WITH THE GREAT SOCIETY

Murray's analysis in *Losing Ground* certainly goes a long way toward explaining what happened in the black ghettos of America in the decades following the major policy changes of the late 1960s. No one who wants to understand the breakdown in black family life following the Great Society period can ignore the weight of what Murray has to say on these matters. Nevertheless, there are limitations to the *Losing Ground* approach that should be obvious to anyone who has ever read the Moynihan Report or any number of other accounts of inner-city black slum life during the pre-*Losing Ground* period of the late 1950s and early 1960s. The simple fact of the matter is that such trends in the inner-city black ghettos as family dissolution, out-of-wedlock births, low labor force participation, poor academic performance, and rising crime and delinquency were cause for alarm among knowledgeable observers years before any of the Great Society programs or liberal policy changes that Murray criticizes were ever instituted.

As early as 1961, for instance, Harvard educator James Bryan Conant responded with shock and horror at the situation he had observed in many inner-city black slums in the final years of the Eisenhower administration. In his widely read and influential book, *Slums and Suburbs*, Conant wrote:

> I am convinced we are allowing social dynamite to accumulate in our large cities. . . . In some slum neighborhoods I have no doubt that over a half of the boys between sixteen and twenty-one are out of school and out of work. Leaving aside human tragedies, I submit that a continuation of this situation is a menace to the social and political health of the large cities. . . .
>
> In some [Negro slums] there are very bad gangs with gang warfare among the boys. There are also vicious fights outside of school between Negro girls. The condition in

one such neighborhood was summed up to one of my staff by a principal of a junior high school who said even he was shocked by the answers to a questionnaire to the girls which asked what was their biggest problem. The majority replied to the effect that their biggest problem was getting from the street into their apartment without being molested in the hallway of the tenement. He went on to say that the area had a set of social customs of its own. The women, on the whole, work and earn fairly good wages, but the male Negro often earns less than the woman and would rather not work at all than to be in this situation. As a consequence, the streets are full of unemployed men who hang around and prey on the girls. The women are the centers of the family and as a rule are extremely loyal to the children. The men, on the other hand, are floaters, and many children have no idea who their father is. Similar reports from principals and teachers can be heard by the attentive and sympathetic visitor to the Negro slums of any one of several cities. . . . What is terrifying is that the number of male *youth* in this category is increasing almost daily.[232]

Such descriptions sound all too familiar. An equally depressing picture of inner-city black slum life during the immediate pre-Great Society period was offered by Charles Silberman in his book *Crisis in Black and White*:

In Northern industrial centers one out of every three Negro workers has suffered unemployment in the last several years. . . . In some Negro neighborhoods, the unemployment rate may run as high as 40 percent. To anyone walking through the Negro neighborhoods of any large city—and

232. James Bryant Conant, *Slums and Suburbs* (New York: McGraw-Hill, 1961), pp. 2, 19–20.

to the children who grow up in them—few sights are more
familiar than the groups of idle Negro men congregating at
street corners, or the lonely Negroes sitting on their front
stoops all day long, sipping wine from bottles discretely hidden in brown paper bags.[233]

Descriptions similar to those of Bryant and Silberman can be
found in the writings of many other observers (Claude Brown's
account of growing up in Harlem in the 1950s in his *Manchild
in the Promised Land*[234] and the description of the disorganized
black lower class in early 1940s-era Chicago in Horace Cayton
and St. Clair Drake's *Black Metropolis*[235] are two of the best), but
there is no need to belabor the point. Contrary to the impression one would get from *Losing Ground*, the problem of black
urban-family disintegration is one that first reached alarming
proportions during the Great Depression, and although the
situation improved considerably during the high-employment
years of the Second World War, it began a gradual deterioration
throughout the 1950s and early 1960s that would continue at
an accelerated pace after this period. Charles Murray makes a
very impressive case for the view that this process of deterioration intensified in the late 1960s and early 1970s in response
to major changes in public policies and elite attitudes. But he is
wrong in suggesting that it all started with the Great Society, or
that most problems that existed in poor black neighborhoods
prior to the Great Society would have worked themselves out
except for the changes of this period. ("It is genuinely an open
issue," Murray wrote in 1982, "whether we should be talking
about spending cuts, or whether we should be considering an

233. Silberman, *Crisis in Black and White*, p. 40.
234. Claude Brown, *Manchild in the Promised Land* (New York: New American
Library, 1965).
235. Horace Cayton and St. Claire Drake, *Black Metropolis* (New York: Harper and
Row, 1945).

overhaul of the entire welfare system as conceived in the Great Society. If the War on Poverty is constructed as having begun in 1950 instead of 1964, it may fairly be said that we were winning the war until Lyndon Johnson decided to wage it." (TWAP, p. 16)

Daniel Moynihan was certainly correct when he criticized *Losing Ground* on this score. "Murray's work is concerned primarily with the growth of an urban minority underclass," Moynihan remarked in his Godkin lectures as Harvard (later published as *Family and Nation*). "But that is precisely what I did predict in 1965, using data series that ended in 1964, before any of the events that he asserts have brought about these 'turns for the worse' . . . *Losing Ground* attributes developments that trouble the author to government actions that mostly began *after* these developments had commenced as clearly recognizable statistical trends."[236] Whatever one may say of Murray's work, it seems that more must be considered in understanding the catastrophe of the inner-city black ghettos in America than the bad public policies and bad elite opinions of the Great Society era of the 1960s.

WILLIAM JULIUS WILSON AND THE CHANGING STRUCTURE OF THE URBAN ECONOMY

If the factors Murray analyzed in *Losing Ground* only partially explained the deteriorating situation in the inner-city black slums, and if certain long-term trends were apparently involved that predate the reforms of the Great Society period, what other factors needed to be explored? After the publication of *Losing Ground,* by far the most important work to address this question was William Julius Wilson's *The Truly Disadvantaged.*[237]

---

236. Daniel Patrick Moynihan, *Family and Nation* (New York: Harcourt Brace Jovanovich, 1986), pp. 134–5.
237. William Julius Wilson, *The Truly Disadvantaged* (Chicago: University of Chicago Press, 1987).

Wilson, a University of Chicago-trained sociologist and past president of the American Sociological Association, viewed himself in this work as a reseacher trying to restore an older approach to the problem of black family dissolution and neighborhood decline, one that would place much of the blame for the deterioration of the ghetto on certain fundamental changes in the nature of the modern urban economy. Wilson spends a good deal of time addressing the arguments in *Losing Ground*, and while he doesn't dismiss Murray's work entirely, his review of the anti-Murray literature, together with his own studies of the urban poor in Chicago and elsewhere, convinced him that Murray greatly overemphasized the effect of Great Society policies in explaining the growth of an urban underclass and greatly underestimated or ignored what Wilson sees as the most important explanatory variable, namely, black male unemployment brought about by the decline in the number of low-skilled inner-city manufacturing jobs.

Although Wilson writes from the perspective of a left-oriented social democrat, he is highly critical of the behavior of many left and left-liberal-oriented writers, who, he charges, ignored for many years the deteriorating conditions in the inner-city ghettos and left the field open for conservative theorists like Murray to propound views that he considers of doubtful validity. In Wilson's own words:

> The liberal perspective on the ghetto underclass and inner-city social dislocations is less persuasive and influential in public discourse today, because many of those who represent the traditional liberal views on social issues have failed to address straightforwardly the rise of social pathologies in the ghetto. . . . Some liberals completely avoid any discussion of these problems, some eschew terms such as *underclass*, and others embrace selective evidence that denies the very existence of an underclass and behavior associated with

the underclass or rely on the convenient term racism to
account for the sharp rise in the rates of social dislocation
in the inner city. . . . The combined effect of these tendencies, is to render liberal arguments ineffective and to enhance
conservative arguments on the underclass, even though the
conservative thesis is plagued with serious problems of interpretation and analysis. (TD, pp. 12–13)

Like Murray, Wilson in *The Truly Disadvantaged* finds
theories that would try to explain underclass growth in terms
of ongoing racism and discrimination thoroughly unpersuasive.
The underclass increased the most in size, he points out, during
the decade of the 1970s, a period following the enactment of
the most comprehensive civil rights legislation in the nation's
history,and one that also saw the implementation of affirmative-
action policies designed to grant special preference to black job
applicants. Discrimination in the post-civil rights era, Wilson
says, has certainly been less than it was in the 1940s, yet the
black male employment picture then was much better than it
was in the 1970s and 1980s. Moreover, the racism and discrimination theory, Wilson points out, cannot explain the very considerable success of the black middle class during the very period
when the condition of the black lower class was deteriorating
most rapidly. Wilson also rejects theories of the underclass, such
as those proposed by Edward Banfield in *The Unheavenly City*,
which would stress differences in individual moral or behavioral factors or the existence of a "culture of poverty" as causal
agents. Poor inner-city black males, Wilson says, share values
and aspirations similar to those of mainstream society, although
their aspirations, he contends, are usually thwarted by circumstances beyond their control.

If Great Society policy changes, continuing racism, or a "culture of poverty" don't offer much of an explanation for the disintegration of the lower-class black family and the many other

pathologies of the inner-city ghetto, how is the situation to be explained? In answer to this question Wilson develops at length his thesis concerning the basic changes in the structure of American industry and the impact these changes have had in increasing the joblessness of young black males. Wilson's argument goes something like this: When the hordes of European immigrants poured into America in the early decades of the twentieth century, America was an industrializing nation with an expanding blue-collar job market that offered great employment opportunities for those with little skills and without even a command of the English language. A healthy body and an eagerness to work were all that were usually necessary to find employment in the great industrial centers of the Northeast and Midwest, and what involuntary unemployment did exist was usually brief in duration and tied to the ups and downs of the business cycle.

In the last several decades, however, American industry has undergone a major restructuring. This restructuring has been characterized by a dramatic decline in the number of manufacturing jobs in the older central cities, as steel, rubber, autos, and other traditional smokestack industries have declined in size due to foreign competition and the movement of manufacturing facilities abroad. Where increases in manufacturing jobs have occurred, they happen not in the central cities but in the suburbs, where lower taxes, less congestion, and improved road transportation have provided a more congenial environment than that available in the urban metropolis. For example, in the 25-year period between 1947 and 1972, the number of manufacturing jobs in the 33 largest metropolitan areas declined by 880,000 at the same time that manufacturing employment in the surrounding suburbs grew by 2.5 million. Over the same period, these cities lost 867,000 jobs in retail and wholesale trade while their suburbs added millions of jobs in these same categories.

As the central cities were losing many jobs in manufacturing, as well as in retail and wholesale trade, the black population of these same cities was burgeoning, due both to natural population growth and to the enormous influx of unskilled agricultural laborers from the rural South. Between 1950 and 1980, for instance, the black population of the 33 largest metropolitan areas increased by over five million. Since most young blacks living in the inner cities do not own automobiles and are not tied to the sorts of information networks that would enable them to exploit many of the opportunities for employment in the surrounding suburbs, the result of these simultaneous changes has been increasing black joblessness, particularly among black male youth.

The central cities have, it is true, gained jobs in many categories other than manufacturing and trade. But the job growth has been in such areas as information processing, financial services, business administration, and various high-tech fields, all of which have educational and training requirements that place them beyond the reach of most inner-city black residents. Inner-city black residents are thus mismatched for jobs both geographically and educationally, and the result is ever lower levels of participation in the regular urban labor force. Unlike the situation confronting the Southern and Eastern European immigrants who came to America before the First World War, blacks today living in America's largest cities confront an employment situation where there seems little room for those who do not possess a special skill or a minimum of two years of college education. Even a high school diploma doesn't go very far nowadays.

Such, in briefest outline, is the substance of Wilson's "deindustrialization" argument. Black male joblessness caused by basic changes in the nature of urban jobs and urban job requirements, he explains in his book, is the key to understanding the pathologies of the ghetto, particularly the rise in female-headed households and out-of-wedlock births. Since the possibilities of a steady job are so poor for so many unskilled black youth, many young black women, Wilson says, see very limited prospects for being able to marry a black male who will be capable of fulfilling the traditional male role of breadwinner and provider. Wilson constructs what he calls a "male marriageable pool index," which relates the rates of employed civilian men to women by race and age group, and he uses this index to show how the proportion of young black males in an economic position enabling them to support a family has steadily declined since the 1950s. The number of marriageable men is much lower among black men than among whites due to greater black male joblessness and much higher black rates of mortality and incarceration. Lacking the prospect of marrying a man with a stable job, young black women, Wilson says, turn to out-of-wedlock births as the only means of fulfilling their natural human desire to have children. Out-of-wedlock births and female-headed households, while not seen as an ideal situation, are nevertheless accepted within the inner-city black community because of the absence of a better alternative. Wilson quotes in this context from Kenneth Clark's *Dark Ghetto*:

> In the ghetto, the meaning of the illegitimate child is not ultimate disgrace. There is not the demand for abortion or for surrender of the child that one finds in more privileged communities. In the middle class, the disgrace of illegitimacy is tied to personal and family aspiration. In lower-class families, on the other hand, the girl loses only some of her already limited options by having an illegitimate child; she is not going to make a "better marriage" or improve her economic and social status either way. On the contrary, a child is a symbol of the fact that she is a woman, and she may gain from having something of her own. Nor is the boy

who fathers an illegitimate child going to lose, for where is
he going? The path to any higher status seems closed to him
in any case. (TD, pp. 73–4)

The destructive effect of male joblessness on family and
community life in the ghetto has been made worse, according
to Wilson, by the exodus of the more stable middle-class and
working-class elements from inner-city ghetto communities.
Throughout the 1940s and 1950s and even into the 1960s, he
explains, middle-class and working-class blacks often lived in
the same inner-city neighborhoods as the poor and the unemployed. Black professionals—doctors, lawyers, teachers, social
workers, etc.—not only had poor blacks as clients but also lived
very near those whom they served. Their children attended the
same schools, played on the same playgrounds, and sometimes
attended the same churches. It was this stable middle and working class, Wilson says, that provided most of the community
leadership in the ghettos and helped to establish strong community sanctions against aberrant behavior. Black inner-city communities in these earlier decades were often a source of positive
identification for the residents who lived there, Wilson explains,
and the more stable and hard-working elements tended to set
the standards for the community as a whole.

Ironically, it was partially as a result of certain civil rights
victories, according to Wilson's analysis, that ghetto communities were deprived of this critically important stable element.
As long as access to more desirable neighborhoods in the suburbs or in predominantly white sections of the cities was denied
to the more successful blacks, they were forced to remain in
the all-black central city ghettos. But with the invalidation of
racially restrictive covenants by the Supreme Court (the critical case was *Shelly v. Kraemer* in 1948) and the passage of fair
housing laws by many states and by the federal government in
the 1960s, many middle-class and working-class blacks began

to move out of the ghettos, leaving behind the worst-off elements. As a result of this exodus, ghetto communities became dominated by female-headed households, unemployed or only episodically employed young men, drug addicts, alcoholics, the mentally disturbed, and a large criminal population. Growing up in neighborhoods with few male breadwinners to serve as role models for the youth, the youth of the ghettos, Wilson says, were not able to develop the kinds of habits of regularity, punctuality, cooperativeness, etc., which would enable them to succeed at a mainstream job. "In neighborhoods in which most families do not have a steadily employed breadwinner," Wilson writes, "the norms and behavior patterns associated with steady work compete with those associated with casual or infrequent work. . . . The combination of unattractive jobs and lack of community norms to reinforce work increases the likelihood that individuals will turn to either underground illegal activity or idleness or both." (TD, p. 61)

The inner-city youth of the post-60s period, according to Wilson's analysis, differ from the inner-city youth of earlier generations, not because of changes in their basic attitudes or cultural values, but because of their greater social isolation. The most disadvantaged elements of the black lower class are now concentrated in neighborhoods where they have little access to people who are capable of providing the young with information about available jobs or initiating them into the norms and behavioral patterns required of a reliable worker. This social isolation and concentration effect only serves to exacerbate the problem of declining blue-collar jobs in the central city. And when the youth no longer aspire to mainstream jobs, Wilson says, they no longer have much of an incentive to prepare themselves in school to gain the basic literacy skills and other qualifications necessary to acquire such jobs. Teachers in inner-city schools where such youth predominate become demoralized and begin to lose interest in teaching. As a result, inner-city schools almost cease to be educational institutions, and drop-out rates often reach 50 percent or more.

Toward the end of *The Truly Disadvantaged* Wilson makes a series of policy proposals designed to enhance the life chances of the worst off among blacks in the inner cities, although he acknowledges that his proposals, intended to bring the American welfare state more into line with the more highly developed welfare states of Northern and Central Europe, lack current political feasibility. His proposals include a program of universal child care for working mothers; universal family assistance payments to all families with children; vastly expanded job training and education programs; and better enforcement of child-support judgments. Wilson stresses that to gain widespread acceptance, such programs must be universal in scope rather than race-specific, and like the policies of the New Deal—but unlike the policies of the Great Society—they should try to help the most seriously disadvantaged in ways the better off can positively relate to. Wilson is highly critical of affirmative-action policies in this regard, since they lack support among most white people, he says, and generally help only the better-off blacks, not "the truly disadvantaged." Wilson also supports a policy of national economic planning designed to promote, simultaneously, full employment, economic growth, and low inflation, although he offers no blueprint or theory as to how this is all to be achieved, and few people, it would seem, except the most naïve of the older-style Keynesians would find his recommendations on this score at all helpful.

ASSESSMENT OF WILSON

In focusing on the structural changes in the American economy, Wilson in *The Truly Disadvantaged* certainly adds to our understanding of the problem of the black ghetto. Whether one speaks of "automation," as analysts did in the 1950s and

1960s, or "deindustrialization," as they did in the 1970s and 1980s, there can hardly be any doubt that in the largest urban areas in America the number of high-paying factory jobs that require little skill has been diminishing for many decades. The sociologist John Kasarda, whose studies Wilson relied on heavily, has demonstrated this fact with abundant evidence. To give an example from Kasarda's data: Over just one short decade—between 1970 and 1980—the number of jobs in Boston requiring less than a high school education decreased by 58.7 percent, in Chicago by 41.8 percent, in Cleveland by 48.2 percent, in Detroit by 55.0 percent, in New York by 40.4 percent, and in Philadelphia by 47.2 percent. The number of jobs requiring only a high school diploma also dropped over this period in each of these same cities, though at a considerably lower rate.

By contrast, the number of jobs requiring some college study *increased* very substantially in each of the six cities (in Boston by 32.1 percent, in Chicago by 43.9 percent, in Cleveland by 53.5 percent, in Detroit by 48.4 percent, in New York by 61.0 percent, and in Philadelphia by 57.4 percent), as did the number of jobs requiring a four-year college degree or more (the increases for the six cities were 71.4 percent, 56.7 percent, 31.0 percent, 35.3 percent, 47.3 percent, and 57.4 percent, respectively). In all, between 1970 and 1980 the six cities lost a total of almost 1.45 million jobs requiring a high school education or less, while they gained a total of more than 995,000 jobs that require at least some college experience.[238] These figures indicate employment shifts of very considerable magnitude, and any theory of black family disintegration and underclass growth must certainly take them into consideration. With Wilson's basic contention there can be little argument: It is unquestionably more difficult today for an inner-city youth to find a good-paying job

---

238. John Kasarda, "Urban Industrial Transition and the Underclass," in William Julius Wilson, *The Ghetto Underclass: Social Science Perspectives, The Annals of the American Academy of Political and Social Science,* 501 (Jan. 1989): 26–47.

without a special skill or some college training than it was in the 1940s or in the decade preceding the Great Depression.

Wilson's argument about the exodus of stable middle-class elements from the ghetto and the resulting social isolation of the lower-class families that remained there is also important and draws attention to the often neglected element of neighborhoods in understanding the quality of life in the inner city. Youth from broken homes or single-parent families have a much easier time assimilating mainstream values and integrating into mainstream society—particularly into the world of regularized work—if they are fortunate enough to live in neighborhoods where most other families have working fathers present than they are in neighborhoods where most of their friends and schoolmates come from families similar to their own. This is a simple, common-sense observation, though one easy to overlook. Conversely, even an intact husband-wife family, with a working father present, that lives in an area where 80 or 90 percent of the children come from households led by unwed mothers will have great difficulty insulating its offspring—particularly its male offspring—from the destructive effects of local street gangs and the local teenage peer-group culture, no matter how conscientious the family may be in trying to raise its children according to general American norms. Unless it can construct a countervailing environment centered on a socially conservative church or a small network of stable relatives and friends, there is a very high probability that even children from intact families will be lost to the negative forces of the ghetto. Again, this is a common-sense observation that nevertheless is easy to overlook, and we have Wilson to thank for drawing our attention to these important facts.

Wilson's analysis, however, can be criticized on a number of grounds. One obvious criticism, made by Christopher Jencks in a long review of *The Truly Disadvantaged* for *The New Republic*, is Wilson's tendency to dismiss or ignore important moral and cultural changes since the late 1960s that have surely had a significant impact on the decay of stable family life in the black ghetto. Specifically, Wilson gives short shrift to the enormous changes in attitudes toward divorce, out-of-wedlock births, and the obligations of responsible parenthood among the supposedly stable middle class, both black and white, who are expected to provide the role models and set the norms for inner-city black communities. Wilson does acknowledge in one or two places that the sexual revolution among the middle class may have had some harmful effects in the ghetto, but he drops the matter almost as soon as he mentions it on the grounds that there is no way to measure the effect. Precise measurement in the area of cultural and attitudinal changes may not be attainable, but an inability to measure a phenomenon precisely is hardly a reason for ignoring it.

A decline in marriage, an increase in divorce and spouse abandonment, and an increase in out-of-wedlock births have been pervasive throughout American society since the mid-1960s, and they have been accompanied by, and in part have resulted from, radical changes in the older cultural values, which had prescribed lifelong marriage, sexual fidelity within marriage, and dedication to spouse and children as the only proper mode of family existence. The disintegrating forces that observers noted in the black ghetto in the late 50s and early 60s were surely reinforced by the decline in these once pervasive cultural norms, which were weakened by successive attacks, first from the *Playboy* philosophy of the late 50s and early 60s, then from the drug-and-drop-out culture of the later 60s, from the antifamily feminism of the late 60s and early 70s, and finally from the "me generation" hedonism and narcissism of the late 70s and beyond. The 25-year period from 1965 to 1990 might be described as one in which much of the middle class itself lost its moorings and progressively abandoned its attachment to traditional middle-class values. The sturdy bourgeois family man of the 1950s was to give way to the cocaine-snorting yuppies and buppies of a later date, who were hardly in a position to teach the lower classes about the sanctity of home and hearth even if they had lived in the same neighborhood.

In his review of Wilson's book, Jencks described these general cultural changes and their effects on lower-class family life, providing an important addition to Wilson's economic interpretation. What Jencks wrote in this regard is worth quoting at some length:

> My own calculations show that the marriage rate among black men with steady, well-paid jobs declined almost as much between 1960 and 1980 as the marriage rate among all black men. Marriage must, therefore, have been losing its charms for non-economic reasons as well.
>
> The stable two-parent family is losing ground throughout American society. The trend is the same in Beverly Hills as in Watts. . . . Single parenthood began its rapid spread during the 1960s, when elite attitudes toward sex, marriage, divorce, and parenthood were undergoing a dramatic change. This change was obvious in the mass media, in the law, and in the widely publicized activities of celebrities. In the space of a decade we moved from thinking that society ought to discourage extramarital sex, and especially out-of-wedlock births, to thinking that such efforts were an unwarranted infringement on personal liberty. . . .
>
> Americans have always believed that every couple had a God-given right to conceive children, but until recently we assumed that this right carried with it an obligation to marry, to live together, and to support these children. To enforce this obligation we exerted very strong social pressure on couples to marry if they conceived children, and to stay married thereafter. . . . Even when almost every "respectable" adult thought unwed parenthood, desertion, and

divorce immoral, it was hard to keep families together in poor communities. Now that the mass media, the schools, and even the churches have begun to treat single parenthood as a regrettable but inescapable part of modern life, we can hardly expect the respectable poor to carry on the struggle against illegitimacy and desertion with their old fervor. They still deplore such behavior, but they cannot make it morally taboo. Once the two parent norm loses its moral sanctity, the selfish considerations that always pulled poor parents apart often become overwhelming.

In making this "cultural" argument, I do not mean to deny the importance of the economic factors that concern Wilson. I only want to suggest that economic factors alone cannot explain the changes that began in the 1960s. It is the conjunction of economic vulnerability and cultural change that has proved disastrous.[239]

The remarks above are stated with Jencks's characteristic lucidity, and to anyone who lived through the trends described, such claims are hard to ignore. Huge cultural changes in marriage and family life that began in the mid-1960s almost certainly had a negative impact on black families and black neighborhoods, especially those in the poorer sections of America's major cities.

Another important cultural trend Wilson does not consider but that certainly had a negative impact on black ghetto youth, was the decline in the once-venerable American work ethic, which demanded of all able-bodied people not caring for children that they seek gainful employment, even if at a modest wage. Wilson does not consider supply-side factors in explaining the low labor force participation rates of black youth, but certainly during upswings in the business cycle the conclusion is inescapable that many young blacks fail to seek employment

---

239. Christopher Jencks, *The New Republic*, June 13, 1988, pp. 28–30.

not because of a lack of jobs but because the jobs that are actually offered are in the low-paying service sectors of the economy and are often seen as too demeaning or too unremunerative by African American youth to be worth the effort. Wilson had drawn attention to this fact in his earlier book, *The Declining Significance of Race*, but for reasons that are not clear, he ignored these problems entirely in *The Truly Disadvantaged* and does not in that work distinguish sufficiently between a situation in which there is a lack of jobs for the unskilled and a situation in which there is a lack of *high-paying* jobs. Certainly in the high-employment years of the late 1980s there was no lack of unskilled jobs in most of the Northern cities—indeed, many security guard agencies, janitorial services, fast-food chains, and other employers of unskilled workers at this time found themselves forced to raise their starting wages considerably above the official minimum wage in order to attract sufficient numbers of employees—and any conscientious youth at this time who was willing to work had little difficulty finding employment.

But inner-city African American youth, like American youth more generally, are often choosier than their parents and grandparents were in the sort of work they are willing to do (in one 1980 study of unemployed youth 16 to 21 years old, almost half listed an amount 50 percent or more above the minimum wage as the minimum they would accept before working), and the result of this greater choosiness is often a spotty employment record and generally poor work habits and work attitudes that make it difficult for young people to take advantage of a "good job" even if such should come their way. Wilson had treated these issues very candidly in his earlier book, although perhaps so as not to give ammunition to his conservative critics he fudged over these same issues in his later work and failed to consider the impact of important attitudinal changes in this area. Some of Wilson's statements in his earlier book are worth recalling, for like Jencks's comments, they supplement without negating the structural economic interpretation of *The Truly Disadvantaged*:

> Unlike the occupational success achieved by the more talented and educated blacks, those in the black underclass find themselves locked in the low-paying and dead-end jobs of the non-corporate industries. . . . Many of these jobs go unfilled, and employers often have to turn to cheap labor from Mexico and Puerto Rico. As Nathan Glazer has pointed out, "Expectations have changed, and fewer blacks and whites today will accept a life at menial labor with no hope for advancement, as their fathers and older brothers did and as European immigrants did."
>
> It is not surprising . . . that recent studies of unemployment in the urban core reveal that blacks do not experience any special employment barriers in the casual, low-paid, and menial jobs of the low-wage sector. In fact, many of these jobs remain unfilled despite the extremely high unemployment rate of blacks in the inner city. Employers constantly complain of the difficulty of attracting and keeping a stable work force and often comment that some blacks seem to be more willing to go on welfare than to accept available work. . . . It is no doubt true that in recent years, attitudes concerning low-status work have changed. Workers today are less wiling to accept the kinds of low-paying and menial jobs that their grandfathers or fathers readily accepted. . . . The underclass also knows that illegal activities, in many respects, provide a more lucrative alternative to low-wage employment. It was estimated in a recent study that roughly 20 percent of the adult residents in Harlem lived entirely on illegal income.[240]

---

240. William Julius Wilson, *The Declining Significance of Race: Blacks and Changing American Institutions* (Chicago: University of Chicago Press, 1978), pp. 16, 106–8.

BEYOND MURRAY, WILSON, AND JENCKS

The research of Murray and Wilson has unquestionably enhanced our understanding of the problems of the inner-city black poor, and although neither writer thinks very much of the work of the other, their analyses should be seen as complementary rather than contradictory. Combining their two perspectives, we get a picture of an inner-city environment in which high-paying blue-collar jobs have been steadily shrinking since the 1950s; better-off middle-class blacks have been moving out to the suburbs or at least away from the older inner-city black areas; numerous changes in government policy have made welfare a more attractive option for an unwed mother than was the case in the 1950s; welfare recipiency for the able-bodied and unwed motherhood have lost their social stigma; there are many fewer status rewards accruing to the working poor who carry their own weight and refuse to take government handouts than was the case previously; crime has gotten out of control due in part to lax law enforcement and a belief that the poor and disadvantaged are not responsible for their actions; and discipline in the inner-city schools has collapsed so that little learning takes place. To this picture we can add the insight of Jencks that the reduced commitment to marriage, children, and family life on the part of the cultural elite and a broad spectrum of the white middle class encouraged the general growth of individual selfishness, which, in combination with the other problems of the ghetto, helped create a social disaster.

What are we to make of this composite picture? Does it really explain the catastrophe of the inner-city black ghetto in the latter half of the twentieth century? Surely it is part of an explanation, but it fails to address itself to one of the obvious questions involved here, namely, why is it that American-born blacks, but not to the same extent the members of many other ethnic groups, have been so susceptible to the destructive social, economic, and cultural forces in the inner city that Murray, Wilson, and Jencks describe? No other ethnic group in America's cities has a problem with crime, delinquency, poor school performance, and out-of-wedlock births nearly as severe as that of black Americans, nor as much difficulty seeing to it that their children advance into the ranks of the (broadly defined) middle class. If generous welfare benefits, lack of high-paying blue-collar jobs, the movement of wealthier and more successful people to better neighborhoods, a decline in status rewards for being poor-but-independent, along with changing cultural attitudes toward sex and marriage, can produce an underclass—as the reader of Murray, Wilson, and Jencks might reasonably infer—why hasn't such a class emerged on anything like the scale one finds in America in the more highly developed European welfare states? Many of the welfare states of Northern and Western Europe—Sweden and Denmark, for instance—never had as strong a tradition of self-reliance as in America; they have undergone similar structural economic changes as in America; their more successful citizens presumably like nicer neighborhoods just as much as Americans do; they have had similar changes in attitudes toward sex and marriage as in America; and they offer much more extensive welfare benefits than in America. Yet by all accounts they do not have a problem nearly as serious as America's with a permanent inner-city underclass. Moreover, if the factors that Murray, Wilson, and Jencks describe produce an underclass, why do most of the current immigrants to the United States, including the vast bulk of nonwhite immigrants from Asia, Africa, and the Afro-Caribbean, seem so less susceptible to this process? Why, in short, the reader of Murray, Wilson, and Jencks must ask, has it been pre-eminently American blacks who have shown such a high degree of susceptibility to being trapped by the welfare system and the many cultural and policy changes since the 1960s and who have displayed such low levels of adaptability to structural changes in the economy?

To answer questions such as these one must turn to certain salient features of black history, black culture, and the black experience in America, none of which Murray, Wilson, or Jencks show much interest in investigating. One can only speculate on the reasons for their disinterest in such matters—residual fallout from the Moynihan Report controversy may be part of an explanation, as well as the general bias against cultural and historical approaches by much of contemporary social science. But it is certain that even by combining the rational-choice type of incentive and disincentive model that Murray offers to analyze the many policy changes of the late 1960s with Wilson's structural unemployment and middle-class-exodus models and adding Jencks's account of the changes in family morality and cultural values among the white American middle class, something is radically missing from our understanding of the "dark ghettos" of the inner cities.

In his Labor Department memorandum, Daniel Moynihan had tried to explain how the legacy of past brutalization and oppression continued to have a great impact on black communal life in the urban North long after black people had escaped from the horrors of slavery and life in the Jim Crow South. Here Moynihan was continuing in a tradition of interpretation that had held the historio-cultural and historio-psychological dimensions of the black experience in America to be of utmost importance for understanding contemporary black problems. Moynihan drew much of his thinking on these matters from the pioneering research of the black scholar E. Franklin Frazier, whose *The Negro Family in the United States* was the standard work on its subject for a generation of social scientists.[241] Virtually every social scientist of note who wrote on African American

---

241. E. Franklin Frazier, *The Negro Family in the United States* (Chicago: University of Chicago Press, 1939).

issues from the 1930s through the 1960s shared Moynihan's and Frazier's view in this regard, and indeed, to anyone whose mind is not constrained by methodological dogma or a partisan political agenda their view here would seem to be a simple postulate of common sense. History and culture do matter, and the idea that one can gain a good understanding of what has happened in the black neighborhoods of Harlem, Bedford-Stuyvesant, Detroit, Watts, or South Chicago by explanations that ignore African American specific factors should be viewed with utmost skepticism.[242]

---

242. In subsequent books both Murray and Wilson realized that there was something missing from their respective accounts of black ghetto disintegration, and they sought to provide what they saw as some of the missing element. For Murray in *The Bell Curve* (co-authored with Richard Herrnstein), the missing element was distributional differences in the kind of intelligence measured by IQ tests and the difficulties posed for low-IQ individuals in gaining employment, raising children, obeying the law, and other social outcomes. Ethno-racial groups were shown to possess different mean IQ scores, with Jews at the top, followed in rank order by Asians, whites, Latinos, African-Americans, and sub-Saharan black Africans. The black/white IQ difference was attributed to some unknown combination of genetic and environmental factors. *The Bell Curve: Intelligence and Class Structure in American Life* (New York: The Free Press, 1994).

Wilson, in a follow-up book to *The Truly Disadvantaged* titled *When Work Disappears: The World of the New Urban Poor*, moved in a culturalist rather than a genetic/hereditarian direction. While still stressing the "deindustrialization" theory of his earlier book, Wilson in this later book was struck by huge differences between poor blacks and poor Mexican immigrants in the inner cities in terms of their marriage and family arrangements and their work habits. He came to believe that cultural differences between the two groups put African Americans, especially the males, at a distinct disadvantage in terms of maintaining stable marital relations and stable work habits. "A brief comparison between inner-city blacks and inner-city Mexicans (many of whom are immigrants) . . . provides some evidence for these cultural differences," Wilson writes. He continues: "Mexicans come to the United States with a clear conception of a traditional family unit that features men as breadwinners. Although extramarital affairs by men are tolerated, 'a pregnant, unmarried woman is a source of opprobrium, anguish, or great concern.' Pressure is applied by the kin of both parents to enter into marriage. The family norms and behavior in inner-city black neighborhoods stand in sharp contrast. . . . Inner-city black women routinely say that they distrust men and feel strongly that black men lack dedication to their families. They argue that black males are hopeless as either husbands or fathers and that more of their time is spent on the streets than at home. . . . The women in the inner city tend to believe that black men get involved with women mainly to obtain sex or money, and that once these goals are achieved women are usually discarded." Wilson also contrasts the black male and Mexican-immigrant male work ethic: "The ethnographic data [from our Chicago study]

Within the context of the present survey it is not possible to

suggest that the Mexican immigrants are harder workers because they 'come from areas of intense poverty and that even boring, hard, dead-end jobs look, by contrast, good to them.' . . . The data . . . reveal that the black men are more hostile than the Mexican men with respect to the low-paying jobs they hold, less willing to be flexible in taking assignments or tasks not considered part of their job, and less willing to work as hard for the same low wages." *When Work Disappears* (New York: Alfred A. Knopf, 1996), pp. 98–9, 140–1.

Both Daniel Patrick Moynihan and E. Franklin Frazier believed that the fragility of family bonds among African Americans in the urban North was at least partially a legacy of the slavery and Jim Crow eras, where a strong sense of the father as provider and protector of his family never had a chance to develop or to become strongly internalized or institutionalized. This idea has been more recently developed by James Q. Wilson in his book *The Marriage Problem*, where he goes beyond Moynihan and Frazier in tracing certain black family patterns back to those the black slaves brought with them from West Africa. Here J.Q. Wilson continues in a tradition of interpretation popularized in the early twentieth century by the anthropologist Melville Herskovits, who believed there were many New World survivals of African customs. Like W. J. Wilson, J. Q. Wilson is struck by the different pattern of family formation and stability between recent Mexican immigrants and lower-income African Americans. He writes on this: "Controlling for income, the rate at which Latinos take welfare benefits is only about one-fifth the rate at which African Americans do. They are poorer and less educated than blacks, and many are certainly in a risky legal situation, but they are not nearly as likely to have children living without two parents. . . . The high rates of out-of-wedlock births for black women cannot be explained by intelligence, for holding IQ constant, black women are three times as likely as Latinos and five times as likely as Anglo white women to have out-of-wedlock children. There is, of course, an easy explanation for this difference—culture." *The Marriage Problem* (New York: HarperCollins Publishers, 2002), p. 108.

In recent years, genetic-based theorists have bought into the "African legacy" theory but given it a heriditarian twist. The high rates of infant deaths endemic to a disease-ridden tropical climate, in combination with the ease of obtaining plant foods to sustain life, they argue, led to a genetic propensity among sub-Saharan African males for following a reproductive strategy involving multiple partners, high numbers of offspring, and a corresponding low level of parental investment in the rearing of each child. Males developing in much colder, less disease-ridden environments, they say, evolved a genetically programmed reproductive strategy focused on fewer offspring and the greater male parenting-involvement needed for each cold-climate-reared child to survive. Climate and local ecology, they say, can, over time, genetically influence mating strategies in surviving offspring. It is possible—and likely—they say, that culture and genes interact, and that genetic propensities will influence cultural values, so that sub-Saharan African populations and their recent descendants will be naturally more tolerant of widespread out-of-wedlock births than populations that have evolved over the millennia in much colder climates (such as northern Asia). This, they say, is why black populations not only in Africa but also in the U.S., South America, and the Caribbean are more tolerant of out-of-wedlock births than the Asian-descendant and European-descendant populations living next to them. The most influential proponent of this view is the Canadian psychologist J. Philippe Rushton in his book *Race, Evolution and Behavior*, 3rd ed., (New Brunswick, NJ: Transaction Publishers, 2000).

deal with all the cultural, historical, and psychological factors that need to be explored in order to understand the catastrophe of the black ghetto. Some of the more salient of these factors, however, can be set forth in rough outline. It must first be understood that most of the black inhabitants of America's ghettos are direct descendants of a displaced rural peasantry, forced out of the cotton-agricultural economy of the rural South in the 25-year period following the end of the Second World War.[243] We might call this the era of the Great Automation Migration, since

---

Some find Rushton's ideas incendiary, although like any theory in social science they must be validated or refuted based on the best evidence, not the most widely shared ideology.

243. See Nicholas Lemann, *The Promised Land* (New York: Alfred A. Knopf, 1991), and his earlier two-part article in the *Atlantic*, "The Origins of the Underclass," June 1986, pp. 31–6, and July 1986, pp. 54–68. Lemann's thesis, which is identical to Daniel Moynihan's, is that much of the problems of the inner-city black ghettos of America in the latter half of the twentieth century are the result of the rapid migration of rural blacks ill-prepared for the challenges of urban life. His thesis was later attacked by the *U.S. News and World Report* urban specialist David Whitman on the ground that ample statistics show Southern-born blacks to have done better in the North in terms of getting and holding a job and staying out of jail than blacks born in the North (David Whitman, "The Great Sharecropper Success Story," *The Public Interest*, 104 (1991): 3–19). But Whitman's attack on Lemann's thesis was based on an error, since Whitman failed to take account of the "second-generation dynamic" and as a result misinterpreted the indisputable fact that first-generation black migrants often did better than many in the second and third generation. Whitman failed to understand the connection between the downward mobility of the second and third generations and the parenting and socialization failures of the first. The problems with displaced peasant cultures, such as the Irish in the nineteenth century and the Southern-reared African Americans in the second half of the twentieth, are often most acutely seen in the second and subsequent generations when urban-reared children and grandchildren, especially the males, need guidance and discipline in a new, bewildering, and challenging environment—guidance their parents are ill-equipped to provide. The problem is particularly acute with "push-driven" migrations, where the immigrants have not been highly self-selected for ambition, drive, future-orientation, desire to see their children get ahead, etc. The analysis presented in the text confirms the basic Moynihan-Lemann insight, which has not received the appropriate consideration it deserves among social scientists specializing in urban problems. The "second-generation problem," however, has been taken up recently in conjunction with the latest immigrant groups to America by a number of leading academic sociologists. See, for instance, Alejandro Portes and Ruben G. Rumbaut, *Legacies: The Story of the Immigrant Second Generation* (Berkeley: University of California Press, 2001); Alejandro Portes, ed., *The New Second Generation* (New York: Russell Sage Foundation, 1996); and Ruben G. Rumbaut and Alejandro Portes, eds., *Ethnicities: Children of Immigrants in America* (Berkeley: University of California Press, 2001).

it resulted from the introduction into Southern agriculture of tractors and automatic cotton-picking machines, which, in conjunction with the introduction of chemical weed-killers, practically eliminated the need for black agricultural labor, and more than any other factor in the twentieth century, was responsible for the massive migration of black people from the Southern farms and rural areas to the Northern and Midwestern cities. The Great Automation Migration differed from the first great migration of blacks out of the rural South that began during the First World War—the migration that produced so many of the vibrant black working-class communities in the Northern and Midwestern cities of the 1920s—in two important ways. It was much greater in size, and unlike the earlier migration in which the northward-bound blacks were driven by the allure of greater opportunity for self-improvement and upward mobility, it was what demographers call a "push-driven" migration, caused by the involuntary displacement of black farm workers and sharecroppers from the agricultural regions of the South brought about by the rapid mechanization of Southern agriculture in the immediate post-World War II era.[244]

To give some indication of just how massive the exodus from Southern agriculture was during the period after the Second World War, consider the following figures: According to the 1940 U.S. Census more than 40 percent of blacks worked

---

244. As late as the 1910 Census, almost 9 out of 10 blacks lived in the South, most of them in small towns or rural areas. The first large migration of African Americans out of the South began in earnest during the years of the First World War (1914–1918), when the supply of cheap immigrant labor flowing into America from Southern and Eastern Europe was abruptly cut off as the European belligerents conscripted most of their young men into the military, resulting in huge labor shortages in many Northern and Midwestern American cities. Many ambitious Southern blacks at this time heeded the call of Northern industrialists to leave their Southern abodes and create a new life for themselves and their families in the urban North. On balance this Great Migration (as it is called) was a considerable success and went on to create decent working-class communities in places like the South Side of Chicago and New York's Harlem with an élan and morale that later older ghetto residents would look back upon nostalgically with a sad yearning.

on farms, the vast bulk of the farms being in the South; when the 1970 Census was taken, this figure had plummeted to a minuscule 4.4 percent. Over the decade of the 1950s, the net black out-migration from the six Deep South states, Mississippi, Alabama, Georgia, South Carolina, Arkansas, and Louisiana, was a staggering 1.2 million, with Mississippi and Alabama accounting for 547,000 of these. The state of Mississippi alone during the 1950s had a net loss of 323,000 blacks, almost a quarter of its entire black population, and a figure roughly equal to the total net out-migration of blacks from the entire South during the decade of the 1930s. Charles Silberman has rightly described the post-World War II black migration out of the agricultural South as one of the great migrations of history, and the authors of the most important demographic history of blacks in America do not exaggerate when they describe the rural-to-urban migration that took place during the 1950s as "the relocation of black America."[245] Not surprisingly, the most frequent destinations of the black migrants were the states with the largest industrial cities, with New York, Illinois, California, Ohio, Michigan, and New Jersey showing the greatest net gain in their black populations over this period.

As Oscar Handlin and other students of human migrations have documented, the problem of adjusting to life in a complex, competitive, work- and achievement-oriented urban environment is always difficult for people from a rural peasant background, but at least four salient factors distinguished the post-World War II black migrants from the Deep South from many other rural immigrants, which, when taken together and in conjunction with the various factors analyzed by Wilson, Murray, and Jencks, made it extremely difficult for either the migrants or their children to meet the pressing challenges

---

245. Rex Campbell and David Johnson, *Black Migration in America: A Social Demographic History* (Durham, NC: Duke University Press, 1981).

of the new urban environment. These factors were a) the general poverty, illiteracy, and social isolation of the population; b) the lack of an entrepreneurial tradition or experience with buying and selling, and more generally, the lack of a tradition of self-improvement; c) the involuntary nature of the migration itself and the resulting nonselectivity of much of the migrant population in terms of such important personal characteristics as ambition, self-discipline, and future-orientation; and, d) the legacy of Southern violence, oppression, and extreme negative psychological conditioning. Each of these factors requires further elaboration.

To begin with the first, it is important to realize just how impoverished, socially isolated, and intellectually backward the typical black sharecropper or rural black farm worker was who lived in the cotton- and tobacco-growing regions of the Deep South before the massive out-migration of the postwar years. Other than a few pieces of usually second-hand household furniture, assorted housewares, and a tiny amount of inexpensive clothing and other inexpensive personal items, the typical sharecropper or farm worker owned virtually nothing. He usually lived in a small decrepit shack lent to him by his landlord, lacking both electricity and indoor plumbing; he received an amount of food and money from the landlord that was just enough to keep himself and his family going; he owned no tools, no capital, no draft animals; and he had almost no savings other than the few dollars he might have in his home for personal items and foodstuffs. Though not subject to periodic famines, the typical sharecropper or farm worker family led a truly subsistence-level existence, little better than that of a medieval serf. When forced to migrate north, the family had almost no financial resources with which to begin life in the new environment.

Most sharecroppers and rural farm worker were not much better off in terms of their educational resources or exposure to knowledge and ideas. In 1940 the average black adult in the

South had less than five years of education, and even this low figure offers an exaggerated picture of the level of intellectual achievement among Southern blacks. Black schools in rural areas of the South were typically operated for only six or seven months out of the year (white schools were usually run for nine months), and per pupil expenditures were usually only a small fraction of what they were for white schools, despite the fact that per pupil expenditures for white schools in the South were the lowest in the nation. One study of black schools in Alabama in the late 1930s showed a per pupil expenditure that was less than 15% of the national average for all students. Throughout the 1930s and 1940s the pay for teachers in many rural Southern black schools was so low that in many cases schools had to employ teachers who themselves were only barely literate and barely able to do grammar school-level arithmetic. A standard achievement test administered to over 300 black Alabama schoolteachers in the early 1930s resulted in an average test score that was below the national average for ninth-graders.

The typical farm worker's home contained no books, periodicals, or newspapers. In his classic study of 612 black sharecropper families in the cotton-growing regions of the South,[246] sociologist Charles S. Johnson found that only nine of the families—less than 1.5 percent—received a daily newspaper. The vast majority of sharecropper homes—over 85 percent—received no newspapers, magazines, or periodical literature of any kind, not even a monthly farm journal. As Johnson remarked of these families: "Reading and writing are not a serious part of the routine of daily life for either adults or children." The displaced sharecroppers and farm workers who migrated north could bring with them no more intellectual resources than they could financial ones.

---

246. Charles S. Johnson, *Shadow of the Plantation* (Chicago: University of Chicago Press, 1934).

Poverty and illiteracy by themselves have certainly not been an insuperable barrier to social and economic advancement for immigrants to America. Many immigrants have been poor, and in the English language at least the vast majority have been illiterate. But the poor and illiterate blacks who migrated to the Northern cities from the Deep South in the 1950s and early 1960s also lacked what was often so decisive to the success of many foreign immigrants to these shores, namely some rudimentary experience in buying and selling and in the ways of a market economy. Small business has often been a lifeline for many ethnic minority immigrants—the Chinese, Jews, Italians, Armenians, Greeks, and West Indians in the early decades of this century, for instance; Koreans, Vietnamese, Asian Indians, and Arabs today. But Southern-born blacks and their offspring never developed the kind of enterprising business spirit that one finds in these other groups. The few African American-owned businesses existing in the Northern cities have usually been confined to personal services or to specialty products purchased mainly by a black clientele (e.g., barber shops, beauty parlors, funeral homes, black-oriented cosmetic shops, etc.), and only rarely has black business been able to compete successfully in non-black markets.

Even in the inner-city ghetto itself, the proprietors of small businesses have most frequently been foreign-born immigrants—Jews in the 20s and 30s, for example, and Asians today—while one of the few cases where there was a large black business presence in the inner city, that is, in New York's Harlem between the world wars, the businesses were usually owned not by Southern-born blacks but by Jamaicans and other West Indian immigrants. Many reasons have been offered to explain the low participation of African Americans in small business, and each must be carefully evaluated, but part of the reason is certainly to be sought in the rural Southern background from which most African Americans have come.

Unlike many European peasants, black sharecroppers and black rural farm workers not only owned nothing but also had little experience in selling at market even small quantities of produce. In the cotton-growing regions of the South, all buying and selling operations on the plantations were conducted by the landowner, who alone was responsible for all business and financial matters. The Southern sharecropper and farm labor system was specifically intended, in fact, to discourage individual initiative and entrepreneurship among blacks, and to keep the black laborer dependent on the landlord for his day-to-day sustenance. Together with the general rules of caste subordination extant in the South, the Southern farm labor system seems to have been successful in producing exactly what Southern cotton growers wanted it to produce—a black labor force that was extremely docile, dependent, and submissive. Our best source for understanding the effect of this Southern system on Southern black attitudes, habits, and personality formation is John Dollard, whose masterful *Caste and Class in a Southern Town*,[247] first published in 1937, is still indispensable reading for anyone who wants to understand the genesis of many of our contemporary black urban problems.

According to Dollard, the institution of the "furnish," in which the landlord, in addition to providing the farm laborer with a small shack to live in, advanced him a small monthly allotment of money or credit to take care of his basic subsistence-level needs, was specifically designed to instill in the poor black agricultural laborer a sense of infantile dependency and subservience. According to Dollard's own observations and the testimony of many of his informants, the system was very successful in achieving its goals:

247. John Dollard, *Caste and Class in a Southern Town* (New Haven: Yale University Press, 1937.

Middle class Negro informants uniformly deplored the passivity of lower class Negroes and often reproached them with it. One said he believed that many tenant farmers do not care much whether they make money out of a crop or not. They are satisfied with a secure furnish, take it easy, and let the white man worry. . . . A bird in the hand is worth two in the bush to lower class Negroes. Informant believed that habits which might lead to advancement are especially weakened by the security of the furnish. So long as they have a living, however meager, and the indefinite guarantee of this living, [Negro farm workers] are not forced to save; they always know that they will be furnished a house the year round and food for six or seven months while the crop is growing. Under these circumstances the Negro cropper experiences none of that institutional pressure which produces an ambitious and aggressive attitude toward economic life. . . .

The furnish system is a kind of permanent dole which appeals to the pleasure principle and relieves the Negro of responsibility and the necessity of forethought. Very important in the above account are the personal dependence and attitude of passive expectation of the tenant toward his landlord. . . . One can think of the lower class Negroes as bribed and drugged by this system. The effect of the social set-up seems to be to keep [lower class] Negroes infantile, to grant them infantile types of freedom from responsibility, and also to exercise the autocratic control over them which is the prerogative of the patriarchal father. The shift from a clinging, dependent adjustment to parents over to an independent attitude toward the world is always perceived as slightly traumatic by children. Parents at least are careful to enjoin the child to "act like a big boy," and so on, as a means of persuading him to abandon infantile adjustments. The southern caste set-up, on the other hand, encourages the lower class Negro to "act like a little boy," and this in fact he does. (CCST, pp. 402–5)

Besides the infantile dependency encouraged by the practice of the furnish, the Southern caste system itself, Dollard says, provided ample disincentives to socioeconomic advancement not only for poor black sharecroppers but for all blacks, regardless of their occupation. Southern whites generally believed that blacks had a definite "place" in society, and, as Dollard explains, any attempt to rise above this place by efforts to improve one's social and economic position might be interpreted by whites as a hostile act of aggression against the caste system itself and a threat to specifically white prerogatives:

> Strange as it may seem, this effort on the part of Negroes [to improve their socio-economic position] is perceived by the white caste as an affront. Holding a prestigeful job, owning a large tract of land, having a special talent by which the Negro competes with white people are forms of activity which are defined as aggressive. It is plain to see how the caste situation tends to discourage or prevent vertical social mobility in Negroes. In Southerntown, at least, resentment at Negro "rising" is felt not only by lower class white people, but by the middle class people as well. . . .
>
> Every Negro who has achieved advancement beyond lower class status in Southerntown has been made aware of this envy and resentment at his aggressive mobility. Such Negroes are said to get ideas beyond their station, that is, to threaten the fixed inferior and superior positions of Negro and white castes. The individuality and independence which go with landownership, for example, seem to be defined as aggressive behavior on the part of a Negro. . . . Although it does not happen often, the threat of being driven off one's own land is always there. . . . The homes and barns of the

innocent and upright may be destroyed. The knowledge that
this can happen has a tendency to discourage the capable
Negroes from saving and building up farms of their own.
(CCST, pp. 297–9, 428–9)

One doesn't need much of a sociological imagination to predict that people with the sort of background and past experience that Dollard describes in these paragraphs are not likely
to become successful and aggressive entrepreneurs should they
find themselves moving to the urban industrialized centers of
the North. Those whose skills are limited to picking cotton, hoe-
ing weeds, milking cows, and running errands for the boss man
but who have had little experience with money and markets, or
with the risks and rewards of private economic initiative, are
not likely to take advantage of new entrepreneurial opportunities in small businesses even if such opportunities should present
themselves in abundance.

Poverty and illiteracy, together with a total absence of a
tradition of entrepreneurship and self-improvement, are background characteristics that under any circumstances would provide formidable obstacles to an immigrant population's upward
social and economic advancement in an urban economy. The
members of the Great Automation Migration, however, were
handicapped by two additional factors, each of which was
probably of significantly greater importance than the total combined impact of these other two forces. The first of these was the
involuntariness of the migration itself and the resulting (relative)
nonselectivity of those transplanted in the process. If we define a
"voluntary" economic immigrant as one who has the opportunity to remain employed at his traditional occupation without
his basic livelihood being threatened, but despite this possibility
chooses to migrate in order to improve the social and economic
position of himself and his family, and if we define an "involuntary" economic immigrant as someone who does not have

such a stay-as-you-are option but is forced to move because of loss of employment and the destruction of a traditional way of life, then it is clear that there are major differences between the typical voluntary and the typical involuntary economic immigrant that will be of major significance in terms of their ability to succeed in an achievement-oriented market economy.[248] The self-selection process that determines who migrates and who stays behind in the case of voluntary immigrants will result in an immigrant population very different in character than one in which this self-selection process has not operated or has not operated to the same degree.

Voluntary economic immigrants migrate for the specific purpose of getting ahead in life and seeing to it that their children and grandchildren get ahead. They are often single-minded in the pursuit of this goal and are often willing to adapt themselves to whatever is necessary to achieve their ends. Compared with the stay-at-homes and the involuntarily uprooted, voluntary immigrants typically show a greater degree of dissatisfaction with their lowly economic and social position; they display higher levels of ambition, aspiration, and energy; they have higher levels of self-confidence and a correspondingly lower level of self-doubt and feelings of inferiority; they display a greater willingness to take calculated risks to further their economic advancement; they have more clearly defined life-goals and a more focused direction to their efforts to achieve these life-goals; they have greater confidence in their ability to alter their personal situation positively though personal sacrifice and hard work; they have a higher degree of optimism and greater faith in the future; and in general, they display a more creative use of their varying talents

---

248. The terms "voluntary immigrant" and "involuntary immigrant," as set forth here, are, of course, intended as "ideal types." Like "monopoly," "oligopoly," and "perfect competition" in economics, or "upper-class," middle-class," and "working class" in sociology, they paint with a broad brush and obviously don't capture all the richness of the real world. Crude as they are, they are useful in capturing many of the social world's salient features.

and energies. Those among their compatriots lacking these characteristics typically choose to stay home when that is possible. (Recall Tocqueville's observation in this context about economic ambition being less of a driving force in many men than a desire for a simpler life of greater idleness and leisure.)

Involuntary immigrants, on the other hand, particularly if they come from peasant backgrounds or other premodern, fixed-status-order societies radically different from the U.S., rarely display these features, or display them to a much lesser extent. Moreover, by the very fact that they have been involuntarily uprooted and forced to move to a strange and often bewildering environment where they do not necessarily desire to be, involuntary immigrants will be more inclined to be fatalistic about life, to believe that most things depend on "luck," to be more pessimistic and self-pitying, to have less faith in a benign future, and to have less confidence in their own capacities to alter their life for the better. Although such characteristic are not what economists and quantitatively oriented social scientists like to study, these differing attitudes, motivations, and psychological characteristics can be enormously important in determining who gets ahead and who does not in a competitive capitalist environment.

Motivational and attitudinal disadvantages, however, are not the only ones from which the involuntarily uprooted suffer. Compared with voluntary immigrants, involuntary immigrants will be less likely to have planned long in advance and to have saved up money to help support themselves in their emigration; they will be less likely to possess marketable skills; and they typically will not have as capable a support network of family and friends in the area to which they have migrated that will be able to help them make a successful adjustment. This last factor is particularly important, since it is often these individual support networks that provide new immigrants and their families with valuable information about jobs and the ways of getting

ahead in new surroundings, and they can often lend the immigrants money or provide other goods and services in time of
need. Success or failure in the new urban environment can often
depend on the degree of support an immigrant receives from
such private networks.

The difference between voluntary and involuntary immigrant
groups is well illustrated in the relative success (compared with
many inner-city African Americans) of recent black immigrants
from Haiti. Haiti is one of the poorest countries in the Western hemisphere; its people are largely illiterate; they have darker
racial features than most American blacks; they speak a French
patois first, maybe some fragmentary English. Yet the poor Hai-
tians who have immigrated to the United States in recent years
seem to be displaying patterns of upward social and economic
mobility clearly superior to those of earlier African Americans.
In Miami, for instance, where the Haitian population is very
substantial, a struggling but surviving working-class community
has emerged that stands in marked contrast to the city's African American ghettos of Overtown and Liberty City. Many of
the small businesses in the Haitian area are Haitian-owned, and
employers throughout Florida are said to prefer Haitian workers
to native Americans, whether black or white, because of their
greater reliability and greater eagerness to work. Haitian parents
often try to keep their own children away from African American children, whose influence they feel is often harmful.[249]

The example of the Haitian immigrants and, indeed, of successful black immigrants from many other areas of Africa and
the Afro-Caribbean, also helps to illustrate the final handicap
under which the members of the Great Automation Migration

---

249. See Alex Stepick, "The Haitian Informal Sector in Miami," *City and Society* 5
(1991): 10–22; Alejandro Portes and Alex Stepick, *City on the Edge: The Transformation
of Miami* (Berkeley: University of California Press, 1993); and Margarita Mooney, *Faith
Makes Us Live: Surviving and Thriving in the Haitian Diaspora* (Berkeley: University of
California Press, 2009).

had to labor in their attempted adjustment from a rural to an urban environment. This is the fact that the black migrants from the Deep South, unlike foreign-born black immigrants from Africa or the Afro-Caribbean, had been socialized into the ways of a white-dominated caste society that not only had a subordinate place assigned to blacks but also tried to convince blacks through generations of brutal and pervasive negative conditioning that this was their rightful place because of their alleged mental inferiority and innate childlike immaturity. The destructive effect of the inferiority doctrine on black-self-confidence and the black self-image can hardly be underestimated, and of the four factors distinguishing the members of the Great Automation Migration from many other rural immigrants who have come to America, it is this which arguably has had the most harmful and the most lasting effects in preventing black adjustments to the demands of an increasingly high-tech and information-oriented economy.

Every aspect of social life in the Deep South was designed to convince black people that they occupied a lower order of humanity than that occupied by the superior whites. Whether it was the requirement that blacks allow whites to be waited on first in retail establishments; that they give up their seats on crowded buses and trains to white people; that they address white people by such honorific titles as "Mr.," "Mrs.," "Sir," or "Boss," while they themselves, no matter how prominent or mature in years, were addressed by their first names in the manner in which one would address a child; that they enter a white household only through the back door and never shake the hand of a white person—these and numerous other social customs in the Deep South were intended to reinforce the general Southern view that black people were so lowly and degraded, so animal-like and inferior, so mentally and morally unfit for any kind of higher civilization, that they would never be capable of living together with white people on a level of social equality.

For understanding some of the psychological effects of Deep South customs on black development, John Dollard is once again one of our best sources. His description of the brutality of some of these customs, together with the social and psychological effects they were intended to have, is chilling, especially when one considers how widespread such customs were and how generally accepted within the dominant white society:

Violations of caste custom may also lead to the beating of a Negro. A local informant told me of a Negro physician who came down from the North to practice in a southern town. He had resolved to accept the situation and do the right thing. But one day in talking to a drugstore clerk he occasionally forgot and said "yes" and "no." The clerk flew into a rage and bellowed at him, "Say, nigger, can't you say 'Yes, sir'?" The doctor corrected his mistake. That evening a group of young white men called at his house, took him out into the country, and beat him severely. Subsequently he had to leave town. . . .

Southern white informants are not reticent about the use of assault on Negroes; rather they talk about it with a self-confident satisfaction. One declared, for example, that the "nigger" is all right in his place. . . . He mentioned the case of a "nigger" who once worked for him and refused to do something he was told to do. Informant got his black-jack and beat him about the head until he was unconscious. When the "nigger" woke up, informant asked him if he wanted any more. The Negro replied, "No, boss, Ah's got enough." Informant did not discharge the Negro but sent him back to the job and "he was one of the best niggers I have ever had." Informant said he has, on occasion, broken all the knuckles of his right hand, exhibiting same, hitting "niggers." Another white man said that the only thing to

do with "uppity niggers" is to smash them down. If they get
"sassy," hit them: that is all they understand.

A Negro man related the story of a friend who was
appointed postmaster of a little town in the South. The white
people resented the appointment and threatening rumors
began to circulate concerning what the whites would do if
the postmaster did not get out. Informant worked occasionally with his friend but finally, in face of hostility of the
white people, decided to quit. The postmaster stayed on.
A few weeks later he was caught by a gang of whites and
beaten so badly that he died shortly afterwards. . . .

There are, are of course, other forms of aggression
besides the direct physical violence which we have been
discussing. One of them is undoubtedly moral intimidation,
that is, an attack on the self-esteem of another individual.
This type of aggression is a chronic policy of the white caste
in the South; its aim seems to be to humiliate the Negro, to
put him on another and lower scale of humanity. . . . One
of [the forms of personal derogation of Negroes] is the caste
etiquette which is compulsory for Negroes. A white friend
gave me some instruction on this score immediately after
I arrived in Southerntown. . . . Of course, at first I made
mistakes and on one occasion a white friend gently reminded
me, "You know, down here we never refer to a Negro as
'Mr.' or 'Mrs.'; they don't expect it and we never do it. We
always call them by their first names no matter if they are
doctor or preacher or teacher or anything else. If we should
call them 'Dr.' or Mr.' or 'Mrs.,' they would get the idea that
they were somebody and get real cocky." . . .

Another form of personal derogation of Negroes is to
apply the special and unfavorable designation, "nigger," to
them. It stamps the Negro as an inferior man and seems to
isolate him from the community of human sympathy and

cooperation. At first it was jarring to hear the word used, but I heard it repeated so often that eventually it lost its shock for me. . . . There are many forms of personal derogation of Negroes which are hard to classify. One of these, for example, is that Negroes are expected to "wait" or stand at the end of the line until white persons are through. In the case of Negroes and whites waiting in a professional or business office, it is taken for granted that whites are served first. A Negro employee of a white boss was much irked by having eternally to wait for conferences until no white people were about. The white employer understood quite well, as indeed did his employee, that he could not afford to let it be said that he let a white person wait while he talked to a Negro. This sort of thing is extremely discouraging and disheartening, as probably it is meant to be. It is difficult to keep up a tone of active self-feeling and self-respect when one constantly receives these signs of negative evaluation from others. (CCST, pp. 339–44)

It is often said that under the constraints of the Jim Crow system, black people developed two faces (or two personalities), a role-playing one which they displayed before white people, and their true face (or true personality) which they exhibited only when they were alone among each other. There is no doubt much truth in this observation, and certainly for anyone who wanted to preserve even a minimal sense of human dignity, such a double life was an absolute necessity. But it would be the height of foolishness to suppose that the efforts to convince black people that they were innately inferior to whites was without its harmful effects. On the contrary, it would seem to be only the very exceptional person, or the person fortunate enough to have a very exceptional and supportive family, who could come through such an experience psychically unscathed. In the great majority of cases, the more reasonable assumption would seem to be that the systematic effort over generations to convince black people that they were inferior to whites had just the effect it was intended to have, and that, at the very least, the inferiority doctrine sowed the seeds of self-doubt among black people that has served to undermine the self-confidence of even some of the most able and ambitious. As the previously quoted Andrew Billingsly (in a more characteristically lucid moment) reminds us: "It should not be difficult to discern that people who, having been told for 200 years—in ways more effective than words—that they are subhuman, should begin to believe this themselves and internalize these values and pass them on to their children and their children's children." (BFWA, p. 49) The rural, Deep South farm hand, the most backward, illiterate, isolated, and poorest of all blacks in the South, no doubt internalized these negative values more readily than anyone else.

DISPLACED SHARECROPPERS AND THEIR DELINQUENT SONS: WHEN THE CHILDREN AND GRANDCHILDREN NO LONGER REMEMBER THE SOUTH

What happened to the displaced sharecroppers and rural farm hands when they came to live in the big city in the 1950s and 1960s? How successful were they at getting and keeping a job, at establishing and maintaining a stable family, and most important of all, at preparing their children and grandchildren for the great challenges posed by life in a new competitive urban environment where one's "place" was no longer ascribed (at least not in the same way it was in the rural South), and upward socioeconomic mobility was not only permitted of immigrants and their children but also expected of them? While a comprehensive history of the Great Automation Migration has yet to be written, from what we do know it seems that for many displaced sharecroppers and other rural blacks, the move to the great Northern metropolis proved to be a disaster—frequently for the Southerners themselves but much more frequently for their children and grandchildren. When the displaced share-croppers and other rural blacks entered the world of the North-ern industrial city, one populated by immigrants from many parts of the world who had come to America explicitly to get ahead, they entered an alien universe, where a new competitive work-and-achievement game was being played that they were singularly ill-prepared to master. Indeed, they were almost pre-programmed to fail. Their background and conditioning, the circumstances of their migration, their poverty, illiteracy, and lack of useful urban skills, together with the racial discrimina-tion they inevitably faced (which was often greater than that faced by members of other immigrant groups) conspired to insure that they would not do very well in terms of the self-improvement values of the new urban culture.

The results were predictable: Some men got discouraged by their inability to secure a high-paying job or one that offered the possibility for advancement. Others were resentful over the fact that while they had important tasks to do on the farm, which women could not do as well, in the urban North, where a man's status primarily depends upon earning power, they can earn no more at most of the low-skilled jobs available to them than their wives can earn as domestics. And in the impersonal atmosphere of the big city, of course, many succumb to the all-too-human vices of gambling, alcoholism, and womanizing, which had pre-viously been kept under a much greater degree of social control in small Southern towns and rural areas through the general surveillance of the local community and the influence of the local black church. Family desertion by the males seems to have been a common response to many of these developments.

Still, for the Southern-reared sharecropper and other rural blacks life in the urban metropolis was often experienced in more positive terms. After all, the standard of living the Southerner encountered in the urban North, even at the wages of the lowest paid janitor, hotel worker, elevator operator, or other service worker, was a vast improvement over the abject poverty of the rural South, and since the rural black Southerner was conditioned in his formative years not to have high aspirations or ambitions, the fact that he might not do as well as the members of certain other immigrant groups in America was not always a problem. In the urban North, even the poorest Southern migrant usually lived in a structurally sound building—one with glass windows and efficient indoor heating, electric lighting and electric refrigeration, hot and cold running water, and even a flush toilet. Most of these apartments, moreover, were outfitted with serviceable second-hand furniture, and in time many migrants were able to add to their household items their own radios and television sets. Although such living arrangements may seem shabby by middle-class standards, compared with their former existence in the falling-down shacks of the cotton plantations and impoverished Southern "nigger quarters"—with their dirt floors, leaking roofs, stinking outhouses, sparse furnishings, and lack of electricity—these new homes in the urban North offered many distinct amenities.

There were other advantages as well. In the North black people no longer had to face the daily humiliation of the Jim Crow system; they were no longer subject to lynching or mob violence (or to the legal lynching that often passed for justice under the Southern court system); they had access to much better medical care; and both their rights and their interests were much better cared for by the urban political systems that had become increasingly solicitous of black votes. All in all, life under such circumstances for the transplanted rural black, even if he had to toil for the rest of his days at a low-status job, might be seen as quite tolerable.

Where the real problems begin to emerge, and indeed on such a scale that they will eventually overwhelm and ultimately destroy the black inner-city ghettos as decent places to live, are in the second and subsequent generations. One might speak here of a bewildered-father/delinquent-son syndrome. Children who have been raised in the urban North will typically develop Northern-style aspirations and desires. They will see that upward mobility is possible in the North and that no white caste system will try to instill in them the conviction that they must stay in their assigned "place." Given a normal level of youthful energy and enthusiasm, they will probably want to rise up in the world, "make something of themselves," and advance according to the accepted American pattern. However, their parents will be almost totally useless to them in terms of providing them with the guidance, discipline, knowhow, and resources necessary to achieve their desired ends. Whether one is talking about money or start-up capital, a dedication to educational advancement, above-average levels of self-discipline, entrepreneurial skills, high levels of self-confidence, familial supervision and "push," or the special habits of perseverance and dedication to long-range plans, the displaced sharecroppers and rural farm workers will not be able to provide their offspring with what it takes to advance in the Northern industrial city.

Moreover, the children of the Deep South migrants no longer remember the poverty of the rural South, so what may have satisfied their parents in terms of their improved socioeconomic status in the North cannot possibly satisfy them. Their frustrations will grow. The problem will be particularly acute in the case of males, since it is males in America—as in virtually all societies—who have traditionally held the role of breadwinners and providers and have been under the most social pressure to advance themselves in terms of their occupational and income status. However successful he may be at holding down a low-paying menial job, given his ignorance of the ways of an urban industrial society and his past conditioning to be docile and passive, the black migrant from the rural South will often prove a failure as a guide and role model to his male offspring under the new competitive conditions of the urban North.

As the sons of the Deep South migrants begin to enter their critical teen years, where rebelliousness is normal and forceful and creative parenting most critical, they begin to lose respect for their fathers and mothers, who will increasingly appear to them as ignorant country bumpkins, if not contemptible Samboes and Uncle Toms. The situation will be even worse, of course, if the father has deserted the family and their mother alone is responsible for their discipline and upbringing. Confronted with the intolerable situation of rising desires and expectations that have been induced by growing up in an upwardly mobile society and a realization of the fact that, given their meager familial cultural and financial resources, they will have little chance of succeeding along a conventional career and achievement path, the male teenagers will have a very powerful incentive to drop out of mainstream society and renounce the traditional male husband/provider role. Since such teenagers will typically live in neighborhoods where there will be large numbers of other teenagers from similar backgrounds as themselves, the stage will be set for the emergence of delinquent gangs and deviant teenage peer group cultures that will provide alternative conceptions of what it means to be a man. And such alternative conceptions will surely prove more alluring and more in tune with the impulsiveness, thrill-seeking, and short time horizons of male youth than will most mainstream conceptions.

THE SECOND GENERATION IN NEW YORK CITY'S HARLEM

Perhaps nowhere is the conflict between the bewildered, Southern-reared parents and their rebellious, gang-and-delinquency-prone sons better illustrated than in Claude Brown's classic account of his growing up in Harlem in the 1950s. Brown's reminiscences can add flesh and specificity to what has been said so far in more general terms. His autobiographical *Manchild in the Promised Land* is a classic of second-generation estrangement literature and is worth quoting at length. With great pathos he explains below the inability of his parents to guide their children in the bewildering environment of urban New York:

> [I knew that Pimp, my younger brother, had problems now]. He had that problem of staying home and taking all that stuff from Dad. Mama had told me that he had had a fight with Dad. He was fighting back now. He was declaring his independence. I didn't know what to do when he started complaining about how Dad and Mama and Papa, my grandfather, were still in the woods and he was growing up. He was getting away from all that old down-home [down South] stuff, and he didn't go for hearing it all the time around the house. I knew he was right, because I'd had the same feeling. You feel as though they're trying to make something out of you that you couldn't be and didn't want to be if you could, as though they're trying to raise you as a farm boy in New York, in Harlem. I knew he was right. . . . I tried to talk to [Mama]. I said, "Look, Mama, Pimp grew up here in New York City. . . . He didn't grow up on all that salt pork, collard greens, and old-time religion. You can't make a chitterlin' eater out of him now." . . . It seemed as though [Mama and Dad] . . . were going to bring the South up to Harlem with them. I knew they had had it with them all the time. Mama would be telling [my sisters] Carole and Margie about the root workers down there. . . .
>
> It seemed as though Mama and Dad were never going to get out of the woods until we made them get out. . . . I wanted to say, "Look, Mama, we're in New York. Stop all this foolishness." She and Dad had been in New York since

1935. They were in New York but it seemed like their minds were still down there in the South Carolina cotton fields. Pimp, Carole, and Margie had to suffer for it. I had to suffer for it too, but because I wasn't at home as much, I had suffered less than anybody. . . . I guess I had an arrogant attitude toward the family. I saw them all as farmers. . . . Living in that house wasn't too hard on Carole and Margie but for a boy it must have been terribly hard. Everybody was far away, way back in the woods. . . . They didn't seem to be ready for urban life. They were going to try to guide us and make us do right and be good, and they didn't even know what being good was. When I was a little boy, Mama and Dad would beat me and tell me, "You better be good," but I didn't know what being good was. To me, it meant that they just wanted me to sit down and fold my hands or something crazy like that. Stay in front of the house, don't go anyplace, don't get into trouble. I didn't know what it meant, and I don't think they knew what it meant, because they couldn't ever tell me what they really wanted. . . .

They needed some help. The way I felt about it, I should have been their parents, because I had been out there on the streets, and I wasn't as far back in the woods as they were. . . . I remember how Dad thought being a busboy was a real good job. . . . To him it was a good job because when he was nine years old, he'd plowed the fields from sunup to sundown. I came in one night and told Mama. I said, "Mama, I'm gon quit this job at Hamburger Heaven, because it's getting too damn hard on me." . . . I said I was going to school, and that plus the job was kind of tough on me. After Dad couldn't take any more, he lifted his head out of the paper and said, "Boy, you don't need all that education. You better keep that job, because that's a good job." . . .

I guess I could understand their feeling in this way. Their lives were lived according to the superstitions and fears that they had been taught when they were children coming up in the Carolina cotton fields. It was all right for them down there, in that time, in that place, but it wasn't worth a damn up in New York. . . . Mama and Dad and the people who had come to New York from the South about the time they did seemed to think it was wrong to want anything more out of life than some liquor and a good piece of cunt on Saturday night. This was the stuff they did in the South. This was the sort of life they had lived on the plantations. They were trying to bring the down-home life up to Harlem. They had done it. But it wasn't working. They couldn't understand it, and they weren't about to understand it. . . .

I could sense the fear in Mama's voice when I told her once that I wanted to be a psychologist. She said, "Boy, you better stop that dreamin' and get all those crazy notions outta your head." She was scared. She had the idea that colored people weren't supposed to want anything like that. You were supposed to just want to work in fields or be happy to be a janitor. . . . I remember the times I tried to explain these things to Mama, just what was happening in Harlem, just what was happening between my generation and hers. I would tell her, "Look, Mama, don't you remember when I used to play hooky from school, steal things, and stay out all night? Do you know why I was doin' that?" . . . I'd tell her about rebellion. . . . I'd say, "Look, Mama, when people start ruling people and they rule 'em wrong, in a way that's harmful to them, they have to stop them. They've got to rebel; they've got to get out from under their rule. . . . I had to rebel. I had to get away from all that old down-home nonsense you been talking.'"[250]

---

250. Claude Brown, *Manchild in the Promised Land* (New York: New American Library, 1965), pp. 279–93.

REACHING CRITICAL MASS: THE 60S AND BEYOND

To understand the disintegration of the ghettos that took place in the 1960s, 1970s, and beyond—the explosion in out-of-wedlock births and in crime, the decline in male parental responsibility, the exodus of the better-off away from the chaos of the inner cities—one must understand, in addition to the factors that Murray, Wilson, and Jencks analyze, that it was during this period that the Northern-reared male offspring of the Great Automation Migration entered the turbulent period of their adolescent years and the years of their young adulthood. One must also understand the enormous attractiveness that the teen-age gang and the values of the male street culture can have for lower-class adolescents, even for those who come from fairly stable homes. Compared with the humdrum existence of life along a more conventional work and achievement path (even if one has confidence that one can succeed along such a path), the thrills and excitement of being together with one's buddies on the street can be enormously alluring. Hell-raising and gang-banging are seductively attractive for many young men, offering charms that a more sedate lifestyle can hardly match.

For those who are corrupted by their influence, however, the gangs and deviant peer group cultures will virtually destroy a young man's chances of becoming an effective husband or family man. The values of the gangs and adolescent peer groups represent a complete inversion of the bourgeois family ethic: Maleness comes to be identified with sexual prowess and the ability to con and exploit a string of transient sexual partners; women are referred to contemptuously as "bitches" and "ho's," while fathering children out of wedlock for whom one takes no responsibility comes to be seen as a crucial rite of passage and proof of one's manhood; students who work hard at school in order to advance themselves according to mainstream norms are taunted for "acting white"; pimping, drug-dealing, numbers-running, fencing stolen goods, and other forms of street hustles and criminal activities come to be seen as vastly preferable to the less exciting (and much less remunerative) conventional jobs; getting high on dope becomes the major form of recreation; an emphasis on toughness, manipulation, and violence comes to dominate relationships with outsiders; and Superfly comes to replace the church-going family man as the dominant figure to emulate.

In a community where such values come to prevail, it is not hard to understand why there are so few "marriageable black males," why young black women might give up on finding a stable husband, and why the level of crime, delinquency, and street violence reach such a point that normal community life becomes impossible and those with the financial means move away. The problem of the second generation was compounded in the 1960s by the sheer number of black youth in the ghetto. During this decade, the number of black teenagers living in central cities increased by almost 75 percent, thus compounding the "second-generation effect" with a "critical-mass" effect. As more and more black male youth dropped out of mainstream society and hung out in street gangs and other deviant peer groups, the more stable elements of the ghetto community were simply overwhelmed and could not control the destructive explosion that so large a number of improperly guided adolescents unleashed. When the number of teenage Claude Browns and Pimp Browns reach critical mass, all hell breaks loose—and with a fury that the more stable elements in the community are powerless to contain.

The "second-generation effect," it should be understood, is not peculiar to rural Southern black migrants, nor is it a phenomenon that has appeared only since the Second World War. Oscar Handlin, one of our acutest observers of immigrant life in the nineteenth and early twentieth century, sees the problem of second-generation delinquency as one that to some extent affected *all* of the immigrant groups that came to America's large cities, although of course, it was a vastly more manageable problem in the case of some groups than others. Speaking of the high rates of "intemperance, prostitution, pauperism, gambling, criminality, and juvenile delinquency" that observers complained of in New York City's slums during the latter part of the nineteenth century and early part of the twentieth, Handlin says that such problems were in part "the results of the destruction of old habits and of the shocking effects of new conditions." He goes on:

> The disruption of family ties and the dissolution of the authority of accepted values unsettled the norms of personal behavior and left the individual confused and therefore vulnerable at moments of crisis. That was why the second generation was in a particularly precarious situation. Compelled to devise their own standards, its members often found those in conflict with the rules of established society, so that street sports and gang activity verged almost imperceptibly over into crime and vice. The degree of susceptibility to one or another of these disorders varied from ethnic group to ethnic group, although none was altogether free of them.[251]

The closest historical parallel to the experience of the Great Automation Migration was undoubtedly that of the potato famine generation of Irish Catholic immigrants. The similarities are indeed striking: like the displaced sharecroppers and rural black Southerners of the Great Automation Migration, the Irish Catholic immigrants of the late 1840s potato famine generation were an involuntarily uprooted rural peasantry, who came to the urban centers of America less because they wanted to than because they had little choice—their purpose in leaving

---

251. Oscar Handlin, *The Newcomers: Negroes and Puerto Ricans in a Changing Metropolis* (Cambridge, MA: Harvard University Press, 1959), p. 37.

was more to survive and get by than to thrive or get ahead. And like the black sharecroppers and impoverished rural blacks, they were a destitute population, unskilled and often illiterate, with little experience in the ways of entrepreneurship or self-improvement. And also like the black sharecroppers, they were an oppressed and despised people, ruled by an alien "race" that did everything it could to degrade and humiliate them and to convince them that compared with their English masters they were inferior and animal-like beings.

The Irish response to urbanization in America paralleled that of the rural blacks: family life became disorganized; husbands abandoned their wives; alcoholism and within-group violence became rampant; the male youth turned to crime and delinquency; the areas of the cities in which they lived became dangerous slums from which respectable people fled; many became burdens on private and public eleemosynary institutions; and the more incorrigible among the young men filled up the public jails (whence our terms "paddy wagon"—the police van in which rowdy Irish "paddies" were hauled off to jail—and "hooligan"—a variation on the common nineteenth-century Irish surname Houlihan).

It was, in fact, this close parallel between the trajectories of the potato famine generation of Irish immigrants and the Great Automation Migration of Southern blacks that provided Daniel Moynihan, himself an Irishman who had studied the nineteenth-century Irish immigrant experience in great depth, with the insight and understanding that enabled him to comprehend developments in the black ghettos of America that baffled everyone else.[252] "Country life and city life are profoundly dif-

252. Shortly before its publication, an earlier version of this article (now this chapter) was sent by me to the Washington office of Daniel Patrick Moynihan on the remote chance that the New York senator might actually see it and read it. (I had never before had any previous contact with Senator Moynihan or his office). To my astonishment

ferent," Moynihan wrote in his famous report. "The gradual shift of American society from a rural to an urban basis over the past century and a half has caused abundant strains, many of which are still much in evidence. When this shift occurs suddenly, drastically, in one or two generations, the effect is immensely disruptive of traditional social patterns. It was this abrupt transition that produced the wild Irish slums of the 19th Century Northeast. Drunkenness, crime, corruption, discrimination, family disorganization, [and] juvenile delinquency were the routine of that era. In our own time, the same sudden transition has produced the Negro slum—different from, but hardly better than its predecessors, and fundamentally the result of the same process." (MR, p. 17) [253]

Moynihan not only read the article but also called me personally on the telephone in the office I was occupying at that time in Princeton's Woodrow Wilson School in order to discuss at length various points I had made in the piece. I remarked to Moynihan that I thought the reason he was able to understand so much better than most other observers the disintegrating process taking place in the black urban ghettos of the early 1960s was because he had seen it all before in his earlier studies of the nineteenth-century Irish. "Yes, absolutely!" was his reply. "That was the reason." He then said he'd once acknowledged this in print (in a work I hadn't read and now can't remember the title of).

253. In commenting on the Moynihan Report, Martin Luther King, Jr., who seems to have agreed with much of Moynihan's analysis, also traced the current ghetto problems of blacks to the rapid rural-to-urban transition. Although he doesn't specifically draw the Irish analogy, King, like Moynihan, believed that, regardless of skin color, involuntarily uprooted rural peasants face a daunting task in an urban environment and are in danger of losing control of their children to the surrounding allure of the street. In an address delivered in Westchester County, New York, soon after the publication of Moynihan's report, King had this to say: "[Some Negro families] found their way to the North in a movement [sociologist E. Franklin Frazier] aptly describes as 'into the city of destruction.' Illiterate, undisciplined, afraid, and crushed by want they were herded into slums. City life then, as now for migrant groups, has been ruinous for peasant people. The bewilderment of the complex city undermined the confidence of fathers and mothers, causing them to lose control of their children whose bewilderment was even more acute." Martin Luther King, Jr., from an address delivered at Abbott House, Westchester County, New York, Oct. 29, 1965, reproduced in Lee Rainwater and William Yancey, *The Moynihan Report and the Policy of Controversy* (Cambridge, MA: MIT Press, 1967), pp. 402–9, 406.

IRISH EYES ARE SMILING (BUT THE GHETTO ANGELS HAVE YET TO SING)

Depressing as it may seem, the analogy with the displaced Irish peasants of the nineteenth century gives cause for hope, for although the movement was arduous and painful, proceeding at a very slow, intergenerational pace, with the aid of their church the Irish did go on in the third, fourth and subsequent generations to develop strong community and family structures that eventually conformed to the general American middle-class pattern. What will become of inner-city black families and their neighborhoods is, of course, impossible to predict. On some measures, at least, it would seem as if the situation could hardly get any worse. Although tough law enforcement has helped to reduce dramatically crime in the ghetto from the Wild West days of the heroin and crack epidemics, the decline has meant that there are currently more black men in prison or otherwise under supervision of the criminal justice system than in college. Young black males face odds of almost one in three of spending at least a year behind bars sometime during their lifetime. The odds for ghetto males can be as high as one in two.

The black family situation is equally dire. Currently almost seven out of ten black babies are born out of wedlock, and the rate in the more impoverished inner-city communities is substantially higher. With the dominant middle-class society itself in American having reached a low point in its own family stability, the task of reconstructing the two-parent black family is more daunting than ever.

One thing can be said with a fair amount of certainty, however, and that is that for improvement to take place a candid assessment of what has gone wrong and what needs to be done must be undertaken by all interested parties. We have people such as Murray, Wilson, and Jencks to thank—like Moynihan, Frazier, Dollard, and Myrdal before them—for shedding light on important aspects of this continuing American dilemma.

INDEX

abolitionist personalism, 53–58

Abrams, Elliot, 66n

academic disengagement, 212–213

acting white, 212, 323, 326, 340, 475

Adarand v. Pena (1995), 29–30, 101, 373

Adelson, Joseph, 71n

adolescent peer groups, 475–476

affirmative action
  in college admissions, 10, 12, 105–110
  defenses of, 69–74
  earliest use of term, 81
  emergence of, 63
  in employment, 10–11, 15, 25, 34–38, 46–47, 65–66, 91–94
  myths and pathologies of, 74–90

  as used by L. B. Johnson, 74–75
  See also racial preferences in college admissions

Affirmative Discrimination (Glazer), 18

African Americans
  becoming college professors, 148–154
  family dissolution and, 388–397
  incarcerated males, 399–400
  inferiority, feelings of. *See* inferiority doctrine/ stereotype
  journalistic discrimination against, 59–61, 61–62n
  law school student mismatching, 222–233
  male joblessness, 442–444
  middle class growth of, 15
  in military, 127

out-of-wedlock births, 398–399, 402, 418–420, 422, 434, 440, 449n, 480

rewarding college underachievement of, 119–215

role models, need for, 72–73

SAT scores of, 106–109, 155–156

scholastic underperformance of, 16–17

in sports, 126

studying science and engineering, 189–199

underperformance of, 319

white and Asian attitudes toward affirmative action, 376–379

See also black underclass in inner cities

African immigrants, 462–463

African legacy theory, 449n

Afro-Caribbean immigrants, 446, 462–463

All Our Kin (Stack), 396

Allen, Walter W., 166n, 268–270

Allport, Gordon, 301

altruism, 22

alumni legacy college admissions, 360

American Apartheid: Segregation and the Making of the Underclass (Massey and Denton), 332

An American Dilemma (Myrdal), 249, 386

American Enterprise Institute, 136

Andrew W. Mellon Foundation, 21, 133, 135–137, 148–149, 163, 277

Antidiscrimination Law and Social Equality (Koppelman), 97

Arcidiacono, Peter, 218–222

armed forces. *See* military

Asians

as honorary whites, 239–240

positive effect of presence on college campus, 266

post-college employment benefits of undergraduate affirmative action, 215–222

SAT scores of, 106–109, 155–156, 195, 199–203, 201n

self-esteem and, 281

work ethic and high achievement of, 213–214, 313, 333–340, 342–343

athletics. *See* sports, diversity in

Bakke, Allan, 244
See also Regents of the
University of California v.
Bakke (1978).
Banfield, Edward, 18, 431
Bar Passage Study, 224
Barber, Elinor, 148–154, 163–
168, 194, 292
Barker, Ernest, 40–41n
baseball, integration of, 62,
249
Behind Ghetto Walls
(Rainwater), 396
"On Being a Good Neighbor"
(King), 52–53
Bell, Derrick, 124–125
The Bell Curve (Murray and
Herrnstein), 448n
Berghe, Pierre van den, 21
Berry, Mary Francis, 33
best black syndrome, 357
bewildered-father/delinquent-
son syndrome, 470–471
Billingsly, Andrew, 396–397,
467
Birmingham marches, 57
Black American Students in
an Affluent Suburb—A
Study of Academic
Disengagement (Ogbu),
212
Black Education: Myths and
Tragedies (Sowell), 13

Black Families in White
America (Billingsly), 396
black family dissolution. See
urban-family disintegration
black feminist writers, 398
Black Metropolis (Cayton
and Drake), 428
black middle class, 15
black pride movement, 394–
395
black underclass in inner
cities, 383–480
from crisis to catastrophe,
397–400
displaced sharecroppers and
delinquent sons, 467–
471
future of, 480
before Great Society, 426–
429
growing up in Harlem,
471–474
Moynihan Report, 388–393
Moynihan Report, response
to, 393–397
Murray, assessment of,
417–426
Murray on, 400–411
overview, 383–393
second-generation effect,
475–479
status rewards and, 411–
417

unique factors contributing to, 445–467

Wilson, assessment of, 437–444

Wilson on, 429–437

Blood and Belonging (Ignatieff), 370

Bloom, Alan, 185–187

Bok, Derek, 133–135, 138–140, 147, 157, 161–162, 167–168, 182–184, 195, 204, 214, 218, 233, 275, 277, 301, 305, 380

Bowen, William, 133–135, 138–140, 147, 157, 161–162, 167–168, 182–184, 195, 204, 214, 218, 233, 275, 277, 284, 301, 346

Bowling Alone: The Collapse and Revival of American Community (Putnam), 255–256

Bradley, Bill, 189

Brightman, Edgar S., 48

Broom, Leonard, 386

Brown, Claude, 385, 428, 471–474

Buber, Martin, 39

Bumpass, Larry, 399

bureaucrats, federal, and desire for power, 90

Cabrini Green, 400

campus diversity, attitudes toward, 172–189

Canada, Geoffrey, 384

Carter, Jimmy, 244–245

Carter, Stephen, 102–103, 104, 357

Case, Clifford, 36–37

Caste and Class in a Southern Town (Dollard), 301–302, 456-458

Cato Institute, 136

Cayton, Horace, 428

Chang, Mitchell, 196–199

Christian roots of American personalism, 43–44

civic engagement, 254–260

Civil Rights Act of 1964, 34–38, 43–47, 65–66, 74–75, 116, 273, 387

civil rights, origins of term, 84, 84n

Civilian Infrastructure Corps, 26

Clark, Joseph, 36–38, 44, 46–47

Clark, Kenneth, 341, 384, 394, 434–435

cognitive impairment from ghetto stress, 329–340

Cole, Stephen, 148–154, 163–168, 194, 292

The Color Purple (Walker), 398

Coming Up Black (Schultz),
396
compassion, 84–86
Conant, James Bryan, 426–
427
contact hypothesis
defined, 241–243
origins of, 247–250
Putnam's challenge to,
253–262
revised, 250–253
Council of Ivy Group
Presidents, 135, 149, 333–
334
crime in inner city black
neighborhoods, 399–400
crime-control policy changes
1960-1970, 409–410
Crippen, Timothy, 367–368
Crisis in Black and White
(Silberman), 387, 427–428

Dale, Stacy Berg, 136–148
Dark Ghetto (Clark), 394,
434–435
Daughters of the American
Revolution, 58
*The Death and Life of Great
American Cities* (Jacobs), 18
Death at an Early Age
(Kozol), 409
Declaration of Independence,
44–45

*The Declining Significance of
Race* (W. J. Wilson), 443
DeFunis v. Odegaard (1974),
29–30, 33, 101, 103
deindustrialization, 432–434,
438, 448n
Depth of souls and being,
42–43
Dershowitz, Alan, 245–246,
273
detribalization and immigrant
experience, 58–61
DeWolf, L. Harold, 48
discrimination
in Civil Rights Bill of 1964,
34–38
in journalism, 59–61,
61–62n
as justification for
affirmative action, 66
"The Disease as Cure"
(Scalia), 101
disruptive students, 407–409
The Disuniting of America
(Schlesinger), 18, 376
diversity on college campuses,
241–274
in the academy, 262–271
attitudes toward, 172–189
contact hypothesis defined,
241–243
contact hypothesis, origins
of, 247–250

contact hypothesis,
Putnam's challenge to,
253–262
contact hypothesis, revised,
250–253
in law schools, 222–233
mismatching and
downward raiding, 271–
274
overview, 241–243
racial preference policies
and, 14–15
rationale for, 243–247
Dollard, John, 24, 301–302,
302n, 456–458, 464–465
Douglas, William O., 29, 101,
103
downward raiding, 271–274,
296–304
See also institutional
mismatch effect
Drake, St. Clair, 428
D'Souza, Dinesh, 342, 374
DuBois, W.E.B., 328

economic immigrants, 459–
462
economic limits of
preferentialist policies,
127–131
educational policy changes in
late 1960s, 407–409
Eibl-Ebesfeldt, Irenäus, 366

elite universities and racial
preferences, 136–148
Elliott, Rogers, 190–196,
199
entrepreneurship, 18, 217,
344, 453, 456, 459, 470,
478
Equal Employment
Opportunity Commission
(EEOC), 65
Escape from Freedom
(Fromme), 43n
"Estimating the Payoff to
Attending a More Selective
College: An Application of
Selection on Observables
and Unobservables" (Dale
and Krueger), 136–137
ethnic nepotism, 22
The Ethnic Phenomenon (van
den Berghe), 21–22
ethnic rage, 23–24
Ethnicity Indifference
Principle, 92–93
ethnicity vs. race, 361–376
ethnicly homogeneous
Hispanic minority myth, 79
ethnicly homogeneous white
majority myth, 78–79
ethnocentrism, 22, 366–367
evolution, 449n
evolutionary psychology, 24,
362–369

Executive Order 10925 (Kennedy), 387

Executive Order 11246 (Johnson), 65–66, 74–76, 176, 176n, 373, 373n, 387

Executive Order 11375 (Johnson), 65–66, 75–76, 116, 373, 373n

fair housing laws, 435

fairness and reciprocity, 112–128

family destabilization, 448–449n, 477, 480
See also Moynihan Report

fear of the poor and oppressed, 87–88

Federal Aid to Families with Dependent Children program (AFDC), 404–406, 418–419

federal bureaucrats and desire for power, 90

female-headed black families, 396–398, 418, 427, 434–436, 441–442

feminism, 63–64

Fischer, Claude, 345n

Fleming, Jacqueline, 166n, 266–267

Food Stamps, 404, 406, 418–419, 421

Ford Foundation, 135

Fordham, Signithia, 326

foreign-born black immigrants, 462–463

Forty Years of Economic Progress for Blacks (Welch and Smith), 129–130

14th Amendment to U.S. Constitution, 36, 84n, 245

Fox, John B., Jr., 162

Frazier, E. Franklin, 18, 24, 447–448, 449n

Fromme, Erich, 43n

Fryer, Roland, 321n

furnish system, 456–458

The Game of Life: College Sports and Educational Values (Bowen and Schulman), 346–356

gangs, 475–476

Gardner, Howard, 345n

Garrison, William Lloyd, 54–56

Gault v. Arizona (1967), 409

General Social Survey, 256

genetics, 345, 345–346n, 449n

ghettos, 83, 329–340

Gibson, Margaret, 339

Gifford, Bernard, 425

Glazer, Nathan, 18, 44, 79, 444

Glenn, Norval, 386

Goldwater, Barry, 388, 422

Gordon, Milton, 26
government policy in
  employment, suggested
  principles of, 92–94
grade inflation, 208–209
Great Automation Migration,
  450–452, 459, 462–463,
  467, 475, 477–478
Great Society, 386, 403
Greenstein, Robert, 417
Grutter v. Bollinger (2003),
  216, 243, 317
guilt, white collective, 80–86,
  235–240

Haitian immigrants, 462
Handlin, Oscar, 452, 476–477
Hannerz, Ulf, 396
Harlan, John Marshall, 28,
  273
Harlem, growing up in, 471–
  474
Harlem Children's Zone, 384
Harrison, Lawrence, 233–235
Hayek, Friedrich, 18, 417
Head Start, 124
Hegel, 48n
Heritage Foundation, 136
Herrnstein, Richard, 111n,
  333–334, 345n
Herskovits, Melville, 449n
high-rise public housing,
  17–18
Hill, Lister, 37

Hispanics
  ethnicly homogeneous
    Hispanic minority myth,
    79
  piggybacking on 60s-era
    black struggle, 238–239,
    341
  rise of militants, 63–64
  role models, need for,
    72–73
  SAT scores of, 106–109,
    155–156
  studying science and
    engineering, 189–199
homogenization of the poor,
  413–417
Horowitz, Donald, 374
Horowitz., Donald, 24
Humphrey, Hubert, 36, 388
hypocrisy, 86

"I Have a Dream" (King),
  51–52
iconographic reforms, 235–
  236
Ignatieff, Michael, 370
immigrants and
  detribalization, 58–61
incarcerated black males,
  399–400
*Increasing Faculty Diversity:
  The Occupational Choices
  of High-Achieving Minority
  Students*, 148

Independent Institute, 136

Inequality by Design: Cracking the Bell Curve Myth (Fischer), 345n

inferiority doctrine/stereotype, 101–104, 111–112, 159–160, 170–173, 221, 234, 264, 284–286, 302, 319, 463–467

institutional affirmative action, 287–288, 287–288n

institutional mismatch effect, 154, 162–163, 165, 182, 192–199, 222–223, 228–230, 271–274, 278, 288n

involuntary immigrants, 461–462

IQ tests, 448n

Irish immigrants, 477–480

I-Thou relationships, 39

Jacobs, Jane, 18

Jeffersonian (liberal) roots of American personalism, 43–53

Jencks, Christopher, 24, 384, 440–441, 445–447

Johnson, Charles S., 454

Johnson, John H., 424

Johnson, Lyndon, 18, 44–46, 74, 116, 373, 383, 387, 388, 422, 429

journalistic discrimination, 59–61

juvenile offenders, 410

Kane, Thomas, 221n

Kasarda, John, 438

Katzenstein, Mary, 374

Keeley, Lawrence, 364n

Kemp, Jack, 189

Kennedy, John F., 387

Kennedy, Randall, 245, 247, 273

Kerner Commission, 81–82, 82n

King, Martin Luther, Jr., 33, 40n, 42n, 44, 47–53, 56–58, 63, 327–328, 385, 479n

King v. Smith (1968), 404

Klitgaard, Robert, 155–156

Koppelman, Andrew, 97–98

Kozol, Jonathan, 409

Kristol, Irving, 238n, 387

Krueger, Alan, 136–148

Ku Klux Klan, 58, 67, 88

Ladner, Joyce, 396

Latinos. *See* Hispanics

Law School Admission Council, 224

Law School Admissions Test (LSAT), 224–225, 317

law school student mismatching, 222–233

law schools admissions, 316–318

legacy college admissions, 360

legal myth of affirmative action, 74

Lemann, Nicholas, 450n

Leonard, Jonathan, 128

Li, Jian, 357–359

liberal roots of American personalism, 43–53

liberalism, in 1960s, 81, 81n

Liebow, Elliot, 396

Lindsay, John, 82

Lipset, Seymour Martin, 180–183

Lopreato, Joseph, 367–368

"Losing Faith in *Losing Ground*" (Greenstein), 417

Losing Ground: American Social Policy 1950–1980 (Murray), 401–411, 417–426

Loury, Glenn, 104–105, 321n

low effort syndrome, 212–213

male joblessness, 394, 432–435, 432–436, 442–444

male marriageable pool index, 434

Malkiel, Nancy Weiss, 208–209

The Man Without Qualities (Musil), 43n

Manchild in the Promised Land (Brown), 428, 472–474

man-in-the-house rule, 404, 406, 421

manufacturing, restructuring of, 432–434, 438

The Marriage Problem (J.Q Wilson), 449n

Marshall, Thurgood, 33

Massey, Douglas, 168–173, 264–265, 332

materialist-careerist ethic, 91

McArdle, John, 195–196

McGuiness, Kenneth C., 77n

McWhorter, John, 187, 206–209, 265, 312, 319, 323

Meaning, humans as centers of, 40–42

Medicaid, 404

Medical College Admissions Test (MCAT), 316

medical school admissions, 315–316

"Memoir on Pauperism" (Tocqueville), 423–424

merit, lack of, in college admissions policy, 275–381
  black underperformance and, 319
  cultural factors and, 340–346
  disincentive effects of racial preferences, 305
  dysfunctional subcultures and, 329–340

middle class complacency and, 324–329

overview, 275–284

race vs. ethnicity, 361–376

recruitment and corruption of educational standards, 346–356

stigma harm of racial preferences, 284–296

tribal loyalties and enmities, 356–361

upward ratcheting/ downward raiding, 296–304

white and Asian attitudes toward blacks re affirmative action, 376–379

middle class complacency, 324–329

military

blacks as disciplined officers, 355n

integration of, 62, 248–249, 251

veterans preference bills, 11, 127

Mill, John Stuart, 39

Mirandola, Pico della, 44n

mismatching in higher education. *See* institutional mismatch effect

Moral Man and Immoral Society (Niebuhr), 42n

mother-only black families, 396–397, 418, 427, 434–436, 441–442

motivation, student, 204–206

Moynihan, Daniel Patrick, 18, 24–25, 341, 384, 388–397, 429, 447–448, 449n, 478–479

Moynihan Report, 25, 388–393

response to, 393–397

Murray, Charles, 24, 104, 110–111, 111n, 345n, 384, 400–411, 417–426, 448n

Musil, Robert, 43n

Myrdal, Gunnar, 249, 386

Mystery, humans as centers of, 40–42

National Labor Relations Act (Wagner Act) of 1935, 74n

National Longitudinal Study of Freshmen, 277

The Nature of Prejudice (Allport), 301, 302n

Naylor, Gloria, 398

negative stereotyping, 98, 100, 103, 112–113, 241, 247–248

The Negro Family in the United States (Frazier), 447–448

The Negro Family: The Case for National Action

(Moynihan). *See* Moynihan Report

"The Negro Today Is Like the Immigrant Yesterday" (Kristol), 387

nepotism, 22

Nevitte, Neil, 180–183

New Frontier, 386

"new racists," 110–111

Niebuhr, Reinhold, 42n

"nigger," use of term, 465–466

Nisbett, Richard, 345n

Nixon, Richard, 383

No Proxy Principle, 92

nonpersistence rate, 190–191, 195

O'Connor, Sandra Day, 216, 219, 243, 246–247

Office of Federal Contract Compliance (OFCC), 65

Ogbu, John, 211–212, 326, 345, 352

Orfield, Gary, 182

out-of-wedlock births, 398–399, 402, 404–405, 418–420, 422, 434, 440, 449n, 480

parental demands on student performance, 213, 306–308, 313, 324, 338–340

parental guidance, 470–474
  See also Moynihan Report

Patterson, Orlando, 345n

Peabody Picture Vocabulary Test, 155

personalism
  abolitionist, 53–58
  Christian roots of, 43–44
  defenses of, 69–74
  defined, 39
  detribalization and immigrant experience, 58–61
  and emergence of affirmative action, 62–69
  explained, 40–43
  King and, 40n, 44, 47–53, 48n
  liberal roots of, 43–54
  myths and pathologies of, 74–90
  public policy and, 91–94

Piazza, Thomas, 376–379

"pipeline problem" in college education, 151–154, 172

Plaut, Steven, 68n

Plessy v. Ferguson (1896), 10, 28–29, 273

post-college employment, 215–222

Powell, Colin, 355, 355n

Powell, Lewis, 215, 219, 243, 245

power, desire for among
  federal bureaucrats, 90
"the projects," 17–18
The Promised Land
  (Lemann), 450n
public housing assistance, 404
public housing, highrise,
  17–18
Punjabi Sikh immigrants,
  339–340
Purdy, Larry, 305
Putnam, Robert, 243–262

quotas, harm done by, 13,
  160–161n

Race, Evolution and Behavior
  (Rushton), 449–450n
*Race, Racism and American
  Law* (Bell), 124–125
race vs. ethnicity, 361–376
racial preferences as antidote
  to racism
  definitions, 99–111
  economic limits of, 127–
    131
  reciprocity and fairness,
    112–128
racial preferences in college
  admissions, 133–240
  benefitting whites and
    Asians in post-college
    employment, 215–222

black scientists and
  engineers, dearth of,
  189–199
blacks becoming college
  professors, 148–154
campus diversity, attitudes
  toward, 172–189
conclusions, 233–240
at elite universities, 136–
  148
law school student
  mismatching, 222–233
overview, 133–136
rewarding
  underachievement, 199–
  215
stereotype vulnerability and
  underperformance, black,
  154–163
stereotype vulnerability,
  research on, 163–172
racism
  as blasphemy, 46–47
  defined, 99–100, 112–113
  as explanation for
    underclass growth,
    431
  racial preference policies
    and, 13–14
  as way of life, 365–366
  See also racial preferences
    as antidote to racism
Rainwater, Lee, 341, 396

reciprocity and fairness, 112–128

recruitment of school athletes, 346–356, 359

Regents of the University of California v. Bakke (1978)., 215, 243, 273, 299n

Reuther, Walter, 38

Revised Order No. 4., Department of Labor, Office of Federal Contract Compliance, 77, 77n

Rickey, Branch, 249

Rieder, Jonathan, 118–123

Rivers, Eugene, 26

The Road to Serfdom (Hayek), 18, 417

Robinson, Jackie, 62, 249

role models, 72–74

romanticism, 87

Rothman, Stanley, 180–183, 266

Rudenstine, Neil, 148–149

Rushton, J. Philippe, 365–366, 449–450n

Russell Sage Foundation, 135, 149

Rustin, Bayard, 67

Ryan, William, 394

Sander, Richard H., 223–232

Sanderson, Stephen, 22

SAT scores, 105–110, 152–153, 155–158, 160–161, 163–164, 191–193, 195–203, 201n, 287–288n, 287–289

Scalia, Antonin, 29, 101

Schlesinger, Arthur, Jr., 18, 376

school vouchers, 26

Schulman, James, 284, 346

Schultz, David, 396

second-generation effect, 475–479

segregation
    and cognitive impairment, 329–340
    King on, 50–51
    in military, 62

Self-Representation Only Principle, 92

self-righteous hypocrisy, 86

"The Selling of Joseph" (Sewall), 53–54

Sewall, Samuel, 53–54

sexual discrimination, 76

The Shape of the River (Bowen and Bok), 133–148, 157, 161, 275, 277

sharecroppers, 451–459, 467–471

Shelley v. Kraemer (1948), 435

Silberman, Charles, 387, 427–428

Skrentny, John David, 11

Slave and Citizen (Tannenbaum), 61

Slums and Suburbs (Conant), 426–427

Smith, James P., 129–130

Smyth, Frederick, 195–196

Sniderman, Paul, 376–379

social capital, 256, 258–259

Social Capital Community Benchmark Survey, 257

social engagement, 254–260

social mythology of affirmative action, 74–90

socioeconomic homogeneity of blacks and Hispanics myth, 78

Soulside (Hannerz), 396

The Source of the River (Massey et al.), 168, 264, 275, 277

Southern caste system, 458, 464–466

Sowell, Thomas, 13, 24, 95n, 160–161n, 165, 232–234, 278, 335, 345, 374

Spheres of Justice (Walzer), 11–12, 131

Spielberg, Steven, 145

sports, diversity in, 62, 126, 184–185, 188–189, 249, 251, 346–356, 359

Stack, Carol, 396

standardized testing, 155

status rewards, 411–417

Steele, Claude, 158–159, 159n, 161–165, 207, 211, 352

Steele, Shelby, 17, 134, 160, 209, 235–238, 296n, 314, 327

Steinberg, Laurence, 212, 313

stereotype vulnerability, 154–163, 163–172, 207, 348, 352

stereotyping, 39, 70, 82, 165, 247–249, 352, 397

stereotyping, negative, 98, 100, 103, 112–113, 241, 247–248

stigma, 100–103, 284–296

stress hormones effect on developing brains, 329–340

Stride Toward Freedom (King), 49

student discipline, 407–409

student motivation, 204–206

Student Nonviolent Coordinating Committee (SNCC), 56

student work ethic, 204–206

Summers, Clyde, 304n

Sumner, William Graham, 366

Swain, Carol, 318n

Tally's Corner (Liebow), 396

Taming the River (Charles et al.). *See* merit, lack of, in college admissions policy
Tannenbaum, Frank, 61
test anxiety, 158–159
Thatcher, Margaret, 253–254
Thernstrom, Abigail, 214, 305, 328
Thernstrom, Stephen, 214, 305, 328
thirty-and-a-third rule, 404, 407, 421
Title VI, Civil Rights Act of 1964, 34–37, 65
Title VII, Civil Rights Act of 1964, 34–38, 65, 74–75, 116
To Be Equal (Young), 387, 391–392
Tocqueville, Alexis de, 423–424
Tomorrow's Tomorrow (Ladner), 396–397
tribalism, 38–40, 64–65, 356–361
The Truly Disadvantaged (W. J. Wilson), 429–437, 448n assessment of, 437–444
Truman, Harry, 62, 248
trust, 254–259
two-faced personalities, 466

Underdog Equality Principle, 92–93

The Unheavenly City (Banfield), 18, 431
upward ratcheting, 296–304 *See also* institutional mismatch effect
urban housing projects, 400
urban-family disintegration, 199–215, 279–280, 430

Vars, Fredrick, 161
veterans preference bills, 11, 127
victimization of the poor, 413–417
Vietnamese immigrants, 336–339
Vigdor, Jacob, 218–222
visceral universalism, 119–120, 123
voluntary economic immigrants, 459–462
Voting Rights Act of 1965, 387

Walker, Alice, 398
Wallace, George, 36
Walzer, Michael, 11–12, 99, 124, 131
War Before Civilization (Keeley), 364n
War On Poverty, 429
Watts riots, 394
wealth-donor admissions preferences, 360

Weber, Max, 262
Weiner, Myron, 23–24, 374
Welch, Finis, 129–130
welfare, 279, 342n, 384, 402–407, 410–425, 444–446
"What Antidiscrimination Law is Against" (Koppelman), 97–99
When Work Disappears: The World of the New Urban Poor (W. J. Wilson), 448n
Where Do We Go from Here: Chaos or Community (King), 49–51, 51n
white "liberals," 84–89
white society, defined, 82–83
Whitman, David, 450n
Who Prospers? (Harrison), 233
Williams, Robin M., 392
Williams, Walter, 355
Wilson, James Q., 333–334, 449n
Wilson, William Julius, 24, 383–384, 429–437, 437–444, 445–447, 448n
Wolfe, Alan, 304n
women
academic underperformance among athletes, 348
as centers of black families, 427, 448–449n
difficulty in finding mates among blacks, 281–282, 435, 448n, 476
disrespected by black men, 475
role models, need for, 72–73
SAT scores of, 195
welfare and, 404–405, 418–421
See also female-headed black families; out-of-wedlock births
The Women of Brewster Place (Naylor), 398
Woods, Tiger, 184
work ethic, 204–206, 266, 442
working poor, 412, 416–417, 419, 424, 445
Wright, Richard, 385

xenophobia, 22, 366–367

Young, Whitney M., Jr., 387, 391–392